Lecture Notes in Artificial Intelligence 3374

Edited by J. G. Carbonell and J. Siekmann

Subseries of Lecture Notes in Computer Science

T0224608

Danny Weyns H. Van Dyke Parunak
Fabien Michel (Eds.)

Environments for Multi-Agent Systems

First International Workshop, E4MAS 2004
New York, NY, July 19, 2004
Revised Selected Papers

 Springer

Volume Editors

Danny Weyns
Katholieke Universiteit Leuven
Department of Computer Science, AgentWise, DistriNet
3001 Leuven, Belgium
E-mail: danny.weyns@cs.kuleuven.ac.be

H. Van Dyke Parunak
Altarum Institute
3520 Green Court, Suite 300, Ann Arbor, MI 48105-1579, USA
E-mail: van.parunak@altarum.org

Fabien Michel
LIRMM - Université de Montpellier II
161 rue Ada, 34592 Cedex 5, Montpellier, France
E-mail: fmichel@lirmm.fr

Library of Congress Control Number: 2005920458

CR Subject Classification (1998): I.2.11, I.2, C.2.4

ISSN 0302-9743
ISBN 3-540-24575-8 Springer Berlin Heidelberg New York

Springer is a part of Springer Science+Business Media

springeronline.com

© Springer-Verlag Berlin Heidelberg 2005
Printed in Germany

Typesetting: Camera-ready by author, data conversion by Scientific Publishing Services, Chennai, India
Printed on acid-free paper   SPIN: 11389903   06/3142   5 4 3 2 1 0

Preface

The modern field of multiagent systems has developed from two main lines of earlier research.

Its practitioners generally regard it as a form of artificial intelligence (AI). Some of its earliest work was reported in a series of workshops in the US dating from 1980, revealingly entitled, "Distributed Artificial Intelligence," and pioneers often quoted a statement attributed to Nils Nilsson that "all AI is distributed." The locus of classical AI was what happens in the head of a single agent, and much MAS research reflects this heritage with its emphasis on detailed modeling of the mental state and processes of individual agents. From this perspective, intelligence is ultimately the purview of a single mind, though it can be amplified by appropriate interactions with other minds. These interactions are typically mediated by structured protocols of various sorts, modeled on human conversational behavior.

But the modern field of MAS was not born of a single parent. A few researchers have persistently advocated ideas from the field of artificial life (ALife). These scientists were impressed by the complex adaptive behaviors of communities of animals (often extremely simple animals, such as insects or even microorganisms). The computational models on which they drew were often created by biologists who used them not to solve practical engineering problems but to test their hypotheses about the mechanisms used by natural systems. In the artificial life model, intelligence need not reside in a single agent, but emerges at the level of the community from the nonlinear interactions among agents. Because the individual agents are often subcognitive, their interactions cannot be modeled by protocols that presume linguistic competence. The French biologist Grassé observed that these interactions are typically achieved indirectly, through modifications of a shared environment [1].

All interaction among agents of any sort requires an environment. For an AI agent whose interactions with other agents are based on speech act theory, the environment consists of a computer network that can convey messages from one agent's outbox to another agent's inbox. For an ALife agent, the environment is whatever the agent's sensors sense and whatever its effectors try to manipulate.

In most cases, AI agents (and their designers) can take the environment for granted. Error-correcting protocols ensure that messages once sent will arrive in due course. Message latency may lead to synchronization issues among agents, but these issues can be discussed entirely at the level of the agents themselves, without reasoning about the environment. As a result, the environment fades into the background, and becomes invisible.

Not so for ALife agents. Simon observed long ago that the complex behavior of an ant wandering along the ground is best explained not by what goes on inside the ant, but by what happens outside, in the structure of the ground over which the ant moves [2]. When a termite interacts with other termites by depositing and sensing pheromones, the absorption and evaporation of the pheromone by the environment plays a critical role in the emergent structure of the colony's behavior. There are no error-correcting protocols to ensure that an agent who tries to push a rock from one place to another will in fact be able to realize that objective. From the ALife perspective, the environment is an active participant in agent dynamics, a first-class member of the overall system.

One happy result of the confluence of AI and ALife in MAS is the emergence of hybrid agents that draw on the best of both earlier traditions. This volume, and the workshop of which it is the archival record, is evidence of that hybridization. The agents described in these papers are not artificial ants constructed to test a biologist's theories about insect behavior, but components of systems engineered to fly airplanes, or analyze sensor data, or produce plausible human-like behavior in a video game. Like AI agents, many of them have cognitive, symbolic internal structures. Like ALife agents, all of them interact explicitly and deliberately with the environment through which they coordinate their behaviors.

The notion of the environment in MAS is still young, but the number of papers contributed to this volume suggests the potential of this concept for engineered systems, and their breadth sketches the broad framework of what a mature discipline of environments for multiagent systems might resemble. The entire life cycle of environmental engineering is represented here: conceptual models and languages for the design and specification of environments, simulation environments that admit environments as first-class objects, analysis of the role played by an explicit environment in agent coordination, and examples of full applications that exploit the power of an active environment. The introductory survey pulls these themes together to offer an integrated overview of this emerging discipline.

This volume shows the wide range of exploration typical of a nascent discipline as pioneers discover the best ways to frame problems and approach solutions. It will enable other researchers to take build on this body of initial exploration, and should form the foundation for a fruitful new set of tools and methods for developing multiagent systems.

[1] Grassé, P.P.: La Reconstruction du Nid et les Coordinations Inter-individuelles chez Bellicositermes Natalensis et Cubitermes sp. La theórie de la Stigmergie: Essai d'Interpreétation du Comportement des Termites Constructeurs. Insectes Sociaux 6 (1959) 41-84
[2] Simon, H.A.: The Sciences of the Artificial. Cambridge, MA, MIT Press (1969)

December 2004   H. Van Dyke Parunak
                                                      Ann Arbor, MI, USA

Organization

E4MAS 2004 was organized in conjunction with the 3rd International Joint Conference on Autonomous Agents and Multi-agent Systems (AAMAS 2004), New York City, July 19, 2004.

Program Co-chairs

Danny Weyns	Katholieke Universiteit Leuven, Belgium
H. Van Dyke Parunak	Altarum Institute, Ann Arbor, USA
Fabien Michel	Université de Montpellier II, France

Program Committee

Eric Bonabeau	Icosystem, Boston, USA and Paris, France
Sven Brueckner	Altarum Institute, Ann Arbor, USA
Paolo Ciancarini	University of Bologna, Italy
Yves Demazeau	Laboratoire Leibniz, IMAG, Grenoble, France
Marco Dorigo	Université Libre de Bruxelles, Belgium
Alexis Drogoul	Laboratoire d'Informatique de Paris 6, France
Jacques Ferber	Université de Montpellier II, LIRMM, France
Tom Holvoet	DistriNet, K.U.Leuven, Belgium
Franziska Klügl	University of Wurzburg, Germany
Marco Mamei	University of Modena and Reggio Emilia, Italy
Jean-Pierre Müller	CIRAD–LIRMM, Montpellier, France
James Odell	James Odell Associates, Ann Arbor, USA
H. Van Dyke Parunak	Altarum Instutute, Ann Arbor, USA
Karl Tuyls	COMO Lab, V.U.B., Belgium
Paul Valckenaers	PMA, K.U.Leuven, Belgium
Franco Zambonelli	University of Modena and Reggio Emilia, Italy

Website

http://www.cs.kuleuven.ac.be/~distrinet/events/e4mas/

Acknowledgements

Many thanks to the PC members for their critical review work. We also thank Elke Steegmans, Alexander Helleboogh, Kurt Schelfthout, Tom De Wolf, Koen Mertens, Nelis Boucké and Tom Holvoet for their efforts for E4MAS. A special word of thanks to Tom De Wolf for managing the web site.

Table of Contents

Survey

Conceptual Models

Languages for Design and Specification

Simulation and Environments

Mediated Coordination

Applications

Environments for Multiagent Systems
State-of-the-Art and Research Challenges

Danny Weyns[1], H. Van Dyke Parunak[2], Fabien Michel[3],
Tom Holvoet[1], and Jacques Ferber[3]

[1] AgentWise, DistriNet, K.U.Leuven, B-3001 Leuven, Belgium
{danny.weyns, tom.holvoet}@cs.kuleuven.ac.be
[2] Altarum Institute, Ann Arbor, MI 48105-1579, USA
van.parunak@altarum.org
[3] LIRMM, CNRS, Montpellier, 34392 Montpellier Cedex 5, France
{fmichel, ferber}@lirmm.fr

Abstract. It is generally accepted that the environment is an essential
compound of multiagent systems (MASs). Yet the environment is typically assigned limited responsibilities, or even neglected entirely, overlooking a rich potential for the paradigm of MASs.

Opportunities that environments offer, have mostly been researched
in the domain of situated MASs. However, the complex principles behind
the concepts and responsibilities of the environment and the interplay
between agents and environment are not yet fully clarified.

In this paper, we first give an overview of the state-of-the-art on environments in MASs. The survey discusses relevant research tracks on
environments that have been explored so far. Each track is illustrated
with a number of representative contributions by the research community. Based on this study and the results of our own research, we identify
a set of core concerns for environments that can be divided in two classes:
concerns related to the structure of the environment, and concerns related to the activity in the environment. To conclude, we list a number
of research challenges that, in our opinion, are important for further
research on environments for MAS.

1   Introduction

There is a general agreement in the multiagent research community that environments are essential for multiagent systems (MASs). Yet most researchers neglect
to integrate the environment as a primary abstraction in models and tools for
MASs, or minimize its responsibilities. As a consequence, a rich potential of
applications and techniques that can be developed using MASs is overlooked.

Popular frameworks such as Jade [9], Jack [44], Retsina [79] or Zeus [58]
reduce the environment to a message transport system or broker infrastructure.
Well-known methodologies such as Message [25], Prometheus [66] or Tropos [12]
offer support for some basic elements of the environment, however they fail to
consider the environment as a first-class entity. Standard literature on MASs

D. Weyns et al. (Eds.): E4MAS 2004, LNAI 3374, pp. 1–47, 2005.
© Springer-Verlag Berlin Heidelberg 2005

used for education, including [73, 93, 45], only deals very briefly with the topic of environments. Even in the FIPA [34] specifications it is hard to find any functionality for the environment beyond message transport or broker systems. Restricting interaction to inter-agent communication neglects a rich potential of possibilities for the paradigm of MASs.

Researchers working in the domain of situated MASs traditionally integrate the environment as a first-class entity in a MAS. In situated MASs, the environment is an active entity with its own processes that can change its own state, independent of the activity of the embedded agents. Inspired by biological systems, several researchers have shown that the environment can serve as a robust, self-revising, shared memory for agents. This can unburden the individual agents from continuously keeping track of their knowledge about the system. Moreover, it enables the agents to use their environment as an excellent medium for indirect coordination. Gradient fields and evaporating marks in the environment can guide agents in their local context and as such facilitate the coordination in a community of agents in a decentralized fashion. Several practical applications have shown how the environment can contribute to manage complex problems. There are examples in domains such as supply chain systems, network support, peer-to-peer systems, manufacturing control, multiagent simulation etc. Since the exploitation of the environment in MASs results in better manageable solutions, it is a promising paradigm to deal with the increasing complexity and dynamism of future system infrastructure and more advanced problem domains, e.g. ad hoc networks or ubiquitous computing.

Despite the large amount of work in the domain of situated MASs, we are just at the very beginning of understanding the complex principles behind the concepts related to the environment and the interplay between agents and the environment. This paper aims to contribute in three ways. First we give an overview of the state-of-the-art on environments for MASs. Based on this study as well as the results of our own research, we identify a set of core concerns for environments, as a second contribution. Third, we outline a number of research challenges that, in our opinion, are important for the future development of environments for MASs.

2 Organization of the Paper

In Sect. 3, we start with an overview of the state-of-the-art on environments for MASs. Studying MAS literature with a focus on environments is a tough job. During our study, we encountered two types of difficulties: (1) the term *environment* has several different meanings, causing a lot of confusion, (2) the functionalities associated with the environment are often treated implicitly, or integrated in the MAS in an ad-hoc manner.

The confusion on what the environment comprises is mainly caused by mixing up concepts and infrastructure. Sometimes, researchers refer to the environment as the logical entity of a MAS in which the agents and other objects/resources are embedded. Sometimes, the notion of environment is used to refer to the software infrastructure on which the MAS is executed. Sometimes, environment even refers to the underlying hardware infrastructure on which the MAS runs.

The fact that functionalities of the environment are often treated implicitly, or in an ad-hoc manner, indicates that in general, the MAS research community fails to treat the environment as a *first-class entity*. [36] defines a first-class module as: "a program building block, an independent piece of software which [...] provides an abstraction or information hiding mechanism so that a module's implementation can be changed without requiring any change to other modules." Thus, the environment is in general not treated as an independent building block that encapsulates its own clear-cut responsibilities in the MAS, irrespective of the agents.

Starting from this perspective, the overview of the state-of-the-art on environments for MASs we discuss in Sect. 3 is not just a summary of representative papers on the topic of environments for MASs. In fact, the number of research papers that are devoted to the environment is very limited. The overview is rather a reflection on MAS research literature in which we have put the spotlight on models and concepts associated with the environment. The survey is structured as follows:

3.1 General models for environments (Russell and Norvig, Ferber, Odell et al., Environments for mobile agents)
3.2 Inter-agent facilities
   − Communication infrastructure (Huhns & Stephens, FIPA, Jade, Retsina)
   − Models for indirect interaction
      • Classical blackboard communication
      • Tuple-based interaction models (JavaSpaces, Lime)
      • Stigmergy (Synthetic ecosystems, Network routing)
      • Interaction models related to space in MASs (MMASS)
   − Environment as an organizational layer (AGR)
3.3 Agent-Environment interaction
   − Perception of the environment (Robocup Soccer Server, Model for active perception)
   − Dealing with actions in the environment (Synchronous model for action, Action model with regional synchronization)
   − Task-environments (Wooldridge, TAEMS)
3.4 Environments in agent-oriented methodologies (Gaia)

For each track we selected a number of relevant contributions from the research community, specified in brackets. It is not a primary goal of the survey to be complete, but rather to give an overview of the wide range of different conceptions associated with the environment for MASs and its various uses.

In Sect. 4, we extract, from the listed research tracks, a set of core concerns for environments in MASs. We have divided the concerns in two classes:

4.1 Concerns related to the structure of the environment (Structuring, Resources, Ontology)
4.2 Concerns related to the activity in the environment (Communication, Actions, Perception, Environmental processes)

Each concern represents a *logical functionality* for which the environment may have a *natural responsibility*. Our goal is to make the logical functionalities *explicit*, i.e. as concerns of environments as first-class entities. We want to underline that the proposed list of concerns is not intended to be complete. Our aim is to give an initial impetus to explore the rich potential of environments for MASs.

Next in Sect. 5 we outline a number of research challenges that, in our opinion, are important for the further development of environments for MASs. We have divided the list in three categories:

5.1 Definition and scope of environments
5.2 Agent-environment interrelationship
5.3 Engineering environments

Each category discusses a number of applicable research challenges. These challenges may serve as a source of inspiration for future exploration of environments for MASs.

Finally, in Sect. 6 we draw conclusions.

Conventions. In the remainder of the paper, we use the following style conventions:

- Quotations are put in "quotation marks."
- Specific terms used in literature are marked in `teletype`.
- Terms of concepts we want to emphasize are marked in *italic*.

3   Environments for MASs: A Survey of the State-of-the-Art

In this section we give an overview of a number of important research tracks that, in one way or another, include some notion of environment. We start with discussing a couple of general models for environments that have been proposed in literature. Then we zoom in on various concepts and functionalities related to inter-agent facilities in the environment and agent-environment interaction. We conclude the section by discussing the position of environments in agent-oriented software engineering. Each track is illustrated with a number of relevant contributions from the research community.

3.1   General Models for Environments

We start our study on environments for MASs with a number of representative models for environments that have been proposed in the research community.

Russell and Norvig. In chapter 2 of [73], S. Russell and P. Norvig discuss how an intelligent agent relates to its environment: "An agent is anything that can be viewed as perceiving its environment through sensors and acting upon the environment through effectors." This generally acknowledged relationship between an agent and its environment is schematically depicted in Fig. 1.

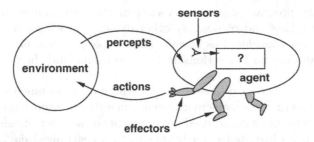

Fig. 1. Agent interaction with the environment [73]

Russell and Norvig discuss a number of key properties of environments that are now adopted by most researchers in the domain:

- Accessible versus inaccessible: indicates whether the agents have access to the complete state of the environment or not.
- Deterministic versus nondeterministic: indicates whether a state change of the environment is uniquely determined by its current state and the actions selected by the agents or not.
- Static versus dynamic: indicates whether the environment can change while an agent deliberates or not.
- Discrete versus continuous: indicates whether the number of percepts and actions are limited or not.

The most complex class of environments are those that are inaccessible, nondeterministic, dynamic and continuous. The first three properties of this list are properties typically occurring in MASs.

Russell and Norvig also define a "generic environment program", see Fig. 2. The program periodically gives the agents percepts and receives back their ac-

```
procedure RUN-ENVIRONMENT(state, UPDATE-FN, agents, termination)
    inputs: state, the initial state of the environment
            UPDATE-FN, function to modify the environment
            agents, a set of agents
            termination, a predicate to test when we are done

    repeat
        for each agent in agents do
            PERCEPT[agent] ← GET-PERCEPT(agent, state)
        end
        for each agent in agents do
            ACTION[agent] ← PROGRAM[agent](PERCEPT[agent])
        end
        state ← UPDATE-FN(actions, agents, state)
    until termination(state)
```

Fig. 2. A generic environment program [73]

tions. Next, the program updates the state of the environment based on the actions of the agents and of possibly other dynamic processes in the environment that are not considered as agents. This simple program for environments clearly illustrates the basic relationship between agents and their environment.

Ferber. In [28], J. Ferber discusses the modelling of environments for MAS at length. According to Ferber, an environment can either be represented as a single monolithic system, i.e. a centralized environment, or as a set of cells assembled in a network, i.e. a distributed environment. In a centralized environment, all agents have access to the same structure. In a distributed environment, each cell behaves like a centralized environment in miniature. However, a cell of a distributed environment differs in a number of ways from a centralized environment: (1) the state of a cell in a distributed environment depends on the surrounding cells, (2) the perception of agents in a distributed environment typically goes beyond one cell, (3) when agents move from cell to cell, the agent's link with the cells has to be managed and (4) the propagation of signals over the network of cells has to be managed. Orthogonal to the difference between a centralized or a distributed representation of environment, Ferber distinguishes between "generalized" and "specialized" models for environments. A generalized model is independent of the kind of actions that can be performed by agents. A specialized model is characterized by a well-defined set of actions. Ferber further distinguishes between purely communicative MASs (in which agents can only communicate by message transfer), purely situated MASs (in which agents can only act in the environment) and the combination of communicating and situated MASs.

Central to Ferber's model of an environment is the way actions are modelled. The action model of Ferber distinguishes between `influences` and `reactions` to influences. Influences come from inside the agents and are attempts to modify the course of events in the world. Reactions, which result in state changes, are produced by the environment by combining influences of all agents, given the local state of the environment and the laws of the world. This clear distinction between the products of the agents' behavior and the reaction of the environment provides a way to handle simultaneous activity in the MAS.

Ferber uses the BRIC formalism (Block-like Representation of Interactive Components) to model a MAS as a set of interconnected components that can exchange messages via the links. BRIC components encapsulate their own behavior and can be composed hierarchically. Fig. 3 depicts a model for a combined communicating and situated MAS in BRIC notation. In the BRIC model depicted in Fig. 3, the activity cycle of the MAS starts when the environment sends "perceptions" to the agents. As soon as the Synchronizer sends "synchronization of perceptions" signals to the agents, the agents are triggered to interpret the perceptions. Then, each agent produces an influence in the environment and possibly transmits a message to another agent. Next, the agent informs the Synchronizer it has finished its action by sending an "synchronization of actions" message. When all agents have sent their "synchronization of actions" messages, the Synchronizer sends a "synchronization of reactions" message to the Environ-

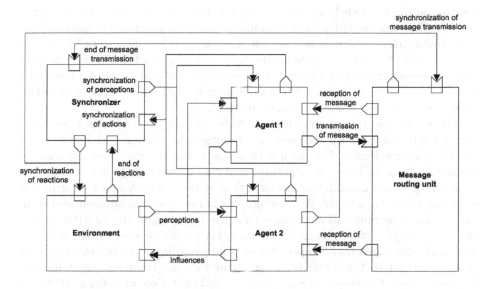

Fig. 3. BRIC model of communicating and situated MAS [28]

ment and simultaneously it sends a "synchronization of message transmission" to the Message routing unit. As a consequence, the Environment calculates the reactions to the collected influences, i.e. state changes of the Environment, and the Message routing unit delivers the messages. When the reactions are calculated, the Environment sends an "end of reactions" message to the Synchronizer. Analogously, the Message routing unit sends an "end of message transmission" when all messages are delivered. After that, the Environment sends the next perceptions to the agents and the whole cycle repeats. In the MAS model of Fig. 3, messages are synchronized with actions, i.e the messages are transmitted at the same time as the influences. A variant to this model is discussed in [87].

Odell et al. A classic paper on environment modelling for MAS is [61]. According to J. Odell and his colleagues, "an environment provides the conditions under which an entity (agent or object) exists". The authors distinguish between the **physical environment** and the **communication environment**.

The physical environment provides the laws, rules, constraints and policies that govern and support the physical existence of agents and objects. An example of a law in the agent system is that two agents are not allowed to occupy the same place at the same time. In accordance with [68], an environment is defined as a tuple $< State, Process >$. $State$ is a set of values that completely define the environment, including the agents and objects within the environment. $Process$ indicates that the environment itself is an active entity. It has its own process that can change its state, independently of the actions of the embedded agents. The primary purpose of $Process$ is to implement dynamism in the environment, e.g. the aggregation, diffusion and evaporation of pheromones that ant-like agents use to coordinate. Odell and his colleagues argue for a "common processing platform [...] that would provide a foundation upon which agent applications could build to leverage their own specific environmental requirements." However, they conclude, "In spite of the acronym, the FIPA (Agent Platform) architecture focusses almost entirely on the electronic environment, and does not address the physical environment. As such, it does not address the real potential of an active environment [...] to get more powerful interaction."

The communication environment provides (1) the principles and processes that govern and support the exchange of ideas, knowledge and information, and (2) the functions and structures that are commonly employed to exchange communication, such as roles, groups, and the interaction protocols between roles and groups. Basically, communication is the conveyance of information from one entity to another. A difference exists between transmission and communication. Communication requires that the information transmitted by one agent results in a state change of another, i.e. an act of sensing and deciding (although the latter may simply choose to do nothing). An interesting point of view related to this issue is discussed in [82]. L. Tummolini and his colleagues propose the notion of Behavioral Implicit Communication (BIC) as a parasitical form of communication that exploits both environmental properties and the agents' capacity to interpret each other's actions. To enable BIC, the environment needs to support the observability of the actions of the agents.

Odell and his colleagues define an agent's social environment as "a communication environment in which the agents interact in a coordinated manner". The social environment consists of (1) the social units (groups) in which the agent participates, (2) the roles that are employed for social interaction and (3) all the other members who play roles in these social groups. A group can be empty if no agents participate in the group; its collection can also contain a single participating agent or multiple agents. Groups have a unique identity in the overall system. As such, groups can become social actors, e.g. a business organization that interacts with sector groups in industry. The authors define a role as an abstract representation of an agent's function, service or identification within a group. Roles determine the patterns of dependencies and interactions among agents.

Environments for Mobile Agents. Since the mid nineties, mobile agents have been an active area for research and development communities. Mobile agents have the ability to migrate autonomously across a network, based on the principle of code mobility. A mobile agent is capable to suspend its execution at one node (at an arbitrary moment or at particular points in its life time), to move along with its code and its execution state to another node, and to resume its execution seamlessly. As such, a mobile agent is not bound to the network host where it begins execution. This permits a mobile agent to move to a destination node that contains the resources or services with which it wants to interact. As such mobile agents provide flexibility inside a distributed network to reduce network load and optimize service performance. Support for mobil-

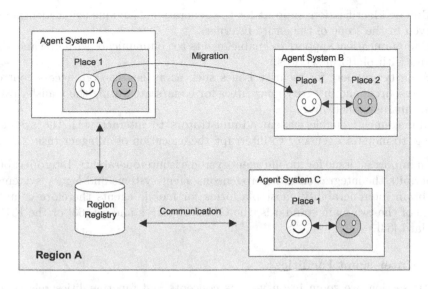

Fig. 4. Structure of a Distributed Agent Environment [65]

ity introduces additional requirements for the multiagent platform. During the last decade, many **platforms for mobile agents** have been developed. Some representative examples are Aglets from IBM [1], Voyager from Objectspace [83], Grasshopper from IKV++ [39], Ajanta from University of Minnesota [2] or SOMA developed at the University of Bologna [76].

Mobile agent platforms realize a distributed processing environment that is usually referred to as **Distributed Agent Environment** (DAE). DAEs typically support a hierarchy of locality abstractions to model physical network resources. Fig. 4 depicts an abstract overview of a DAE. The white agents symbolize mobile agents, the gray symbolize stationary agents.

On each host, at least one **agent system** has to run to support the execution of agents. Each agent system provides one or more **places**. A place is an executing context that offers specific services. An example is a trading place where agents can offer or buy information and service access. A **region** groups a number of agent systems (typically in a local area network). Each region has a **region registry** that maintains information about all registered agent systems, places and the hosted agents. The current location of mobile agents is updated in the corresponding region registry after each migration. The terminology used in Fig. 4 (region, place and agent system) is standardized by the OMG MASIF standard [63]. [65] enumerates a number of common capabilities for mobile agent platforms:

1. Agent execution: basic provisions to put incoming agents into execution, taking into account the binding to local resources.
2. Transport: mobility support to facilitate the network transport of agent code and execution state.

3. Unique identification: support for the generation of unique agent identifiers, even in the scope of the entire Internet.
4. Communication: support to enable agents to communicate with one another and with platform services.
5. Security: support for security issues such as authentication, access control of resources and integrity guarantees for code/state during the transfer over an untrusted network.
6. Management: enable system administrators to interact with the system, e.g. to monitor agents or to interrupt the execution of an agent task.

An important issue for mobile agent systems is interoperability. Interoperability permits the integration of heterogeneous agent systems and legacy systems. To obtain interoperability, most platforms for mobile agents therefore comply to one of the two main standards, the OMG MASIF standard [63] or the FIPA standard [34].

3.2   Inter-agent Facilities

In this section, we zoom in on various concepts and functionalities related to inter-agent facilities in the environment. We have organized the material in line with the taxonomy of agent interaction mechanisms proposed in [69]. We start with studying traditional infrastructure for direct message transfer between agents. The most commonly used form of direct message flow are peer-to-peer conversations, but also a distinguished agent that commands a subordinate is an example. Next, we discuss several models for indirect interaction, including blackboard systems, tuple-based interaction models and stigmergy. To conclude we look at models in which the environment serves as an organizational layer.

Communication Infrastructure. Communication is without any doubt a basic aspect of any MAS. In this section, we focus on communication infrastructure for message transfer between agents. We start with some general reflections on agent communication from Huhns and Stephens. Then we look at the FIPA agent platform for communication. In connection we discuss two concrete architectures for communication: the FIPA compliant middleware platform Jade, and the Retsina MAS infrastructure.

Huhns and Stephens. In the 2nd chapter of [45], M. Huhns and L. Stephens discuss characteristics and concerns of multiagent environments. The authors list the following characteristics:

1. Multiagent environments provide an infrastructure specifying communication and interaction protocols
2. Multiagent environments are typically open and have no single centralized designer
3. Multiagent environments contain agents that are autonomous and distributed and may be self-interested or cooperative

Next the authors list a brief summary of a number of concerns of multiagent "execution environments":

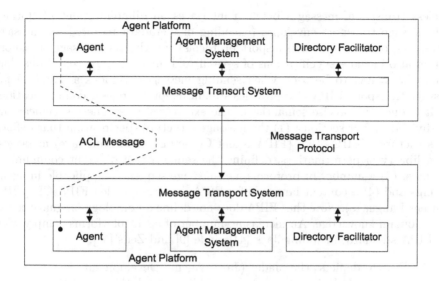

Fig. 5. FIPA agent platform reference model [34]

1. Design autonomy: relates to the platform, interaction protocols and agent architecture
2. Communication infrastructure: relates to type of communication medium and the type of connection
3. Directory service: white or yellow pages
4. Message protocol: refers to language (e.g. KQLM) and technology (e.g. CORBA)
5. Mediating and Security services: e.g., support needed for transactions or authentication
6. Operations support: refers e.g. to archiving

Hunhns and Stephens look at the environment as a *computational infrastructure* that enables agents to *communicate* with one another.

FIPA. The FIPA (Foundation for Intelligent Physical Agents) agent platform reference model [34] illustrates a typical communication infrastructure for direct message exchange, see Fig. 5.

The key building block of an environment in FIPA is the `agent platform`. An agent platform includes a "run-time environment" that defines the life cycle of the agent system, and executes e.g. on a Java virtual machine. The building blocks of the agent platform are: (1) a `directory facilitator` acting as a yellow pages service for the agents to advertise and discover services offerings, (2) an `agent management system` that enables agents to register on the platform and to locate one another (i.e. a white pages service) and that controls resource usage, and (3) a `message transport system`, i.e. a communication service for local and inter-platform message exchange. The message transport system is specified in great detail. It specifies transport protocols (low level details for wired and wireless transfer of messages between interfaces on different agent platforms) and message transport envelopes (encoding of metadata required for message forwarding over individual transport protocols). Lastly, the message transport system also includes specifications of several ACL message representations that define the syntax to be used when sending messages. Besides a standard for message transport, FIPA also provides standards for interagent communication, i.e. it defines the precise semantics of the exchanged bits. These specifications are divided in four sections: (1) the message structure specification that defines the structure of FIPA-ACL (FIPA Agent Communication Language) messages, (2) a library of performatives, defining the semantics of different communicative acts, (3) a number of protocols, i.e. message sequences applicable in agent systems and (4) a content language for FIPA messages, called FIPA-CL (FIPA Content Language). Note that FIPA does not define an ontology language to express domain knowledge. An increasing number of agent platforms comply with the FIPA standard, including Jack [44], Jade [9] and Zeus [58].

JADE. Fig. 6 depicts the Jade (Java Agent Development Environment) architecture [9]. Jade is a pure Java, middleware platform intended for the development of distributed multiagent applications based on peer-to-peer communication. Jade includes Java classes to support the development of application agents and the "run-time environment" that provides the basic services for agents to execute. An instance of the Jade run-time is called a container, and the set of all containers is called the platform. The platform provides a layer that hides from agents the complexity of the underlying execution system. Jade includes a naming service ensuring that each agent has a unique name, and a yellow pages service that can be distributed across multiple hosts.

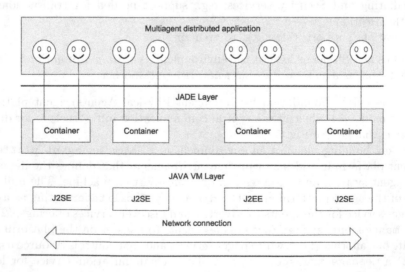

Fig. 6. The Jade architecture [9]

Agents can dynamically discover each other and communicate by exchanging asynchronous messages. The structure of the messages complies with the FIPA-ACL language definition. Jade provides a set of skeletons of typical interaction protocols. The platform also supports mobility of code and execution state (exclusive the data on the JVM -Java Virtual Machine- stack). This enables agents to stop running on a host, migrate to a different remote host and restart execution from the point they stopped. Jade is widely used in the academic community and several companies are using Jade for their internal projects, including Telecom Italy [81], Whitestein Technologies AG [90] and Rockwell Automation [72].

RETSINA. Retsina (Reusable Environment for Task-Structured Intelligent Network Agents) [79] is a well-known MAS infrastructure, see Fig. 7. Retsina is an open MAS infrastructure that supports communities of heterogeneous agents. The Retsina MAS infrastructure is build up in several layers. The operating environment provides the platform on which the infrastructure components and the agents run. Retsina supports a broad range of execution platforms and it automatically handles different types of network transport layers.

The communication infrastructure provides two types of communication channels: one for message transfer between peers, the other for multicast that is

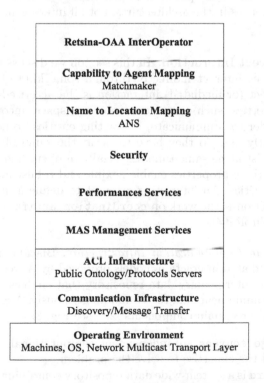

Fig. 7. The Retsina MAS infrastructure [79]

used for a discovery process to let the agents find infrastructural components. The ACL used in Retsina is KQML (Knowledge Query and Manipulation Language) [33]. Retsina provides an ontology derived from the Wordnet Ontology [27] and a protocol engine with a protocol language. The MAS management services offer tool support to monitor the activity of the agents and to debug and launch the applications. Retsina provides a service for performance monitoring in simulation. The security module supports agent authentication, secure communication and integrity of the Retsina infrastructure components. A first basic high-level infrastructural support is offered through ANSs (Agent Name Services). An ANS provides a means to abstract away from physical locations by mapping agent identifiers to network addresses. ANSs do not participate in the transactions between agents, they only provide the agents with addresses that they can cache, removing the need for unnecessary lookups. A second level of infrastructural support is offered by middle agents, i.e. matchmakers. Matchmakers provide a mapping between agents and services. Service providers can advertise their services at the matchmakers and agents can request the matchmakers to get contact information of relevant providers. Advertisement and requests have to be formulated in a special language called LARKS (Language for Advertisement and Request for Knowledge Sharing) [78]. The Retsina-OAA InterOperator on top of the Retsina MAS architecture bridges the Retsina MAS infrastructure with the OAA platform (Open Agent Architecture) [18]. Due to fundamental differences in the architectures, not all inter-agent interactions can be translated.

Models for Indirect Interaction. In this section we discuss interaction models in which entities interact indirectly through some kind of communication abstraction. Indirect (or mediated) interaction is characterized by a number of fundamental properties, such as name uncoupling, space uncoupling and time uncoupling. In order to communicate, interacting entities do not have to know each other explicitly, nor do they have to be at the same place, they do not even have to co-exist at he same time. Especially in open, highly dynamic, distributed systems, these properties enable flexible and robust interaction among the cooperating entities. An interesting attempt to define a unified framework for indirect interaction is the work on `coordination artifacts` of A. Omicini, A. Ricci and M. Viroli [64].

Classical Blackboard Communication Infrastructure. Blackboard systems were the first type of mediated interaction models proposed by AI researchers [24][20]. A blackboard is an intermediary data repository that enables cooperating software modules to communicate indirectly and anonymously. A classic blackboard system consists of three main components [20], see Fig. 8:

1. The `knowledge sources` are independent computational modules that together contain the expertise to solve the problem.
2. The `blackboard` is a system-wide data repository containing the shared data; interaction between knowledge sources only happens via the blackboard.

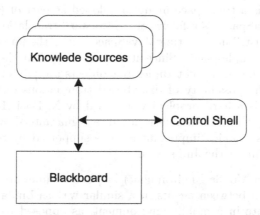

Fig. 8. Components of a classical blackboard system

3. A `control component` makes runtime decisions about the course of problem solving. When the currently executing knowledge source completes, the control component selects the most appropriate pending knowledge source for execution. To guide its selection, knowledge sources provide the control component with the necessary control knowledge.

Traditional MASs contrast with blackboard systems since they emphasize autonomy of agents, coordinated interaction between the agents, distribution (thus no central data repository) and organization as an emergent global phenomenon. As such, MASs and blackboard systems are two technologies with different application domains. Traditional blackboard systems are most appropriate for closely collaborating problem solving, while the focus of MASs is on solving large-scale distributed problems.

Tuple-based Interaction Models. In contrast to blackboard systems, tuple-based technologies use associative access to a shared dataspace for communication and synchronization purposes. `Tuplespaces` were first introduced in Linda [16]. Linda is a coordination language, where coordination is defined in the spirit of separation of concerns: computation, i.e. the internal behavior of the active entities in the system, and coordination, i.e. the management of the interdependent active entities, especially their communication and synchronization, should be separated as much as possible. Linda attains this by providing a coordination language that enables communication between agents. Agents in Linda communicate by putting tuples in, and removing them from a shared space, i.e. the tuplespace. The Linda language is in essence composed out of three primitives: *in*, allows to take a tuple out of the tuplespace that matches with a given template; *out*, allows to put a tuple in the tuplespace; and *rd* that allows to nondestructively read a tuple based on a template. Throughout the years variants for distributed computing appeared, such as MARS [15], Sun's JavaSpaces [77] and LIME [57]. We take a closer look at the latter two.

JavaSpaces. [77] is a tuplespace model developed as part of (and as base of) Sun's Jini [35]. JavaSpaces is a fairly straightforward translation of the original Linda model to a distributed setting. JavaSpaces offers the possibility of several remotely accessible tuplespaces. Since it was developed in the context of the Java programming language, not tuples but objects are put in the tuplespace. JavaSpaces adds the possibility of distributed transactions on the tuplespace. The fact that this is a hard problem was raised by N. Busi [14]. Busi showed that the serializability of transactions is not always guaranteed by the JavaSpaces system. JavaSpaces remains important as it is supported by Sun and used as discovery mechanism for the Jini system.

LIME. (Linda In a Mobile Environment) [57] is a middleware system that allows communication between agents in a similar way as Linda does. However, it is built to operate in a mobile environment, as opposed to Linda which is conceived for parallel computing. Instead of communicating through one centralized tuplespace, in Lime each agent carries its own tuplespace. The traditional tuplespace operations are available, augmented with other operations such as the *non-blocking read* and *non-blocking in* operations. The originality of the approach is that, when agents reside on the same or a connected host, their tuplespaces are merged transparently, i.e. agents have the illusion of a locally shared tuplespace. The Lime middleware can be used for applications where both the agents are mobile (i.e. moving from host to host) and the hosts are mobile (i.e. physically moving). In order to make this possible a location parameter is added to the operations, so that agents can select the tuplespace they wish to interact with. Also, to cope with the dynamic environment, `reactions` can be defined, i.e. code that is executed by the tuplespace when specific tuples are inserted in the tuplespace.

In recent years, a number of tuple-based systems were proposed for ad hoc and mobile computing. ObjectPlaces [74], EgoSpaces [47] and TOTA [49] add mechanisms for sharing tuples across tuplespaces. ObjectPlaces maintains an agent defined view on a host's surroundings. A view is an up-to-date representation of the state of tuplespaces on neighboring nodes in the network, and this representation is maintained as the network and the contents of the tuplespaces change. This can be done efficiently since the interface to the tuplespaces in ObjectPlaces is asynchronous (i.e. operations do not block, but their result is returned when it is available), as opposed to the synchronous interface common in other tuplespace-like systems. In the EgoSpaces system, a view is similarly a description of neighboring hosts in the network, and the system allows agents to execute Linda-like operations on the tuplespaces gathered from the view specification. EgoSpaces is built upon the Lime system. TOTA takes a different approach. The TOTA middleware maintains distributed tuples: a distributed tuple can for example represent a gradient field that decays as it is propagated on the network. This tuple is thus spread out over different distributed tuplespaces, and the TOTA middleware maintains the tuple as the network topology changes.

Stigmergy. The term stigmergy is coined by Grassé [38] to explain nest construction in termite colonies. The concept indicates that individual entities interact indirectly through a shared environment: one individual modifies the environment and others respond to the modification, and modify it in turn. [68] discusses several uses of stigmergy for MAS.

A popular means for such indirect interaction is through pheromones. A pheromone is a chemical substance (or a software counterpart) deposited in the environment. A pheromone has three interesting properties: (1) it aggregates, i.e. newly dropped pheromone merges with/reinforces already existing pheromone, (2) it diffuses, meaning it propagates in its local environment, and (3) it evaporates, meaning it decays over time. A pheromone is thus a representation of shared agent knowledge: it spreads to other nearby agents, allowing a local information transfer; it can be reinforced by other agents, allowing the MAS to incrementally build a solution; and disappears over time, which is a natural way to cope with dynamism in the environment.

Some applications using stigmergy include solving constraint problems, used by Dorigo's Ant Colony Optimization [23]; routing calls through telecommunication networks [11]; manufacturing control [13] and peer to peer systems [56]. For more application examples and more in-depth technical discussion, we refer to [10]. Here we take a closer look at two representative uses of stigmergy. First we zoom in on synthetic ecosystems presented in [13], than we look at the telecommunication network routing infrastructure presented in [11].

Synthetic Ecosystem. In [13], S. Brueckner considers a synthetic ecosystem where on the one hand agents control physical entities in the real world, but on the other hand, agents act among each other in a software environment. To enable indirect coordination among software agents in the same way social ants coordinate, the software environment emulates the "services" provided by the real world of ants. The part of the software environment realizing the services is called the **pheromone infrastructure**.

The pheromone infrastructure models a discrete spatial dimension. It comprises a finite set of places and a topological structure linking the places. A link connecting two places has a downstream and an upstream direction. Thus, for each place there is a set of downstream and a set of upstream neighbor places that are directly linked to it. Each agent in a synthetic ecosystem is mapped to a place, i.e. the current location of the agent, which may change over time. The pheromone infrastructure models a finite set of pheromone types. A pheromone type is a specification of a software object comprising a strength-slot (real number) and other data-slots. For each pheromone type, a propagation direction (downstream or upstream) is specified.

The pheromone infrastructure handles a finite set of software pheromones for each pheromone type. Every data-slot, except the strength-slot, is assigned a value of a finite domain to form one pheromone (type, direction etc.) The strength value (i.e. the value in the strength-slot) is interpreted as a specific amount of the pheromone. Different pheromones of a synthetic ecosystem may be stored in each place.

An agent may perform the following activities at its current place in the pheromone infrastructure:

- Access the references to all agents located at a place.
- Perceive the neighbor places of a place.
- Sample the local strength values of a specified set of pheromones.
- Initiate a change in the local strength of a specified pheromone by a specified value.

The pheromone infrastructure manipulates the values in the strength-slot of the pheromones at each place in the following way:

1. External input (aggregation): based on a request by an agent, the strength of the specified pheromone is changed by the specified value.
2. Internal propagation (propagation/diffusion): Assume an external input of strength s into a pheromone g at a place p. The input event is immediately propagated to the neighbors of p in the propagation direction of g. There, the local strength of g is changed by an input weaker than s. An even weaker input propagates to the following neighbors. The stepwise weakening of the input is influenced by g's propagation parameter.
3. Without taking changes caused by external input or propagation into account, the strength of each pheromone is constantly reduced in its absolute value (evaporation). The reduction is influenced by the evaporation parameter of the pheromone.

There is a major difference between the algorithms realized in the pheromone infrastructure and those observed in nature. After an ant deposits pheromones on the ground, evaporation disperses it. Particle by particle the pheromone moves through the continuous space driven by Brownian motion. At the initial location the amount of pheromones is reduced, while it builds up somewhere else or vanishes completely. In the discrete space of the pheromone infrastructure, propagated pheromones have only specific locations on which to "settle down". Furthermore, the structure of the space is not homogeneous. At some places, pheromones may be propagated to many places, while at other places no further propagation is possible. As a consequence, the mechanisms of evaporation and propagation of pheromones are modelled separately. Instead of continuously exchanging particles among places, there is one "wave" of input events running along the links, which is triggered by the original input of the agent.

The pheromone infrastructure realizes an application-independent support for synthetic ecosystems designed according to a number of design principles, such as decentralization, locality, parallelism, indirect communication, information sharing, feedback, randomization and forgetting. In [13], the principles of synthetic ecosystems and the proposed pheromone infrastructure are applied to manufacturing control systems. V. Parunak and his colleagues have applied digital pheromones in several practical applications, for an overview we refer to [67].

Network Routing. In [11], E. Bonabeau and his colleagues present an ant-like mechanism for routing and load balancing in telecommunication networks that builds upon work of R. Schoonderwoerd [75] and S. Guérin [40]. Routing allows calls to be transmitted from a source to a destination through a sequence of intermediate switching nodes. The pathway of a message must be as short as possible, taking into account fluctuations of user traffic and changes of the network structure (e.g. link or switch failures.) To provide fault tolerance and spreading the computational load, the routing functionality should be implemented in a decentralized way. Social insects exhibit flexibility and robustness, solving difficult problems in a highly distributed way. The authors exploit this knowledge to tackle the routing problem in telecommunication networks. In the original routing algorithm of Schoonderwoerd [75], a node N_i (of a network with n nodes), with $k(i)$ neighbors (links being bidirectional) is characterized by a routing table $R_i = [r^i_{l,m}]_{n-1,k(i)}$ that has $n-1$ rows and k columns: each row corresponds to a destination node and each column to the next node. $r^i_{l,m}$ gives the probability that a given message, the destination of which is node N_l, be routed from node N_i to node N_m.

Agents go from their source node to their destination node by moving from node to node. The next node an agent will move to is selected according to the routing table of its current node. Agents update routing tables of nodes viewing their node of origin as a destination node, i.e. agents use certain knowledge about the portion of the network they come from to modify routing tables. For its part, this modification will influence the routing of messages and agents that have this portion of the network as destination. This approach avoids requiring agents to go back all the way to their node of origin to update the intermediate routing tables.

More precisely, an agent modifies the row corresponding to its source node, which is viewed as its destination node. With N_s the source node of an agent, N_m the node it just came from, and N_i its current node at time t, the entry $r^i_{s,m}(t)$ is reinforced while other entries $r^i_{s,l}(t)$ in the same row decay. The modification is determined by a reinforcement parameter δr that depends on the agent's characteristics. The influence of δr of a given agent must depend on how well this agent is performing, e.g. aging can be used to modulate δr. If an agent has been waiting a long time along its route to its destination node, it means that the nodes it has visited and links it has used are congested, so that δr should decrease with the agent's age.

Based on an idea of Guérin [40], Bonabeau and his colleagues propose to update not only the row that corresponds to an agent's source node, but all rows corresponding to all the intermediate nodes visited by the agent. Thereby the reinforcement of an entry associated with a given name is discounted by a factor that depends on the agent's age relative to the time it visited that node. [11] shows that the extended approach yields significantly better performance results. The authors however, point to the simplifications of previously used models and state that realistic tests in complex network models are needed. Therefore a deeper understanding of the limits and constraints of communication networks is necessary.

Interaction Models Related to Space in MASs. The ancestors of agent models providing an explicit representation of the spatial structure of the environment are Cellular Automata (CA) [91][92]. The CA model provides a regular lattice of automata, characterized by a homogeneous state and transition rule. The related structure is naturally suited to represent an abstraction of a physical environment, and CA have been widely used to model problems in which spatial features can play an important role. Some approaches providing the integration of CA and agent systems have been proposed, see e.g. [22]. Several platforms for MAS-based simulation, developed in line with Swarm [55], implement a spatial structure of the environment in terms of regular grids.

The Multilayered Multi Agent Situated System (MMASS) [6] is a MAS model providing an explicit representation of the agents environment and an interaction model strongly related to the agents context. The environment is modelled as a multi-layered structure, where each layer is represented as a connected graph of sites. Layers may represent abstractions of a physical environment, but can also represent logical aspects, e.g. the organizational structure of a company. Between the layers specific connections (interfaces) can be defined that are used to specify that information generated in one of these layers, may propagate into a different one. In MMASS, agents can (1) interact through a reaction among adjacent entities, (2) emit fields that are diffused in the environment, and (3) can be perceived by other agents. After experiments for the simulation of complex systems, the MMASS model has been recently proposed for applications in the ubiquitous computing scenario [50]. This type of application requires software architectures and tools based on models comprising some notion of space. Among other approaches sharing this viewpoint, it is important to mention Co-Fields [48] (Computational Fields) of M. Mamei, L. Leonardo and F.Zambonelli. Co-Fields supports the coordination of agents in an environment by means of distributed data structures (i.e. the co-fields) that can be spread either by the agents themselves or by other elements of the environment. Agents can sense the intensity of co-fields and are constantly guided by them, e.g. by moving towards local minima.

Environment as an Organizational Layer. Recently a particular interest has been given to organizational concepts within MAS such as "organizations", "groups", "communities", "roles" etc. [21, 29, 46, 37, 95, 59]. From an organizational perspective, a MAS can naturally be considered and designed as a *computational organization* [94] that defines a framework for agent activities, i.e. the organization imposes a set of constrains for the behavior of agents, and offers a set of facilities and services that agents may use. In [30] J. Ferber and his colleagues make a distinction between ACMAS or agent-centered MAS and OCMAS or organizational-centered MAS. In OCMAS, the organization acts (1) as a "dynamic framework" where agents may enter and leave organizations at will, and (2) as an environment for resources, services, communications and tasks, through the concepts of both groups and roles.

Thinking in terms of organizational design differs from the agent-centered approach that has been dominant during many years. When building an OC-

MAS, the designer first concentrates on the organizational level by specifying the structures and pattern of activities among agents, based on abstractions such as groups, roles, interaction protocols, authority constraints between roles, etc. At this stage, no mental issues such as beliefs or goals are considered. It is only when the organization has been specified that the MAS developer focusses on the agent's internal architecture.

Several models of OCMAS have been proposed [4, 30, 60]. Here, we briefly examine the AGR model (previously called Aalaadin) [29, 30] which is a very simple organizational model.

AGR. The AGR model is based on three primitive concepts: *Agent, Group* and *Role.* In the AGR model, agents play roles within groups. An agent may play multiple roles at the same time and may be a member of several groups. A group, as a part of an organization, is used as a context for patterns of activity. Agents are only allowed to communicate with agents of the same group. Suppose that an agent a of group G wants to communicate with an agent b of group H, but a does not belong to H and b does not belong to G. Communication can only be established when agent a joins group H, or agent b joins group G, or an agent c exists that is member of both groups G and H, and that can act as a mediator for this communication. This restriction on the scope of communication supports the creation of well-defined organizational structures such as hierarchies.

Groups act as environments for agents. An agent may enter or leave a group as a human may enter or leave a house or a social structure such as a firm or a lab. Within a group, agents provide services and facilities that the other agents of the group may use. Partitioning a society of agents into several groups enables a designer to build secure systems where secured groups of agents protect themselves by requesting authorization to be joined.

AGR provides a set of diagrams to describe organizations [30]. In the "cheeseboard diagram", a group is represented as an oval that imitates a board. Agents are represented by skittles that are positioned on a board and cut across a board when they belong to several groups.

A role is represented as a hexagon and a line links the role to agents. Fig. 9 illustrates a concrete organization using the cheeseboard diagram. In this exam-

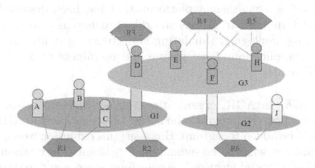

Fig. 9. The "cheeseboard" diagram in AGR for describing concrete organizations

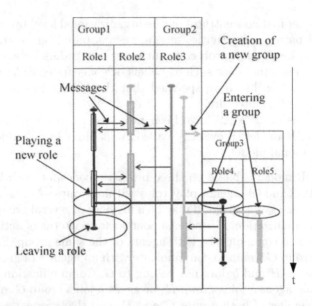

Fig. 10. The organizational sequence diagram in AGR

ple, the agent F is a member of both groups, $G2$ and $G3$, and the agent plays roles $R4$ and $R5$ in group $G2$, and role $R6$ in group $G3$.

The "organizational sequence diagram" describes the dynamics of organizations, i.e. the temporal relationships between organizational events, such as the creation of a group, an agent that enters a group or leaves it, or the acquisition of a role. The organizational sequence diagram can be seen as an extension of UML sequence diagram that incorporates the dynamics of roles and groups.

Contrary to an AUML sequence diagram where the life-line of an agent is represented by a single vertical line, in an organizational sequence diagram the life-line of an agent may consists of several (possibly parallel) segments. Each segment describes the *life* of an agent playing a specific role in a specific group. Parallel segments represent the fact that an agent plays several roles simultaneously. Fig. 10 depicts an example of a organizational sequence diagram.

MadKit [41, 52] is a multiagent platform, that has been designed according to the AGR model. In MadKit, groups and roles are used as core mechanisms for building, launching, deploying, simulating and observing multiagent programs. Several practical applications have proven the usefulness of MadKit and the underlying AGR model.

Extensions of AGR. In AGR, organizations do not encompass the notions of situatedness and action. To integrate the notion of situatedness in AGR, a spatial relationship could be added to a group. However, this extension would raise many difficult problems: e.g. what is the semantics of "distance" in relation to roles, is a role representing a "social location" as coordinates represent spatial locations? This approach has not been followed so far. To include the notion of action in

AGR, it is necessary to reify the concept of environment and to integrate it with the organizational concepts.

In [70], V. Parunak and J. Odell propose an extension of AGR by reifying the environment. In this model, an agent is both a member of (possibly several) groups, and an element of an environment. This work is interesting, but needs further exploration. In [32], J. Ferber and F. Michel propose another approach and consider an organization as a special kind of environmental zone, called an area. Actions are associated with organizations, i.e. communicating, entering a group or leaving it, playing a role, and creating a group.

In summary, the main idea of the research track on AGR is to offer an organizational-centered approach to build MASs. In AGR, the designer first considers the organization of the MAS as an accessible organizational structure in which agents have to behave, i.e. the designer builds the agent system according to the roles the agents play in the organization. Afterwards, the designer can focuss on the agent internal architectural details.

3.3   Agent-Environment Interactions

In this section, we discuss different models related to agent-environment interaction. First we look at agents' perception of the environment. Then we zoom in on a couple of models for actions. The section concludes with a brief discussion of the notion of task-environments.

Perception of the Environment. Perception is the ability of an agent to observe its neighborhood, resulting in a percept of the environment. Percepts describe the sensed environment in the form of expressions that can be understood by the agent. Agents use percepts to update their knowledge about the world or use it directly for decision making. In the case of an agent situated in the physical world, perception can be implemented in hardware: for example, it might be a video camera or a laser sensor on a mobile agent. For software agents situated in a virtual environment, perception must be implemented in software. Although perception is very common for any MAS, relatively little research work has been done in this area. Most of the research on perception can be found in robotics and cognitive science. For virtual environments, where all aspects of perception must be modelled explicitly, only a couple of theories and generic models for perception have been proposed. First, we illustrate perception in the RoboCup Soccer Server, then we discuss a domain independent model for active perception.

RoboCup Soccer Server. The RoboCup Soccer Server [71] supports three kinds of sensors in its sensor model: the aural sensor, the visual sensor and the body sensor. The aural sensor detects messages sent by the referee, the coaches and the other players. All messages are received immediately. The format of an aural sensor message is:

(*hear Time Sender Message*)

Time indicates the current time, *Sender* refers to the sender and *Message* to the content of the received message. Several server parameters affect the aural sensor. E.g., a player can only hear a message if the player's hear capacity is at least *hear_decay*, since the hear capacity of the player is decreased by that number when a message is heard. Every cycle, the hear capacity is increased with *hear_inc*, but is limited to *hear_max*. Players can receive more than one message at the same time. A message of a player is transmitted only to the players within *audio_cut_dist* meters from that player.

The visual sensor reports objects currently seen by the player. The information is automatically sent to the player every *sense_step*, a fixed period of time. Visual information arrives from the server in the following format:

(*see ObjName Distance Direction DistChng DirChng BodyDir HeadDir*)

ObjName refers to the name of the observed object, *Distance* and *Direction* are self-explaining. *DistChng* and *DirChng* refers to information about the relative velocity of the target object. *BodyDir* and *HeadDir* are only included if the observed object is another player and indicate the head and body direction of the other player relative to the observing player. The visible sector of a player is dependent on several parameters such as *sense_step*, which determines the basic time step between received visible information, *visible_angle*, i.e. the player's view cone, and *visible_distance* being the number of meters a player is able to see an object. If an object is within the distance but not in the view cone, then the player can only perceive the type of the object (ball, player, goal etc.) but not the exact name of the object. The player itself can influence the frequency and quality of the information by changing *ViewWidth* and *ViewQuality*.

Finally, the body sensor reports the current "physical" status of the player. This information is automatically sent to the player every *sense_body_step*. The transmitted information contains different kinds of player-specific information, such as: *AmountOfSpeed*, i.e. an approximation of the player's current speed, *HeadDirection*, i.e. the relative direction of the player's head, and *MoveCount*, i.e. a counter that indicates the number of move commands the player has executed so far.

The Robocup Soccer Server supports a rich and flexible model for perception, however the model is confined to the Robocup domain.

Model for Active Perception. In [89], D. Weyns, E. Steegmans and T. Holvoet propose a generic model for active perception that focusses on software agents situated in a virtual environment. Active perception enables an agent to direct its perception at the most relevant aspects of the environment according to its current task, facilitating better situation awareness and helping to keep processing of perceived data under control. The authors state that their model is generic in the sense that (1) it is independent of any domain or specific topology of the environment; (2) it offers reusable core abstractions for active perception in situated MASs, and (3) it offers support to model domain specific properties of perception. Fig. 11 gives a high level overview of the model. The model de-

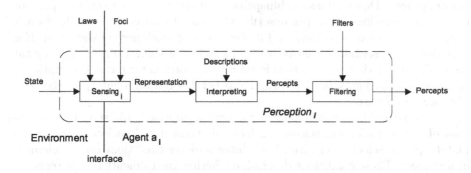

Fig. 11. Model for active perception

composes active perception in three functional modules: sensing, interpreting and filtering.

Sensing maps the state of the environment onto a representation. A representation is defined as a structured assembly of symbols that refers back to something in the environment, i.e. external to the agent. The mapping of state to representation depends on two factors. First the agent can select a set of foci. Each focus is characterized by its sensibility, but may have other properties too, such as an operating range, a resolution etc. Focus selection enables an agent to direct its perception, it allows it to sense the environment only for specific types of information. E.g., in an ant-like MAS, one agent may be interested in a "visible" perception of his environment, while another agent may be interested in "smelling" pheromones. To sense the desired type of information, both agents have to select a different appropriate focus. Second, the representation of the state is composed according to a set of perceptual laws. A perceptual law is an expression that constrains the composition of a representation according to the requirements of the modelled domain. As such, perceptual laws are an instrument for the designer to model domain specific constraints on perception. Contrary to physical sensing that incorporates such constraints naturally, such constraints have to be modelled explicitly in software MASs. Examples are a perceptual law that specifies how an area behind an obstacle is out of the scope of a perceiving agent or a law that under certain conditions adds some noise to perception. Besides the modelling of domain specific sensing, perceptual laws also permit the designer to introduce "synthetic" constraints on perception. E.g., for reasons of efficiency one could introduce default limits for perception in order to restrain the amount of information the agents have to process. It is important to notice that the model supports parallel sensing of the environment. Since agents can select different foci simultaneously, sensing typically results in a compound representation of the environment. This property is important to enable agents to sense their environment in a multi-mode manner.

The second functionality of active perception is interpretation. Interpretation maps a representation to a percept. To interpret a representation, agents use descriptions. Descriptions are blueprints that enable agents to extract percepts from representations. Percepts describe the sensed environment in the form of expressions that can be understood by the internal machinery of the agent. E.g., consider a representation that contains a number of similar objects in a certain area. The agent that interprets this representation may use one description to interpret the distinguished objects and another description to interpret the group of objects as a cluster.

The third and final functionality of active perception is filtering. By selecting a set of filters an agent is able to select only those data items of a percept that match specific selection criteria. Each filter imposes conditions on the elements of a percept. These conditions determine whether the elements of a percept can pass the filter or not. E.g., an agent that has selected a focus to perceive its environment visually and is currently interested in only the agents within its perceptual range can select an appropriate filter that matches only agents for its percept.

An important remark concerns dynamism of perception. In the context of open systems, it is important that the components of the perception system can change (or be changed) dynamically, by the engineer or by the agents themselves. According to the authors, in the model for active perception, the agent can change the set of selected foci and filters dynamically according to its ongoing tasks. On the other hand, perceptual laws are pre-defined by the designer. As such, perceptual laws can not cope with unpredictable changes in the environment. To deal with run-time changes of domain specific constraints on perception, the model can be extended with infrastructure to adapt the set of perceptual laws (according to the changes in the system) or to replace laws dynamically.

Models for Actions. The classical approach to deal with actions is based on the (environmental) transformation of states, i.e. an action is defined as a transition of state, that is, as an operator whose execution produces a new state. From an observational point of view, the result of the behavior of an agent -its action- is directly modelled by modifying the environmental state variables. Whereas this approach suffices in classical AI where only one agent is acting, it fails for MASs were several agents are acting concurrently on a shared environment.

In [28], J. Ferber indicates a number of weaknesses of the classical approach to action. A first limitation is that only very elementary actions can be described. Complex composite actions can hardly be described. A harder problem is the static nature of actions as state transformations. Dynamic processes in the environment, such as the evaporation of pheromones, cannot be described, only the transformation obtained by the application of actions can. Another drawback is the lack of (flexible) support for simultaneous actions. E.g., to deal with a possible collision, explicit tests (as well as their possible consequences) must be added to the action code to verify whether two agents step to the same location or not. While the MAS community always assumes that the actions of different agents are carried out in parallel, the classical models for action do not offer an adequate formal basis to represent collective actions. Finally, the approach does not distinguish between the actions themselves (what the agents do) and the consequence of the actions. Thus, traditional approaches to actions leave the description of how actions happen aside and only take into account the results of the actions.

Hereafter, we zoom in on two models for action that deal with these drawbacks. First, we zoom in on the action model for situated MASs of Ferber and Müller, described in [31]. Next, we look at the action model of Weyns and Holvoet, described in [86], that builds upon the Ferber-Müller model. From the scarce other work that is done on explicit models for action, we point to the work of F. Okuyama, R. Bordini and A. da Rocha Costa [62], which presents an XML based description language for actions and its effects, called ELMS (Environment Description Language for Multi-Agent Simulations). For more background information on action models we refer to [28].

Synchronous Model for Action. The action model of J. Ferber and J.P. Müller is based on three main principles. First, it distinguishes between influences and reactions to influences. Influences come from inside the agents and are attempts to modify the course of events in the world. Reactions, which result in state changes, are produced by the environment by combining influences of all agents, given the local state of the environment and the laws of the world. This clear distinction between the products of the agents' behavior and the reaction of the environment enables the handling of simultaneous actions. Second, the model decomposes the system dynamics in two parts, the dynamics of the environment and the dynamics of the agents situated in the environment. Third, the model describes the different dynamics of the MAS by means of abstract state machines.

Contrary to classical theories that only use the state of the world to describe evolution in a MAS, in Ferber and Müller's model evolution is described as the transformation of what they call **dynamical state**. Such a dynamical state is defined as a tuple consisting of the state of the environment and the set of influences simultaneously produced in the environment. The evolution of the MAS is defined as a function called *Cycle*, that in each step transfers the dynamical state to the next dynamical state. The *Cycle* function is further split in two sub-functions, *React* and *Exec*. A set of laws of the world describe how the next state of the world is computed given the previous state and the set of influences. In addition, a set of operators is defined for the agents that allow them to produce influences in the environment. The *React* function takes the influences and according to the current state of the world and its laws, produces the next state of the world. The *Exec* function produces the influences in the next dynamical state.

To describe the overall dynamics of the system, Ferber and Müller integrate the *React* and *Exec* functions in the *Cycle* function. The *Cycle* function then expresses the evolution of a MAS with n agents, i.e. in each cycle the function produces (1) a new state of the environment as reaction of the environment to the set of produced influences and (2) a new set of influences produced by the agents and the dynamics of the environment. A global synchronizer is responsible for the synchronization of the cyclic evolution of the MAS. This synchronizer ensures that, "at a given moment, all the agents are treated as acting simultaneously, and that the environment reacts only subsequently, before handing over to the agents in an endless loop" [28].

The Ferber-Müller model deals with complex interactions in the environment and between agents, solving the fundamental problem of simultaneous actions in an elegant way. Besides, the model is applicable to purely reactive agents as well as to agents with memory. The model is basically restricted to synchronous MAS evolution, i.e. the MAS evolves at one global pace. Because the influences of *all* agents are treated as if they happened together, each influence can potentially interfere with any other influence.

Action Model with Regional Synchronization. As an alternative to the centralized synchronization model of Ferber-Müller, D. Weyns and T. Holvoet [86] propose an action model based on regional synchronization. With regional synchronization, there is no longer one global synchronizer, but instead each agent is equipped with his own local synchronizer. Each synchronizer is responsible to handle all synchronization issues for its associated agent. Before each action, the agent's synchronizer synchronizes with the other synchronizers in its neighborhood. The result of the synchronization algorithm is the formation of a group of agents, called a `region`. Agents of the same region act simultaneously, but independent of the other agents of the MAS. An algorithm for regional synchronization is discussed in detail in [85, 88].

The action model that integrates regional synchronization, describes the dynamics of a MAS composed of a set of agents that exist in an environment and act simultaneously based on their locality. Besides the actions invoked by the agents, other activities may be going on in the environment too. In [86], such activities are denoted as `ongoing activities`. Examples of ongoing activities are a moving object or, in the context of ant-like systems, an evaporating pheromone. Weyns and Holvoet use a different notion of dynamical state than the Ferber-Müller model. Dynamical state is defined as a tuple consisting of the state of the environment, and a set of `consumptions`. A consumption[1] is an effect from the environment reserved for a particular agent. Such consumption results from the reaction of the environment to the most recently produced influences for that agent. When an agent "consumes" a consumption, the consumption can be absorbed by the agent (e.g. food that is turned into energy), the agent may simply hold an element (e.g. an object he has picked up) or the consumption may affect the agent's state (e.g. the arm of a robot is wrenched through an external force).

The dynamics of the system is defined as the *Cycle* function that maps a dynamical state to the next dynamical state. To clarify the activities invoked by the agents A and the ongoing activities D in the environment on the one hand and the reaction of the environment upon both activities on the other hand, the *Cycle* function is split up in two parts. The first part is composed of two sub-functions: $Exec^A$ and $Apply^D$. The second part is a single function *React*

---

[1] The notion of consumption is introduced by Ferber in [28].

that represents the reaction of the environment to the simultaneously performed activity of agents and ongoing activities.

$Exec^A$ represents the activities invoked by the agents. The subset of simultaneous acting agents consume their consumptions and produce a set of influences through the application of operators. The effects of the ongoing activities in the environment are induced by the $Apply^D$ function. Depending on the state of the environment, the set of ongoing activities produce a set of influences in the environment through the application of a set of parallel composed operators that are associated with the ongoing activities.

Since the activities invoked by the agents and the ongoing activities in the environment happen simultaneously, the influences resulting from $Apply^D$ and $Exec^A$ have to be combined. The reaction of the environment to the simultaneously performed activity of the agents and the ongoing activities in the environment is described by the *React* function, i.e. in the state of the environment, for the united sets of influences, and according to the set of parallel composed laws, *React* determines the next state of the environment and produces a new set of consumptions.

The evolution of the dynamical system is then defined as a sequence of cycles. In each cycle the *Cycle* function transfers the dynamical state into the next dynamical state, i.e. it produces (1) a new state of the environment and (2) a new set of consumptions. This twofold transfer is the result of the *reaction* of the environment to the *execution* of a set of operators invoked by a subset of agents that exist in the system together with the application of a set of operators resulting from the ongoing activities in the environment, given the state of the environment, a set of consumptions, and a set of laws of the world.

Comparison. In [86], Weyns and Holvoet compare the two discussed models for action. Two obvious differences between the models are the definition of dynamical state and the granularity of the groups of synchronized agents. The models are compared from the perspective of the typical execution-reaction cycle for situated MASs, graphically depicted in Fig. 12.

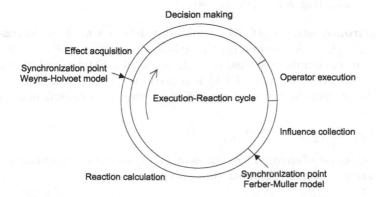

Fig. 12. Comparison of the two model for action based on the execution-reaction cycle

In the Ferber-Müller model, dynamical state is composed of state and *influences*. As such, the dynamics of the MAS can be expressed as the reaction of the environment to the set of influences and subsequently the production of a new set of influences, given the state of the environment and the laws of the world. So, the execution-reaction cycle runs from the point where the influences are collected to the next point where influences are collected, indicated by the "Synchronization point Ferber-Müller model" in Fig. 12. The start of the cycle is initiated by the environment and as such the model takes an *environment-centered* view on MAS evolution. The granularity of synchronously acting agents in the Ferber-Müller is the whole group of agents in the MAS. All agents act at one global pace, i.e. the influences of all agents in each cycle are considered as happening simultaneously. Thus, in the Ferber-Müller model, all agents synchronize in each passage of the execution-reaction cycle at the "Synchronization point Ferber-Müller model" and act simultaneously.

In the regional synchronized model for action, dynamical state is composed with state and *consumptions*. The dynamics of the MAS can be expressed as the consummation of a subset of consumptions and the production of a set of influences to which the environment subsequently reacts (according to the applicable laws) by updating its state and producing a new set of consumptions. So in the Weyns-Holvoet model the execution-reaction cycle runs from the point where the reactions are calculated to the next point where the reactions are calculated, indicated by the "Synchronization point Weyns-Holvoet model" in Fig. 12. Here the agents (on a per region basis) take the initiative to start their cycles, and as such the model takes an *agent-centered* view of MAS evolution. In this model agents of different regions can consume their consumptions independently and run asynchronously through the execution-reaction cycle. In the Weyns-Holvoet model, the granularity of synchronous acting agents are regions of synchronized agents. Influences of agents within a region are considered as happening simultaneously, however different regions can act asynchronously. Thus, in the Weyns-Holvoet model, in each passage of the execution-reaction cycle agents synchronize at the "Synchronization point Weyns-Holvoet model" and form regions that act simultaneously.

Task Environments. In [93], M. Wooldridge defines a task environment as a tuple $< Env, \Psi >$. An environment Env is a triple $Env = < E, e_0, \tau >$, where E is a set of environment states, $e_0 \in E$ is an initial state, and τ is a state transformer function. $\Psi : R \to \{0, 1\}$ is a predicate over runs. A run $r \in R$ of an agent in an environment is a sequence of interleaved environment states and actions, i.e.:

$$r : e_0 \xrightarrow{\alpha_0} e_1 \xrightarrow{\alpha_1} e_2 \xrightarrow{\alpha_2} \ldots \xrightarrow{\alpha_{u-1}} e_u$$

with $e_i \in E$ the set of environment states and $\alpha_j \in Ac$ the set of actions available to the agents. A task environment thus specifies:

- The properties of the system the agent will inhabit, i..e. the environment *Env*.
- The criteria by which an agent either failed or succeeded in its task, i.e. the specification Ψ.

According to Wooldridge, the most common types of tasks are `achievement tasks`, those of the form "achieve a state of affairs", and `maintenance tasks` of the form "maintain a state of affairs". An achievement task is specified by a number of goal states. The agent is required to bring about one of these goal states. A well-known achievement task environment is the blocks world, see e.g. [73]. A maintenance task environment is a task environment in which an agent is required to keep (or avoid) some state of affairs. A simple example is a software agent which task it is to maintain the set of available services in a particular context. Complex tasks might be specified by combinations of achievement and maintenance tasks.

A well-known model for task environments is the TAEMS framework (Task Analysis, Environment Modelling, and Simulation), developed by K. Decker and V. Lesser [43]. TAEMS can be used to specify, reason about, analyze, and simulate task environments. TAEMS is independent of the agent architecture and the inherent nature of the modelled domain. For details, we refer to [80].

3.4 Environments in Agent-Oriented Methodologies

Popular methodologies such as Message [25], Prometheus [66] or Tropos [12] offer support for some basic elements of the environment, however they do not consider the environment as a first-class entity. To our knowledge, the only methodology for analysis and design of MASs that considers the environment as a primary abstraction is the extended version of Gaia described in [94]. F. Zambonelli and his colleagues state that "identifying and modelling the environment involves determining all the entities and resources that the MAS can exploit, control or consume when it is working towards the achievement of the organizational goal." The authors distinguish between computational (or virtual) environments (e.g. a Web site) and physical environments (e.g. a manufacturing pipeline). A list of issues is put forward that has to be taken into consideration during the environmental modelling phase:

1. What are the environmental resources that agents can effectively sense and effect? The environment model should distinguish between the existence and the (possibly constrained) accessibility of a resource.
2. How should the agent perceive the environment? This question refers to the representation of the environment according to given circumstances.
3. What of the existing scenario should be characterized as part of the environment? The distinction between the agents and the environment is not always clear cut. For dynamic environmental resources, the designer has to decide whether they should be modelled as agents or as dynamic resources in the environment.

In Gaia, the identification of the environmental model is part of the analysis phase and is intended to yield an abstract, computational representation of the environment in which the MAS will be situated. During the subsequent architectural design phase, the output of the environmental model (together with a primary role model, a preliminary interactions model and a set of organizational rules) is integrated in the system's organizational structure that includes the real-world organization (if any) in which the MAS is situated. The organizational structure is then used to complete the preliminary role and interaction models. During the detailed (and final) design phase, the definition of the agent model and services model are derived from the completed role and interaction models. According to the authors, Gaia does not commit itself to specific techniques for modelling roles, environment and interactions etc. The outcome of the Gaia process is a technology-neutral specification that should be easily implemented using an appropriate agent-programming framework of a modern object or a component-based framework. With respect to the development of the environmental model, the authors state "it is difficult to provide general modelling abstractions and general techniques because the environments for different applications can be very different in nature and also because they are somehow related to the underlying technology." Therefore the authors propose a "reasonable general approach (without the ambition to be universal), and treat the environment in terms of *abstract computational resources*, such as variables or tuples, made available to the agents for sensing (e.g. reading their values), for affecting (e.g. changing their values) and for consuming (e.g. extracting them from the environment)." As such the environmental model is represented as a list of resources, each associated with a symbolic name, characterized by the type of actions that the agent can perform on it and possibly associated with additional textual comments and descriptions. A notation is used that is based on the Fusion [19] notation, e.g. :

> *reads*   *Var*1   *//readable resource of the environment*
> *Var*2   *//another readable resource*
> *changes*   *Var*3   *//a variable that can also be changed by the agent*

The authors indicate that "in realistic development scenarios, the analyst would choose to provide a more detailed and structured view of environmental resources." In particular, specific issues related to the modelling of environmental resources may be required to enrich/complement the basic notation. Some examples are:

- the representation of the logical/physical relationships between the resources in the environment. A graphical schema may be of help to model and to identify how and from where a resource can be accessed.
- the dynamics of the environment. The authors propose additional annotations to the basic notation to deal with this issue.
- dealing with a priori unknown availability of resources. The authors suggest an associative access model as the Linda tuple space to suit this purpose.

To deal with active components (services and computer-based systems) as part of the *operational environment*, the authors give some general guidelines.

When the role of the active components is simply that of a data provider (e.g. a Web server or a computer-based sensor), they should be modelled in terms of resources. However, if the environment contains components that are capable to perform complex operations (e.g. active databases or active control systems), the components should not be treated as part of the environment but, instead, they should be agentified.

4   Concerns for Environments

The survey described in the previous section shows us that the environment includes a broad diversity of functionalities. In this section we extract a number of core concerns for environments from the survey. We focus on concerns that represent *logical functionalities* of the environment.

As we already mentioned in the introduction section, researchers have highly different views on the concept of environment, causing a lot of confusing what the environment comprises. As a start to disentangle the confusion, we propose a 3-layer model for MASs[2] as depicted in Fig. 13.

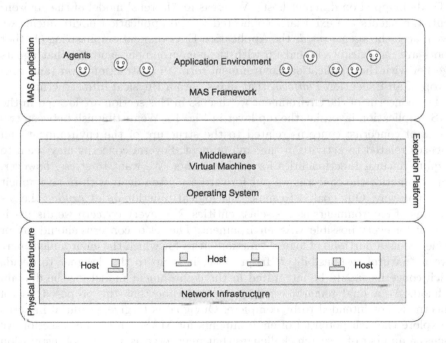

Fig. 13. 3-layer model for MASs

The MAS Application layer typically consists of two sub-layers: (1) the domain specific application logic containing the `Application Environment` with

---

[2] The focus of the proposed model is first of all on software agents.

the embedded Agents, and (2) a supporting MAS framework that offers high-level programming abstractions for the MAS developer such as support for communication or a pheromone infrastructure. The MAS Application runs on top of an "Execution Platform" that typically is composed of a generic (distributed) Middleware infrastructure and Virtual Machines that execute on top of an Operating System. The Execution Platform is mapped onto the "Physical Infrastructure" that comprises the hosts with processors and the connecting Network Infrastructure.

In [51], K. Mertens and his colleagues identify two levels of environments: the "application environment" and the "execution environment." According to the authors, the application environment provides the context for the agents to perform their actions, to communicate with one another and to acquire information about the problem they have to solve. The application environment is the translation of the problem situation, e.g. a grid world with tiles and holes for the Tileworld or a graph structure of locations with accessible files for a peer-to-peer file sharing system. The execution environment is the platform that is used to execute the MAS. The execution environment is mapped onto the physical layout of the hardware, e.g. a JVM that is mapped onto a single host or a number of JVMs mapped on different hosts. Whereas in Mertens' model of the environment, the agents are externally connected to the application environment, we have placed the agents *inside* the Application Environment emphasizing (1) that agents are inextricably bound up with their environment, and (2) that agents together with the Application Environment form an abstraction layer (and run) on top of an Execution *Platform* that maps onto a Physical Infrastructure.

The concerns of the environment we discuss in this section are located in the MAS Application layer, i.e. the top layer in Fig. 13. We distinguish between two classes of concerns: concerns related to the structure of the environment and concerns related to activity in the environment. Several concerns may seem to be quite natural functionalities for environments. We want to stress, however, that in practice the concerns we put forward are often dealt with in an implicit or ad hoc way. Our goal is to make the logical functionalities *explicit*, i.e. as concerns of environments as first-class entities. Not every concern we discuss is relevant for every possible MAS environment. The set of concerns should rather be viewed as a portfolio of logical functionalities for which the environment may have a "natural responsibility." In practice, it is up to the designer to decide which concerns should be integrated in the environment model for the domain at hand. As a final remark, we want to underline that the proposed list of concerns is not intended to be complete. Our goal is to give an initial impetus to explore the rich potential of environments for MASs. In the next section we discuss a number of research challenges that may serve as a source of inspiration for further exploration.

4.1   Concerns Related to the Structure of the Environment

We start with discussing a number of concerns related to structural features of the environment. Successively we look at structuring, resources and ontology.

Structuring. Agents and objects of a MAS share a common environment. The agents as well as the objects are dynamically interrelated to each other. It is the role of the environment to define the rules under which these relationships can exist and can evolve. As such the environment acts as a *structuring* entity for the MAS. This structuring can take different forms: it can be spatial, see e.g. [5, 13, 7, 54], but also organizational, e.g. [30, 94], or the environment can be structured as a mediating entity as e.g. in [16, 57, 74]. Structuring is a fundamental functionality of the environment. The structure of the environment is a design choice that depends upon the requirements of the domain at hand, and should be dealt with explicitly.

Resources. Besides the agents, an environment typically comprises different types of objects or (logical) resources. It is a responsibility of the environment to control the access to the resources. In general, resources can be read/perceived, writed/modified or consumed by agents. The extent to which agents are able to access a particular resource may depend on several factors such as the nature of the resource itself, the resource's current relationship to other resources or agents, the neighborhood of the agent to the resource, the capabilities of the agent etc. In general, the access to the resources can be described by a set of laws defined by the domain at hand, see e.g. [28, 86].

Ontology. In [17], P. Chang and his colleagues state: "agents must be able to understand their environment." Therefore, an environment must specify an ontology that provides a conceptual representation of the domain at hand. The ontology must cover the structure of the environment as well as the observable characteristics of objects, resources and agents, and their interrelationships. For symbolically-oriented agents, an explicit ontology should be available to the agents to enable them to interpret their environment and reason about it. For reactive/behavior-based/stigmergic agents, the designer/developer applies the ontology to encode the agents' internal structures. As such, these kinds of agents have an implicit ontology that enables them to make decisions.

4.2   Concerns Related to the Activity in the Environment

Next we discuss a number of concerns related to activity performed in the environment. First we look at concerns related to activity produced by the agents: communication, actions and perception. We conclude with the responsibilities of the environment related to activity produced by resources or objects.

Communication. As stated in the state-of-the-art overview, communication is inextricably bound up with MASs. Communication can take very different forms, ranging from direct message transfer over anonymous mediated communication via a shared space to indirect communication through stigmergy. Each of these types of communication has its own pros and cons. Designers should be aware of the potency as well as the impact of each type of communication for their solution. Selecting a particular type of communication should be an architectural choice, determined by the requirements of the problem domain at hand.

Actions. Dealing with actions in MASs in general is a very complex matter. If we allow multiple agents to act in the environment in parallel, we need explicit models to deal with actions that range far beyond the scope of state changes based on simple individual manipulation of objects. More than a decade ago, S. Hanks, M. Pollack and P. Cohen already raised in [42] the problem of "how the effects of simultaneous actions differ from the effects of those actions performed sequentially." In the state-of-the-art section we discussed a couple of models for action for MASs. Central to these models are (1) the distinction between the products of the agents' behavior on the one hand and the reaction of the environment on the other hand, and (2) a set of explicitly defined laws that govern the effects of the actions of the agents. These models resolve a number of fundamental issues with respect to actions in MASs, however, dealing with actions in MAS needs extensive further research to grow into full maturity.

Perception. Perception implies that the environment must be an *observable* entity. Agents must be able to inspect their neighborhood. In general, agents should be able to inspect the environment according to their current preferences. In the state-of-the-art overview, we discussed several examples of selective perception, such as "foci" proposed in [89] or "views" as proposed in [47] and [74]. Perception is constrained not only by agents' capabilities, but also by environmental properties (which in fact reflect properties of the problem domain). In [89] the environmental constraints are made explicit in the form of "perceptual laws". As for action models, there is still a wide (unexplored) field open to the concern of perception.

Environmental Processes. Besides the activity of the agents, resources or objects can produce activity in the environment too. A digital pheromone, for example, is a dynamic structure as it aggregates with additional pheromone that is dropped, it diffuses in space and it evaporates over time. Other examples are a rolling ball that moves on, or the local temperature that evolves over time. Maintaining such dynamics is an important functionality of the environment, see e.g. [13, 86].

5   Challenges

To conclude this paper, we list a number of research challenges that, in our opinion, are important for the further exploration of environments for MAS. We have divided the list in three categories: issues with respect to the definition and scope of environments, issues with respect to the interrelationship between agents and their environment, and finally issues concerning the engineering of environments for MASs.

5.1   Definition and Scope of Environments

In Sect. 2, we noted that the term "environment" is vague and ill-defined in relation to MASs. An ongoing research challenge will be developing a clearer understanding of what we mean by an "environment." Defining anything requires relating it to other entities. In the case of environments, their definition requires relating them first to the agents that inhabit them, then to one another, and finally to different application domains.

Environments and Agents. What is the difference between the environment and the agents that inhabit it? A wide variety of distinctions have been proposed. Here are only a few examples:

- What the developer writes for a specific application are the agents. The software or hardware infrastructure on which the agents run is the environment.
- The environment provides the logical context for the agents to perform their actions, to communicate with one another and to acquire information about the problem they have to solve.
- Agents are autonomous, in that they proactively pursue objectives. The environment has no objectives.
- In a refinement of the previous suggestion, agents have achievement goals, while the environment can have only maintenance goals.
- The environment is extensive and unbounded, while the agents are bounded and localized in the environment.
- The environment embodies the given dynamics or "laws of physics" of a problem domain. The agents react to those laws in contingent ways.
- The environment is open to inspection. Individual agents are opaque. In other words, the environment implements what everyone is presumed to be able to see about the domain, while agents hide local decisions that should not be open to direct inspection or manipulation by others.

Each of these distinctions (and others that might be proposed) will yield different conclusions about the relative responsibilities of the agents and the environment, how they are mapped onto a given problem domain, and the life cycle of the design and implementation of a real system. These distinctions deserve formalization and analysis. Certainly, they are not orthogonal to one another. How many truly distinct views are there of the relation between agent and environment?

Taxonomy of Environments. With a formal understanding of the different ways that agents can be related to their environment, we can then classify environments with respect to one another. This level of understanding will enable researchers to be sure that they are talking about the same kind of environment in describing their systems and arguing for the relative merits of alternative approaches.

Environments and Domains. One reason that definitions of "environment" have proliferated is that MASs have been applied to a wide range of different applications domains, which impose differing constraints and afford different resources for interactions among agents. For example, it is natural for designers of a MAS intended to provide packet routing and quality of service management on a communications network to associate the environment with the existing infrastructure of hardware and software that makes up the network and on which the agents will have to execute. In another domain, such as an agent-based simulation of an ecosystem, the environment as well as the agents will be custom-built for the application, and the distinction between agent and environment will be driven more by the differences between bounded vs. unbounded scope and given vs. contingent dynamics. In yet another domain, such as electronic commerce, the distinction between a transparent environment and opaque agents that can hide proprietary details of individual participants becomes paramount.

With a taxonomy of environments in hand, we can begin to develop systematic principles for relating a specific kind of environment to a particular domain. A number of research questions address the question of the relation between a taxonomy of environments and a taxonomy of domains. These include:

- Are there domains that do not need an explicit distinction between environment and agent?
- Are there domains that are particularly well suited to this distinction?
- What features of domains make them particularly amenable or hostile to this distinction?
- Are there particular functions of environments that are valuable regardless of the application domain?
- In general, how can a specification of a domain be mapped to a specification of a particular environment that will best support MASs serving that domain?

5.2   Agent-Environment Interrelationship

As our understanding of the space of possible environments becomes more refined, we need to explore in more detail the relation between agents and their environments. This relationship can be elaborated along at least three dimensions: architecture, protocol, and topology.

Architecture. In many applications, both agents and their environment will be software running on some physical computing system. What is the relationship between the agent software, the environment software, and the software and hardware that make up the computational substrate? In some cases, the agents may be completely dependent on the environment for their access to computational services, so that the environment (whatever other services it provides) becomes an "operating system" for the agents. In other cases, agents and the environment may have independent access to computational services (perhaps on different physical CPU's, as in robotic applications), and will interact with one another as computational peers. In this latter case, the question of how to distinguish the agents from the environment becomes particularly important, since at one level the environment is just another program executing architecturally at the same level as the agents.

These two cases are not mutually exclusive. One can imagine an architecture in which agents and environment execute on separate CPU's, but in which some services (such as inter-agent communications) are only available through the shared environment. Still other configurations are possible, such as the case of a purely physical two-dimensional arena that provides the environment for soccer robots. The exploration of architectural alternatives for relating agents to environments offers ample scope for a new discipline within software engineering.

Protocol. By "protocol," we mean the set of conventions by which agents interact with the environment. The issue of protocol governs the degree to which an environment is open to heterogeneous agents, or to agents that are designed without advance knowledge of the environment. Protocols can vary along at least two dimensions: physical vs. digital and natural vs. arbitrary.

 – In a physical protocol, agents must have physical sensors and effectors that can change and sense the state of the physical world. In a digital protocol, agents need only a way to read and write a register, such as a message mailbox or a communication channel.
 – In a natural protocol, the structure of the interaction is constrained by the broader laws of physics, and any agent that complies with these laws can interact. In an arbitrary protocol, the signs exchanged by the agents are defined by some engineered language that each agent must understand in order to interact. The more natural the protocol, the more open the system will be to other agents that were constructed without detailed knowledge of the environment.

All four combinations of these dimensions are possible, illustrated in Tab. 1.

Table 1. Taxonomy of agent-environment protocols, with examples

	Physical	Digital
Natural	Agents try to push a ball toward their goal in a soccer arena.	An agent trying to communicate on a shared channel detects whether or not there is traffic on the channel (similar to Ethernet). It is unnecessary for the agent to understand the traffic that it detects.
Arbitrary	The goal is marked by a visual target of a designated color.	Agents exchange KQML messages through the environment.

This taxonomy of agent-environment protocols is very preliminary, and offers several directions for further research:

 – What other dimensions distinguish the different ways in which agents interact with their environments?
 – How do those dimensions impact the degree to which the system is open or closed?

- What responsibilities does the environment have, and what services can it provide, to increase its openness to heterogeneous agents?
- Alternatively, in applications that must be highly secure, how can environments ensure that only authorized agents have access to their services?

Topology. One characteristic of many environments is that they define a topology within which agents exist locally. A soccer agent is at only one location within the arena; a network agent lives on a specific router; an information retrieval agent visits only one database at a time. Such topological constraints can simplify agent reasoning (by restricting the range of information an agent must consider to that which is locally available) and system deployment (by restricting interaction to nearby entities and thus enabling the use of low-bandwidth communications), but may also pose challenges in achieving timely, long-range interactions. Research questions involving the relation between agents and the environment's topology include:

- What topologies does each kind of environment naturally induce? In robotics, environments naturally conform to low-dimensional manifolds, such as the surface of the earth or (for flying robots) the atmosphere. Computer networks cannot be mapped to such manifolds, but are typically power-law graphs [8] or more complex structures [3]. In some information retrieval applications, the topology may conform to the semantic structure of natural language [84].
- What does it mean for an agent to be "local" in an environment? In other words, how should the topology constrain agent actions? In some cases, agents may be able to access information only about their current location in the topology, but may be able to communicate with other agents that are remote from them. In other cases, direct inter-agent communications may be restricted to agents at the same location.
- What constraints do different topologies impose on agent interactions with the environment, and with one another through the environment? The existence of such phenomena as small-world shortcuts or highly varying node degrees can lead to interactions that vary widely from what our intuitions lead us to expect in low-dimensional manifolds or planar graphs.
- What is the environment's responsibility with regard to locality? Is it responsible, for instance, to enforce locality of agent interaction? Should all agents be equally localized, or can agents have different degrees of scope? For example, in a tree-structured environment, one can imagine that each agent can interact directly with all agents at its nodes and at lower-level nodes. How should agent scope be related to environment structure?

5.3   Engineering Environments

The previous two areas of research challenges provide ample scope for theoretical exploration, and will lead to many intriguing intellectual issues. The ultimate social benefit from these insights, though, requires their application to concrete problems, and the challenge of engineering environments for such problems will pose significant challenges in both the design and implementation of practical systems.

Design. Disciplined design practices for agents in general are in their infancy, and extending these techniques to environments greatly increases the scope of work to be done. A first step is gaining recognition for environments as first-class entities in MAS design. A number of the points discussed above directly impact design, such as how different sorts of domains map to different types of environments, and how agents are related to their environments. The results of studies in these areas need to be captured in tools such as description languages and other representational mechanisms that will enable engineers to communicate unambiguously about alternative designs. In many cases, the environment may incorporate physical as well as digital elements, and design tools need to support the integration of these domains.

Implementation. The growth of agent-oriented programming led to the proliferation of frameworks and development platforms for agents. Similarly, growing recognition of the importance of environments will stimulate extensions to these tools, or even the development of new tools that can support environments within which agents from different platforms can interact. Inevitably, embodying the services of an environment in a platform will collapse some of the dimensions we have explored in the previous paragraphs. For example, it is unlikely that a single platform will support all of the architectural options discussed above. The success of rival platforms in the market will itself be an important tool to assessing which of these dimensions are most important for practical use, and which can safely be removed from the developer's inventory. A critical question for implementation concerns the relationship between the logical and physical distribution of the environment. In some cases, it will make sense for an environment that represents a physically distributed topology to be distributed physically itself, while in other cases many of the benefits of the agent-environment distinction can be retained even if the environment is hosted on a single machine.

In sum, recognizing the distinction between agent and environment opens up new horizons for research and development comparable to those inaugurated by the development of the agent metaphor itself in the 1990's. These suggestions may help to inspire the next generation of researchers to explore directions that, at this point, seem the most promising. A measure of their success will be the degree to which the natural momentum of the research community overtakes them and leads to a self-sustaining body of science and technology that recognizes environments as first-class entities in the study of multi-agent systems.

6   Conclusions

Environments for MASs are too often assigned limited responsibilities, overlooking a rich potential for the paradigm of MASs. In this paper we have given a survey on the use of environments for MASs. From the study we learned that environments include a broad diversity of functionalities.

We used the insights from the survey to extract a first set of general concerns for environments, each concern representing a particular logical functionality for environments. A fundamental concern of the environment is that it *structures* the MAS. The environmental structuring can take different forms, such as spacial or organizational. Since agents must be able to understand their environment, an explicit ontology is required that covers the structure of the environment as well as the observable characteristics of objects, resources and agents, and their interrelationships. Besides structural aspects, we identified a set of concerns related to the *activity* in the environment. The most common activity of agents in the environment is communication. We discussed several types of communication for MASs. The designer should be aware of the potency as well as the impact of each form of communication and select the appropriate form according to the requirements of the problem domain. Next to communication, agents typically perform actions in the environment. It is the responsibility of the environment to *define the rules* for, and *enforce the effects* of, the agents' actions. Agents must also be able to perceive their environment. As such, the environment is an *observable* entity, contrary to the agents themselves. The environment should enable agents to observe their neighborhood according to their preferences, however, perception is constrained by environmental properties that reflect limitations in the modelled domain. Finally, we clarified that agents are not the only entities that can produce activity in the environment. Objects or resources too may be active in the environment (for example, a pheromone or a moving object). Maintaining such dynamics is an important responsibility of the environment.

The set of concerns we have proposed is not complete, but intended as a start to make the potential responsibilities for environments for MAS explicit. We listed a number of research challenges that may serve as a source of inspiration for further exploration.

We hope that this paper may contribute to extend the exploration of environments for MASs. Environments carry a rich potential for the paradigm of MASs. However, as long as researchers and software developers limit the functionality of environments, or deal with its responsibilities in an implicit or ad hoc manner, the full potential of environments will not be revealed. To discover and exploit the full potential of environments, we must treat environments as first-class entities. Recognizing environments as first-class entities opens up new horizons for research and development in MASs.

Acknowledgments

We would like to thank the attendees of the First International Workshop on Environments for Multiagent Systems [26] for the valuable discussions that have contribute to the work presented in this paper. A special word of appreciation also goes to Kurt Schelfthout, Alexander Helleboogh and Guiseppe Vizzari for their kind cooperation.

References

1. Aglets: http://www.trl.ibm.com/aglets/
2. Ajanta: http://www.cs.umn.edu/Ajanta/home.html
3. Alderson, D., Doyle, J., Govindan, R., Willinger, W.: Toward an Optimization-Driven Framework for Designing and Generating Realistic Internet Topologies. ACM SIGCOMM Computer Communications Review (2003)
4. Amiguet, M., Müller, J.P., Baez-Barranco, J.A., Nagy, A.: The MOCA Platform. Multi-Agent-Based Simulation II, Lecture Notes in Computer Science, Vol. 2581. Springer-Verlag, Berlin Heidelberg New York (2003)
5. Bandini, S., Manzoni S., Simone C.: Dealing with Space in Multi-Agent Systems: a Model for Situated MAS. Second International Joint Conference on Autonomous Agents and Multiagent Systems, ACM Press, Bologna, Italy (2002)
6. Bandini, S., Manzoni, S., Simone, C.: Heterogeneous agents situated in heterogeneous spaces. Applied Artificial Intelligence, Taylor & Francis 16(9-10) (2002)
7. Bandini, S., Manzoni, S., Vizzari, G.: A Spatially Dependant Communication Model for Ubiquitous Systems. First International Workshop on Environments for Multiagent Systems, New York (2004)
8. Barabasi, A., Albert, R.: Emergence of scaling in random networks. Science, 286(509) (1999)
9. Bellifemine, F., Poggi, A., Rimassa, G.: Jade, A FIPA-compliant Agent Framework. 4th International Conference on Practical Application of Intelligent Agents and Multi-Agent Technology, (1999)
10. Bonabeau, E., Dorigo, M., Theraulaz, G.: Swarm Intelligence: From Natural to Artificial Systems. SFI Studies in the Sciences of Complexity, Oxford University Press (1999)
11. Bonabeau, E., Henaux, F., Guérin, S., Snyers, D., Kuntz P., Theraulaz, G.: Routing in Telecommunications Networks with "Smart" Ant-Like Agents. Intelligent Agents for Telecommunications Applications (1998)
12. Bresciani, P., Giorgini, P., Giunchiglia, F., Mylopoulos, J., Perrini, A.: Tropos: an Agent-Oriented Software Development Methodology. Technical Report DIT-02-0015, University of Trento, Italy (2002)
13. Brueckner, S.: Return from the Ant. PhD Dissertation, Humboldt-Universität Berlin, Germany (2000)
14. Busi, N., Zavattaro, G.: On the Serializability of Transactions in JavaSpaces. Electronic Notes Theoretical Computer Science, Vol. 54 (2001)
15. Cabri, G., Leonardi L., Zambonelli, F.: MARS: a Programmable Coordination Architectue for Mobile Agents. IEEE Internet Computing (2000)
16. Gelernter, D., Carrierro, D.: Coordination Languages and their Significance. Communications of the ACM, 35(2) (1992)
17. Chang, P., Chen, K., Chien, Y., Kao, E., Soo, V.: From Reality to Mind: A Cognitive Middle Layer of Environment Concepts for Believable Agents. First International Workshop on Environments for Multiagent Systems, New York, 2004.
18. Cheyer, A., Martin, D.: The Open Agent Architecture. Journal of Autonomous Agents and Multi-Agent Systems, 4(1) (2001)
19. Coleman, D., Arnold, P., Bodoff, S., Dollin, D., Hayes, H., Jeremas, P.: Object Oriented Development: the Fusion Method. Prentice-Hall International, Hemel Hampstead, UK (1994)
20. Corkill, D.: Collaborating Software. International Lisp Conference, New York (2003)

21. Demazeau, Y., Rocha Costa, A.C.: Populations and organizations in open multi-agent systems. 1st National Symposium on Parallel and Distributed AI (1996)
22. Dijkstra, J., Timmermans, H.J.P., Jessurun, A.J.: A Multi–Agent Cellular Automata System for Visualising Simulated Pedestrian Activity. 4th International Conference on Cellular Automata for Research and Industry (2001)
23. Dorigo, M., Maniezzo, V., Colorni, A.: The Ant System: Optimization by a Colony of Cooperating Agents. IEEE Transactions on Systems, Man, and Cybernetics-Part B, **26(1)** (1996)
24. Englemore, R.S., Morgan, A. (eds.): Blackboard Systems. Addison-Wesley (1988)
25. Evans, R., Kearney, P., Caire, G., Garijo, F., Gomez Sanz, J., Pavon, J., Leal, F., Chainho, P., Massonet, P.: MESSAGE: Methodology for Engineering Systems of Software Agents. EURESCOM, EDIN 0223-0907 (2001)
26. E4MAS: First International Workshop on Environments for Multiagent Systems. New York (2004) http://www.cs.kuleuven.ac.be/~distrinet/events/e4mas/
27. Fellbaum, C.: WordNet: An Electronic Lexical Database. MIT Press (1998)
28. Ferber, J.: Multi-Agent Systems, An Introduction to Distributed Artificial Intelligence. Addison-Wesley, ISBN 0-201-36048-9, Great Britain (1999)
29. Ferber, J., Gutknecht, O.: A Meta-Model for the Analysis and Design of Organizations in Multi-Agent Systems. 3rd International Conference on Multi Agent Systems, Paris, France (1998)
30. Ferber, J., Gutknecht, O., Michel, F.: From Agents to Organizations: an Organizational View of Multi-Agent Systems. Agent-Oriented Software Engineering IV. Springer-Verlag, Berlin Heidelberg New York (2003)
31. Ferber, J., Müller, J.P.: Influences and Reaction: a Model of Situated Multiagent Systems. 2th International Conference on Multi-agent Systems, Japan, AAAI Press (1996)
32. Ferber, J., Michel, F.: Integrating Environments with Organization-Centered Multiagent Systems, Environments for Multiagent Systems, Weyns, D., Parunak, H.V.D, Michel, F. (Eds.), Lecture Notes in Artificial Intelligence Vol. 3477, Berlin Heidelberg New York, Springer (2005)
33. Finin, T., Labrou, Y., Mayfield, J.: KQLM as an Agent Communication Language. Software Agents, MIT Press (1997)
34. FIPA: Foundation for Intelligent Physical Agents. http://www.fipa.org/
35. Freeman, E., Hupfer, S., Arnold, K.: JavaSpaces: Principles, Patterns an Practice. The Jini Technology Series, Addison-Wesley (1999)
36. Free On-Line Dictionary of Computing. http://foldoc.doc.ic.ac.uk/foldoc/index.html
37. Gasser, L.: Perspectives on Organizations in Multi-Agent Systems, Multi-Agent Systems and Applications: 9th ECCAI Advanced Course ACAI 2001 and Agent Link's 3rd European Agent Systems Summer School, EASSS. Luck, M., Mark, V., Stpnkov, O., Trappl, R. (Eds.), Lecture Notes in Artificial Intelligence, Vol. 2086. Berlin Heidelberg New York, Springer (2001)
38. Grassé, P.P.: La Reconstruction du nid et les Coordinations Inter-Individuelles chez Bellicositermes Natalensis et Cubitermes sp. La theorie de la Stigmergie: Essai d'interpretation du Comportement des Termites Constructeurs. Insectes Sociaux, Vol. 6 (1959)
39. Grasshopper: http://www.grasshopper.de/
40. Guérin, S.: Optimisation multiagents en environment dynamic: application au routage dans les réseaux de télécommunications. Dissertation, University of Rennes I and Ecole Nationale Supérieure des Télécommunications de Bretange (1997)

41. Gutknecht, O., Ferber, J., Michel, F.: Integrating tools and infrastructures for generic multi-agent systems, 5th International Conference on Autonomous agents, Montreal, Quebec, Canada, ACM Press (2001)
42. Hanks, S., Pollack, M., Cohen, P.: Benchmarks, Testbeds, Controlled Experimentation, and the Design of Agent Architectures, AI Magazine 14(4) (1993)
43. Horling, B., Lesser, V., Vincent, R., Wagner, T., Raja, A., Zhang, S., Decker, K., Garvey, A.: The Taems White Paper, Multi-Agent Systems Lab University of Massachusetts.
44. Howden, W., Ronnquist, R., Hodgson, A., Lucas, A.: JACK Intelligent Agents, http://www.agent-software.com/shared/home/
45. Huhns, M.N., Stephens, L.M.: Multi-Agent Systems and Societies of Agents. G. Weiss (ed.), Multi-agent Systems, ISBN 0-262-23203-0, MIT press (1999)
46. Jennings, N.R.: On agent-based software engineering. Artificial Intelligence 117(2), Elsevier Science Publishers (2000)
47. Julien, C., Roman, G.C.: Egocentric Context-Aware Programming in Ad Hoc Mobile Environments. 10th International Symposium on the Foundations of Software Engineering, Charleston, USA (2002)
48. Mamei, M., Leonardi, L., Zambonelli, F.: Co-Fields: Towards a Unifying Approach to the Engineering of Swarm Intelligent Systems. Lecture Notes in Artificial Intelligence Vol. 2577. Springer-Verlag, Berling Heidelberg New York (2003)
49. Mamei, M., Zambonelli, F., Leonardi, L.: Tuples On The Air: A Middleware for Context-Aware Computing in Dynamic Networks. ICDCS Workshops (2003)
50. Manzoni, S., Nunnari, F., Vizzari, G.: Towards a Model for Ubiquitous and Mobile Computing. Theory And Practice of Open Computational Systems, TAPOCS. IEEE Computer Society (2004)
51. Mertens, K., Holvoet, T., Berbers, Y.: Adaptation in a Distributed Environment, First International Workshop on Environments for Multiagent Systems, New York (2004)
52. Michel, F., Ferber, J., Gutknecht, O.: Generic Simulation Tools Based on MAS Organization, 10th European Workshop on Modelling Autonomous Agents in a Multi Agent World MAMAAW'01, Annecy, France (2001)
53. Michel, F., Gouaich, A., Ferber, J.: Weak Interaction and Strong Interaction in Agent Based Simulations. 4th Workshop on Multi-Agent Based Simulation, MABS'03 at AAMAS 2003, Melbourne, Australia (2003)
54. Mili, R., Leask, G., Shakya, U., Steiner, R., Oladimeje, E.: Architectural Design of the DIVAS Environment. First International Workshop on Environments for Multiagent Systems, New York (2004)
55. Minar, N., Burkhart, R., Langton, C., Askenazi, M.: The swarm simulation system: A toolkit for building multi-agent simulations. Working Paper 96-06-042, Santa Fe Institute (1996)
56. Montresor, A.: Anthill: a Framework for the Design and Analysis of Peer-to-Peer Systems. 4th European Research Seminar on Advances in Distributed Systems, Bertinoro, Italy (2001)
57. Murphy, A., Picco, G.P., Roman, G.C.: LIME: a Middleware for Physical and Logical Mobility. 21th International Conference on Distributed Computing Systems (2001)
58. Nwana, S., Ndumu, D.T., Lee, L.C., Collis, J.C.: Zeus: A Toolkit for Building Distributed Multi-Agent Systems. 3th International Conference on Autonomous Agents, Seattle, WA, USA (1999)

59. Odell, J., Parunak, H.V.D., Breuckner, S., Fleischer, M.: Temporal Aspects of Dynamic Role Assignment. Agent-Oriented Software Engineering IV: 4th International Workshop, Melbourne, Australia. Springer-Verlag, Berlin Heidelberg New York (2003)

60. Odell, J., Parunak, H.V.D., Fleischer, M.: The Role of Roles in Designing Effective Agent Organizations. Software Engineering for Large-Scale Multi-Agent Systems, Lecture Notes in Computer Science Vol. 2603. Springer-Verlag, Berlin Heidelberg New York (2003)

61. Odell, J., Parunak, H.V.D., Fleischer, M., Breuckner, S.: Modeling Agents and their Environment. Agent-Oriented Software Engineering III, Giunchiglia, F., Odell, J., Weiss, G. (eds.) Lecture Notes in Computer Science, Vol. 2585. Springer-Verlag, Berlin Heidelberg New York (2002)

62. Okuyama, F., Bordini, R., da Rocha Costa, A.C.: ELMS: An Environment Description Language for Multiagent Simulation. First International Workshop on Environments for Multiagent Systems, New York (2004)

63. OMG MASIF: http://www.fokus.gmd.de/research/cc/ecco/masif/index.html

64. Omicini, A., Ricci, A., Viroli, R., Castelfranci, C., Tummolini, L.: Coordination Artifacts: Environment-based Coordination for Autonomous Agents, 3th Joint Conference on Autonomous Agents and Multi-agent Systems, ACM Press, New York (2004)

65. Omicini, A., Zambonelli, F., Klusch, M., Tolksdorf R., (eds.): Coordination of Internet Agents: Models, Technologies and Applications. Springer Verlag, Berlin Heidelberg New York (2001)

66. Padgham, L., Winikoff, M.: Prometheus: A methodology for Developing Intelligent Agents. 3th Agent-Oriented Software Engineering Workshop, Bologna, Italy (2002)

67. Parunak, H.V.D.: Altarum Institute, http://www.altarum.net/~vparunak/

68. Parunak, H.V.D.: Go to the Ant: Engineering Principles from Natural Agent Systems. Annals of Operations Research, Vol. 75 (1997)

69. Parunak, H.V.D., Brueckner, S., Fleischer, M., Odell, J.: A Design Taxonomy of Multi-Agent Interactions. Agent-Oriented Software Engineering IV, Melbourne. Springer-Verlag, Berlin Heidelberg New York (2003)

70. Parunak, H.V.D., Odell, J.: Representing social structures in UML, Agent-Oriented Software Engineering II, Wooldridge, M., Weiss, G., Ciancarini, P. (Eds.) Lectue Notes in Computer Science Vol. 2222, Berlin Hiedelberg New York, Springer (2002)

71. RoboCup: http://www.robocup.org/

72. Rockwell: http://www.rockwell.com/

73. Russell, S., Norvig, P.: Artificial Intelligence: A Modern Approach, Prentice Hall (2003)

74. Schelfthout, K., Holvoet, T.: An Environment for Coordination of Situated Multi-Agent Systems. First International Workshop on Environments for Multiagent Systems, New York (2004)

75. Schoonderwoerd, R., Holland, O., Bruten, J., Rothkrantz, L.: Ant-based load balancing in telecommunication networks. Adaptive Behavior, Vol. 5 (1997)

76. SOMA: http://www-lia.deis.unibo.it/Research/SOMA/

77. Sun Microsystems, Inc.: The JavaSpaces v1.2.1 Specification (2002)

78. Sycara, K., Klusch, M., Widoff, S., Lu, J.: Dynamic Service Matchmaking Among agents in Open Environments. ACM SIGMOD Record 28(1) (1999)

79. Sycara, K., Paolucci, M., van Velsen, M., Giampapa, J.: The Retsina MAS Infrastructure, Kluwer Academic Publishers (2001)

80. TAEMS: http://dis.cs.umass.edu/research/taems/

81. Telecom Italia: http://www.telecomitalialab.com/
82. Tummolini, L., Castelfranchi, C., Omicini, A., Ricci, A., Viroli, M.: "Exhibition-ists" and "Voyeurs" do it better: a Shared Environment for Flexible Coordination with Tacit Messages. First International Workshop on Environments for Multia-gent Systems, New York (2004)
83. Voyager: http://www.recursionsw.com/voyager.htm
84. Weinstein, P., Parunak, H.V.D., Chiusano, P., Brueckner, S.: Agents Swarming in Semantic Spaces to Corroborate Hypotheses. Joint Confer-ence on Autonomous Agents and Multiagent Systems, New York (2004) http://www.altarum.net/ vparunak/AAMAS04AntCAFE.pdf
85. Weyns, D., Holvoet, T.: Regional Synchronization for Situated Multi-agent Sys-tems. 3rd International/Central and Eastern European Conference on Multi-Agent Systems, CEEMAS 2003, Prague, Czech Republic, Lecture Notes on Computer Sci-ence, Vol. 2691. Springer-Verlag, Berlin Heidelberg New York (2003)
86. Weyns, D., Holvoet, T.: A Formal Model for Situated Multi-agent Systems. Formal Approaches for Multi-Agent Systems, Special Issue of Fundamenta Informaticae, 63(2) (2004)
87. Weyns, D., Holvoet, T.: Look, Talk, Do: A Synchronization Scheme for Situated Multi-Agent Systems. UK Workshop on Multi-agent Systems, Liverpool (2002)
88. Weyns, D., Holvoet, Y.: A Colored Petri Net for Regional Synchronization in Sit-uated Multiagent Systems. First International Workshop on Petri Nets and Coor-dination, PNC'04, Bologna, Italy (2004)
89. Weyns, D., Steegmans, E., Holvoet, T.: Towards Active Perception in Situated Multi-agent Systems. Journal on Applied Artificial Intelligence 18(9-10) (2004)
90. Whitestein: http://www.whitestein.com/pages/index.html
91. Wolfram, S.: Theory and Applications of Cellular Automata. World Press (1986)
92. Wolfram, S.: A New Kind of Science. Wolfram Media, ISBN 1-57955-008-8 (2002)
93. Wooldridge, M.: An Introduction to MultiAgent Systems. ISBN 0-471-49691-X. John Wiley and Sons, Ltd. England (2002)
94. Zambonelli, F., Jennings, N., Wooldridge, M.: Developing multiagent systems: The Gaia Methodology. Transactions on Software Engineering and Methodology, 3(12), ACM Press (2003)
95. Zambonelli, F., Parunak, H.V.D.: From design to intention: signs of a revolution. First International Joint Conference on Autonomous agents and Multiagent Sys-tems, Bologna, Italy, ACM Press (2002)

AGRE: Integrating Environments with Organizations

J. Ferber, F. Michel, and J. Baez

LIRMM, CNRS 161 rue Ada
34392 Montpellier Cedex 5, France
{ferber, fmichel, baez}@lirmm.fr

Abstract. This paper presents an extension of the AGR (Agent-Group-Role) organizational model, called AGRE (AGR + Environment), which includes physical (or simply geometrical) environments. This extension is based on the concept of a space which can be seen either as a physical area or as a social group, and on a clear distinction between an agent and its mode, i.e. the way it appears and interacts into a space with other agents. A notation which encompasses both social and physical environments is given.

1 Introduction

Recently a particular interest has been given to the use of organizational concepts within multiagent systems (MAS) where the concepts of 'organizations, 'groups, 'communities, 'roles', 'functions', etc. play an important role [1, 2, 3, 4, 5, 6].

The use of organizations provides a new way for describing the structures and the interactions that take place in MASs. The organizational level, the way organizations are described is responsible for the description of the structural and dynamical aspects of organizations. It stands for an abstract representation of concrete organizations, i.e. as a specification of the structural and dynamical aspects of a MAS. The organizational level describes the expected relationships and patterns of activity which should occur at the agent level and therefore it defines the constraints and potentialities that constitute the horizon in which agents behave.

1.1 Organization Centered General Principles

The principles for designing true organizational centered multiagent systems as explained in [7] are the following:

Principle 1: The organizational level describes the "what" and not the "how". The organizational level imposes a structure into the pattern of agents activities, but does not describe how agents behave. In other terms, the organizational level does not contain any "code" which could be executed by agents, but provides specifications, using some kind of norms or laws, of the limits and expectations that are placed on the agents behavior.

D. Weyns et al. (Eds.): E4MAS 2004, LNAI 3374, pp. 48–56, 2005.

Principle 2: No agent description and therefore no mental issues are provided at the organizational level. The organizational level should not say anything about the way agents would interpret this level. Thus, reactive agents as well as intentional agents may act in an organization. In other words, ant colonies are as much organizations as human corporations. Moreover, seen from a certain distance, or using an intentional stance it is impossible to say if the ants or the humans are intentional or reactive. Thus, the organizational level should get rid of any mental issues such as beliefs, desires, intentions, goals, etc. and provide only descriptions of *expected* behaviors.

Principle 3: An organization provides a way for partitioning a system, each partition (or group) constitutes a context of interaction for agents. Thus, a group is an organizational unit in which all members are able to interact freely. Agents belonging to a group may talk to one another, using the same language. Moreover, groups establish boundaries. Whereas the structure of a group A may be known by all agents belonging to A, it is hidden to all agents that do not belong to A. Thus, groups are opaque to each other and do not assume a general standardization of agent interaction and architecture.

These principles are not without consequences:

1. An organization may be seen as a kind of dynamic framework where agents are components. Entering a group/playing a role may be seen as a plug-in process where a component is integrated into a framework.
2. Designing systems at the organizational level may leave implementation issues, such as the choice of building the right agent to play a specific role, left opened.
3. It is possible to realize true "Open Systems" [8] where agents architecture is left unspecified.
4. It is possible to integrate multiple aspects of a system and make them interact together, considering each group as a "black boxes" which represents a specific perspective of a system: what happens in a group cannot be seen from agents that do not belong to that group.

However, the general concept of environment which is one of the main concepts of a MAS [9] is not taken into account with these principles. If we consider an environment as *the conditions under which an entity exists* [10], these principles provide only support for social environments [11, 7]. They do not say anything about physical (or even simply geometrical) environments, and entities which are not agents (e.g. documents, objects to be grasped, etc.) are not considered. Several attempts have been made to integrate environments with AGR (Agent-Group-Role). In [11] a model has been proposed. But this model has not really been analyzed in detail and nothing has been said about the way to practically integrate environments with groups. Thus, it is still necessary to extend the AGR model to take physical environments into account, without losing the expressiveness and simplicity of this model.

1.2 Content of the Paper

Section 2 will summarize the main concepts of AGR and of the UML meta-model one can use to implement AGR in various platforms. Section 3 will present the AGRE (Agent-Group-Role-Environment) model which is an extension of the AGR model and which allows for the design of social and physical environments in an integrated way. We will see that both groups and areas (parts of the physical environments) may be considered as specializations of more general spaces in which agents are embedded through what we call 'modes'. This presentation will include the basic concepts and the notation one can use to describe both social and physical environments. Section 4 will draw conclusions and present some perspectives.

2   AGR: A Basic Model of Organization Centered MAS

In order to show how these principles may be actualized in a computational model, we have presented the Agent-Group-Role model, or AGR for short, also known as the Aalaadin model [4] for historical reasons, which complies with the organization centered general principles that we have proposed in the previous section. The AGR model is based on three primitive concepts: Agent, Group and Role that are structurally connected and cannot be defined by other primitives. They satisfy a set of axioms that unite these concepts.

- **Agent:** an agent is an active, communicating entity playing *roles* within *groups*. An agent may hold multiple roles, and may be a member of several groups. An important characteristic of the AGR model, in accordance with the principle 2 above, is that the architecture of an agent is left unspecified, and that no cognitive abilities are assumed. Thus, an agent may be as reactive as an ant, or as clever as a human.
- **Group**: a group is a set of agents sharing some common characteristic. A group is used as a context for a pattern of activities, and is used for partitioning organizations. Following principle 3, two agents may communicate if and only if they belong to the same group, but an agent may belong to several groups. This feature will allow the definition of organizational structures.
- **Role:** the role is the abstract representation of a functional position of an agent in a group. An agent must play a role in a group, but an agent may play several roles. Roles are local to groups, and a role must be requested by an agent. A role may be played by several agents.

The AGR meta-model is represented in Fig. 1 in UML.

A **group type** (or **group structure**), defined at the organizational level, describes a particular type of **group**, how a group is constituted, what are its roles, its communication language, and the possible norms that apply to this type of group. A group is thus a kind of instance of a group type. A **role type** is part of the description of a group structure and describes the expected behavior of an **agent** playing that **role**. Role types may be described as in Gaia [12] by attributes such as its cardinality (how many agents may play that role). It is also

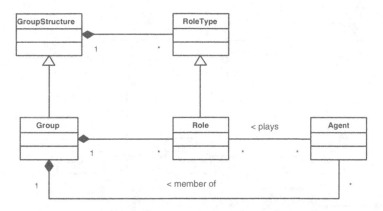

Fig. 1. The UML meta-model of AGR

possible to describe *interaction protocols* and *structural constraints* between roles (not viewed in the figure, but presented in [7]). A structural constraint describes a relationship between roles that are defined at the organizational level and are imposed to all agents.

A role, which is part of a group, is an instance of a role type defined for an agent. We can see the role as a representative of an agent or as a kind of social body that an agent plays when it is a member of a group, the interface by which an agent is able to communicate and more generally to perform actions in a group.

Several notations may be used to represent organizations. In [7] we have proposed a set of diagrams to represent both static and dynamic aspects of organizations.

3   AGRE: Integrating Environments to AGR

First, we will give a general overview of AGRE, and then we will present the principles on which this model is based.

3.1   Description of AGRE

In this section we provide an extension of the AGR model to take into account both physical and social environments. This extension, called AGRE, for Agent-Group-Role-Environment, is based on the idea that agents are situated in domains, that we call **spaces**. A space may be physical (i.e. geometrical) or social. Geometrical spaces will be called **areas**, and social spaces represent AGR **groups**. There may be other kinds of spaces but we will not discuss them here.

Agents are situated in spaces and are able to perform actions in these spaces through **modes**. A mode should be seen as the manifestation of an agent in a specific domain, as its way of existence and appearance in a space. A mode describes the agent's location and the way it perceives and acts within a space. A mode in an area is called a **body**, and a mode in a group is called a **role**.

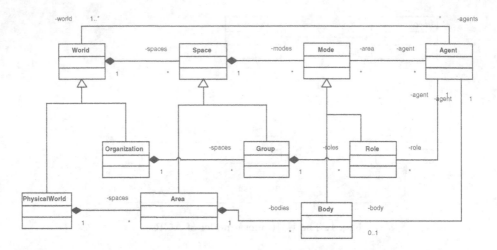

Fig. 2. The UML meta-model of AGRE at the concrete level

Spaces are regrouped in **worlds**. A world is simply a collection of spaces of the same kind. For the moment we will only consider two type of worlds: organizations which represents social environments and are composed by sets of groups, and physical worlds which represent physical environments and are made of areas. It could be possible to consider other worlds: worlds for displaying agents in a specific manner, worlds made of places for describing agent mobility, etc. In this paper we will consider only two types of worlds: physical worlds made of areas, and organizations made of groups.

Figure 2 shows the simplified UML diagram which represents the relations between world, spaces, areas, groups, modes, bodies and roles at the concrete level. For each concept at the concrete level (e.g. group, area, role, body) there is a related abstract concept at the organizational level (e.g. group structure, area structure, role description, mode description), except for the concept of agent which does not have any corresponding concept at the organizational level.

The aggregation relation that links space to mode, are overridden by the same relation that links area to body and group to role. In the same idea, the aggregation which relate world to space is overridden by an aggregation which link organization to group on one hand, and physical world and area on the other hand.

A world proposes the required primitives that are necessary for an agent to enter a space and get its mode. Because the mode is the only way through which an agent can act in a space, it is necessary for an agent to have the ability to enter a space. This is done through the world which gives the necessary primitives that an agent needs for entering a space and acquire a mode. An agent may live in several worlds at once. Worlds are used as starting points for agents to enter groups and areas. When an agent is created, it must register to a world. For instance, a social agent, i.e. an agent that plays roles in groups, has to register first to an organization. Let us suppose that the agent is registered to an organization o, then, to enter a group, the agent may use the primitive[1]:

```
Role r = o.requestRole(GroupName, RoleType, RoleName, a);
```

which gives it the ability to request the entrance to a group for playing the role of the type `RoleType` with the authorization `a`. If this is possible, the agent will get a role through which it will have the possibility to act within this group. All the skills associated to this role will be available to it, and naturally it will be able to send messages to agents within this group, using a primitive of the following kind:

```
r.sendMessage(RoleName,Message);
```

which expresses a request for the role to send a message to the agents having the role `RoleName`. One can see that agents are only referenced by their `RoleName` in a group. There is no way to send messages to the "real" agent, because formerly there are no agents in a group: only roles by which agents are connected to groups. To get an idea of the concepts involved, a role instantiated in a group is like a registered login name in an internet e-commerce site. An agent may act only through its login name which constitutes its mode. Of course there are primitives by which an agent may acquire information about the different agents related to a specific `RoleType` such as the following:

```
List<RoleName> l = r.getAgentsWithRoleType(RoleType);
```

which will return a list of all the local `RoleName` (i.e. all the logins) of all the agents that play a specific `RoleType` in the group where the agent has the role `r`.

The same idea applies to physical worlds and areas. To enter an area, an agent must register to a physical world p which contains this area and use a primitive such as

```
Body b = p.requestBody(AreaName, BodyType, Location, a);
```

which gives it the ability to enter an area using a specific `BodyType` at the location Location, with the authorization `a`. A reference to a body is returned. Then, according to the capabilities of the body, the agent may move, grasp things, etc. with commands like the following:

```
b.move(30,10);
```

Figure 3 shows the graphical notation used to represent items in the AGRE model, which is an extension of the "cheeseboard" notation proposed in [7].

The following figure shows a snapshot of two agents playing roles in groups and having bodies in areas. One can see that agent A1 plays two different roles in G2 and one role in G1, while agent A2 plays only one role in G1. Both agents have a body in area A1. These bodies are instances of the body type B.

---

[1] We use a Java-like notation to give an idea of how such a model may be practically realized. But obviously, this could be expressed in any language.

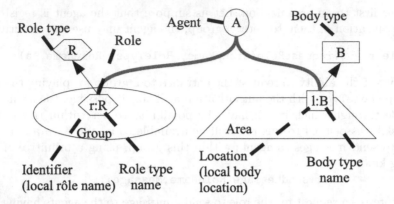

Fig. 3. Notation used to represent an instance diagram of agents, areas and groups

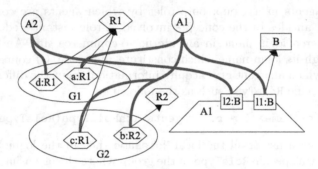

Fig. 4. A simple example with two agents playing roles in groups and having bodies in areas

3.2   Principles of AGRE

In this section, we will summarize the principles applying to the AGRE model that we have introduced in previous sections.

Principle 1: a multiagent world is constituted of agents (individuals) that may perceive and act in spaces and manifest their existence through their mode. This statement, when it is reduced to social world may be expressed as the following:

> **Principle 1a:** An organization is a kind of world in which spaces are groups and in which agents perceive and act through their roles.

> **Principle 1b:** A physical world is a kind of world in which spaces are areas and in which agents perceive and act through their bodies.

Principle 2: an agent may belong simultaneously to a social world and to a physical world. The number of roles an agent may play is not restricted, but the number of bodies an agent may possess is constrained by obvious conditions that an agent can act in a world through only one body.

Principle 3: An agent may possess several modes of different kinds. The constraints about the number of modes an agent possesses depend of the world in which it has been registered.

> **Principle 3a:** an agent may have several roles in a group and may belong to several groups.

> **Principle 3b:** an agent may possess only one body for a given world. This principle expresses the fact that an agent may not live in two different places at the same time. However, this constraint may be relaxed, when two areas overlap.

Let us note by s : m.op(a1,..,an) the action of an agent with mode m executing the operator op with args a1,..,an in space s. Let us also note the following assertion:

- mode(x, m, s)[role(x,r,g)] : the agent x has a mode m in space s [has a role r in group g]
- type(m, M) [type(r, R)] : the mode m is of type M [the role r is of type R]
- op(o(a1,..,an), M) : the operator o(a1,..,an) is defined in mode[role] type M

Principle 4: The mode is the way for an agent to act in a space. An agent may act in a space if one of its mode in the space gives it the power to do so. Thus, an agent a may perform an action u in a space s, if there exist a mode m of a in s such that the type of m (its ModeType) allows for u.

$$s : m.o(a1, .., an) \Rightarrow \exists x : \mathsf{Agent}, \mathsf{mode}(x, m, s) \land \mathsf{type}(m, M) \land \mathsf{op}(o(a1, .., an), M)$$

> **Principle 4a:** an agent may communicate only if it plays a role in a group. This communication is performed through its role, and the receiver is necessarily another role within the same group.

$$s : r1.\mathsf{send}(r2, msg) \Rightarrow \exists x, y : \mathsf{Agent}, \mathsf{role}(x, r1, g) \land \mathsf{role}(y, r2, g)$$

4   Conclusion

We have proposed a simple model, AGRE, which is an extension of AGR and which integrates smoothly physical and social environments. This extension respects the main principles of organizational centered multiagent systems. Both groups and areas may be seen as specializations of spaces in which agents may act through modes. Because roles and bodies are modes, it is possible to consider social and physical embedding as a general manner for an agent to manifest itself in a world. We have proposed some notations for this model and a set of principles which describe the basic elements for understanding AGRE.

These concepts may be used for practical implementations. The MadKit platform [13] that we have designed is built around the AGR model. Since its first release, hundreds of users (thousands of downloads) have been able to use these organizational concepts (presented in a less rigorous way than here) to build applications in various areas. We plan to extend the MadKit platform to integrate this new AGRE model.

References

1. Jennings, N.R.: On agent-based software engineering. Artificial Intelligence **117** (2000) 277–296
2. Zambonelli, F., Van Dyke Parunak, H.: From design to intention: signs of a revolution. In: Proceedings of the first international joint conference on Autonomous agents and multiagent systems, ACM Press (2002) 455–456
3. Demazeau, Y., Costa, A.R.: Populations and organizations in open multi-agent systems. In: 1st National Symposium on Parallel and Distributed AI (PDAI96). (1996)
4. Ferber, J., Gutknecht, O.: A meta-model for the analysis and design of organizations in multi-agent systems. In: Proceedings of the 3rd International Conference on Multi Agent Systems, IEEE Computer Society (1998) 128–135
5. Odell, J., Parunak, H.V.D., Breuckner, S., Fleischer, M.: Temporal aspects of dynamic role assignment. In Giorgini, P., Muller, J.P., Odell, J., eds.: Agent-Oriented Software Engineering IV: 4th International Workshop, Aose 2003. Lecture notes in computer science LNCS, Melbourne, Australia, Springer Verlag (2003) 47–59
6. Gasser, L.: Perspectives on organizations in multi-agent systems. In Luck, M., Mak, V., tpnkov, O., Trappl, R., eds.: Multi-Agent Systems and Applications : 9th ECCAI Advanced Course ACAI 2001 and Agent Link's 3rd European Agent Systems Summer School, EASSS 2001. Volume 2086 of LNAI., Prague, Czech Republic, Springer-Verlag Heidelberg (2001) 1–16
7. Ferber, J., Gutknecht, O., Michel, F.: From agents to organizations: an organizational view of multi-agent systems. In Giorgini, P., Muller, J.P., Odell, J., eds.: Agent-Oriented Software Engineering IV: 4th International Workshop, Aose 2003. Lecture notes in computer science LNCS, Melbourne, Australia, Springer Verlag (2003) 185–202
8. Hewitt, C.: Offices are open systems. ACM Trans. Inf. Syst. **4** (1986) 271–287
9. Weyns, D., Parunak, H.V.D., Michel, F., eds.: The First International Workshop on Environments for Multiagent Systems E4MAS. In Weyns, D., Parunak, H.V.D., Michel, F., eds.: Environments for Mutiagent Systems. Volume 3477 of LNAI., Springer (this volume, 2005)
10. Weyns, D., Parunak, H.V.D., Michel, F., Holvoet, T., Ferber, J.: Environments for multiagent systems: State-of-the-art and research challenges. In Weyns, D., Parunak, H.V.D., Michel, F., eds.: Environments for Mutiagent Systems. Volume 3477 of LNAI., Springer (this volume, 2005)
11. Parunak, H.V.D., Odell, J.: Representing social structures in uml. In: Agent-Oriented Software Engineering II. Volume 2222 of Lecture notes in computer science LNCS., Berlin, Springer (2002) 1–16
12. Zambonelli, F., Jennings, N.R., Wooldridge, M.: Developing multiagent systems: The Gaia methodology. ACM Transactions on Software Engineering and Methodology (TOSEM) **12** (2003) 317–370
13. Gutknecht, O., Ferber, J., Michel, F.: Integrating tools and infrastructures for generic multi-agent systems. In: Proceedings of the fifth international conference on Autonomous agents, AA 2001, ACM Press (2001) 441–448

From Reality to Mind: A Cognitive Middle Layer of Environment Concepts for Believable Agents

Paul Hsueh-Min Chang[1], Kuang-Tai Chen[1], Yu-Hung Chien[1], Edward Kao[2], and Von-Wun Soo[1,2]

[1] Department of Computer Science
[2] Institute of Information Systems and Applications
National Tsing-Hua University,
101 Section 2, Kuang-Fu Road, Hsinchu, Taiwan
{pchang, fuchs, sot, edkao, soo}@cs.nthu.edu.tw

Abstract. The environment is an important but overlooked piece in the construction of multiagent-based scenarios. Richness, believability and variety of scenarios are inseparable from the environment because every action and interaction of agents is based around the environment they are situated in. The prerequisite, however, is that agents must be able to understand the environment and capture its dynamic nature. This paper proposes a cognitive middle layer between agent minds and the environment. Aspects of the reality are mapped to concepts in the middle layer, through which agents can feel and reason about the real environment. The middle layer is modelled with a structured specification based on Web Ontology Language (OWL) to be extensible and reusable. Environmental concepts are integrated into the goal processing of agents to trigger intentions. This paper also reports our initial investigation about the design of a simulation system for multiple environment-aware agents and multiple users.

1 Introduction

Computational models of story scenarios are gaining importance lately [14] [11] [6]. With intelligent agent technologies, characters of the scenarios can be made autonomous and express human-like behaviors [9]. Therefore, instead of a static story shown in movies or novels, a flexible scenario construction can be obtained, where agents behave intelligently and respond to the behaviors of the user intelligently. Such scenarios are useful for many purposes, including digital entertainment [18], simulation-based training [16], and education [6] [7]. Although the multiagent paradigm helps developing agents that exhibit believable behavior through interaction, the importance of environment is often overlooked. To evaluate agent designs incorporated with complex cognitive or social characteristics, a rich dynamic environment is needed [8]. The environment is therefore an important part of a convincing scenario not only because agents can interact with the environment and other agents, but also because the environment provides foundations for richer agent interactions. In other words, agent interactions

D. Weyns et al. (Eds.): E4MAS 2004, LNAI 3374, pp. 57–73, 2005.

are not confined to exchange of messages; the agents interact through many alternative media provided by the environment. The changes an agent makes to the environment can either convey a message to or directly affect other agents. We propose the idea of believable environments, which agents can interact with. The believability of an environment depends on how well it can express agent behaviors in a human-like and realistic way. The challenge is that agents must be able to understand and reason about the environment in order to exploit it. Also, the agents must be able to sense the changes in the environment and affect it with actions. However, it is difficult for agents to understand the environment as a continuous entity or numerical values. Psychological studies show that human beings form discrete concepts (also known as schemata) from the environment and use them to think. Cantor and Kihlstorm [1] argue that the schemata in the human brain has a complex hierarchical structure, while Trafimow and Wyer [15] describes schemata as abstract concepts and some concrete instances of them. There are two major advantages of modelling agent cognition in a similar way. First of all, agents that think on concepts are understandable to human beings because humans can comprehend the feelings of and decisions made by the agents. Second, the connection among concepts enables agents to infer state transitions of the environment without going into complex numerical calculation.

However, contrary to human beings, we believe that agents' concept model of the world should be constructed as a part of the environment instead of inside the mind of agents. Here we propose a three-layer architecture. The bottom layer is the physical environment that works according to physical laws. The middle layer is the concept model, in which concepts are identified and connected. The concept model is merged into the environment and shared among all agents in the scenario because doing so avoids redundancy of concepts and gives all agents a common conceptual basis so that they can reason about the actions among one another. The topmost layer is the subjective mind, which resides in an agent. Physical environments map to concepts, which in turn trigger the sentiments and intents of agents. With this architecture, the agents have a high-level representation of the environment which is integrated in the scenario seamlessly.

The rest of this paper is organized as follows. Section 2 describes the background and reviews related work. Section 3 introduces the three-layered cognitive architecture and explains how an agent maps the reality to concepts and concepts to its mind. Section 4 discusses the design of such a simulation system. Section 5 concludes this paper.

2   Background and Motivation

Research efforts that can be ascribed as construction of believable scenarios consist of diverse application domains including simulation-based training, storytelling and entertainment, as mentioned in section 1. Nevertheless, an explicit model of environment is missing in most of the research efforts related to believable scenarios. Riedl's Mimesis system [13] for scenario control in an interactive drama is built on top of the Unreal Tournament engine, a commercial 3D gaming environment. Although the environment of Mimesis provides a background for narrative stories, it is more like a drama stage for actor agents who have already decided what to do than a realistic environment that agents can dynamically interact with. The simulation system of Norling and Sonenberg [8] [9] is built on a similar gaming environment, Quake 2. Instead of creating agent-based dramas, Norling and Sonenberg focus on creating agents that mimic human game-playing behaviors. There is no explicit notion of environment modeling, and therefore believability of their agents is specific to the game environmment allowing only a small set of combat actions such as running and shooting.

The background environment has an important role in Mission Rehearsal Exercise project [16], which simulates a traffic accident in a peacekeeping scenario. In this scenario, a human trainee plays a lieutenant and collaborates with intelligent virtual humans enacting the roles of his sergeant and other characters by negotiating plans and tasks. The environment is represented to human trainees with 3D graphical virtual environment and immersive audio. Despite the fact that the environmental factors such as weather and physical surroundings can actually change the situation that the trainee must face, there is no explicit description about how the environment is presented to agents, and it is hard to see how the virtual humans will adjust their behaviors when the environment is changed by a designer. In summary, we observed a tendency toward viewing a believable scenario as a set of virtual characters that exhibit believable behaviors through interacting among themselves or with a human participant; little emphasis is put on the interaction between characters and the environment. Thus, the agents either are able to act in a specific environmental context only, or ignore the environment entirely. We believe that the absence of a model of environment not only leaves a major source of believability unexploited, but also limits the applicability of existing approaches. Although work on environments for multi-agent simulation [5] [21] exists, their focus is on providing a framework for agent development and testing instead of constructing a dynamic and interactive environment.

A notable exception is Doyle [3], who proposed the idea of annotated environment that facilitates building believable agents which guide the user through virtual worlds such as virtual galleries and computer games. The environment is described with annotations on objects, events and contextual information. The annotations inform agents of what operations can be invoked, what emotions should be triggered, and so on. As a result, an agent does not need to carry a lot of environmental information before visiting a different place because the information has already been annotated in the environment. Doyle's work enables agents to be situated in the environment, however, his approach still has two limitations. First, the annotations dictate the functions of objects in the environment and do not provide enough clues for agents to act intelligently and creatively. In Doyle's own example, a spray can of plant killer is annotated with a single purpose which is to kill the plant guardian. This annotation tells agents what can be done with the object, but also makes it impossible for agents to infer that the plant killer can also slay other plant monsters, tremove weeds, or simply be thrown at others. Second, static annotations have the risk of washing out behavoral differences among agents. Behavioral differences are expected when different agents enter the same place, or when the same agent stays at or revisits a place that has changed. For example, a room annotated as a romantic place will stop being romantic when too many agents enter it, and agents inside this room will change their moods and behaviors according to their tolerance to noise. The need to create behavioral differences will increase as the scenario becomes larger, longer or more dynamic in nature. We argue that such desirable behaviors can only be modeled with a systematic method to update agents' beliefs about the environment; mere static annotations are unstructure and hence do not suffice. Instead of instructing the agents what they can and what they should feel, we think the environment should provide hints to agents about its effects on them, allowing creative use of the environment and exhibition of different personalities.

Our cognitive architecture defines ontologies as the abstraction of the world, and maps aspects of the environment to concepts in the ontologies. In this aspect, our approach is comparable to Dickinson and Wooldridge's Nuin agent architecture [2] in which BDI agents [12] use the Semantic Web as their knowledge sources. However, our architecture differs from Nuin as our concept model has built-in reasoning capability about the direct causal relations between actions/events and environmental effects. The most significant advantage of our approach is that agents can be designed to know only a subset of concepts while the whole ontology is stored in the environment. Agents can query the concept model about what can be done with an object or what must be done to bring about an effect. The relation between BDI agents and our cognitive architecture is a topic for future investigation. Although this paper does not aim to provide a comprehensive model of multi-agent systems, it can be related to the formal notion of situated multi-agent systems, whose reference can be found in [17] [4].

3   Cognitive Architecture

Figure 1 illustrates the cognitive architecture with a simple example. The architecture consists of three layers. They are, in bottom-up order, reality, concept model and agent mind. We describe each of them in the following subsections.

3.1   Reality Model

This reality layer represents the objective physical environment whose existence does not depend on the agents' minds. To create a realistic scenario, the environment should be modelled in a way similar to how the real world works. Simplifications are necessary since producing a virtual world that functions exactly the same as the real world is notably difficult. Fortunately, in many cases believable scenarios do not require absolute resemblance to real environments; the virtual environments just need to be recognized as realistic. Thus, designers

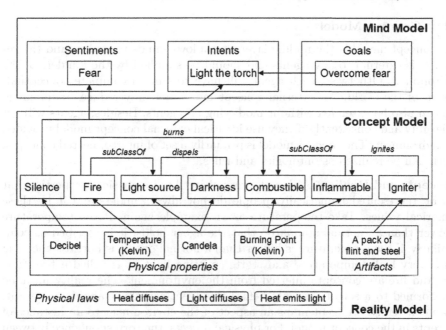

Fig. 1. The cognitive architecture of environmental understanding

of the reality layer can develop their approximations of the environment to suit their target applications.

The reality layer contains two different models, each of which addresses an aspect of the environment. In the first perspective, the environment can be viewed as a set of physical properties, such as the temperature of a point in the location, the hardness of a sword, and the burning point of a wooden chair. Physical properties can change with time according to some physical laws. For example, heat diffuses from places with high temperature to those with low temperature. Physical laws also tell that when the temperature of an object is higher than its burning point, it burns and produces more heat. With simple physical laws, a large set of possible phenomena and consequences can be derived.

However, artificial objects are often complex, and their functions cannot be explained by simple physical laws. For example, the seemingly simple relation between keys and locks has delicate craft behind it. Thus, the second perspective that views environment objects as artifacts (man-made items) is necessary. An artifact directly maps to specific concepts in the concept model as its usage functions (to be described in the next subsection); the functions of an artifact do not need to be explained with physical properties. Nevertheless, an artifact is still a physical object and possesses physical properties. The key in the example above is an artifact because it opens doors, but it still is made of metal and has a melting point. The general principle is that the more delicate and complex an item is, the more likely it is modelled as an artifact.

3.2   Concept Model

The concept model is the middle layer that allows minds to understand the reality. It is external to any agents and should be supplied by the builders of the environment. Otherwise, each agent will have to store a complete conceptualization of the world. An external concept model not only reduces redundancy but can also be extended without modifying all agents. Besides, agents will act believably and consistently if they use identical external concept model provided by environment. The concept model is primarily a set of interconnected concepts, which can be realized as ontologies and rules.

Concepts and Reality. Although every object has its physical properties that can be represented numerically, people do not always understand it by these numerical values. Take temperature as an example again. If the temperature is lower than a "normal standard" that the agent holds, it is ascribed as cold. Similarly, if the temperature is higher than a normal one, it is hot. If something has a very high temperature and starts emitting light, it is called a fire. Hot, cold and fire are concepts inferred from the environment. The reality must be transformed to a set of concepts before the agent can think about and use it. More concretely, an agent maps an aspect of the environment to an instance of concepts in the concept model. For physical objects, the correspondence between reality and concepts is obtained through a set of mapping functions. Artifacts, on the contrary, are directly assigned as instances of concepts during design time. Note that although the qualitative concepts of hot and cold are in most cases shared among human beings, each agent can have its own standard about the normal temperature. Thus, the mapping functions should sometimes take the personal traits of the agent as a parameter that affects the outcome. The system design described in section 4 reflects this.

It is also important to note that although artifacts always match a concept perfectly, the matching between a physical object and a concept is usually imperfect. In the case of artifacts, people have concepts first and then build the instances later. For example, people invented locks and keys because they only want to allow those who are authorized to access certain properties. Conversely, physical objects exist before any conceptual abstractions emerge, and therefore the categorization is usually ambiguous. Thus, the mapping functions return a similarity value that indicates the accuracy of classification. With the mapping function, the similarity value of an object to a concept can be computed. For example, a crossbow is an artifact, and therefore its similarity value to the concept "weapon" is always 1. A decoration sword, even if not designed as a weapon in its usage functions, can still be inferred as a weapon because its physical properties (sharpness, hardness and weight) can easily be exploited to harm people. A glass bottle, although not as effective as a sword, also possesses harmful properties (being hard and somewhat heavy). Whether the agents will consider a glass bottle a weapon is not so obvious because its similarity value to the weaponry concept is lower than that of a sword. In principle, agents will take into consideration the concepts that are better matched by an object. Thus, in a bar fight agents will look for instances that map to the concept of weapon with a high similarity value, such as a sword. They will consider utilizing things like a glass bottle only when a good match cannot be found.

Concept and Perception. The difference between traditional perception-based approaches and the concept-matching approach deserves elaboration. The examples mentioned above can be used to explain the difference between the two approaches. Although fire is very hot, an agent cannot sense fire by temperature. Instead, the agent tells that something is on fire by the shape and the color of light, from which the agent can decide the temperature of the fire (although inaccurately) with experience. Similarly, agents have no way to tell the weight and hardness of a glass bottle without grasping it. In summary, there are some aspects of the world that cannot be easily perceived; knowledge and expertise are needed to decide them. To reduce the complexity, the mapping functions between reality and concepts are designed to imply common-sense knowledge. Thus the concept model subsumes perception. Whether this approach can be an adequate basis for model human-like perception capabilities is an issue for future investigation.

Concept Structure. Although concepts represent the environment in a way that is meaningful for the agents, they alone do not enable agents to reason about the environment. The important fact that concepts are interconnected is what makes reasoning possible. The connection among concepts is divided into two types: *ontologies* and *causal rules*. Ontologies define both the hierarchy of concepts ("fire is a subclass of light source") and the type of relationship between instances of concepts; the latter is defined through a linking word, also known as a property. A property can be either a purely descriptive property or a *causal property*; the latter is used to define causal relations. For example, suppose the concept *Key* has a causal property *unlocks* on the concept *Lock*, the ontology can be used to define the causal relation that key k unlocks lock l. Causal rules, on the contrary, describe the effect that all instances of a concept can cause on all instances of another. "Fire burns inflammable" is such a rule, for instance. Causal properties and causal rules are nevertheless defined through the same set of linking words. A linking word marks the type of the rule/relation and is associated with an action and the effect triggered by the action. An effect can be an addition or a removal of a state or a type of the target. For example, the linking word *unlock* mentioned above is associated with the action *Unlock* and the effect *Unlocked*. Suppose key k can be used to open lock l, the causal relation between them can be represented as a triple $(k, l, unlock)$, which has the following semantics:

$$Unlock(k, l) \rightarrow Unlocked(l) . \tag{1}$$

Note that, although the set of possible relations is defined in the concept model through linking words, actual relations between instances are a part of the reality layer. As would be explained later, agents cannot perceive every actual relation.

The general form of all rules is defined as a triple (C, C, L), where C is set of all concepts and L is the set of all linking words. For any rule $(Source, Target,$

Link), *Source, Target* $\in$ *C, Link* $\in$ *L*, the semantics of the rule is defined as follows:

$$\forall s \; Source(s), \forall t \; (Target(t) \; (Action_{Link}(s,t) \rightarrow Effect_{Link}(t)) \; . \qquad (2)$$

For example, the linking term *burn* in figure 1 is associated with the action *Touch* and the effect *Fire*. Thus the rule "fires burn combustibles" is defined as:

$$\forall s \; Fire(s), \forall t \; Combustible(t) \; (Touch(s,t) \rightarrow Fire(t)) \; . \qquad (3)$$

Similarly, the rule "igniters burn inflammables" is defined as:

$$\forall s \; Igniter(s), \forall t \; Inflammable(t) \; (Use(s,t) \rightarrow Fire(t)) \; . \qquad (4)$$

The rule "light source eliminates darkness" is defined as:

$$\forall s \; LightSource(s), \forall t \; Darkness(t) \; (Noop(s,t) \rightarrow Destroyed(t)) \; . \qquad (5)$$

Note that in (5) the agent does not need to do anything to lighten the darkness, and therefore the action is *Noop*. Actions are also hierarchical; the action *Hit* implies *Touch* and therefore can be defined as a subclass of *Touch*. Combining ontologies and rules results in a wide range of causal reasoning. For example, the agent can infer that an instance of fire (which is a subclass of light source) can eliminate darkness.

As concepts are abstractions of physical properties and artifacts, rules are abstractions of physical laws. Ideally, rule defines the causal effect between every instance of two concepts, and therefore every instance of fire can burn every instance of combustible. However, this is not always true since the instances may not be a perfect match for the concept. Tissue papers and hard wood both can be instances of combustible, but the former has a higher similarity value than the latter and is more likely to catch fire. Thus, when reasoning about rules an agent must take the similarity value into consideration. Agent will apply rules that have a higher chance to succeed since they consider better matches of concepts first. Note that, even if an agent applies a small fire on an combustible and it does not burn, that agent still succeeds in behaving believably, because human themselves can also lead to failures of the same kind.

Selective Information Exposure. Though the concept model provides cues for agents to interact with artifacts and other existences in the reality layer, not all concepts should be acknowledged by every agent. We briefly explain and classify these conditions into two conditions as below.

Different Cultures. The social norms in different societies may not be the same, and hence the usage of artifacts produced in one civilization may not be recognized properly by the outsiders. In this case, the agents can only speculate the artifact usage from its physical features, and can only result in primitive usage such as eat or throw. However, an outsider may gain the knowledge of artifacts from certain methods, such as personally observing others using them. To define the relation between civilization and its artifacts, we take a bottom-up approach. Designers must design artifacts with their usages, and then assign these artifacts to one existing civilization in the current scenario. In other words, a civilization is established by containing various artifacts and other social concepts, or it would simply be an empty set. No artifact is created without associated civilization.

Causal Relations. The agent does not see specific causal relations between an artifact and another one, even the agent and artifacts come from the same society. For example, an agent without previous knowledge cannot ensure whether key k can open lock l by mere looking at them, though he identifies this artifact correctly as a key. Such knowledge has to be gained through instruction manuals, other agents, or simply trial and error. The knowledge is then stored in the memory of the agents as their beliefs, and the agent will stop trying different keys when he encounters this lock again.

3.3   Mind Model

The agent mind represents intelligent agent components, and the architecture consisting of them. Once the agents are in position, they would be able to interact with the believable environment, and therefore strengthen their own believability. Here we explain how concept model informs agents with traditional agent architecture design, and reserves the space for emotion cognition.

Instances of concepts are cues that trigger the activities of the minds of agents. Compare to the concepts, which (relatively) objectively represent the reality, mental activities are subjective because each agent can have different interpretations about the concepts. Mental activities include two major types: *sentiments* and *intents*. A concept can map to multiple sentiments, while multiple sentiments can also map to one concept. For example, Figure 1 shows that the presence of both darkness and silence *in general* trigger the emotion of fear. The mapping between concepts and sentiments can be put inside the concept model because certain commonness among human beings can be assumed. However, darkness and silence instill different degrees of fear into different agents, and the weights of darkness and silence vary from agents to agents. Thus, the personalities of agents must be taken into consideration when calculating the triggering of sentiments. Moreover, some agents may fear a particular thing that others do not necessarily fear, such as a rat, a gecko, or something more personal. Such personal emotional triggers can be placed inside an agent to override the default mapping in the concept model.

The triggering of intents involves two additional components of agent mind: goals and knowledge. Agents first have goals, and then look for knowledge that can be exploited to attain the goals. Knowledge is basically the connections between concepts [10]; isolated concepts cannot help generating the intents since agents rely on the causal effects of the environment to reach the goals. For the purpose of this paper, a goal is defined as a desired effect on a particular target instance. Omitting the target instance means the goal is to apply the desired effect on an arbitrary individual. The following algorithm shows how causal rules in the concept model can be used in the process of triggering new intents. Causal relations that are remembered in the memory of the agent can also be used in a way similar to this algorithm.

```
1 function triggerIntent(goal)
2    targetSet := intentSet := ruleSet := goalSet := {}
3    for all rules r, r.link.effect = goal.effect do
4        add r to ruleSet
5    if ruleSet = {} then return failed
6    if goal.targetInstance != null then
7        add goal.targetInstance to targetSet
8    else
9        for all t, t instanceOf goal.targetConcept do
10           add t to targetSet
11   if targetSet = {} then return failed
12   target := getOneWithMaxSimilarity(targetSet)
13   for all rules r, r belongTo ruleSet do
14       sourceSet := {}
15       for all s, s instanceOf r.sourceConcept do
16           add s to sourceSet
17       if sourceSet != {} then
18           source := getOneWithMaxSimilarity(sourceSet)
19           for all a belongTo r.link.actions do
20               add a new Intent (a, source, target) to intentSet
21       else
22           add a new Goal (r.sourceConcept, null)
             to goalSet. The effect of the new goal is
             r.sourceConcept, while target instance is null,
             which means the target is arbitrary.
23   if intentSet != {} then
24       intent := choose(intentSet)
25       add intent to the agent's intent pool
26       return successful
27   else
28       add a new Goal OR(goalSet) to the agent's
         goal pool
29       add an ordering constraint that OR(goalSet)
         must be executed before goal
30       return suspended
```

Take the intent illustrated in figure 1 for example. To overcome fear, the agent generates a subgoal of dispelling darkness with internal planning. Suppose d is an instance of darkness, the subgoal can be specified as $Destroyed(d)$. Then the intent of agent is triggered through *triggerIntent* algorithm. The process is described as follows:

First Call of triggerIntent(Destroyed(d)):

1. The agent looks for causal rules in the concept model. Any rules or relations whose effects satisfy the goal are retrieved. In this case, rule (5) defined in subsection 3.2 is discovered.
2. The agent checks whether anything in the environment is an instance of the source concept of the rule. In this case, the agent cannot find one because there is no light source in the environment.
3. If no instance of the source concept is found, the agent adds a new goal to create such an instance. In this case, the new goal can be specified as LightSource(null).
4. The original goal is suspended since the new goal must be accomplished before the original goal.

First Call of triggerIntent(LightSource(null)):

1. The agent executes *triggerIntent* with the new goal *LightSource(null)*. It looks for a rule whose effect creates an instance of either light source or a subclass of light source such as a fire. In this case, rules (3) and (4) are discovered.
2. Since the agent cannot find a fire to start another fire, rule (3) is filtered. Thus the agent starts searching for an instance of *Combustible* which is the target concept of (4). A torch o is found.
3. The agent also looks for an instance of igniter, which is the source instance of (4). A matchbox m is found.
4. The agent retrieves the triggering actions of the rule/relation. If multiple possible actions exist, the agent can choose one of them due to other considerations such as the cost of the action, the side effects, etc. In this case the action is *use*.
5. The agent successfully generates an intent to use the matchbox on the torch.

Second Call of triggerIntent(Destroyed(d)):

1. The agent revisits the goal *Destroyed(d)* again after the goal *LightSource(null)* is accomplished. It manages to find a light source this time (the burning torch o).
2. In this special case, the only action is to trigger rule (5) is *Noop*.
3. The agent generates a new intent to perform *Noop* on d with o.

The agent then tries to carry out the intent and find that it does not need to do anything since the action is *Noop*. Thus the agent considers the goal attained internally. The agent can ensure the accomplishment of the goal by observing whether the instance of darkness really disappears.

4   System Design

This section discusses issues about the design and implementation of multi-agent systems realizing the three-layer cognitive architecture described in above sections. Our goal is to provide a concrete implementation of the concept middle layer, enabling the agents to reason about the environment. We do not want to develop a general model of the reality (i.e. the environment itself) because each scenario can have a different model of the environment. Instead, an adapter interface is provided to allow the concept layer to be "plugged" onto different environments. Hence, agents can perform concept-based reasoning by interacting with the concept layer plugged onto different environments, including existing ones, without knowing the implementation details of each environment.

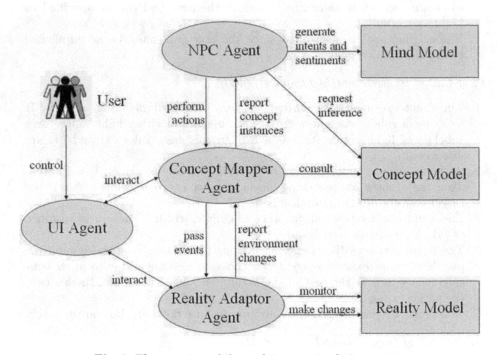

Fig. 2. The overview of the multi-agent simulation system

4.1   Pluggable Architecture

Currently a primitive simulation system of the above scenario of dispelling darkness is created to show how a scenario can be constructed with the pluggable middle layer of environment concepts. Figure 2 illustrates the system architecture. Agents in the system are built upon the JADE agent platform [19]. There are four types of agents in the system: *non-player-character* (NPC) *agents, user interface* (UI) *agents, concept mapper agents* and *reality adapter agents*. The NPC agents are believable characters which realize the mind layer of the cognitive architecture. Human participants can interact with both the NPC agents and the concept mapper agent through UI agents. NPC agents and UI agents are on equal stance in that they can perceive the same data and act in the same way except that NPC agents are driven by artificial minds while UI agents are controlled by human. The reality adapter agent is responsible for monitoring the changes in the reality model and translates them into a form recognizable by the concept mapper agent. For this scenario we created our own the reality model that simulates temperatures, burning points and brightness of objects with simple formulae, but specific reality adaptor agents can be built to connect with existing environments such as computer games if the environment provide an application interface for retrieving environment states. The concept mapper agent manages the interaction between NPC/UI agents with the reality layer and thus has a central role in the system. Unlike the other three types of agents, which are specifically tailored for different scenarios or environments, the concept mapper agent has a fixed implementation and can be introduced to systems without modification.

Concept Mapper Agent. The concept mapper agent is in charge of both perception and action; it maps aspects of reality to instances of concepts and maps action instances to events. The scenario of dispelling darkness is used again as an example of how the concept mapper agent works with other agents. When an NPC agent intends to light a torch, it sends the concept mapper agent an action request to use a pack of flint and steel on the torch. The concept mapper agent translates the action to an event the reality adapter agent recognizes. For example, the action "touch" is interpreted as an event that the source object becomes adjacent to the target object for a short time. The reality adapter agent receives the event, according to which the agent applies actual changes to the environment. The environment changes according to the reality model, which determines that the temperature of the torch becomes higher than its burning point, and the reality adapter agent monitors changes in temperature and brightness. The reality adapter agent then reports these changes to the concept mapper agent, which maps the changes to instances of concepts. Suppose each NPC agent has the same standard about light. Then the concept mapper agent maps the increase in brightness to a new instance of the concept "light" and report the instance to all NPC agents. Each NPC agent, however, has a different standard about being hot, and thus the concept mapper agent must first retrieve the traits of the NPC agents and then use them as input arguments of the mapping function of the concept "hot". The concept mapper agent calculates the mapping function for each NPC agent and reports an instance of "hot" to the NPC agent if and only if the mapping function returns a positive result. The instances are stored in the knowledge base of NPC agents and may invoke a new intent or sentiment.

Realizing Concept Structures. The ontologies in the concept model are written in OWL [23], which is expressive enough for the concept hierarchies and causal properties. The Jena Semantic Web tool [20] is used to parse the OWL ontologies. Jena contacts the RACER description logic reasoner [22] to perform ontological inference. Figure 3 depicts a sample ontology for describing the relationship between keys and locks. Causal rules and linking words are explicitly defined in separate tables. Rule-based inference is achieved with a simple program since the rules currently are in a simple fixed format. There is also an action ontology, also

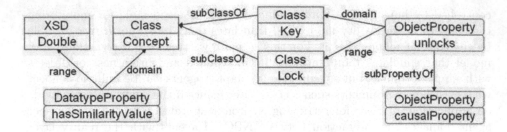

Fig. 3. Sample ontology for representing the causal property of keys on locks

written in OWL, that defines the hierarchy of actions. For example, to hit is a sub-action of to touch because hitting A with B implies that A touches B. NPC agents obtain the concept structure through the concept mapper agent and use inference to trigger intents and sentiments, and to decide what actions to invoke.

Utilizing a Semantic Web language such as OWL is a key to the extensibility of our concept model. Reuse of ontologies can be easily attained by importing existing OWL documents. The reuse can facilitate the creation of new worlds and the integration of multiple existing worlds. In principle, the same NPC agent can travel to and from different worlds created by different authors because the knowledge needed for action and emotion is encoded in the environments. In this aspect, we share the view of Doyle's "knowledge-in-the-world" approach [3], which decouples agents and environments so that they both can be developed independently.

4.2   Discussion on Scalability

This subsection discusses the scalability issues that can result from our system design of the three-layered architecture. The design decision of separating the concept model from agents has the advantage that agents do not need to carry environmental concepts with them. The separation removes redundancy and gives the agents a common basis of environmental understanding even when the size of the concept model grows.

An obvious issue is that the performance may downgrade significantly when the number of concepts and environmental aspects becomes high. For example, suppose there are 1000 concepts in the concept model and 100 aspects of environment in a room. At the first sight, the system will have to perform 200000 operations when two NPC agents enter the room if every aspect of environment is matched against every concept for every agent. The number of operations can cause the system to be overloaded.

However, we argue that not all operations are needed to be done at the same time. Only the few basic concepts related to the crucial background information, such as visual appearance, sound, or other defined concepts in the global settings are to be mapped and sent to the agents in the first place. Other more advanced concepts can be resolved in an incremental way as the time goes by. What kinds of concepts needs to be resolved afterward, are determined by the cognition strategy of agent mind, which is beyond the scope of this paper.

Moreover, the problem can be further alleviated with offline computation. For a concept whose mapping functions does not take traits of NPC agents as parameters, an inverted list can be computed that contains all objects that are instances of the concept. The objects in the list are sorted in descending order according to the similarity values. For example, the concept mapper agent returns the elements in the inverted list of fire if requested with instances of fire. For concepts whose mapping functions take the traits of NPC agents as inputs, offline computation is still possible if the set of all possible values of the trait is a finite enumeration.

5 Conclusion

Environment modeling is an essential part of building a believable multiagent scenario not only because a realistic environment itself contributes to believability, but also because the characters are more believable if they interact with the environment in a convincing way. A three-layer cognitive architecture is proposed as a unified model of agents and environments. The bottom of the architecture is the reality layer that models the dynamic environment as either continuous values or discrete items. The top layer is the agent mind that generates emotions and makes plans. This paper focuses on the middle layer of concepts that bridges the mind and the reality. The concepts, which represent the aspects of the reality, are formulated as ontologies and rules through which agents can reason about the environment. The concept layer also includes a set of mapping functions that maps the reality to instances of concepts. A prototype system is built to allow agent-based characters to create intentions from instances sensed through the concept layer. The specification of the concept layer is based on OWL, and therefore has the advantage of being extensible and reusable. Developing large-scale virtual environments is possible since different environments designed by different authors can be connected by combining the concept models. We are planning to increase the scale of scenario of the prototype system and developing criteria for evaluation and performance analysis. We are also planning to further formulate the causal rules and integrate them within a formal BDI agent architecture. Another topic for future investigation is to incorporate the believable agents themselves as a part of the environment and use the same model for cognition about agents.

Acknowledgements

This research is supported in part by National Science Council of ROC under grant number NSC 93-2213-E-007-061 and also by Ministry of Economic Affairs of ROC under grant number 93-EC-17-A-05-S1-030. The authors appreciate the reviewers' comments and corrections.

References

1. Cantor, N., Kihlstorm, J. F.: Personality and Social Intelligence. Prentice Hall, Englewood Cliffs, USA (1987)
2. Dickinson, I., Wooldridge, M.: Towards Practical Reasoning Agents for the Semantic Web. Proceedings of the Second International Joint Conference on Autonomous Agents and Multiagent Systems (AAMAS 2003). Melborne, Australia (2003)
3. Doyle, P.: Believability through Context: Using "Knowledge in the World" to Create Intelligent Characters. Proceedings of the First International Joint Conference on Autonomous Agents and Multiagent Systems (AAMAS 2002). Bologna, Italy (2002)
4. Ferber, J., Müller, J.P.: Influences and Reaction: a Model of Situated Multiagent System. Proceedings of the 2nd International Conference on Multi-agent Systems. Kyoto, Japan (1996)
5. Klein, J.: breve: a 3D Simulation Environment for the Simulation of Decentralized Systems and Artificial Life. Proceedings of Artificial Life VIII, the 8th International Conference on the Simulation and Synthesis of Living Systems. The MIT Press (2002)
6. Ligorio, B., Mininni, G., Traum, D.R.: Interlocution scenarios for problem solving in an educational mud environment. Proceedings of the First European Conference on Computer-Supported Collaborative Learning (Euro-CSCL 2001). (2001)
7. Marsella S., Johnson, W.L., LaBore, C: Interactive Pedagogical Drama for Health Interventions. Proceedings of the Eleventh International Conference on Artificial Intelligence in Education (AIED 2003). Australia (2003)
8. Norling, E., Sonenberg, L: An Approach to Evaluating Human Characteristics in Agents In Gabriela Lindemann, Daniel Moldt, Mario Paolucci, Bin Yu (eds.): Proceedings of the International Workshop on Regulated Agent-Based Systems: Theories and Applications (RASTA'02). Bologna, Italy (2002)
9. Norling, E., Sonenberg, L: Creating Interactive Characters with BDI Agents. In Australian Workshop on Interactive Entertainment. Sydney, Australia (2004)
10. Novak, J. D.: The Theory Underlying Concept Maps and How to Construct Them. http://cmap.coginst.uwf.edu/info/printer.html. Cornell University (2001)
11. Prendinger, H., Descamps, S., Ishizuka, M. MPML: A markup language for controlling the behavior of life-like characters, Journal of Visual Languages and Computing 15 (2004) 183–203
12. Rao, A. S., Georgeff, M. P.: BDI Agents: From Theory to Practice. Proceedings of the First International Conference on Multi-agent Systems. San Francisco, USA (1995)
13. Riedl, M., Saretto, C. J., Young, R. M.: Managing Interaction Between Users and Agents in a Multi-agent Storytelling Environment. Proceedings of the 2nd Joint International Conference on Autonomous Agents and Multiagent Systems (AAMAS 2003). Melbourne, Australia (2003)
14. Swartout, W., Hill, R.W. Jr., Gratch, J., Johnson, W.L., Kyriakakis, C., LaBore, C., Lindheim, R., Marsella, S., Miraglia, D., Moore, B., Morie, J.F., Rickel, J., Thiebaux, M., Tuch, L., Whitney, R.: Toward the Holodeck: Integrating Graphics, Sound, Character and Story. Proceedings of 5th International Conference on Autonomous Agents. Montreal, Canada. (2001)
15. Trafimow, D., Wyer, R. S. Jr.: Cognitive Representation of Mundane Social Events. Journal of Personality and Social Psychology 64 (1993) 365–376

16. Traum, D., Rickel, J., Gratch, J., Marsella, S.: Negotiation over Tasks in Hybrid Human-Agent Teams for Simulation-Based Training. Proceedings of the 2nd Joint International Conference on Autonomous Agents and Multiagent Systems (AAMAS 2003). Melbourne, Australia (2003)
17. Weyns, D., Holvoet, T.: A Formal Model for Situated Multi-Agent Systems. Fundamenta Informaticae **63**(2-3) (2004) 125-158
18. Full Spectrum Warrior, http://www.fullspectrumwarrior.com (2004)
19. Java Agent Development Framework, http://jade.tilab.com/
20. Jena Semantic Web Toolkit, http://jena.sourceforge.net/
21. Quicksilver 1.2, http://quicksilver.tigris.org/
22. RACER System Description, http://www.sts.tu-harburg.de/ r.f.moeller/racer/
23. W3C Web Ontology Working Group, http://www.w3.org/2001/sw/WebOnt/

A Spatially Dependent Communication Model for Ubiquitous Systems

Stefania Bandini, Sara Manzoni, and Giuseppe Vizzari

Dipartimento di Informatica, Sistemistica e Comunicazione,
Università degli Studi di Milano–Bicocca,
Via Bicocca degli Arcimboldi 8, 20126 Milano, Italy
{bandini, manzoni, vizzari}@disco.unimib.it

Abstract. Models and conceptualizations are necessary to understand and design ubiquitous systems that are context–aware not just from a technological point of view. The current technological trend depicts a scenario in which space, movement, and more generally the environment in which the computation takes place, represent aspects that should be considered as first class concepts. The aim of this paper is to propose the Multilayered Multi-Agent Situated System (MMASS) model as a suitable support for the definition of conceptual architectures for ubiquitous systems. The model provides a strong concept of agent environment, which represents an abstraction of a physical environment possibly interfaced with representations of conceptual aspects as well. The agent interaction model provides two basic mechanisms (reaction and field emission) that are strongly dependent on the spatial structure of the environment. After a brief presentation of MMASS, related concepts and mechanisms, a sample application domain illustrating how it can be adopted to model an ubiquitous system will be given.[1]

1 Introduction

The current trend of technological innovations is transforming the environment where human actors live and the way in which they perceive their interactions. Computers are "disappearing", their computational power is no more concentrated in identifiable spots, rather it is ubiquitous and can be potentially embedded in almost every object populating the environment. Interaction is also changing its nature, since it is not necessarily performed through traditional devices connected to traditional computers. Computation is spread in the environment, actors move in it carrying mobile devices of different kinds and access the "network" in different ways. In this new scenario the movement in a space and the related possibility to interact with other actors, according to the current location, represent new dimensions that must be taken into account as first

---

[1] The work presented in this paper has been partially funded by the Italian Ministry of University and Research within the FIRB project 'Multichannel Adaptive Information Systems'

D. Weyns et al. (Eds.): E4MAS 2004, LNAI 3374, pp. 74–90, 2005.
© Springer-Verlag Berlin Heidelberg 2005

class concepts. The environment influences what can be done and how tasks are performed, as the location influences communication capabilities and resources.

Technological evolution is not combined with an equally rapid evolution of the conceptualization necessary to understand and govern the new situation [27]. The term *context–aware* has been introduced to represent new challenges and possibilities, but it is usually interpreted in technological terms, mainly, of physical localization and available resources (e.g. network connectivity). However the concept of context is a continuum of physical and logical aspects that do not only involve communication as an isolated event but also coordination and cooperation among actors moving in a logical space related to collaborative tasks. Interpreting the physical and logical space as separated worlds is a serious impediment to consider space as a basic dimension for computing systems adaptability. What we call "logical space" received a lot of attention and many approaches have been proposed to model the involved actors and their coordination as well as the involved informational entities (see, e.g., [17, 21]). The emphasis is mainly on their mutual logical relationships, while the spatial one is simulated and managed in the same way as any other one, specifically without considering topology and metrics in an explicit way. On the other hand, the approaches primarily oriented to model the space give, at different degrees, a semantics to the various spatial entities and to their spatial relationships (see, e.g., [13]) but are not open to represent relationships of a different nature. Therefore a model able to handle space as a first class concept, but also to consider in a uniform way both physical and logical spaces, is still needed. These different spaces should both be considered, but not in a mixed way: a good model should reach the above goal by distinguishing the two kinds of space and at the same time by guaranteeing their interoperability (thanks to the above mentioned uniformity).

The design of ubiquitous systems cannot rely on global states or actors owning a global view of the system. On the contrary, control is fully distributed among entities owning a local state and a partial, subjective perception of their situation. Locality, perception, point of view are concepts that, once again, require a space where they can be defined. Fully distributed control and local autonomy is a typical characteristic of many agent based models [6]. Moreover the Multi-Agent Systems (MASs) approach has often been indicated as a suitable abstraction for the analysis and design of complex systems characterized by an inherent distribution of control and information sources [16]. Agent technology has also been considered an instrument to promote software interoperation (see, e.g., [9]), and the concepts and methodologies used for analysis and design of MASs (see, e.g., GAIA [26, 28]) can be adopted in general for the modelling and design of complex distributed systems that, strictly speaking, are not agent-oriented from a software engineering point of view. Hence this approach can be applied to the design of a variety of systems. Agent interaction models however generally do not consider the spatial dimension of agent environment in an explicit way (topology and metrics).

The presence of different reference spaces, representing different classes of relationships among autonomous entities, requires a model able to represent a variety of spaces without imposing a hierarchy among them. In fact the behavior of a system exploiting different layers representing logical spaces and abstractions of the physical one emerges from the mutual interactions among them. The aim of this paper is to propose a model that incorporates features fulfilling the above requirements for the modelling of complex context–aware ubiquitous systems: the Multilayered Multi–Agent Situated System (MMASS) [1] model. The MMASS model provides a rich interaction model for agents, including synchronous *reaction* among adjacent entities and asynchronous interaction through the *field* emission–diffusion–perception mechanism. Both interactions are dependent on the spatial structure in which agents are placed, that can represent a physical space abstraction but also conceptual environments as well. The following section will briefly describe the MMASS model, highlighting the relationships with related works in agent interaction models and introducing the main concepts defined by the model. Section 3 will exploit MMASS in order to define a specific conceptual architecture for ubiquitous computing applications in the automotive area. Conclusions and future developments will end the paper.

2   MMASS Model

The Multilayered Multi-Agent Situated Systems (MMASS) model [1] is a formal and computational framework for the definition of systems made up of a set of autonomous entities acting and interacting in a structured environment. This section does not represent a formal description of the model (that can be found in [2]), but will briefly introduce its main concepts, specifically focusing on the environmental structure. In fact the latter deeply influences agents behaviour, as the environment is the source of their perceptions, a constraint limiting their actions (e.g. their movement), but it also provides them a medium to interact with other entities. First of all related works and their relationships with agent environment modelling will be described, then the MMASS and its main concepts will be introduced.

2.1   Agent Environment in Agent Interaction Models

Most models for agent–based systems generally provide direct–interaction mechanisms that do not consider the circumstances and context of the interaction. Agent environment is generally represented by a communication infrastructure, often implemented through a facilitator agent that is well–known by other entities. It acts as a directory, supplying agents with information related to other entities currently active in the system (often referred to as *social knowledge*), and allowing a direct information exchange among them. In some approaches in this area, the issue of agent discovery is tackled with more complex techniques, providing a set of middle agents collaborating to collect, maintain and provide social knowledge. In particular, some of these approaches provide a thorough analysis of the structure of this organization of middle agents in order to provide specific features (e.g. robustness) [22], other propose a self-organization approach to ob-

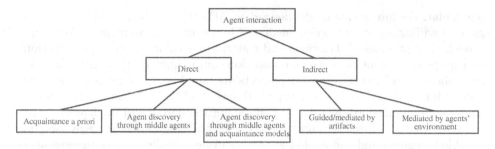

Fig. 1. A possible taxonomy of agent interaction models

tain a flexible, dynamic, yet effective, way of obtaining a robust infrastructure for social knowledge [23]. Other results of the research in this area led to the specification of acquaintance models [14] defining more precisely how this kind of agent social knowledge should be managed. However communication is generally conceived as an indiscriminate point–to–point message transfer, where messages comply to rules defined by a specific Agent Communication Language (ACL) (see, e.g., [11]). The concept of environment is thus rather weak, and in order to obtain a communication that is aware of the context in which interlocutors are placed, the involved elements (spatial or conceptual features of the environment) must be modelled and included in an agent (that can be one of the communication partners, or both of them, or even another facilitator playing the role of the environment). In this way conceptual elements (i.e. interaction and spatial context management) are mixed–up with other aspects related to domain specific issues (e.g. agents behaviour) and often delegated to ad–hoc implementations.

Other approaches provide an indirect agent interaction model, in which agents exchange information through specific artifacts and mechanisms. These artifacts represent agents' environment, at least for what concerns their means of interaction. Some models are not aimed at bringing this metaphor to the extreme, and do not mean to represent a comprehensive environmental model, but are only meant to provide a unified framework for agent interaction and coordination. In fact many of them provide extensions to the basic tuple-space-based approaches (see, e.g., Lime [19]), in order to support developer of agent based and distributed applications with a technical support for coordination in distributed and mobile environment. An interesting approach to indirect agent interaction is represented by the notion of Agent Coordination Context [17], which represents a first class abstraction to model a specific part of agents' environment focused on their social activities. In fact it captures concepts like roles, permissions and other organizational abstractions, representing also a mean for managing them at runtime, for instance in order to enforce the compliance to specific social rules.

The interaction model described in this paper differs from the previously introduced approaches as it offers interaction mechanisms that are strongly dependent on the spatial structure of the environment in which the involved entities are placed. Fig. 1 illustrates a possible taxonomy of agent interaction models, which is inspired and partly based on the one that can be found in [18]. In particular, the interaction model defined by MMASS can be placed in the category providing agent interaction mediated by agents' environment. A MAS approach that provides abstractions and concepts for environment representation and space–dependent form of communication comparable to the MMASS action–at–a–distance is Swarm [15]; other projects are based on it and propose the same kind of interaction model (e.g. Ascape [2], Repast [3], MASON [4]). Swarm is a multi–agent software platform focused on supporting the design and implementations of MASs that are based on purely reactive agents. The idea that agents should be able to understand and exploit an ACL can be unrealistic (and unnecessary) when one has to model biological systems made up of very simple entities for simulations. Moreover very simple entities exploiting their environment in order to interact among each other are able to generate fairly complex emergent behaviours. However this approach provides an explicit representation of the environment in which agents are placed, and even a mechanism for the diffusion of signals (i.e. digital pheromones) in particular versions of these structures. Recent results in the area of self-organizing systems (see, e.g., [10]) are aimed at a thorough formalization and a generalization of this kind of interaction model (often referred to as stigmergy) and its application in the engineering of MASs.

Another approach [13] provides a physically grounded model for agent interaction based on the concept of computational fields (Co-Fields). Co-Fields are signals that may be emitted either by the agents or by other elements of the environment, which supports the diffusion of those signals and thus agent interaction. In this model, agents are constantly guided by fields, that represent a mean of motion coordination, while in MMASS every perception of a field triggers a single generalized action (i.e. not strictly related to agent motion).

A different situated MASs approach [24], derived by the Influence/Reaction model [7], focuses instead on the definition of a model for simultaneous agent actions, including centralized and (local) regional synchronization mechanisms for agent coordination. In particular, actions can be independent or interfering among each other; in the latter case, they can be mutually exclusive (*concurrent* actions), requiring a contemporary execution in order to have a successful outcome (*joint* actions), or having a more complex influence among each other (both positive or negative). However, no specific mechanism for the interaction among agents occupying distant points in the environment is provided. Moreover in this approach agents' environment is related to a single layer of spatial representation.

The MMASS model provides an explicit representation of agent environment, that is made up of a set of interconnected layers whose structure is an undirected graph of sites. These layers may represent abstractions of an actual physical environment but can also be related to "logical" aspects as well (e.g. the organizational structure of a company). Between these layers specific con-

---

[2] http://www.brook.edu/dybdocroot/es/dynamics/models/ascape/README.html
[3] http://repast.sourceforge.net
[4] http://cs.gmu.edu/ eclab/projects/mason/

nections (*interfaces*) can be specified. The latter are used to specify that a given field type, generated in one of these layers, may also propagate into a different one. This mechanism allows to generate interactions among different aspects and levels of the system. *Field based interaction* is the first mechanism for agent interaction, allowing a multicast form of interaction among agents occupying distant points in their environment. Adjacent agents may also perform a coordinated change of their state through a *reaction*, which is the second mechanism for agent interaction.

The model has been successfully applied to several simulation contexts in which the concepts of space and environment are key factors for the problem solving activity and cannot be neglected (e.g. crowd modelling [3], localization problems [4]). The following subsections will briefly introduce the model and the formal definitions of concepts that will be exploited to define conceptual architectures in the ubiquitous computing area.

2.2 An Overview of MMASS Model

According to the MMASS model agents are situated in sites, that is, nodes of the graphs related to a layer of the environment. Every site may host at most one agent (according to a non-interpenetration principle: "two agents cannot occupy the same site at the same time"), and every agent is situated in a single site at a given time (non–ubiquity: : "at a given time an agent occupies a single site"). Agents inherit the spatial relationships defined for the site it is occupying; in other words an agent positioned in site p is considered adjacent to agents placed in sites adjacent to p.

The adjacency relation among agents is a necessary condition for the applicability of *reaction*, the first kind of interaction mechanism defined by the MMASS model. In fact this operation involves two or more agents that are placed in adjacent sites and allows them to synchronously change their state, after they have performed an agreement. This mechanism resembles the one defined by transition rules in Cellular Automata (CA) [25], that also provide an explicit representation of a spatial structure.

CA are the model that has mainly inspired MMASS specification, and one of the main differences between the two models is the possibility to represent *action–at–a–distance*. In fact, the second interaction mechanism defined by the MMASS model provides the possibility for agents to emit *fields*, that are signals able to diffuse through the environment that can be perceived by other agents according to specific rules. This mechanism resembles pheromone approaches to agent communication (see, e.g., [10]), but fields are not just related to an intensity value and may convey more complex kind of information. Moreover for every field type a *diffusion function* can be specified in order to define how related signals decay (or are amplified) during their diffusion in the environment, from the source of emission to destination sites. Other functions specify how fields of the same kind can be *composed* (for instance in order to obtain the intensity of a given field type at a given site) or *compared*. From a semantic point of view fields themselves are neutral even if they can have related information in addition to their intensity; they are only signals, with an indication on how they diffuse in the environment, how they can be compared and composed. Different agent types may be able to perceive them or not and, in the first case, they may have completely different reaction, according to their behavioural specification. With reference to perception, an agent may perceive a field with a non–null intensity active in the site it is situated on according to two parameters characterizing its type and related to the specific field type. The first one is the *sensitivity threshold*, indicating the minimum field intensity that an agent of that type is able to perceive. The second is the *receptiveness coefficient* and it represents an amplification factor modulating (amplifying or attenuating) field value before the comparison with the sensitivity threshold. Thanks to these parameters it is possible to model dynamism in the perceptive capabilities of agents of a give type, since these parameters are related to agent state. In this way, for instance, the same agent that was unable to perceive a specific field value could become more sensitive (increase its own receptiveness coefficient) as a consequence of a change in its state. This allows to model physical aspects of perception, but also conceptual ones such as agent interests.

Reaction and field emission are two of the possible actions available for the specification of agent behaviour, related to the specification of how agents may interact. Other actions are related to the possibility to move (*transport* operation) and change the state upon the perception of a specific field (*trigger* operation). These primitives are part of a language for the specification of MMASS agents behaviour [2]. An important part of the language also provides the possibility to dynamically modify the structure of agent environment, in order to generate new sites and edges (or destroy existing ones) and create (or destroy) agents of a specific type, with a given initial state. *Agent type* is in fact a specification of agent state, perceptive capabilities and behaviour.

2.3   MMASS: Formal Definitions

A *Multilayered Multi–Agent Situated System (MMASS)* is defined as a constellation of interacting *Multi-Agent Situated System* (MASS) that represent different layers of the global system: $\langle MASS_1 \ldots MASS_n \rangle$. A single MASS is defined by the triple $\langle Space, F, A \rangle$ where *Space* models the environment where the set A of agents is situated, acts autonomously and interacts through the propagation of the set F of fields and through reaction operations.

The structure of a layer is defined as a not oriented graph of sites. Every *site* $p \in P$ (where P is the set of sites of the layer) can contain at most one agent and is defined by the 3–tuple $\langle a_p, F_p, P_p \rangle$ where:

- $a_p \in A \cup \{\bot\}$ is the agent situated in p ($a_p = \bot$ when no agent is situated in p that is, p is empty);
- $F_p \subset F$ is the set of fields active in p ($F_p = \emptyset$ when no field is active in p);
- $P_p \subset P$ is the set of sites adjacent to p.

In order to allow the interaction between different MMASS layers (i.e. intra-MASS interaction) the model introduces the notion of *interface*. The latter specifies that a gateway among two layers is present with reference to a specific field type. An interface is defined as a 3–tuple $\langle p_i, p_j, F_\tau \rangle$ where $p_i \in P_i, p_j \in P_j$, with P_i and P_j sets of sites related to different layers (i.e. $i \neq j$). With reference to the diffusion of field of type F_τ the indicated sites are considered adjacent and placed on the same spatial layer. In other words fields of type F_τ reaching p_i will be diffused in its adjacent sites (P_p) and also in p_j.

A MMASS agent is defined by the 3–tuple $< s, p, \tau >$ where τ is the *agent type*, $s \in \Sigma_\tau$ denotes the *agent state* and can assume one of the values specified by its type (see below for Σ_τ definition), and $p \in P$ is the site of the *Space* where the agent is situated. As previously stated, agent *type* is a specification of agent state, perceptive capabilities and behaviour. In fact an agent type τ is defined by the 3–tuple $\langle \Sigma_\tau, Perception_\tau, Action_\tau \rangle$. Σ_τ defines the set of states that agents of type τ can assume. $Perception_\tau : \Sigma_\tau \rightarrow [\mathbf{N} \times W_{f_1}] \dots [\mathbf{N} \times W_{f_{|F|}}]$ is a function associating to each agent state a vector of pairs representing the *receptiveness coefficient* and *sensitivity thresholds* for that kind of field. $Action_\tau$ represents instead the behavioural specification for agents of type τ. Agent behaviour can be specified using a language that defines the following primitives:

- $emit(s, f, p)$: the *emit* primitive allows an agent to *start the diffusion of field f* on p, that is the site it is placed on;
- $react(s, a_{p_1}, a_{p_2}, \dots, a_{p_n}, s')$: this kind of primitive allows the specification a *coordinated change of state* among adjacent agents. In order to preserve agents' autonomy, a compatible primitive must be included in the behavioural specification of all the involved agents; moreover when this coordination process takes place, every involved agents may dynamically decide to effectively agree to perform this operation;
- $transport(p, q)$: the *transport* primitive allows to *define agent movement* from site p to site q (that must be adjacent and vacant);
- $trigger(s, s')$: this primitive specifies that an agent must *change its state* when it senses a particular condition in its local context (i.e. its own site and the adjacent ones); this operation has the same effect of a reaction, but does not require a coordination with other agents.

For every primitive included in the behavioural specification of an agent type specific preconditions must be specified; moreover specific parameters must also be given (e.g. the specific field to be emitted in an emit primitive, or the conditions to identify the destination site in a transport) to precisely define the effect of the action, which was previously briefly described in general terms.

Each MMASS agent is thus provided with a set of sensors that allows its interaction with the environment and other agents. At the same time, agents can constitute the source of given fields acting within a MMASS space (e.g. noise emitted by a talking agent). Formally, a field type t is defined by

$$\langle W_t, Diffusion_t, Compare_t, Compose_t \rangle$$

where W_t denotes the set of values that fields of type t can assume; $Diffusion_t :$ $P \times W_f \times P \rightarrow (W_t)^+$ is the diffusion function of the field computing the value of a field on a given space site taking into account in which site (P is the set of sites that constitutes the MMASS space) and with which value it has been generated. $Compose_t : (W_t)^+ \rightarrow W_t$ expresses how fields of the same type have to be combined (for instance, in order to obtain the unique value of field type t at a site), and $Compare_t : W_t \times W_t \rightarrow \{True, False\}$ is the function that compares values of the same field type. This function is used in order to verify whether an agent can perceive a field value by comparing it with the sensitivity threshold after it has been modulated by the receptiveness coefficient.

3   A MMASS Architecture for Ubiquitous Systems

In order to exemplify the MMASS as a model for the design of conceptual architectures in the ubiquitous computing area, a sample application scenario in the automotive context will be introduced. In fact modern cars are equipped with a large number of sensors (for instance related to the state of brakes, steering and other vehicle subsystems) and are equipped with various microcontrollers (e.g. devoted to engine control, air conditioning [20]). Information related to these devices is generally exploited to allow, enhance or maintain vehicle operation, but is otherwise wasted. The interconnection among these devices is generally developed according to some vehicular network, commonly called Controller Area Network [12]. According to this trend in automotive technology, it is thus possible to design new devices which are able to interface with existing electronic modules, in order to store relevant data, perform some kind of elaboration (e.g. check for crash conditions, perform self diagnosis), and communicate with external systems through wireless communication devices. These new technological devices could be designed in order to support new applications based on the interaction among autonomous mobile computational units spread in the environment and other fixed–position centres, that manage them in order to offer services that are aware of the context of the remote units.

Part of this concept of context is surely represented by an abstraction of the spatial structure of the environment, which may represent a map indicating conceptual communications flows among the various entities. This abstraction may be mapped to a MMASS layer, but also others aspects of the global system may be modelled through different layers interfaced to the previous one. Fig. 2 shows a possible arrangement of three MMASS layers respectively devoted to the management of the spatial aspects, of the emergency management context and to location–aware touristic information provisioning. In the following subsections more details on how these coordinated contexts may me modelled in terms of MMASS will be given.

3.1   Spatial Abstraction Layer

The typical ubiquitous computing scenario provides a number of mobile devices that are able to communicate with other entities, in order to offer some kind of service to end–users. The nature of offered services is a key factor in determining

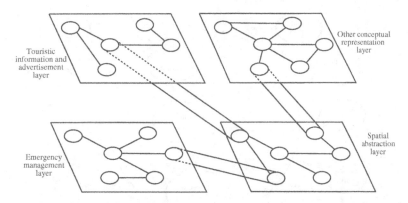

Fig. 2. The multilayered structure of the described application, highlighting interfaces among layers

a possible architecture for such systems, but in general those mobile devices will communicate with another kind of entity, that can be thought to have a fixed position which could even be not particularly relevant to the application. This entity could be a centralized storage and elaboration facility, or it could be part of a composite network, with different nodes that collaborate in order to supply services to the end–user.

A diagram showing this kind of architecture is shown in Fig. 3: in this case the spatial structure is an abstraction of the physical space adopted to define and manage communications in the system. In other words it is used to define which node will manage requests issued by the remote mobile entity. For example, a car fleet management system could be made up of different immobile entities, serving vehicles spread over the territory, connected through a central storage facility; the GSM standard provides a similar architecture with decentralized management of mobile terminals but a centered entity (the Home Location Register [8]) for the storage of subscribers data. In some situations such a central entity is not required, but when acquired and stored data must be analyzed (for instance with data mining techniques in order to derive profiling information) it can be appropriate to have a single data storage facility. On the other hand, if the system only has to supply an emergency assistance service to end–users represented by car drivers, there could be just decentralized centres. The area covered by the service can be partitioned into several sub–areas, and every user should be initially registered to a specific peripheral assistance centre (complex units including people, PCs, computer networks, and so on), at the moment of service subscription. The user can be handled by this unit while he/she remains in this area, and when his/her vehicle moves into another area the two peripheral centres could exchange information related to the user. Even in this case there are similarities with architectures designed for mobile wireless device. In fact this kind of operation involving peripheral centres can be viewed as a non–critical form of handover, and the management of this event could be derived by protocols designed in that area.

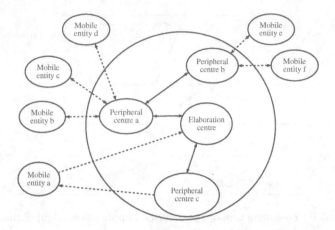

Fig. 3. A possible architecture for ubiquitous applications in the automotive domain

Exploiting the explicit description of the environment that the MMASS approach provides it is possible to take into account the different structures of logical connections (i.e. which peripheral centre is currently managing a specific mobile entity) to model the interactions among entities of the system. From a conceptual point of view, the previously described interactions between peripheral centres and mobile entities (i.e. authentication and login procedure, and mobile entities handover) can be modelled as *reactions*. In fact the initial interaction among mobile entities and peripheral centres can be considered a synchronous agreement process in which the former identifies itself and the latter grants access to the offered services.

In order to model the login procedure a reaction primitive must be included in $Action_{PC}$, the behavioural specification for peripheral centres (PC agents). A compatible reaction should be included in the behavioural specification of agents related to mobile entities(ME agents). In particular, the reaction for PC agents can be specified as follows:

$$action : react\Big(\langle S_a, S\rangle, a_m, \langle S'_a, S\rangle\Big)$$
$$condit : position(p), position(a_m, q), near(p, q), agreed(a_m)$$
$$effect : S'_a = S_a \cup \{a_m\}$$

The state of an agent of type PC is a pair made up of the set of mobile entities that it is currently managing (S_a) and other internal information (S), which is not relevant for the example. The interaction takes place only if the agent and the mobile entity are adjacent in the spatial structure they are placed on and have agreed to react (i.e. the mobile entity has successfully performed an authentication procedure). The effect of the reaction is the inclusion of the mobile entity a_m in the set of the ones that are served by the peripheral centre ($S'_a = S_a \cup \{a_m\}$).

Other possible interactions involving agents situated in the spatial abstraction layer are related to the diffusion of information by the peripheral centre

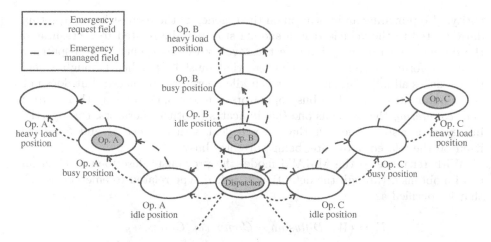

Fig. 4. A model of driver assistance context

to all the mobile entities that are currently present in its area (i.e. which are currently connected to it by an edge and included in the list of authenticated entities included in its state). In this case, the diffusion function should provide that signals reach the mobile entities unmodified, but a perceptive mechanism related to interests of the mobile user could be adopted to filter signals that are not relevant to him/her could be devised. This layer could thus also represent the basic structure for location aware diffusion of information, for instance related to road/traffic condition information or even touristic advertisement. This information could be suitably originated by different layers interfaced to this one: an example of this possibility will be described in Section 3.3.

3.2   Emergency Management Layer

The previously described layer represents just one of the aspects of the whole system, the one related to communication flows, that are dependent on spatial features, but it does not specify anything on the structure of peripheral centres and how they perform the services offered to the end–user. In order to define the behaviour of those peripheral centres a new conceptual spatial structure, interfaced to the physical spatial abstraction layer, should be defined. Fig. 4 shows a possible conceptual representation related to the operation of an organization for the management of emergency signals coming from mobile entities.

The central node, the interface to the spatial abstraction layer, hosts a *dispatcher* agent that must propagate the emergency request issued by a user or by a mobile entity in the structure defined in Fig. 3. This request is augmented with contextual information, such as data related to the user and vehicle, indications on its location, and so on. The latter can be obtained by integrating raw data transmitted by the mobile entity with a cartography and other information that might be obtained by a GIS of by a traditional information system as well. In other words, this node may enhance the information provided by the remote entity, also providing an indication on the urgency of the request by interpreting data related to the vehicle (e.g. a sudden stop may be related to a crash, and the deceleration rate may indicate the severity of this event). The dispatcher diffuses information related to the event that must be handled through a field that reaches all adjacent sites, on which idle operators are placed, but does not reach outer sites, related to busy operators. An idle operator may then *emit* a field *countering* the previous one (i.e. indicates to other operators, through the information system, the fact that he will deal with this event) and *transport* itself on the related outer site, being currently busy.

With reference to the MMASS model the previously described mechanism can be obtained through the definition of a field type related to emergencies F_e that is specified as

$$F_e = \langle W_e, Diffusion_{F_e}, Compare_h, Compose_h \rangle$$

where $w_e \in W_e : w_e = \langle id_e, type_e, int_e, d_e \rangle$ represents the possible values assumed by the field. Its composing parts have the following meaning: id_e represents a unique identifier of the emergency request, $type_e$ (that can assume *request* or *managed* values) indicates that the field is related to the request issued by the dispatcher or represents a counter field emitted by an operator, $int_e \in \mathbb{N}$ is the intensity of the signal, and d_e is the additional data related to the emergency (which is not relevant for the example). The diffusion function specifying how this field is spread into the spatial structure is defined as follows:

$$Diffusion_{F_e}(p_0, f_{p_0}, p) = \begin{cases} f_e & type_e = managed \\ \langle id_e, type_e, int_e - dist(p_0, p), d_e \rangle & dist(p_0, p) < int_e \\ 0 & otherwise \end{cases}$$

The comparison function uniformly returns *true*, as all requests are perceivable by operators, and fields do not compose at all with the exception of the combination of *request* and *managed* field related to the same emergency. Formally $Compose\big(\langle id_e, managed, int_e, d_e \rangle, \langle id_e, request, int_e, d_e \rangle\big) = \emptyset$. With reference to field persistence in the environment, the ones marked as *request* do not vanish while *managed* ones have an instantaneous effect (i.e. they counter related *request* signals) and then are discarded.

The dispatcher performs a diffusion of a *request* field for all fields related to emergencies (which are generated in the spatial abstraction layer and forwarded to this layer thanks to a specific interface) that it perceives. The value of the emitted field is $w_e^1 = \langle id_e, request, 2, d_e \rangle$, as it must be able to reach idle operators but not busy ones. An idle operator perceiving this signal and willing to manage the related request, should thus perform an emission of a counter field $w_e^2 = \langle id_e, managed, k, d_e \rangle$, that will be uniformly diffused in the environment and will cancel the request signal. After that it will *transport* itself on an outer position (the one related to the busy state). Particularly urgent requests may have a higher starting intensity, and could thus reach even outer sites. A busy operator perceiving this field may decide to delay the current lower priority task

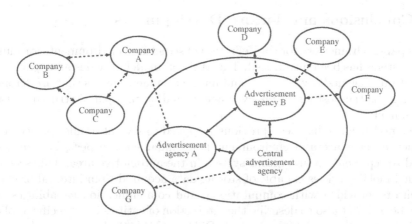

Fig. 5. A model of advertisement management context

to manage the new emergency, moving to the outermost site (related to the heavy load state) in order to be shielded even from these urgent requests.

3.3   Touristic Information and Advertisement Layer

Considering another case, related to touristic information and advertisement, the layer shown in Fig. 3 defines the communication mechanism among the most suitable local information supplier and the active boxes spread over the area it is related to. However, the spatial abstraction layer does not specify anything on how companies may interact among themselves and refer to local or central advertisement agencies, in order to diffuse information related to their offers. Fig. 5 shows a possible conceptual representation related to this kind of scenario.

Thanks to the possibility to modify the spatial structure (e.g. creating or destroying sites and edges), agents related to Companies A, B and C have elected Company A as a representative that is responsible for the interaction with the Advertisement agency A. In other words it is the only one connected to the site related to the agency, with which it will interact through reaction operations. Companies D, E and F are instead interacting directly with Advertisement agency B, which will be able to diffuse information related to policies and offers through a diffusion operation. While these companies operated at a local level, Company G interacts directly with a Central advertisement agency. The latter will perform a reaction involving both Advertisement agencies A and B. The interface among this layer and the one related to the abstraction of agents' physical space, shown in Fig. 3, provides a direct connection among Peripheral centres and local Advertisement agencies, which will be able to emit specific fields that will be perceived by peripheral centres which will in turn emit signals perceivable by mobile entities positioned in their areas.

4   Conclusions and Future Developments

In this paper a framework for the definition of structured environments for multi–agent systems has been introduced. The MMASS model provides an explicit representation of agents' environment and interaction mechanisms that are strongly dependent on the position of involved agents and on the spatial structure of the environment.

The model, which has been previously applied to several simulation scenarios in which agent space and environment is a fundamental aspect, has been exploited to represent an ubiquitous system in the automotive area. This scenario provided mobile entities capable of storing data acquired from internal or external sensors, provided with computational and communication capabilities (i.e. active–boxes), but also to describe the interaction of entities in a specific application (i.e. emergency assistance centre). Different MMASS layers were described representing physical or conceptual abstractions specifying different aspects of the modelled system. The interaction model defined by MMASS was exploited in order to represent the communication among various entities of the system.

The design of a comprehensive software layer implementing a platform for MMASS concepts is the object of current and future developments; a first step in this direction was the analysis of distributed approaches to field diffusion [5]. Another important aspect that must be faced in order to simplify the transition from modelling to design and implementation phases is a mapping between the MMASS interaction model and possible underlying communication technologies, which are often very distant from the mechanism defined by the model.

References

1. Bandini, S., Manzoni, S., Simone, C.: Dealing with Space in Multi–Agent Systems: a Model for Situated MAS. In: Proceedings of the first international joint conference on Autonomous agents and multiagent systems, ACM Press (2002) 1183–1190
2. Bandini, S., Manzoni, S., Simone, C.: Heterogeneous Agents Situated in Heterogeneous Spaces. Applied Artificial Intelligence **16(9-10)** (2002) 831–852
3. Bandini, S., Manzoni, S., Vizzari, G.: Situated Cellular Agents: a Model to Simulate Crowding Dynamics. IEICE Transactions on Information and Systems: Special Issues on Cellular Automata **E87-D(3)** (2004) 669–676
4. Bandini, S., Manzoni, S., Vizzari, G.: MultiAgent Approach to Localization Problems: the Case of Multilayered Multi Agent Situated System. Web Intelligence and Agent Systems **2(3)** (2004) 155–166
5. Bandini, S., Manzoni, S., Vizzari, G.: Towards a Specification and Execution Environment for Simulations Based on MMASS: Managing At–a–distance Interaction. In Trappl, R., ed.: Proceedings of the 17th European Meeting on Cybernetics and Systems Research, Austrian Society for Cybernetic Studies (2004) 636–641
6. Ferber, J.: Multi–Agent Systems. Addison–Wesley (1999)
7. Ferber, J., Muller, J.P.: Influences and Reaction: a Model of Situated Multiagent Systems. In: Proceedings of the 2th International Conference on Multi-agent Systems, AAAI Press (1996) 72–79

8. Gabelgaard, B.: The (GSM) HLR-Advantages and Challenges. In: Third Annual International Conference on Universal Personal Communications, IEEE (1994) 335–339
9. Genesereth, M.R., Ketchpel, S.P.: Software Agents. Communications of the ACM **37(7)** (1994) 48–ff.
10. Hadeli, K., Valckenaers, P., Zamfirescu, C., Brussel, H.V., Germain, B.S., Holvoet, T., Steegmans, E.: Self-Organising in Multi-Agent Coordination and Control Using Stigmergy. In: Engineering Self-Organising Systems: Nature-Inspired Approaches to Software Engineering. Volume 2977 of Lecture Notes in Computer Science., Springer–Verlag (2004) 105–123
11. Labrou, Y., Finin, T.W., Peng, Y.: Agent Communication Languages: the Current Landscape. IEEE Intelligent Systems **14(2)** (1999) 45–52
12. Leen, G., Heffernan, D.: Expanding Automotive Electronic Systems. IEEE Computer **35(1)** (2002) 88–93
13. Mamei, M., Zambonelli, F., Leonardi, L.: Co-fields: Towards a Unifying Approach to the Engineering of Swarm Intelligent Systems. In: Engineering Societies in the Agents World III: Third International Workshop (ESAW2002). Volume 2577 of Lecture Notes in Artificial Intelligence., Springer–Verlag (2002) 68–81
14. Mařík, V., Pěchouček, M., Štěphanková, O.: Social Knowledge in Multi-Agent Systems. In: Multi-Agent Systems and Applications. Volume 2086 of Lecture Notes in Artificial Intelligence., Springer–Verlag (2001) 211–245
15. Minar, N., Burkhart, R., Langton, C., Askenazi, M.: The Swarm Simulation System: a Toolkit for Building Multi-Agent Simulations. Working Paper 96-06-042, Santa Fe Institute (1996)
16. Nwana, H.S., Ndumu, D.T.: A Perspective on Software Agents Research. The Knowledge Engineering Review **14(2)** (1999) 125–142
17. Omicini, A. In: Towards a Notion of Agent Coordination Context. CRC Press (2002) 187–200
18. Omicini, A., Zambonelli, F.: Coordination for Internet application development. Autonomous Agents and Multi-Agent Systems **2(3)** (1999) 251–269 Special Issue: Coordination Mechanisms for Web Agents
19. Picco, G.P., Murphy, A.L., Roman, G.C.: Lime: Linda Meets Mobility. In: Proceedings of the 21st International Conference on Software Engineering (ICSE99), ACM press (1999) 368–377
20. Prasad, V.K.: What Pervasive Computing Brings to Automotive Consumer Experiences, Services, Products & Processes. Presented at *PC2001 NIST*, Gaithersberg, Maryland (2001)
21. Ricci, A., Viroli, M., Omicini, A.: Agent Coordination Context: From Theory to Practice. In Trappl, R., ed.: Proceedings of the 17th European Meeting on Cybernetics and Systems Research, Austrian Society for Cybernetic Studies (2004) 618–623
22. Tichý, P.: Robustness of Social Knowledge in Multi-Agent Systems. In Trappl, R., ed.: Proceedings of the 17th European Meeting on Cybernetics and Systems Research, Austrian Society for Cybernetic Studies (2004) 552–557
23. Wang, F.: Self-Organising Communities Formed by Middle Agents. In: Proceedings of the 1st International Joint Conference on Autonomous Agents and MultiAgent Systems (AAMAS 2002), ACM Press (2002) 1333–1339
24. Weyns, D., Holvoet, T.: Model for Simultaneous Actions in Situated Multi-Agent Systems. In: First International German Conference on Multi-Agent System Technologies, MATES. Volume 2831 of LNCS., Springer–Verlag (2003) 105–119

25. Wolfram, S.: Theory and Applications of Cellular Automata. World Press (1986)
26. Wooldridge, M.J., Jennings, N.R., Kinny, D.: The GAIA Methodology for Agent-Oriented Analysis and Design. Journal of Autonomous Agents and Multi-Agent Systems **3(3)** (2000) 285–312
27. Zambonelli, F., Parunak, H.V.D.: Signs of a Revolution in Computer Science and Software Engineering. In: Proceedings of Engineering Societies in the Agents World III (ESAW2002). Volume 2577 of Lecture Notes in Computer Science., Springer–Verlag (2002) 13–28
28. Zambonelli, F., Wooldridge, M.J., Jennings, N.R.: Developing Multiagent Systems: the GAIA Methodology. ACM Transactions on Software Engineering and Methodology **12(3)** (2003) 317–370

ELMS: An Environment Description Language for Multi-agent Simulation

Fabio Y. Okuyama[1], Rafael H. Bordini[2,1], and Antônio Carlos da Rocha Costa[3,1]

[1] Programa de Pós-Graduação em Computação, Universidade Federal do,
Rio Grande do Sul (UFRGS), Porto Alegre RS, Brazil
okuyama@inf.ufrgs.br
[2,*] Department of Computer Science, University of Liverpool,
Liverpool L69 3BX, U.K
R.Bordini@csc.liv.ac.uk
[3] Escola de Informática, Universidade Católica de Pelotas (UCPel),
Pelotas RS, Brazil
rocha@atlas.ucpel.tche.br

Abstract. This paper presents ELMS, a language used for the specification of multi-agent environments. This language is part of the MAS-SOC approach to the design and implementation of multi-agent based simulations. The approach is based on specific agent technologies for cognitive agent programming and high-level agent communication, as well as ELMS. We here concentrate on introducing ELMS, which allows the description of environments in which agents are to be situated during simulations. The ELMS language also allows the definition of the agents' perceptible properties and the kinds of (physical) interactions, through action and perception, an agent can have with the objects of the environment or the perceptible representations of the other agents in the environment.

1 Introduction

The goal of our overall project is to develop an approach and platform for the development of multi-agent based social simulations, incorporating agent technologies for specifying and running cognitive agents. When a multi-agent system is fully computational (i.e., not situated in the real world, the Internet, etc.), the specification of the (simulated) environment where agents are situated is an important task in the engineering of the system, which is not, however, normally addressed in the literature: environments are usually simply considered as "given", or sometimes environments are themselves modelled as agents. Nevertheless, the characteristics of environments are quite different from those of cognitive agents. Therefore, in our practical work, we identified the need for the use of a language specifically designed for the specification of multi-agent environments.

Based on that experience, we have developed a prototype of an interpreter for an environment definition language, presented in detail in [1] and mentioned in [2]. The

---

* Current affiliation: Department of Computer Science, University of Durham, Durham DH1 3LE, U.K. E-mail: R.Bordini@durham.ac.uk.

D. Weyns et al. (Eds.): E4MAS 2004, LNAI 3374, pp. 91–108, 2005.

language has been designed to support the description of environments for our multi-agent based social simulations (although it may turn out to be useful more generally). Besides the basic environment properties and objects, the language provides the means for the specification of the "physical" representation of a simulated agent, which we refer to as the "body of an agent"[1], as well as the various kinds of physical interactions, through action and perception, among agents and objects or other agents in the environment.

This paper is structured as follows. Sect. 2 covers the main ideas of the MAS-SOC approach to the development of multi-agent based social simulation. We discuss the classes of environments that can be modelled with ELMS in Sect. 3. Sect. 4 presents ELMS itself, the language we introduce in this paper and that is designed specifically for the modelling of multi-agent environments. Then we describe how ELMS environments are run in Sect. 5. Besides small examples given in Sect. 4, we also give a complete example in Appendix A.

2   The MAS-SOC Project

The main goal of the MAS-SOC project (Multi-Agent Simulations for the SOCial Sciences) is to provide a framework for the creation of agent-based social simulations that, ideally, should not require much experience in programming from users [2]. In particular, it should allow for the design and implementation of cognitive agents and their social actions. A graphical user interface facilitates the specification of environments, agents (their beliefs and plans), and the simulation as a whole. It also helps the management of libraries of simulation components. From the information input by the user, the system generates source codes for the interpreter used for agent reasoning (from the representations of agents' mental attitudes), and for the ELMS interpreter, whereby environment objects and agents' bodies are simulated.

Agents' practical reasoning is specified in AgentSpeak(L)[3], using the *Jason* interpreter [4] (see also [5]). We do not discuss here the AgentSpeak(L) programming language, but one can refer to the papers mentioned above, as well as [6, 7], for a complete account of that language. We here concentrate on presenting the ELMS language and its interpreter.

The interaction between the interpreters (for agents and the environment) and the graphical interface for creating and controlling the simulations is made possible by the SACI toolkit, developed as part of the work reported in [8]. This tool also supports the interactions of agents with the environment (perception and action) as well as speech-act based agent communication, including interactions such as plan exchange[2]. SACI also provides the infra-structure that makes it possible for us to run distributed simulations, thus facilitating large-scale simulations with cognitive agents.

---

[1] Note that in referring to agent's bodies we do not mean to say that our approach is only applicable to *embodied agents*. By "body" we simply mean whatever physical properties of an agent that may be *perceptible* by other agents in the environment. This is quite general: if an *environment* metaphor is present at all in the multi-agent system being developed, in all likelihood some characteristics of the agents will be perceivable by other agents.

[2] This will be available in *Jason* soon, as reported in [5].

In summary, when using the MAS-SOC approach to develop a simulation of a social system (where agents have cognitive features), the procedure is as follows: one first defines an environment in ELMS (specifying objects and their interactions, the "bodies" of the agents, and the ways these can interact with the objects through sensors and effectors), then one defines the agents' cognitive aspects with the use of AgentSpeak(L).

Providing mechanisms for specifying social structures explicitly (e.g. groups, organisations) is part of our objectives for future work, which should also include an attempt to reconcile cognition and emergence. This latter objective is inspired by Castelfranchi's idea that only social simulation with cognitive agents ("mind-based social simulations", as he calls it) will allow the study of agents' minds individually and the emerging collective actions, which co-evolve determining each other [9]. In others words, we aim (as a long term objective) to provide the basic conditions for MAS-SOC to be used in the study of a fundamental problem in the social sciences, which is of the greatest relevance in multi-agent systems as well: the micro-macro link problem [10].

3   Multi-agent Environments

According to Wooldridge [11], agents are computational systems situated in some environment, and are capable of autonomous action in this environment in order to meet their design objectives. Agents perceive and interact with each other via the environment, and they act upon it so that it reaches a certain state where their goals are achieved. Therefore, environment modelling is an important issue in the development of multi-agent systems where agents do not act directly on a physical or existing environment (e.g., as robots with real sensors and effectors, or Internet agents). This applies to reactive as well as cognitive agent societies (as discussed below). Nevertheless, the multi-agent systems literature seldom considers this part of the engineering of agent-based systems, in particular when dealing with cognitive agents: environments are simply *assumed* as given.

In a reactive multi-agent system, the environment plays a major role. Since reactive agents have no memory and no high-level (i.e., speech-act based) direct communication with each other, it is only perception of the environment that allows them to make decisions on how to act. On the other hand, cognitive agents have an internal representation of the environment, yet they make decisions (e.g., to adopt new goals, or to change courses of actions) based on the changes that perception of the environment causes on that representation. Thus, environment modelling is equally important for both classes of multi-agent systems. Although some multi-agent systems may be situated in an existing environment, in agent-based simulations the environment is necessarily a computational process too, so modelling multi-agent environments is always an important issue in simulations.

In [12], a number of characteristics that can be used to classify environments is given. We refer to those classifications below so that we can characterise the classes of environments that can be defined with ELMS.

Accessible Versus Inaccessible: Using the ELMS approach, agents have access only to the environment properties that the simulation designer has chosen to make perceptible to them. Thus, making an ELMS environment accessible or inaccessible is a designer's decision.

Deterministic Versus Nondeterministic: As ELMS environments can be inaccessible, and given that there are multiple agents that can change the environment simultaneously, from the point of view of an agent, an ELMS environment can appear to be nondeterministic.

Episodic Versus Non-episodic: In ELMS environments, the current state is a consequence of the previous one and the actions taken by the agents in it. With cognitive agents, past actions may influence future actions, so each simulation cycle is unlikely to be just an isolated episode of perceiving and acting (although it is possible to use this approach for simple reactive agents, this is not its intended use).

Static Versus Dynamic: An ELMS environment is meant to be shared by multiple agents. As various agents can act on this environment, an agent's action may disable another agent's action. Thus, from the point of view of agents, the environment can seem dynamic.

Discrete Versus Continuous: ELMS environments tend to be discrete, through the use of a grid to represent a physical space, although this is not compulsory.

To summarise, ELMS can be used to specify environments that are (from the point of view of the agents): inaccessible, non-deterministic, non-episodic, and dynamic; however, they are usually discrete. This class of environments is the most complex and comprehensive, except for the class of environments that are continuous besides all that. However, continuous environments are notoriously difficult to simulate; although ELMS does not prevent that, it does not give much support in that respect either. We believe that ELMS allows the definition of rather complex environments, supporting a wide range of multi-agent applications (in particular, but not exclusively, for social simulation).

4   The ELMS Language

Agents in a multi-agent system interact with the environment in which they are situated and interact with each other (possibly through the shared environment). Therefore, the environment has an important role in a multi-agent system, whether the environment is the Internet, the real world, or some simulated environment. ELMS is intended as a specification language for the latter form of environments.

We understand as environment modelling, the modelling of external aspects that an agent needs as input to its reasoning and for deciding on its course of action. Also, there is the need to model explicitly the physical actions and perceptions that the agents can do on the environment, as will be seen in Sect. 4.1.

This section introduces the main aspects of the language we defined for the specification of the simulated environment that is to be shared by the agents in a multi-agent system. The language is called ELMS (**E**nvironment Description **L**anguage for **M**ulti-Agent **S**imulation).

4.1   Modelling Environments with ELMS

An environment description is a specification of the properties and behaviour of the environment. In our approach, we also include in such specification the definition of the features of the simulated "bodies" of the agents. The modelling of such "physical" aspects of an agent (or agent class, more precisely) includes the definitions of its properties that may be perceived by others agents, the definitions of the kinds of perceptions that are available for that agent, and the actions that the agent is able to perform in the environment.

The definition of the environment includes mainly sets of: objects, to which we interchangeably refer as *resources* of the environment; reactions that objects display when agent actions affect them; an (optional) grid to allow the explicit handling of the spatial positioning of agents and objects in the environment; and the properties of the environment to which external observers (e.g., the users) have access.

The objects that are part of an environment can be modelled as a set of properties and a set of actions that characterise the object's behaviour in response to stimuli. That is, objects can *react*—only agents are pro-active. Agents can be considered components of the environment insofar as, from the point of view of one agent, any other agent is a special component of the environment (however, only certain properties of an agent can be perceived by other agents, and this must be specified by designers of agent-based simulations). Thus, to define agents from this point of view, it is necessary to list all properties that define their perceptible aspects, a list of actions that they are able to execute (pro-actively), and a list of the types of perception to which they have access. From the point of view of the environment, the deliberative activities of an agent are not relevant, since they are internal to the agent, i.e., they are not observable to the other agents in the environment. As mentioned before, in the MAS-SOC approach the mental aspects of agents are described with the AgentSpeak(L) language.

Quite frequently, spatial aspects of the environment are modelled in agent simulations by means of a grid. Our approach provides a number of features for dealing with grids, if the designer of the environment chooses to have one. In the constructs that make reference to the grid, positions can be accessed by absolute or relative coordinates. Relative coordinates are prefixed by '+' and '−' signs, so $(+1, -1, +0)$, for example, refers to the position at the upper right diagonal from the agent's current position. However, the grid definition is optional, as some simulations may not require any spatial representation. Clearly, there are simulations where the topology resulting from specific types of agent and object positioning is the main issue of interest for the investigation for which the simulations are being used. In contrast, there are also simulations where the existence of a topology is not relevant at all as, e.g., in a stock market simulation, where the main issue under consideration relate to the agent interactions themselves, and perhaps agents' interactions with some types of resources. In order to make ELMS as general as possible, we chose to make the grid an optional feature.

For the definition of the types of perception to which each agent class has access, it is necessary to define which properties of the environment, agents, and objects are to be perceived. The conditions associated with each perceptible property can be specified as well. That is, environment designers can control: which properties of objects will be accessible to the "minds" of the agents that are given access to a certain perception type, and under which conditions each (potentially perceivable) property will be effectively perceived. An action is defined as a sequence of changes in properties (of the environment in general, its resources, or agents) that it causes, along with the preconditions that must be satisfied for the action to be actually executed in the environment.

Note that our approach allows for quite flexible environment definitions. It is the environment designer who decides which properties of the environment can be perceptible by agents, and which are observable by external users (as well as defining how actions change the environment). Any properties associated with objects or with agents themselves can potentially be specified as perceptible/observable properties.

4.2   Language Constructs in ELMS

The ELMS language uses an XML syntax, which can be somewhat cumbersome to be used directly. However, recall that environment specifications are to be obtained from a graphical interface, so users do not need to bother about the language syntax. Still, environment specifications can be written directly in XML with a simple text editor, or some other tool, if the user prefers to do so. The use of XML provides various advantages, for example because of the wide range of XML tools currently available, and it can be useful for the future development of visualisation mechanisms for ELMS-based simulations, particularly if they are to be web-based.

An environment specification in ELMS can make use of constructs of nine main types, and several other constructs that may appear within some of the main ones. There is no special order for the constructs to appear in a specification. The main types of ELMS constructs are listed below.

1. Defining agent bodies:

   Agent Body: This construct defines a class of agent bodies for the agents that may join a simulation with that environment. A specification of an agent-body class contains its name, a list of attributes, a list of actions, and a list of perception types. The list of attributes is defined as before; it characterises the observable properties of this class of agent bodies, from the point of view of the environment and other agents. It is then necessary to specify a list of names for the actions that agents of this type are able to perform in the environment. The set of perceptions is a list of the names of perception types (see below) that are available to agents of this class (i.e., the information that will be accessible to the agent's mind at every reasoning cycle). Note that the same perception and action names can appear in any number of agent-body definitions; that is, they can be used in all the different classes of agent bodies that may execute that type of perception/action (the same applies to reactions for resources). The code sample below defines an agent-body class named `worker_robot` which has as attributes an integer and a boolean value. It is able to perform actions `walk_right`, `walk_left`, `load`, and `unload`. The perceptions that are available for agents belonging to the `worker_robot` class are `vision` and `audition`.

```
<AGENT_BODY   NAME = "worker_robot">
    <INTEGER NAME = "id"> "SELF" </INTEGER>
    <BOOLEAN NAME = "functional"> "TRUE" </BOOLEAN>
    <ACTIONS>
        <ITEM NAME = "walk_right"/>
        <ITEM NAME = "walk_left"/>
        <ITEM NAME = "load"/>
        <ITEM NAME = "unload"/>
    </ACTIONS>
    <PERCEPTIONS>
        <ITEM NAME = "vision"/>
        <ITEM NAME = "audition"/>
    </PERCEPTIONS>
</AGENT_BODY>
```

Perception: This construct allows the specification of perception types to be listed in agent-body specifications. A perception type definition is formed by a name, an optional list of preconditions, and a list of properties that are perceptible. The listed properties can be any of those associated with the definitions of resources, agents, cells of the grid, or simulation control variables. If all the preconditions (e.g., whether the agent is located on a specific position of the grid) are all satisfied, then the values of those properties will be made available to the agent's reasoner as the result of its perception of the environment. Note that perception can be based on the spatial position of the agent, but this is not mandatory; any type of perception can be defined by the environment designer.

```
<PERCEPTION NAME = "vision">
    <PRECONDITION>
        <EQUAL>
            <OPERAND>
                <ELEMENT_ATT NAME = "SELFCLASS" ATTRIBUTE = "functional">
                    <INDEX>"SELF"</INDEX>
                </ELEMENT_ATT>
            </OPERAND>
            <OPERAND> "TRUE" </OPERAND>
        </EQUAL>
    </PRECONDITION>
    <CELL_ATT ATTRIBUTE = "CONTENTS">
        <X> +0 </X>    <Y> +0 </Y>
    </CELL_ATT>
</PERCEPTION>
```

The code sample above defines a perception called vision. This perception has as its precondition that the agent must have its functional attribute equals to TRUE. If the precondition is satisfied, the agent will receive the information about the contents of the cell on the grid where it is currently positioned.

Action: With this construct, the actions that may appear in agent-body definitions are described. An action definition includes its name, an optional list of parameters, an optional list of preconditions, and a sequence of commands which determine what changes in the environment the action causes. The list of parameters specifies the data that will be received from the agent for further guiding the execution of that type of action. The possible commands for defining the consequences of executing an action are assignments of values to attributes (i.e., properties of agents, resources, etc.), and allocations or repositioning of instances of agents or resources within the grid. Resources can also be instantiated or removed by commands in an action. If the preconditions are all satisfied, then all the commands in the sequence of commands will be executed, changing the environment accordingly. To avoid consistency problems, actions are executed atomically. For this reason, they should be defined so as to follow the concept of an atomic action (although this is again not mandatory); recall that more complex courses of actions are meant to be part of agents' internal reasoning[3].

```
<ACTION NAME = "walk_right">
    <PARAMETER NAME="STEPS" TYPE="INTEGER"/>
    <PRECONDITION>
        <LESSTHAN>
            <OPERAND> "STEPS" </OPERAND>
            <OPERAND> 3 </OPERAND>
        </LESSTHAN>
    </PRECONDITION>
    <MOVE>
        <ELEMENT NAME = "SELFCLASS">
                <INDEX>"SELF"</INDEX>
        </ELEMENT>
        <FROM>
            <CELL>
                <X>+0</X> <Y>+0</Y>
            </CELL>
        </FROM>
        <TO>
            <CELL>
                <X>STEPS</X> <Y>+0</Y>
            </CELL>
        </TO>
    </MOVE>
</ACTION>
```

In the example above, an action named walk_right is defined. It has as parameter an integer referred to as STEPS. The precondition defines that this parameter must be lower than 3. As a result of the execution of this action, the agent will walk, to the right, the number of steps specified by the parameter (i.e., the agent's body location will be moved within the environment representation).

2. Defining the environment:

   Grid Options: This is used for a grid definition, if the designer has chosen to have one. The grid can be two or three dimensional, the parameters being the sizes of the grid on the X, Y, and Z axes. Still within the grid definition, a list of cell attributes can be given: the attributes defined here will be replicated for each cell of the grid. Also as part of the cell definition, a list of reactions can be defined for them[4]. The code below exemplifies a definition of a two-dimensional grid that has twenty columns and twenty rows, where each cell has an integer that represents its colour (which defaults to 0) and a boolean variable that keeps the information about whether the cell is occupied (e.g., by an agent) or not. Each of those cells can have the reactions named reaction1 and reaction2.

---

[3] Since agents are constantly perceiving, reasoning, and acting, the actions they execute in the environment should normally be atomic. That is, it is known before the next reasoning cycle whether the previous action was successfully executed, and if it was, its perceptible effects will be noticed by the agent when it does belief revision just before the next reasoning cycle. Although it is possible to make alternative design choices where actions are not atomic, it seems that simulations in particular should be more easily and appropriately engineered this way.

[4] Although the list of reactions is the same for all cells, this does not imply they all have the same behaviour at all times, as reactions can have preconditions on the specific state of the individual cells.

```
<DEFGRID SIZEX="20" SIZEY="20" SIZEZ="1">
    <INTEGER NAME = "cellcolour"> 0 </INTEGER>
    <BOOLEAN NAME = "ocuppied"> "FALSE" </BOOLEAN>
    <REACTIONS>
        <ITEM NAME = "reaction1"/>
        <ITEM NAME = "reaction2"/>
    </REACTIONS>
</DEFGRID>
```

Resources: This construct is used to define the objects in an environment (i.e., all the entities of the environment that are not pro-active). A definition of a resource class includes the class name, a list of attributes, and a set of reactions. The attributes are defined in the same way as for the cell attributes (i.e., by the specification of its name, type, and initial value). The reactions that a class of resources can have is given by a list of the names identifying those reactions (see below how reactions are defined).

```
<RESOURCE NAME = "water">
    <STRING  NAME = "state" VALUE = "liquid"/>
    <INTEGER NAME = "temperature"> 23 </INTEGER>
    <INTEGER NAME = "quantity"> 10 </INTEGER>
    <REACTIONS>
        <ITEM NAME = "solidify"/>
        <ITEM NAME = "melt"/>
    </REACTIONS>
</RESOURCE>
```

The code sample above defines a resource class named water. It has a string attribute that records its state value, and there are two integer values that represent its temperature and quantity. This resource can have the solidify and melt reactions (i.e., the expected reactions to actions changing its temperature).

Reactions: This part of the specification is where the possible reactions of the objects in the environment are defined. For each type of reaction, its name, a list of preconditions, and a sequence of commands is given. The commands are exactly as described above for actions. All expressions in the list of preconditions must be satisfied for the reaction to take place. Differently from actions, where only one action (per agent) is performed, all reactions that satisfy their preconditions will be executed "simultaneously" (i.e. in the same simulation cycle). In the code sample below, the reaction melt is defined. As precondition, the temperature attribute must greater than 273 (Kelvin scale) and the state attribute must be equal to solid. This reaction results in changing the state attribute to liquid. Note the use of the reserved keyword SELFCLASS, which refers to the class of whatever resource type the reaction is associated with, and is useful for programming and code reuse.

```
<REACTION NAME = "melt">
    <PRECONDITION>
        <GREATERTHAN>
            <OPERAND>
                <ELEMENT_ATT NAME = "water" ATTRIBUTE = "temperature">
                    <INDEX> "SELF" </INDEX>
                </ELEMENT_ATT>
            </OPERAND>
            <OPERAND> 273 </OPERAND>
        </GREATERTHAN>
    <EQUAL>
        <OPERAND>
            <ELEMENT_ATT NAME = "SELFCLASS" ATTRIBUTE = "state">
                <INDEX> "SELF" </INDEX>
```

```
                    </ELEMENT_ATT>
                        </OPERAND>
                        <OPERAND> "solid" </OPERAND>
            </EQUAL>
            </PRECONDITION>
                    <ASSIGN>
                        <ELEMENT_ATT NAME = "SELFCLASS" ATTRIBUTE = "state">
                            <INDEX> "SELF" </INDEX>
                        </ELEMENT_ATT>
                        <EXPRESSION> "liquid" </EXPRESSION>
                    </ASSIGN>
        </REACTION>
```

3. Some operational aspects of a simulation are specified using the following constructs:

Observables: This is how the user defines which properties of the agents, resources, and the environment itself will be sent to the MAS-SOC interface as the result of a simulation cycle; that is, the users specify the particular properties of the simulated "world" which they are interested in observing from the simulator interface. The properties to be selected as observable can be any of those associated with instances of resources and agents, cells of the grid, and simulation control variables. The observable items are defined in the same way as the perceptible items in a perception definition.

Initialisation: This part of the specification allows resources in the environment to be instantiated and allocated to grid positions in the initial state of the simulation (resources can also be created in the environment or allocated to the grid dynamically during simulation). All commands in this section are only executed before the start of the simulation. The initialisation is defined in the same way as command sequences in action definitions.

Simulation Values: In this section of an ELMS definition, the values for the attributes of instances of resources and agents that are currently part of a simulation can be defined. The environment controller process (see Sect. 5) can generate a snapshot of a running simulation by filling in such values from those contained in its data structures. With the constructs described above, the classes of agents and resources are simply defined; instantiations can be made in the initialisation section, or in this one for a simulation that is already running. Also in this section, the position of instances of agents and resources on the grid can be defined. The values for environment control variables can be defined by assignment commands over predefined variable names (e.g., the current simulation step number). This feature allows the user to save the simulation state for later execution, or to make on-the-fly changes in the environment (via the interface or by changing the ELMS code manually) to induce various different situations in a simulation. Such simulation snapshots may also be useful for complex forms of visualisation of multi-agent simulations.

Next, we show some of the constructs that are used in ELMS to define commands, expressions, and attributes.

Attribute Definition: The types of attributes supported by ELMS are: boolean, integer, float, and string. Attributes are defined by a specific XML tag for each type and an initial value. The initial value can be a constant or an expression (except for string expressions, which are currently not allowed).

Expressions: In ELMS, some mathematical, logical, and relational operators are available. The available relational operators are EQUAL, UNEQUAL, GREATERTHAN, and LESSTHAN. For mathematical expressions, the following constructs are available: ADD, SUBTRACT, MULTIPLY, DIVIDE, MOD, SUM (summatory), and PROD (product). The available logical operators are: AND, OR, and NOT (negation). Operands of relational operators can be another operation, a constant, and a cell, resource, or agent attribute. It is also possible to use the commands RAND and RANDOM. The former command generates a pseudo-random number between 0 and 1, while the latter command has as parameters a minimum value (inclusive) and a maximum value (exclusive), generating a pseudo-random integer in this range. These commands can be used in all parts of the code, except within the "simulation values" section (where they are not required).

Preconditions: The preconditions for actions, reactions, and perceptions are defined through a sequence of logical operations. If a logical operator is not explicitly defined, AND is assumed (as it is most commonly used). For example, the following code:

```
<PRECONDITION>
    <EQUAL>...</EQUAL>
    <GREATERTHAN>...</GREATERTHAN>
</PRECONDITION>
```

has the same effect as:

```
<PRECONDITION>
    <AND>
        <OPERAND>
            <EQUAL>...</EQUAL>
        </OPERAND>
        <OPERAND>
            <GREATERTHAN>...</GREATERTHAN>
        </OPERAND>
    </AND>
</PRECONDITION>
```

Commands: Below, we use *element* to refer to both resources and agents. The commands available in ELMS are: assignment (ASSIGN), allocation of an element on the grid (IN), random allocation of an element on the grid (IN_RAND), element removal from the grid (OUT), changing the position of an element on the grid (MOVE), instance creation (NEW), instance exclusion (DELETE).

The MOVE command has as parameters an element, its original position, and the destination. Note that one element can occupy more than one position on the grid, but elements have a reference point used for relative position calculation: the cell to which it was first allocated. When using the MOVE command, the whole element is moved by changing its reference point.

5   Running ELMS Environments

The simulation of the environment itself is done by a process that controls the access and changes made to the data structure that represents the environment (in fact, only that process can access the data structure); the process is called the *environment controller*. The data structure that represents the environment is generated by the ELMS interpreter for a specification in ELMS given as input. In each simulation cycle, the environment controller sends to all agents currently taking part in the simulation the percepts to which they have access (as specified in ELMS). Perception is transmitted in messages as a list of ground logical facts. After sending perception, the process waits for the actions that the agents have chosen to perform in that simulation cycle.

The execution of a synchronous simulation in ELMS, from the point of view of the environment controller, follows the steps below:

1. execute the commands in the initialisation section before the start of the simulation;
2. check which percepts from the agent's perception list are in fact available at that time (check which perceivable properties satisfy the specified preconditions);
3. send the resulting percepts (those that satisfied the preconditions) to the agents;
4. wait until the chosen actions (to be performed in that cycle) have been received from all agents[5];
5. the order of the actions in the queue of all received actions is changed randomly to allow each agent to have a chance of executing its action first;
6. check if the first action in the queue satisfies its precondition for execution;
7. execute the action, if the precondition was satisfied;
8. if not, send a message with "@fail" as content to the agent;
9. remove the action at the front of the queue;
10. if there are any actions left in the queue, go to step 6;
11. check and execute all reactions defined for resources in the environment which had their preconditions satisfied;
12. send the set of properties defined as "observables" to the interface or to an output file previously specified;
13. if the step counter has not yet reached the maximum value defined by the user, go to the step 2.

Note that this corresponds to the (default) synchronous simulation mode. An asynchronous mode is also available.

For the communication between the agents, the SACI (Simple Agent Communicaiton Infrastructure) [8] toolkit is used. It supports KQML-based communication and provides an infrastructure for managing distributed agents. All agents participating in a simulation are registered to a SACI society. Through it, every member of the society can communicate with other members by simply sending messages addressed with that member's name in the society (regardless of the host where the agent interpreter is running). This way, it is possible for any SACI-based agent to interact within a simulation, so that, for example, we can make available an interface for human "agents" to interact within a MAS-SOC simulated society (although this is not currently one of the main goals of the MAS-SOC project). This feature (of open SACI societies) can also be very useful for simulation debugging and analysis (e.g., "observer" agents can be introduced to monitor aspects of a simulation).

---

[5] Agents send a message with "true" as its content if they have chosen not to execute an action in that cycle.

SACI is available as free software at http://www.lti.pcs.usp.br/saci/. The ELMS interpreter too will be made available as free software in the near future.

6   Conclusion

This paper introduced the ELMS language, used for the specification of the characteristics of agent "bodies" and the environment to be shared by agents in a multi-agent social simulation. Although the ELMS interpreter is tailored for social simulation implemented according to the MAS-SOC approach, it could be useful for other symbolic approaches as well. The MAS-SOC approach consists of a distinct combination of multi-agent techniques that we consider as the most adequate for the construction of multi-agent based social simulations. We believe that MAS-SOC allows for quite flexible definitions of multi-agent social simulations, taking into considerations not only cognitive agents but also the environment shared by them.

As future work, there are several improvements to the platform that we plan to carry out. In particular, we plan to concentrate on higher-level aspects of agent-based simulations which are particularly important for social simulation, such as the specification of social structures within agent societies, as well as using the ideas of exchange values from [13] to support social interactions. In the long term, we aim at investigating the necessary mechanisms for reconciling cognition and emergence following the ideas of [9], and incorporating such mechanisms into MAS-SOC, thus allowing it to be used in investigations of the micro-macro link problem. We are currently considering the implementation of various social simulation applications.

References

1. Okuyama, F.Y.: Descrição e geração de ambientes para simulações com sistemas multiagente. Dissertação de mestrado, PPGC/UFRGS, Porto Alegre, RS (2003). In Portuguese.
2. Bordini, R.H., Okuyama, F.Y., de Oliveira, D., Drehmer, G., Krafta, R.C.: The MAS-SOC approach to multi-agent based simulation. In Lindemann, G., Moldt, D., Paolucci, M., eds.: Proceedings of the First International Workshop on Regulated Agent-Based Social Systems: Theories and Applications (RASTA'02), 16 July, 2002, Bologna, Italy (held with AAMAS02) — Revised Selected and Invited Papers. Number 2934 in the LNAI Series, Berlin, Springer-Verlag (2004), 70–91.
3. Rao, A.S.: AgentSpeak(L): BDI agents speak out in a logical computable language. In Van de Velde, W,. Perram, I., eds.: Proceedings of the Seventh Workshop on Modelling Autonomous Agents in a Multi-Agent World (MAAMAW'96), 22–25 January, Eindhoven, The Netherlands. Number 1038 in the LNAI Series, London, Springer-Verlag (1996), 42–55.
4. Bordini, R.H., Hübner, J.F., et al.:   *Jason*: A Java-based agentSpeak interpreter used with saci for multi-agent distribution over the net. Manual, first release edn. (2004) http://jason.sourceforge.net/.
5. Ancona, D., Mascardi, V., Hübner, J.F., Bordini, R.H.:   Coo-AgentSpeak: Cooperation in AgentSpeak through plan exchange. In Jennings, N.R., Sierra, C., Sonenberg, L., Tambe, M., eds.: Proceedings of the Third International Joint Conference on Autonomous Agents and Multi-Agent Systems (AAMAS-2004), New York, NY, 19–23 July, New York, NY, ACM Press (2004), 698–705.

6. Moreira, Á.F., Vieira, R., Bordini, R.H.: Extending the operational semantics of a BDI agent-oriented programming language for introducing speech-act based communication. In Leite, J., Omicini, A., Sterling, L., Torroni, P., eds.: Declarative Agent Languages and Technologies, Proceedings of the First International Workshop (DALT-03), held with AAMAS-03, 15 July, 2003, Melbourne, Australia (Revised Selected and Invited Papers). Number 2990 in the LNAI Series, Berlin, Springer-Verlag (2004), 135–154.
7. d'Inverno, M., Luck, M.: Engineering AgentSpeak(L): A formal computational model. Journal of Logic and Computation **8** (1998), 1–27.
8. Hübner, J.F.: Um Modelo de Reorganização de Sistemas Multiagentes. PhD thesis, Universidade de São Paulo, Escola Politécnica (2003).
9. Castelfranchi, C.: The theory of social functions: Challenges for computational social science and multi-agent learning. Cognitive Systems Research **2** (2001), 5–38.
10. Conte, R., Castelfranchi, C.: Cognitive and Social Action. UCL Press, London (1995).
11. Wooldridge, M.: Intelligent agents. In Weiß, G., ed.: Multiagent Systems—A Modern Approach to Distributed Artificial Intelligence. MIT Press, Cambridge, MA (1999), 27–77.
12. Russel, S., Norvig, P.: Artificial Intelligence — A Modern Approach. Prentice-Hall, Englewood Cliffs, NJ (1995).
13. Rodrigues, M.R., da Rocha Costa, A.C., Bordini, R.H.: A system of exchange values to support social interactions in artificial societies. In Rosenschein, J.S., Sandholm, T., Michael, W., Yokoo, M., eds.: Proceedings of the Second International Joint Conference on Autonomous Agents and Multi-Agent Systems (AAMAS-2003), Melbourne, Australia, 14–18 July, New York, NY, ACM Press (2003). 81–88.
14. Bordini, R.H., Fisher, M., Visser, W., Wooldridge, M.: Verifiable multi-agent programs. In Dastani, M., Dix, J., El Fallah-Seghrouchni, A., eds.: Programming Multi-Agent Systems, Proceedings of the First International Workshop (ProMAS-03), held with AAMAS-03, 15 July, 2003, Melbourne, Australia (Selected Revised and Invited Papers). Number 3067 in the LNAI Series, Berlin, Springer-Verlag (2004), 72–89.

Appendix A   Example of an ELMS Specification

We provide below a very simple example so as to illustrate the use of the ELMS language for specifying an environment. A robot (simulated by an AgentSpeak(L) agent) must find garbage in a territory that is modelled as a 10×10 grid. When a piece of garbage is found, the robot collects it and takes it to an incinerator located at the centre of the territory that is to be kept clean. In the environment used in simulations carried out to observe the behaviour of the AgentSpeak(L) agent, garbage randomly "appears" on the grid. We have included some redundant attributes in the example just so that we could show how to use various ELMS constructs. Due to the lack of space, only a few excerpts of the code are explained with accompanying text.

```
<?xml version="1.0" encoding="ISO-8859-1"?>
<!DOCTYPE ENVIRONMENT SYSTEM "elms.dtd">
<ENVIRONMENT NAME = "TERRITORY">

<!-- AGENTS SECTION -->

    <AGENT_BODY NAME="robot">
      <BOOLEAN NAME = "loaded"> "FALSE" </BOOLEAN>
      <PERCEPTIONS>
          <ITEM NAME = "self_info"/>
```

```
            <ITEM NAME = "cur_position"/>
        </PERCEPTIONS>
        <ACTIONS>
            <ITEM NAME = "load"/>
            <ITEM NAME = "unload"/>
            <ITEM NAME = "move_north"/>
            <ITEM NAME = "move_south"/>
            <ITEM NAME = "move_east"/>
            <ITEM NAME = "move_west"/>
        </ACTIONS>
    </AGENT_BODY>
```

This excerpt defines a class of agent bodies named robot. This class has as attribute a boolean value named loaded which is true whenever the robot is carrying a piece of garbage. The robot is able to perform two types of perceptions: self_info and cur_position, which will be defined in the perception section below. Also, it is able to perform six different actions, as listed above and defined later in the action section.

```
<!-- PERCEPTIONS SECTION  -->

    <PERCEPTION NAME="cur_position">
        <CELL_ATT ELEMENT = "garbage" ATTRIBUTE ="size" > // SIZE OF THE GARBAGE
            <X> +0 </X> <Y> +0 </Y>                       // PRESENT IN CURRENT CELL
        </CELL_ATT>
        <CELL_ATT ATTRIBUTE = "colour">
            <X> +0 </X> <Y> +0 </Y>
        </CELL_ATT>
    </PERCEPTION>
```

This perception allows the agent to have an explicit representation of information about the cell where it is currently positioned: the size of the piece of garbage in that cell (if there is any) and the cell's colour, which is represented by an integer. No information about neighbouring cells is perceived.

```
    <PERCEPTION NAME="self_info">
        <ELEMENT_ATT NAME = "SELFCLASS" ATTRIBUTE = "loaded">
            <INDEX>"SELF"</INDEX>
        </ELEMENT_ATT>
    </PERCEPTION>


<!-- ACTIONS SECTION  -->

    <ACTION NAME="move_east">
      <MOVE>
        <ELEMENT NAME = "SELFCLASS">
            <INDEX>"SELF"</INDEX>
        </ELEMENT>
        <FROM>
            <CELL>
                <X>+0</X>
                <Y>+0</Y>
            </CELL>
        </FROM>
        <TO>
            <CELL>
                <X>+1</X>
                <Y>+0</Y>
            </CELL>
        </TO>
      </MOVE>
```

```
</ACTION>

<ACTION NAME="move_north">                          // SUMMARISED
<ACTION NAME="move_south">
<ACTION NAME="move_west">

<ACTION NAME="load">
    <PARAMETER NAME="G1" TYPE="INTEGER" />
    <PRECONDITION>
        <UNEQUAL>                                    // FAIL CHANCE = 1/20
            <OPERAND>
                <RANDOM MIN="0" MAX="20"/>
            </OPERAND>
            <OPERAND> "10" </OPERAND>
        </UNEQUAL>
    </PRECONDITION>
    <OUT>
        <ELEMENT NAME = "garbage">
            <INDEX> "G1" </INDEX>
        </ELEMENT>
        <CELL>
            <X>+0</X>
            <Y>+0</Y>
        </CELL>
    </OUT>
    <ASSIGN>
        <ELEMENT_ATT NAME = "SELFCLASS" ATTRIBUTE = "loaded">
            <INDEX>"SELF"</INDEX>
        </ELEMENT_ATT>
        <EXPRESSION> "TRUE" </EXPRESSION>
    </ASSIGN>
</ACTION>
```

The action above removes the garbage from the cell and changes the loaded attribute of the agent. This action can fail a random number of times, as it has as precondition that a random number between 0 to 20 must not be equals to 10 or else the action will fail. This nondeterminism models possible failures of the robot's grabbing mechanism. The action has as parameter, referred as G1, the index of the garbage that will be loaded.

```
<ACTION NAME="unload">
    <PARAMETER NAME="G1" TYPE="INTEGER" />
    <IN>
        <ELEMENT NAME = "garbage">
            <INDEX>"G1"</INDEX>
        </ELEMENT>
        <CELL>
            <X>+0</X>
            <Y>+0</Y>
        </CELL>
    </IN>
    <ASSIGN>
        <ELEMENT_ATT NAME = "incinerator" ATTRIBUTE = "empty">
            <INDEX>
                <CELL_ATT ELEMENT = "incinerator" ATTRIBUTE ="id" >
                    <X>+0</X>
                    <Y>+0</Y>
                </CELL_ATT>
            </INDEX>
        </ELEMENT_ATT>
        <EXPRESSION> "TRUE" </EXPRESSION>
    </ASSIGN>
    <ASSIGN>
        <ELEMENT_ATT NAME = "SELFCLASS" ATTRIBUTE = "loaded">
            <INDEX>"SELF"</INDEX>
```

```
            </ELEMENT_ATT>
            <EXPRESSION> "FALSE" </EXPRESSION>
        </ASSIGN>
    </ACTION>


<!-- GRID DEFINITIONS SECTION  -->

    <DEFGRID SIZEX="10" SIZEY="10">
        <INTEGER NAME = "colour">
            <RANDOM MIN="0" MAX="16"/>
        </INTEGER>
        <REACTIONS>
            <ITEM NAME ="sprout_trash"/>
        </REACTIONS>
    </DEFGRID>


<!-- RESOURCES SECTION  -->

    <RESOURCE NAME="garbage">
        <INTEGER NAME="size">  5  </INTEGER>
    </RESOURCE>

    <RESOURCE NAME="incinerator">
        <BOOLEAN NAME="empty"> "TRUE" </BOOLEAN>
        <INTEGER NAME="id">    "SELF" </INTEGER>
        <REACTIONS>
            <ITEM NAME ="burn"/>
        </REACTIONS>
    </RESOURCE>


<!-- REACTIONS SECTION  -->

    <REACTION NAME="burn">
      <PRECONDITION>
        <EQUAL>
            <OPERAND>
                <ELEMENT_ATT NAME = "SELFCLASS" ATTRIBUTE = "empty">
                    <INDEX>"SELF"</INDEX>
                </ELEMENT_ATT>
            </OPERAND>
            <OPERAND> "FALSE" </OPERAND>
        </EQUAL>
      </PRECONDITION>
        <DELETE NAME = "garbage">
            <INDEX>
                <CELL_ATT NAME = "garbage" ATTRIBUTE = "id">
                    <X>+0</X>
                    <Y>+0</Y>
                </CELL_ATT>
            </INDEX>
        </DELETE>
    <ASSIGN>
        <ELEMENT_ATT NAME = "SELFCLASS" ATTRIBUTE = "empty">
        <INDEX>"SELF"</INDEX>
        </ELEMENT_ATT>
        <EXPRESSION>
            "TRUE"
        </EXPRESSION>
    </ASSIGN>
    </REACTION>

    <REACTION NAME="sprout_trash">
      <PRECONDITION>
```

```
            <EQUAL>
                <OPERAND>
                    <RANDOM MIN="0" MAX="100"/>
                </OPERAND>
                <OPERAND> 10 </OPERAND>
            </EQUAL>
        </PRECONDITION>
        <NEW NAME = "incinerator">
            <N>1</N>
        <CELL>
            <X>+0</X>
            <Y>+0</Y>
        </CELL>
        </NEW>
    </REACTION>



<!-- OBSERVABLES SECTION  -->

    <OBSERVABLE>
            <CELL_ATT ATTRIBUTE = "colour">
                <X> "ALL"</X>
                <Y> "ALL" </Y>
            </CELL_ATT>
            <CELL_ATT ATTRIBUTE = "CONTENTS">
                <X> "ALL"</X>
                <Y> "ALL" </Y>
            </CELL_ATT>
    </OBSERVABLE>



<!-- INITIALIZATION SECTION  -->

    <INITIALIZATION>
        <NEW NAME = "incinerator">
            <N>1</N>                          //ONE INSTANCE
        <CELL>
            <X>4</X>
            <Y>4</Y>
        </CELL>
        </NEW>
    </INITIALIZATION>
</ENVIRONMENT>
```

The simple AgentSpeak(L) code that could be used for the robot's reasoning has not been included, as the focus here in on modelling environments, but such code can be found in [14] and is one of the examples distributed with *Jason* [4].

MIC*: A Deployment Environment for Autonomous Agents

Abdelkader Gouaïch, Fabien Michel, and Yves Guiraud

LIRMM, CNRS,
161 rue Ada,
34392 Montpellier Cedex 5, France
{gouaich, fmichel, yguiraud}@lirmm.fr

Abstract. This paper presents the MIC* model of autonomous agents deployment environment. A practical social software engineering framework based on AGR is also presented to show how MIC* is used to develop MAS applications.

1 Introduction

Multi-agent systems (MASs) are composed by autonomous agents (AAs) that evolve and interact in order to achieve their goals. What is implicit in this definition of MASs is where these AAs live. This containing place of AAs is identified by the generic term of environment. As Odell and colleagues have pointed out in [1], the environment defines the properties of the world in which an agent can and does function.

However, there are different concerns for the environment regarding the level of abstraction at which the attention is focused [2].

At the conceptual level, the environment defines the model of the AAs' world and the practical means by which they perceive and act on it to achieve their goals. At the implementation level, agents are necessarily embedded in a software system that offers them some computing facilities.

As Zambonelli and Parunak have noticed in [3], traditional software engineering approaches usually do not consider the environment at the implementation level as a primary abstraction. In the scope of this paper, the software system containing the AAs and defining their interactions is identified as the *deployment environment* (DE).

This paper relies on the idea that understanding and explicitly representing the DE is a crucial issue for MAS engineering. Moreover, this paper argues that the DE plays a fundamental role in order to guarantee the autonomy property. In fact, we will see that the *internal integrity* of AAs is an objective criterion that guarantees the autonomy at the implementation level.

As an example of DE, this paper presents MIC* (Movement, Interaction, Computation). MIC* is an algebraic model that is independent from both the conceptual and implementation models of the AAs. Hence, AAs are considered

D. Weyns et al. (Eds.): E4MAS 2004, LNAI 3374, pp. 109–126, 2005.

as black-boxes that sense and act through the DE by sending and receiving *inter-action objects* (IOs). The interaction between the AAs is defined contextually in *interaction spaces* (ISs). The whole dynamics of the DE is seen as the composition of three kinds of functions: the movement, the interaction and the computation. MIC* is a DE which is defined at the implementation level. Consequently, MIC* has not to be confused with the modeling of the AAs' application-dependent world. For instance, agent-based simulations which have been developed using MIC* consider the situated environment as a particular active entity operating on the DE [4]. For instance, this entity is in charge of calculating the evapo-rating/aggregating/diffusing of pheromone, giving an operational semantics of simultaneous actions or environmental variables such as temperature and so on.

Finally, as a case study, this paper describes the implementation of a social framework which relies on traditional organizational concepts inspired by the AGR model [5].

The rest of the paper is organized as follows: Sect. 2 presents the backgrounds of the work; Sect. 3 discusses the autonomy property and induces the require-ments that make necessary the explicit representation of the DE within MASs at the implementation level; Sect. 4 presents the MIC* DE; Sect. 5 shows how a social framework is built upon MIC*; Sect. 6 presents an application devel-oped using this social framework; and finally Sect. 7 concludes and gives some perspectives.

2   Backgrounds

2.1   Multi-agent Systems

Few works tackle the general study of DEs. In this perspective, a lot of agent platforms have been developed and are available for the implementation of MASs [2]. However, these DEs are passive within the MAS and are often considered as basic middlewares used to *(i)* access computer resources and *(ii)* delivering messages to agents on the basis of predefined and fixed routing mechanisms. MIC* does not settle the interaction and routing mechanisms, it gives simply general requirements that should be instantiated for each particular MAS.

2.2   Coordination Media

The coordination medium can be considered as a persistent place where the interaction between the coordinating entities takes place. Linda [6] is an example of such a coordination medium where the entities coordinate their activities by writing and retrieving *tuples*. A tuple is a set of typed fields and values. Linda has inspired many other tuple-based coordination media such as Lime [7], Tuscon [8] and MARS [9]. The interesting feature of coordination media is the property of *generative interaction* [10]. This means that the interaction between entities is uncoupled in space and time. MIC* tries to offer the same property for the interaction among AAs. However, unlike Linda-like approaches, MIC* gives an explicit structure of the medium and defines its dynamics according to the MAS paradigm.

3   Why an Explicit Model of Deployment Environment Is Needed?

3.1   Implementing Autonomous Agents

This section uses Wooldridge and Jennings definition of an agent [11]:

> "Perhaps the most general way in which the term agent is used is to denote a hardware or (more usually) software-based computer system that enjoys the following properties:
> - autonomy: agents operate without the direct intervention of humans or others, and have some kind of control over their actions and internal state [12];
> - social ability: agents interact with other agents (and possibly humans) via some kind of agent-communication language [13];
> - reactivity: agents perceive their environment, (which may be the physical world, a user via a graphical user interface, a collection of other agents, the INTERNET, or perhaps all of these combined), and respond in a timely fashion to changes that occur in it;
> - pro-activeness: agents do not simply act in response to their environment, they are able to exhibit goal-directed behavior by taking the initiative."

This definition specifies some features that a physical or software entity must fulfill to be considered as an AA. Still, this definition does not specify how to implement AAs. Consequently, developers may have their own interpretation of the presented features. In [14], Gouaich identifies two main interpretations of autonomy in the MAS literature: autonomy as self-governance and autonomy as independence.

3.2   Autonomy as Self-governance

This interpretation is related to the definition proposed by Steels in [15]. Steels considers the autonomy feature from a biological point of view:

> "It starts from the idea that agents are self sustaining systems which perform a function for others and thus get the resources to maintain themselves. But because they have to worry about their own survival they need to be autonomous, both in the sense of self-governing and of having their own motivations."

The concept of autonomy is thus regarded as a consequence of a survival instinct. For a software agent, it is a question of achieving its own goals while ensuring its functional requirements. Notably, an agent must be able to adapt itself with respect to a modification of the external environment. Castelfranchi [12] shares also this vision and defines an AA as a pro-active entity which has the ability to produce its own laws and to follow them.

3.3   Autonomy as Independence

This interpretation relates the autonomy feature to the social context of an AA. The *Social Dependence Network* (SDN) has been introduced by Sichman and colleagues in [16] to allow AAs to reason about their artificial society. Within SDN, the autonomy concept is used to evaluate the level of the social dependence. Three forms of autonomy are distinguished. An agent is *a-autonomous* for a given goal according to a set of plans, if there is a plan in this set that achieves the goal and every action in each plan belongs to its capabilities. An agent is considered as *r-autonomous* for a given goal according to a set of plans, if there is a plan in this set that achieves the goal, and every resource in each plan belongs to its resources. Finally, an agent is *s-autonomous* when it is both *a-autonomous* and *r-autonomous*. According to this definition, an agent is autonomous for a particular goal if it does not depend for resources or actions on another agent.

3.4   Internal Integrity: An Objective Criterion for Autonomy

Sichman and colleagues define autonomy as being independent on actions and resources from other agents. On the other hand, [12, 15, 17] define agent's autonomy as a behavioral characteristic. From a software engineering perspective, the latter interpretation is more useful and generic since it does not imply to study the MAS social structure. The autonomy is only related to individual characteristics. However, it still remains a subjective point of view because it relies on how the behavior of an agent is evaluated. So, as Weiss and colleagues have pointed out in [18], objective implementation criteria are necessary to define the autonomy of a software agent. We propose the *internal integrity* as an objective criterion to implement AAs [14].

The internal integrity is a programming constraint that considers an AA as a bounded system which internal dynamics and structure are neither controllable nor observable directly by an external entity. In fact, if the AA's software structure is accessed or modified by another entity, the decisional process and behaviors may be altered. Since the decisional process of an AA has to be entirely determined only by its own perception and behaviors, the internal integrity becomes a sine qua none condition to implement AAs.

3.5   Agent Deployment Environment: Ensuring Internal Integrity

The internal integrity criterion also raises some issues with respect to the implementation of MASs: on one hand, the internal integrity has to be taken into account to guarantee the autonomy; on the other hand, the AAs are interacting entities that need to act and modify the perceptions of other agents. Since these perceptions are included within the boundaries of the AAs, this contradicts the internal integrity statement. In other words, the problem is to enable the interaction between AAs which boundaries do not intersect. To avoid this paradox, the DE needs to be a non-agent entity that manages and carries out the interactions.

The next section presents MIC* as an example of a DE that guarantees the internal integrity of the AAs while enabling their interactions.

4   MIC* Algebraic Model

4.1   Introduction to the MIC* Model

In order to fulfill the presented requirements on autonomy, the AAs have to be considered as bounded black-boxes. Thus, no assumption is made on their internal structure. Consequently, the DE only considers the observable processes such as the interaction. The interaction process is independent from the AAs conceptual and implementation models. In fact, heterogeneous AAs are able to interact at least if they agree on a common interaction language or ontology. Within MASs, the word 'interaction' is misused and often refers to a communication process. Communication is defined as exchanging information between several locations; while interaction goes further and assumes that the exchanged information modifies the state of the communicating entities. To be exchanged, information is usually encoded using explicit carriers. Within MIC* these carriers are reified as *interaction objects* (IOs).

For instance, a researcher's ideas can be encoded as words and sentences in an explicit scientific paper which represents the explicit information carrier. Other human agents are able to read this IO and, depending on their competences, to decode the contained information.

Once the paper has been written and published, the emitting agent does not have control on the ongoing communication processes that occur.

For instance, Socrates is still in a communication process with other human agents centuries after his death. Having this intuition about IOs, it would be interesting to look further in their structure. The first abstraction is to define an empty IO that carries no information. For instance, an empty paper is an IO that does not carry any information but just meta-information: it is a paper and it is empty.

The IOs can also be aggregated. For instance, the proceedings of the conference is an IO represented as an aggregation of more elementary IOs. Consequently, IOs naturally have a monoid structure $(\mathcal{O}, +)$ with the composition law $+$ and identity element 0. In an aggregation, we do not want to consider the order as an additional information. So, no matter the order of the IOs in an aggregation, one has to be able to interpret them similarly. This makes the composition operator $+$ commutative.

Now let us consider a situation where a poor-quality paper is rejected by the program committee of a conference and accepted by a national workshop program committee. This IO never reached the perceptions of other agents in the first case and interacts with them in the second case. So, the interaction process are contextually defined. This introduces the concept of *interaction spaces* (ISs). Hence, ISs define a local context for interactions among IOs. Notice that the interaction processes within MIC* only involve IOs and is completely independent from the AAs.

The AAs have coordinates, in terms of IOs, in all ISs. When an agent is not 'present' in a certain IS, its representation is equal to the empty IO 0; when an agent is present in a certain IS its representation differs from 0.

The (logical) mobility of an AA is defined as the movement of its IOs among ISs. In order to easily define this notion of mobility, we introduce negative IOs. Hence, an AA moves outside an IS when its representation is reduced to 0. This can be expressed as $x + (-x) = 0$. So, negative IOs are defined as being IOs that reduce other IOs under the composition law $+$. So, the IOs structure is no more a commutative monoid but a commutative group $(\mathcal{O}, +)$. The group structure is also used in order to define the composition of several MIC* DEs. Thanks to this on-the-fly composition property, MASs for open and ubiquitous contexts are easily modeled and implemented [19].

The MIC* structure $\mathcal{T} = \mathcal{O}^{(\mathcal{A} \times \mathcal{S})} \times \mathcal{O}^{(\mathcal{A} \times \mathcal{S})}$ is composed by two matrices that are described as follows:

1. The outbox matrix: the rows of this matrix represent agents $i \in \mathcal{A}$ and the columns represent the ISs $j \in \mathcal{S}$. Each element of the matrix $o_{(i,j)} \in \mathcal{O}$ is a representation of the agent i in the IS j. This is the only way for an agent to exist and operate in the MAS. So, the elements of this matrix model the means that enable an agent to perceive and influence the universe in a particular IS. Notice that the means used to perceive the universe are distinguished from the result of the perception. The perception results are placed in the inbox matrix. When $o_{(i,j)} = 0$, the agent i neither influences nor perceives the universe in the IS j: agent i does not exist in IS j.
2. The inbox matrix: the rows of this matrix represent agents $i \in \mathcal{A}$ and the columns represent the ISs $j \in \mathcal{S}$. Each element of the matrix $o_{(i,j)} \in \mathcal{O}$ represents the result of the perceptions of the agent i in the IS j.

Each element, or term, T of $\mathcal{T}$ is represented as:

$$
T = \underbrace{\left(\underbrace{\left[\underbrace{[o_1]_a}_{(C)} \atop \vdots \right]_s}_{(B)} \cdots \right)}_{(A)} \underbrace{\left(\underbrace{\left[\underbrace{[i_1]_a}_{(G)} \atop \vdots \right]_s}_{(F)} \cdots \right)}_{(E)}
$$

(A) : the outbox matrix ; (B) : the IS 's' ; (C) : the outbox of agent 'a' ; (E) : the inbox matrix ; (F) : IS 's' ; (G) : the inbox of agent 'a'.

4.2   MIC* Dynamics

An element $T \in \mathcal{T}$ is an instantaneous snapshot of the DE state. Within all potentially functions defined from $\mathcal{T}$ to $\mathcal{T}$, MIC* considers three classes which have special semantics for MASs:

Interaction (ϕ): From an external point of view, two AAs are considered as interacting when the perceptions of an agent are influenced by the emissions of another. Consequently, interaction functions modifies the perception results of an agent (defined in the inbox) according to its perception means and others influences (both defined in the outbox) within a defined IS. The set of all interaction functions is represented as ϕ.

Movement (μ): The mobility of an agent is defined as the mobility of its IOs among different ISs. During a movement no IO is created nor lost. In fact, this is an interesting feature to prevent incoherent duplications by guaranteeing that an AA actually disappears from its original IS and appears in its destination IS. The set of all movement evolutions is represented by μ.

Computation (γ): The computation is an internal process of AAs. The only way to observe that an AA has conducted a computation is when it changes autonomously its outboxes within ISs. To avoid confusion between computation and movement, after a computation, AAs conserve their presence. In other words, an agent is not allowed to appear (respectively to disappear) suddenly in an IS when it was not present (respectively present) before the computation. Besides, agents are rational entities that change their emissions according to their perceptions. So, an agent consumes its perceptions in order to make a computation. This is expressed in MIC* by resetting the inbox of the computing agent to 0. The set of all computation evolutions is represented by γ.

The core idea is that *(i)* the DE dynamics is discrete and *(ii)* any state of the DE is reached from the initial state by a sequence of functions that may be of three classes: (M)ovement, (I)nteraction, and (C)omputation (MIC*).

4.3   Building MAS Deployment Environment with MIC*:

The formal concepts presented above has been implemented as software structures offering a development library for the designers of DEs. To complete the design and implementation of a DE, the designer has to provide the followings:

- IOs type description: the IOs have been used: *(i)* to encode and carry information, *(ii)* to define the perceptions of AAs in ISs, *(iii)* to define the influences of AAs in ISs, and finally *(iv)* to define the movement of AAs among ISs. A typing system of IOs has been introduced to describe the fields contained in an IO and to provide a semantics. The types of IOs have also been used to improve the performances of MIC*, especially when using the dynamics operators. Hence, the operators, which are typed functions, are executed only when the matching IOs are present within the IS. The DE designer has to provide the description of the different IO types used within the MAS and their possible hierarchical relationships. The introduced type system supports multiple inheritance.
- Interaction spaces: the MIC* library offers a default IS where AAs are initially located. The designer has to define its own application specific ISs.

Dynamics Operators. The dynamics of MIC* is realized by the following operators that are defined for ISs:

- Interaction operators: a couple of IOs is passed to the interaction operator, namely the *sensor* and *effector*. The interaction operator returns the *interaction result*. An IS may contain zero or more interaction operators. Consequently, the interaction is defined between the IOs and not between the AAs. The AAs have to set their outboxes to the correct sensors in order to perceive the effectors of other AAs according to the defined interaction operators. The type information is used to match interaction operators with corresponding IOs present in the IS.
- Movement operators: the movement among the ISs is decomposed in two operators which are combined. In fact, each IS defines a set of *movement out* operators that specify which IOs are allowed to get outside the IS; and a set of *movement in* operators that defines which IOs are allowed to enter the IS. A path is created between two ISs when the types of their corresponding movement out and in operators match. If a path is found among two ISs, the IOs may move from the source to the destination IS.

5   Building a Social Framework Upon MIC*

MIC* only offers a generic and low level abstraction of a DE. To build real world applications, one has to provide a higher level engineering framework. This section presents a social framework. The idea is that MAS designers only deal with social concepts which are automatically translated to MIC* concepts.

5.1   Presentation of the Social Framework

The presented social framework is deeply inspired by the AGR model [5]. The MadKit [20] platform already implements the AGR model; here we explore another implementation using only MIC* primitives.

The social abstractions presented by AGR are briefly described as follows:

- (A)gent: an agent may play one or several roles and may be member of one or several groups;
- (G)roup: a group is a collection of roles and consequently a collection of agents that play these roles. The interaction among the agents can occur only when they are located within the same group;
- (R)ole: a role is an abstraction that represents a function or a service within the society; agents playing the role fulfill the desired service.

At this stage, let us sketch a preliminary mapping between AGR and MIC*. As shown in Fig. 1, the group concept may be modeled as an IS: the IS concept may be seen as a logical location where a collection of agents interact. Besides, the agents may move across groups; this is similar to moving across ISs. The agent concept of AGR naturally corresponds to MIC* AAs. Still, there is not a one to one mapping between these concepts (see Sect. 5.2). The role concept is considered as an IO within MIC*. In fact, when an agent plays a certain role,

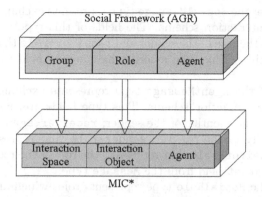

Fig. 1. Mapping between AGR concepts and MIC* concepts

it publishes an IO that describes itself as playing this role. Consequently, other agents can identify its social function and interact with it. The implementation of the AGR model using MIC* is explained in more detail in Table 1.

Two interaction schemes are considered for the social framework:

1. The role-level interaction schema: messages are delivered to agents only by knowing their roles. This mechanism allows implementing one-to-many communications and the discovery of agents' identities by knowing only their roles.
2. The agent-level interaction schema: messages are delivered to agents by knowing their exact identity. This mechanism implements one-to-one communications.

5.2 Implementation of the Social Framework

Interaction Objects. Fig. 2 presents the types of IOs used in the social framework:

- **Message:** the Message type represents IOs used to exchange information encoded as a content. This is the base-type of all other interaction related types; it contains a single field, content, that represents the exchanged information.

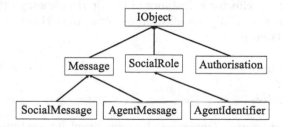

Fig. 2. Type hierarchy of IOs used in the social framework

- SocialMessage: the SocialMessage type represents exchanged messages for the role-level interaction schema. The fields of this type are: sender-role that represents the role of the sender and receiver-role that represents the role of the receiver. This type inherits the content field from the Message type.
- AgentMessage: the AgentMessage type represents exchanged messages at the agent-level interaction schema. This type fields are: sender-agent-id that represents the identity of the sender; receiver-agent-id that represents the identity of the receiver; sender-role that represents the role of the sender; receiver-role that represents the role of the receiver. This type inherits the content field from the Message type.
- SocialRole: the SocialRole type represents roles which are played by the AAs. This type defines only a single field role-id that represents the unique identifier of the role.
- AgentIdentifier: the AgentIdentifier type represents the identity of an agent. In fact, since AAs do not have access to the structure of others, they have to explicitly publish their identity. This type defines only a single field agent-id that represents the unique identifier of the agent; it also inherits the role-id field from the SocialRole type.
- Authorisation: the Authorisation type is used to control group access using movement operators. An agent is allowed to enter an IS by presenting the correct Authorisation instance. The Authorisation contains the name of the played role, namely the played-role field; and the certificate field that represents a signature confirming that the agent is allowed to play this role.

Interaction Operators. Two interaction operators are defined in order to model the interaction schemes:

- Role-level interaction operator: this operator is defined among SocialRole and SocialMessage. A SocialRole interacts with a SocialMessage only and only if the receiver role of the SocialMessage is the same as the role-id field of the SocialRole. This is expressed algorithmically as:

  1: **function** ROLELEVELIOP::INTERACTION(sensor,effector)
     Require: sensor is instance of the SocialRole type
     Require: effector is instance of the SocialMessage type
  2:     **if** sensor['role-id'] == effector['receiver-role'] **then**
  3:         **return** effector
  4:     **else**
  5:         **return** 0   ▷ No interaction.
  6:     **end if**
  7: **end function**

- Agent-level Interaction Operator: the agent-level interaction is defined between AgentIdentifier and AgentMessage. An AgentIdentifier interacts with an `AgentMessage` only and only if the id of the receiver is the same as the id of the agent. This is expressed algorithmically as follows:

1: **function** AGENTLEVELIOP::INTERACTION(sensor,effector)
   Require: sensor is instance of the `AgentIdentifier` type
   Require: effector is instance of the `AgentMessage` type
2:    **if** sensor['agent-id'] == effector['receiver-agent-id'] **then**
3:       **return** effector
4:    **else**
5:       **return** 0   ▷ No interaction.
6:    **end if**
7: **end function**

Movement Operators. The groups are modeled as ISs. Consequently, each IS is associated with a set of roles. To enter the IS, an agent has to play a role that belongs to this set. To realize these movements, the group-entrance operator allows agents to enter inside an IS. The agents have to present an `Authorisation` that describes the played role. On the other hand, the group-leaving operator allows agents to leave the IS.

Interaction Spaces. Besides the default IS defined by MIC*, each group is represented by an extension of MIC* IS, namely the *social interaction space*. Each social IS is defined with a set of authorized roles; the role-level and agent-level interaction operators; and the group-entrance and group-leaving operators.

The Autonomous Agents. Within MIC*, the AAs may have simultaneous activities. For instance, a single AA can sense its surrounding environment and affect it simultaneously. To realize this simultaneity, several MIC* agent entries are used. For instance, Fig. 3 shows this schema where two MIC* agent entries are associated to a single AA: the *sensor* entry and *effector* entry.

From the AA perspective, the sensor entry is dedicated for sensing the universe. Consequently, IOs that perceive the universe are placed in the outbox

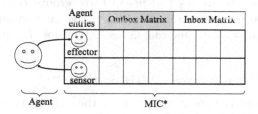

Fig. 3. A single AA have several entries within the MIC* deployment environment: an entry dedicated to sense the universe, i.e. the sensor entry; and an entry dedicated to affect the universe, i.e. the effector entry

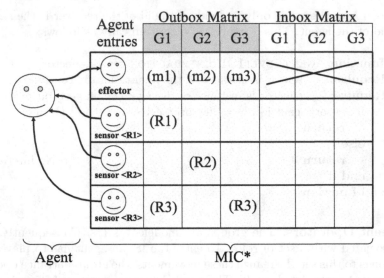

Fig. 4. A social autonomous agent owns an effector entry to affect the universe, and several sensor entries representing its roles

matrix, and the result of their interaction is placed in the inbox matrix. On the other hand, the effector entry is dedicated to affect the universe; consequently, IOs to be perceived by other agents are placed in the outbox matrix and, in this case, the inbox matrix is not used (marked with X, see e.g. Fig. 4). For the MIC* environment, the agent's sensor and effector entries are considered as independent agents; the AA is responsible for making this couple of agents behaving as a single entity. This seems similar to the Holonic approach that considers a set of agents as an single agent [21]; still, here we argue that a set of agents that have been conceived to behave as a single entity can build a global agent.

To represent the fact that an AA plays several roles in groups, the mechanism presented above is extended such that each AA is associated to an effector entry and zero or more sensor entries. Each sensor entry represents a played role. Figure 4 gives an example of an AA that plays three roles R_1, R_2 and R_3. This AA has a single effector to send messages, for instance this agent is sending three messages simultaneously m_1, m_2 and m_3 in three groups G_1, G_2 and G_3. This agent plays simultaneously several roles within the same group: R_1 and R_3 in the group G_1; and plays the same role in several groups: R_3 in G_1 and G_3.

5.3   Mapping Table Between AGR and MIC*:

Finally, by considering the presented concepts, the complete mapping among the AGR concepts and MIC* is described by Table 1.

Table 1. Mapping between AGR concepts and commands to MIC*

AGR	MIC*
Creation of a group named x	This is performed by creating an IS identified as x
Deletion of the group x	This is performed by deleting the IS identified as x
The agent a joins the group x	The agent a's entries (effector and sensors) enter the IS x using the *Authorisation* IO. The involved movement operator is the group-entrance operator.
The agent a leaves the group x	The agent a's entries (effector and sensors) leave the IS x using the group-leaving movement operator.
The agent a acquires the role r	The agent a acquires the *Authorisation* IO with a valid certificate.
The agent a plays the role r within the group g	The agent a moves inside the IS g using the *Authorisation* IO; when this agent is inside the IS, he changes its outbox to the *SocialRole* IO; now this agent is perceived by the others as playing the role r.
The agent a stops from playing the role r within the group g for a short period	The agent a has only to change how the others perceive him; so it changes its *SocialRole* IO to another one; when the agent wants to resume playing the role r, he puts back its *SocialRole* IO.
The agent a drops the role r	The agent a leaves all ISs where he was perceived as playing the role r.
The agent a_1 playing the role r_1 sends a message to the agent a_2 playing the role r_2 within the group g	The message to be sent is an instance of *AgentMessage* type. The agent a_1 puts this message as a computation of its effector in the g IS; then the interaction operator performs the actual interaction among the agent a_1 effector outbox and the agent a_2 sensor corresponding to the role r_2. The result of the interaction is found in the inbox of the agent a_2. In this case, the agent-level interaction operator is used.
The agent a_1 playing the role r_1 sends a message to any agent playing the role r_2 inside the group g	The message to be sent is an instance of *SocialMessage* type. The agent a_1 puts this message as a computation of its effector in the g IS; then the interaction operator performs the actual interaction among the agent a_1 effector outbox and all sensors corresponding to the role r_2. In this case, the role-level interaction operator is used.

6   Example of Application: Ubiquitous Web

The *Ubiquitous Web* is an application that emulates the use of the web in a mobile and ubiquitous environment. The purpose of this section is to present how such an application has been modeled and built using the social framework and to demonstrate its deployment on a simulated 3D virtual world.

6.1   Organizational Modeling:

Systemic Functions. The goal of the application is to emulate the navigation and access of html-based services for ubiquitous environments. There are two systemic functions:

1. Web navigation and access of services: the software system is divided in two main parts, namely the server and client modules. The server module is responsible for delivering web-pages that describe the offered services and forms. The client is responsible for translating the user's commands into requests to the server and displaying the html pages.
2. Discovery of services: the server module of the system is also responsible for delivering a human readable description of the offered services. On the other hand, the client is responsible for discovering all accessible services and for retrieving their description.

Organisational Structure

Roles

1. WEBSERVERROLE: this role responds to the requests of agents playing WEBCLIENTROLE. A WEBCLIENTROLE may request a html presentation; or request a service. When requesting a service, the WEBCLIENTROLE agent can deliver the parameters which have been set by the user.
2. WEBCLIENTROLE: this role represents the intermediary function between the final user and the WEBSERVERROLE. The functions of this role are:
   (a) request a particular html presentation from the WEBSERVERROLE;
   (b) correctly layout the html presentation to the user;
   (c) request services from the WEBSERVERROLE by sending the parameters of the service as imported by the user.
3. SERVICEDISCOVERYSERVERROLE: the main function of this role is to deliver a human readable description of the offered service; and to deliver an access point where to contact the actual service provider.
4. SERVICEDISCOVERYCLIENTROLE: the main function of this role is to check the presence of SERVICEDISCOVERYSERVERROLE agents and to retrieve their description and the service's access point.

Groups

1. WEBGROUP: this group holds agents that play WEBCLIENTROLE and WEBSERVERROLE roles.
2. SERVICEDISCOVERYGROUP: this group holds agents that play SERVICEDIS-COVERYSERVERROLE and SERVICEDISCOVERYCLIENTROLE roles.

6.2   Simulation of Ubiquitous Environments

In order to experiment with the application, a simulator has been developed for ubiquitous environments using computer games technologies. The goal of this

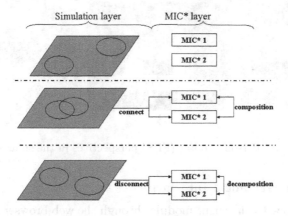

Fig. 5. MIC* DEs are composed and decomposed according to the avatars' communication areas

simulation is to emulate a physical world where the user, represented by an *avatar*, can move and interact with the deployed services which are also represented as avatars. Behind each avatar an entire MAS is running: this includes the AAs and the corresponding MIC* DE. Each avatar has a communication area; when the avatars' communication areas overlap, their corresponding MIC* DE are on-the-fly composed. Similarly, when the avatars' communication areas do not intersect, their corresponding MIC* DE are disconnected. This process is shown graphically by Fig. 5. The user has a 'First Person Shooter' (FPS) perspective and can move around in the virtual world. Figure 6 presents the main views:

- Situation A: there is no service in the immediate surroundings of the user.
- Situation B: the user perceives a service, but the service is too far away to establish a composition of the DEs.
- Situation C: since a communication link can be established, the MIC* DEs are composed. Consequently, AAs located in both deployment environments can interact.

When the user leaves the building of the service (after situation C), the MIC* DEs are immediately decomposed. Consequently, the AAs cannot interact. These are the realistic properties of the ubiquitous environment and the applications have to handle them. Thanks to the on-the-fly composition property of MIC* DEs, the constraints on communication links do not disturb drastically the software systems. In fact, these constraints are handled explicitly in the developed models. For instance, a disconnection is not very different from a silence of an AA that has decided to not reply to external stimuli.

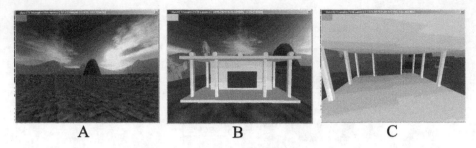

Fig. 6. First-Person-Shooter (FPS) perspectives in the simulator

6.3   End User Graphical Interface

The user interacts with the client module through the web browser presented by Fig. 7:

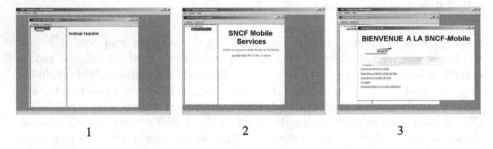

Fig. 7. Ubiquitous web browser GUI

- Situation 1: the agent that plays the role of SERVICEDISCOVERYCLIENTROLE has not discovered any service yet. An empty list is presented to the user. This corresponds to situations A and B of Fig. 6.
- Situation 2: the agent that plays the role of SERVICEDISCOVERYCLIENTROLE has discovered some services by interacting with the agent that plays the role of SERVICEDISCOVERYSERVERROLE in the SERVICEDISCOVERYGROUP group. The list of the available services is presented to the user. This corresponds to situation C of Fig. 6.
- Situation 3: the user has now a web-like interaction with the service. The involved agents are those playing the WEBCLIENTROLE and WEBSERVERROLE roles. This also corresponds to situation C of Fig. 6.

7   Conclusion

This paper has argued that the DE is a key concept for agent-oriented engineering, since it guarantees the autonomy of the agents while it defines their interactions. As an example of such DE, MIC* has been presented.

The notion of DE separates the concerns of MAS engineering. In fact, the engineering of agents is completely separated from the engineering of DEs. The DE is the common structure offered to different developers to deploy AAs and make a global system which functions emerge from the interactions of the individuals.

MIC* offers some interesting features such as the implementation of the internal integrity for AAs; the generative interaction and the on-the-fly composition. These features have provided the basis for engineering open software systems in complex and unpredictable environments such as ubiquitous environments.

However, MIC* has to provide more elaborated control and trust functions. Currently, we are exploring the control of coordination and interaction protocols by MIC*. Hence, MIC* monitors the agents' conversations with regards to interaction and coordination protocols. Any AA that challenges these protocols is identified by the DE and other AAs are prevented from its influences. Consequently, the AAs are offered a normed DE where they can collaborate with autonomous partners.

References

1. Odell, J., Parunak, H.V.D., Fleischer, M., Breuckner, S.: Modeling agents and their environment. In Giunchiglia, F., Odell, J., Weiss, G., eds.: Agent-Oriented Software Engineering (AOSE) III. Volume 2585 of Lecture Notes on Computer Science., Springer, Berlin (2002) 16–31
2. Weyns, D., Parunak, H.V.D., Michel, F., Holvoet, T., Ferber, J.: Environments for multiagent systems: State-of-the-art and research challenges. In Weyns, D., Parunak, H.V.D., Michel, F., eds.: Environments for Mutiagent Systems. Volume 3477 of Lecture Note in Artificial Intelligence LNAI., Springer (to appear, 2005)
3. Zambonelli, F., Parunak, H.V.D.: From design to intention: signs of a revolution. In: Proceedings of the first international joint conference on Autonomous agents and multiagent systems, ACM Press (2002) 455–456
4. Michel, F.: Formalisme, méthodologie et outils pour la modélisation et la simulation de systèmes multi-agents. PhD thesis, Université Montpellier II (2004)
5. Ferber, J., Gutknecht, O., Michel, F.: From agents to organizations: an organizational view of multi-agent systems. In Paolo Giorgini, Jrg P. Mller, J.O., ed.: Agent-Oriented Software Engineering IV: 4th International Workshop, Aose 2003. Lecture notes in computer science LNCS, Springer Verlag (2003) 185–202
6. Gelernter, D., Carriero, N., Chandran, S., Chang, S.: Parallel programming in linda. In: Proceedings of the International Conference on Parallel Programming. (1985) 255–263
7. Picco, G.P., Murphy, A.L., Roman, G.C.: Lime: Linda meets mobility. In: International Conference on Software Engineering. (1999) 368–377
8. Omicini, A., Zambonelli, F.: The tucson coordination model for mobile information agents. 1st Workshop on Innovative Internet Information Systems (1998)
9. Cabri, G., Leonardi, L., Zambonelli, F.: Reactive tuple spaces for mobile agent coordination. Lecture Notes in Computer Science 1477 (1998) 237–247
10. Gelernter, D.: Generative communication in linda. ACM Transaction od Programming Languages and Systems 7 (1985) 80–112
11. Wooldridge, M., Jennings, N.R.: Intelligent agents: Theory and practice. The Knowledge Engineering Review 10 (1995) 115–152

12. Castelfranchi, C.: Guarantees for autonomy in cognitive agent architecture. In: Proceedings of the workshop on agent theories, architectures, and languages on Intelligent agents, Springer-Verlag New York, Inc. (1995) 56–70
13. Genesereth, Ketchpel: Software agents. Communications of the ACM **37** (1994) 48–53
14. Gouaïch, A.: Requirements for achieving software agents autonomy and defining their responsibility. In: The First International Workshop on Computational autonomy - Potential, Risks, Solutions (autonomy 2003). (2003)
15. Steels, L.: The biology and technology of intelligent autonomous agents. Robotics and Autonomous Systems **15** (1995)
16. Sichman, J.S., Conte, R., Castelfranchi, C., Demazeau, Y.: A social reasoning mechanism based on dependence networks. In Cohn, A.G., ed.: Proceedings of the Eleventh European Conference on Artificial Intelligence, Chichester, John Wiley & Sons (1994) 188–192
17. Luck, M., d'Inverno, M.: A formal framework for agency and autonomy. In Lesser, V., Gasser, L., eds.: Proceedings of the First International Conference on Multi-Agent Systems (ICMAS-95), San Francisco, CA, USA, AAAI Press (1995) 254–260
18. Weiss, G., Rovatsos, M., Nickles, M.: Capturing agent autonomy in roles and xml. In: Proceedings of the second international joint conference on Autonomous agents and multiagent systems, ACM Press (2003) 105–112
19. Gouaïch, A., Guiraud, Y., Michel, F.: Mic*: An agent formal environment. In: the 7th World Multiconference on Systemics, Cybernetics and Informatics (SCI 2003), session on Agent Based Computing ABC'03. (2003)
20. Gutknecht, O., Ferber, J., Michel, F.: Integrating tools and infrastructures for generic multi-agent systems. In: Proceedings of the fifth international conference on Autonomous agents, AA 2001, ACM Press (2001) 441–448
21. Parunak, H.V.D., Odell, J.: Representing social structures in uml. In: Agent-Oriented Software Engineering II. Volume 2222 of Lecture notes in computer science LNCS., Berlin, Springer (2002) 1–16

About the Role of the Environment in Multi-agent Simulations

Franziska Klügl, Manuel Fehler, and Rainer Herrler

Dept. of Artificial Intelligence, Universität Würzburg, Würzburg, Germany
{kluegl, fehler, herrler}@ki.informatik.uni-wuerzburg.de

Abstract. Multi-agent Simulation can be seen as simulated multi-agent systems situated in a simulated environment. Thus, in simulations the modelled environment should always be a first order object that is as carefully developed as the agents themselves. This is especially true for evolutionary simulation and simulation of adaptive multi-agent systems, as the agents environment guides the selection and adaptation process. Also, for the simulation of realistic agent behavior complex and valid environmental models have to be tackled. Therefore, a modelling and simulation system should provide appropriate means for representing the environmental status, including spatial representations, and dynamics. On the other side, simulation infrastructure should be as simple as possible, as a modeler with domain expertise is usually no computer scientist. He might neither be trained in dealing with data structures and efficient algorithms, nor in traditional programming.

After going into the details of simulated environments for multi-agent simulations, this paper shows how environments with different characteristics can be represented in a particular modelling and simulation system, named SeSAm, without asking too much from its users.

1 Introduction

Modelling and simulation form a well-known method for studying a system with the aim of for example improving its understanding, its design, or the procedures for its control. The real world system is abstracted into a model. If this abstraction is done in a correct and valid way, this model can be used for answering the relevant questions instead of the original that is not yet or anymore existing, not understood, inaccessible, etc. The main problem is the design and implementation of the model capturing the necessary – but not too much – details of the original. There are diverse modelling paradigms that are suitable for specific types of systems and types of questions. Multi-agent simulation is a rather new modelling paradigm that is specially appropriate for complex systems of flexibly interacting entities, like social science or biological models [1].

Multi-agent simulation is a modelling paradigm based on the concept of a multi-agent system. In contrast to other forms of micro-level simulations with

D. Weyns et al. (Eds.): E4MAS 2004, LNAI 3374, pp. 127–149, 2005.
© Springer-Verlag Berlin Heidelberg 2005

objects, tokens or processes, the active entities in the model are agents interacting with each other and with their environment. Although this higher level of abstraction facilitates modelling in general, dealing with multi-agent models leads to some difficulties due to the large amount of assumptions and parameter in complex and detailed models. This is also due to the fact that the modeler has to deal with the environment for the simulated multi-agent system. Thus, dealing with the notion of the environment in a multi-agent simulation is an interesting and important issue. If one could provide a method to support dealing with the environment in a general applicable yet convenient way, designing and implementing a multi-agent simulation would be facilitated in a highly valuable way.

An important aspect hereby is that the overall environment of the simulated multi-agent system can be divided into two basic parts: the "simulation environment" and the "simulated environment". The simulated environment is the part of the *model* that concerns all non-agent aspects. Thus, it possesses corresponding elements in the original system like the agents do themselves. In general, one may state that the simulated environment is everything that is left when the agents of the multi-agent system are deleted from the simulation model. It may contain simulated resources or dynamics that cannot be associated with the particular agents that the model should be asked about.

On the other side, the simulation environment provides the infrastructure for running the simulation. For example, in an event-based simulation this simulation infrastructure would contain the parts of the overall model and simulation software that manages the event queue. In this case, the simulated environment would be one special process that is also producing events which may affect all agent processes. In contrast to this, the simulation environment contains the infrastructure for running all processes.

However, the distinction between simulated environment and simulation environment is only explicit in simulation models where the simulation software and the model representation are treated separately. Although this property is highly desirable [2], it is not realized in many simulation applications, as it requires an explicit, declarative representation language for the model that is either interpreted or compiled for running the simulation. Many simulations are implemented based on an (extended) programming language or framework where infrastructure functions that manage the simulation, etc. are mixed up with functions that are responsible for the description of the simulated environment, or even with the agent programs. In that case it is not trivial to find out what parts of the code belong to the simulation infrastructure and what parts belong to the simulated environment. Consider the example of a communication infrastructure like a bus: The general functionality of message transport would clearly be provided by the infrastructure, that means the simulation environment; however, probabilities for loosing a message or transportation error that modify the content of the message are part of the specially modelled environment in this multi-agent simulation model. Dealing with modelling and simulation environments the question arises, how the development of a multi-agent simulation model is supported best: What structures and functions should be provided in a generic tool for multi-agent simulations? This has to be based on considerations concerning simulated environments and simulation infrastructure, especially on characteristics and possible representation of the former. As it is clear that every model that should be treated with simulation needs simulation infrastructure, we focus on simulated environments as this is something special for multi-agent simulations - compared to other forms of simulation and also compared to multi-agent systems in general.

Therefore, the remainder of the paper is starting with a short introduction into multi-agent simulation, its basic components and different forms and consequences not only for the simulated environment. There, the distinction between simulated environment and simulation infrastructure will also be taken up again. In section 3 some aspects concerning the simulated environment and its related assumptions are detailed. This is followed by a short characterization of different categories. In section 5 a simulation tool that is based on a flexible framework for different environmental representations is presented. Examples given in section 4 – applications of SeSAm – illustrate the different roles and characteristics that a simulated environment may take. The contribution ends with a short summary.

2   Multi-agent Simulation

A multi-agent simulation – executing a multi-agent model – in general can be seen as a simulated multi-agent system that exists in a simulated environment [3]. The multi-agent system paradigm provides a very natural form of modelling, especially for societies, because active entities in the original system are interpreted as actors in the model. It can be seen as a special kind of micro simulation where the agents are capable of autonomous and flexible acting and are interacting with each other and their common simulated environment.

As mentioned in the introduction, the notion of environment is twofold when dealing with multi-agent simulation. Like in any other form of simulation, a simulation infrastructure is necessary for providing the framework within that the simulation model is executed. In multi-agent simulation an explicit treatment of the simulated environment as a part of the model – separated from the infrastructure – is necessary and has specific relations to the general properties and advantages of a multi-agent model. In contrast to this, the infrastructural part of the environment can be seen in analogy to simulation engines, runtime environments, etc. of standard simulations and is part of the simulator in any case. The fact that the environmental part of the model can be more or less distinctive, does not influence its importance. The necessary consequences for tools for multi-agent simulations are discussed in section 5.

- Multi-agent models facilitate the simulation of variable agent numbers and variable structures. Using a simulated environment, this can be dealt with on the model-level without always referring to infrastructure.
For modelling the "death" and "birth" of agents, either every agent holds a dynamic representation of its integration into the agent system for determining its interaction partners, like e.g. in the modelling framework AgeDEVS [4]. The other possibility is using an explicit model of an environment where agents "live" and encounter. An environmental model that captures the necessary details of the original real-world environment of the simulated multi-agent system, enables the modeler to reproduce the agents behavior – not only its interaction behavior – more realistically without using artifacts like middle agents unless they are also present in the original.
- A multi-agent simulation is well suited, when feedback loops in the agent behavior are important. Those feedback loops – the agents actions amplify or weaken what this or other agents perceive that again triggers actions, and so on – are often mediated by an explicitly represented environment. Examples are found in models of recruitment in social insects (e.g. pheromone trails) When the decision making of the simulated entity is not only based on its local surroundings but relates to more or less global properties or values, then, these values need to be represented in an explicit object that captures the simulated environment as a part of the model.
- If inhomogeneous space is relevant for the simulation question, that means that agents are dependent on local differences, an explicit representation of this environment is required. A critical question here is challenging the distinction between simulated environment and simulation infrastructure. Whereas dynamics and configuration of and on the simulated space clearly can be counted to the simulated environment, the basic framework for representation cannot easily be assigned. 2- or 3-dimensional maps are normally integrated and provided by the modelling and simulation tool. On such a framework level those maps are independent from a particular model and thus can be treated as infrastructure. In section 5 these aspects will be addressed in more detail.

Thus, one may see that the existence of a simulated environment – explicitly treated – is correlated to important advantages of multi-agent simulation in general. However, the drawbacks of multi-agent simulation are also depending on the treatment of an simulated environment. Due to the possible level of detail, the goal of a valid simulation behavior causes an immense effort on justification, modelling and simulation. This has to be done on least two levels of observation and for large parameter spaces, etc. Not only the agent behavior has to be validated, also the structure and behavior of the simulated environment. Both has to happen based on the chosen characteristics of the infrastructure, like time advance, update cycle, etc. The validity of the environmental model is often neglected, as the modeler focusses on the agents model. Testing it can be even more costly than the justification of the as-

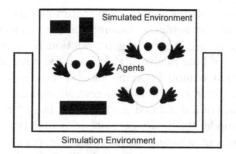

Fig. 1. Ingredients for multi-agent simulations: agents, simulated environment and simulation environment (infrastructure)

sumptions built into the agents. The level of abstraction of the environmental model is determined by the possible actions and perceptions of the agents. An illustrative example is given in section 6.1 where the agent behavior is quite simple whereas the environmental model has to capture complex physical phenomena.

2.1   Basic Ingredients of a Multi-agent Model

Figure 1 shows the ingredients of a multi-agent simulation: Agents, simulated environment containing additional objects that are not belonging to the agent system under examination, and the simulation environment. These components are described in more detail.

Agents. Agents are the most characterizing ingredient in multi-agent simulation. Agents are autonomously active entities. Autonomy can be seen here in relation to the other entities within the simulated environment. There can be no autonomy in relation to the modeler that designed the agents. Agents in multi-agent simulation mostly possess some form of internal representation denoting beliefs or individual state, like age, gender, energy status, etc. The latter may be described by state variables, but may also contain higher level representations of intentions or goals. Their dynamics are given by the model. The way this is done can be distinguished into behavior describing and behavior generating models. The consequences for the environmental model are discussed in section 2.3.

Simulated agents are situated in the simulated environment and in relation to this may possess the well-known agent properties. They are "executed" by the simulation environment.

Simulated Environment. Simulated agents are "living" in a simulated environment that is an abstraction of the original environment and thus part of the model. A single agent may interact with other simulated agents as well as with non-agent entities in this environment or – if explicitly represented as some form of "world"-entity – with the environment itself.

This global entity may carry some global state variables like overall temperature, and even its own dynamics, e.g. temperature changes. These dynamics also can be so complex, e.g. containing production of new entities, that one may assign some form of behavior with the simulated environment. Every environmental dynamic that is model-specific can be counted to it. The simulated environment is unique for a specific multi-agent simulation.

The most basic form of a simulated environment is an "empty world". In this case the simulation model itself just consists of a society of simulated agents, the simulated environment possesses no specific state, nor dynamics. Interaction, e.g. communication using messages, is technically realized using the simulation infrastructure, but without any model-specific characteristics like delay or potential errors. There is no simulated space. Such an empty simulated environment may only be used in very abstract simulation models. Any simulation model replicating more detailed aspects of the real world requires a reproduction of some aspects of the agents environment. The modeler may use some kind of spatial representation populated by non-agent entities like resources, or even other (simpler) agents that are not in the focus of the simulation. The simulated environment as an explicitly represented entity may also contain some state variables and complex dynamics.

As the real world constrains the structure and behavior of the real agents, the simulated environment plays that role for the simulated agent system. The perceptions of the simulated agents need to have some origin in the environment that has to be represented in the environmental model. Thus, complex agent models require rich environmental models that cannot be abstracted to the empty environment without loosing the necessary complexity of the simulated agents.

Simulation Infrastructure. The simulation infrastructure or simulation environment provides all means for executing the model in a runable simulation. It provides all components of a simulator that can be provided by a modelling and simulation framework that are in principle independent from a particular model. It controls the specific simulation time advance – e.g. time stepped or event based, provides message passing facilities or directory services. Also the instrumentation of the model that are means for data gathering during the simulation execution, is part of it. Modelling and simulation tools provide specific simulation infrastructures. Nowadays many tools for developing multi-agent simulations are available. When a modeler is using a standard programming language, then he has not only to implement the model, but also the infrastructure for running the model. This is not advisable.

The simulation environment basically constrains what can be simulated at all. If for example a simulation tool does not provide means for message passing, then message passing has to be reproduced using the means that the infrastructure provides, e.g. some shared memory. Thus, the message passing component has to be realized as a part of the model. An analogous situation occurs when the infrastructure basically is provided, yet not with the flexibility that is required, e.g. when the simulation environment provides a bus system for addressed message passing but all messages are guaranteed to arrive without any loss. If the modelled entities should be able to react on message transfer noise then this noise has to be implemented on the model side by re-building some kind of infrastructure based on the provided one. The situation becomes even worse if the infrastructure that the simulation environment provides, is not apt at all to reproduce the properties necessary for the model. An example are discrete spatial representations provided by the infrastructure, but continuous positioning is necessary for the model. The modeler might ignore all a priori provided spatial representation and re-implement the continuous positioning system based on status information of the agents. However, this is very effortful and error-prone and should be avoided as other tools seem to be more apt for the target model.

The borderline between simulation infrastructure and simulated environment for the agent system cannot be drawn precisely in every case: Is a specific message passing system part of the infrastructure or part of the model? The discretization of space in a map as well as some features of the time advance function can be seen as both. However, this distinction is useful for several reasons:

- The simulated environment is part of the model itself and should be specified with at least the same amount of carefulness as the simulated multi agent system.
- The simulated environment has to be validated as it serves as the mapping of the real environment that contains the multi-agent system.
- Both, simulation infrastructure as well as simulated environment, carry assumptions and abstractions from the original real-world system. Whereas the assumptions concerning infrastructure are more technically dealing with virtual time, update regime, etc, the assumptions concerning the simulated environment are more conceptually constraining the agents possible perceptions and actions.
- The distinctions helps to realize a clear design when implementing a multi-agent simulation, and even more when developing a model-independent tool for them. Especially general purpose simulation tools should not include too many assumptions about the environment – infrastructure and model. In contrast to this, domain specific simulation systems, e.g. a simulation system for biological simulations, may also include specific build-in parts for simulated environments.

By integrating more powerful and flexible basic infrastructure for interaction into a modelling and simulation tool, like configurable message passing systems or special kinds of spatial representations, like 3d-grids, a modeler is allowed to concentrate on the model-specific aspects of the overall environment, namely the simulated environment. However, the more specific representations and tools are given by the simulation environment, the more restricted is the variety of simulation models that can be built using it.

2.2   Assumptions Concerning the Different Environments

Although modelling assumptions are mainly associated with and have to be tested for the simulated environment, a modeler also has to be aware of the assumptions laying behind the simulation environment.

- Abstractions concerning time advance are part of the simulation environment, whereas ontological definitions, like one simulation tick corresponds to one year in realtime, are part of the model and therefore part of the simulated environment.
- Assumptions concerning implementation of parallelism, e.g. update sequence, process control belong also to the infrastructure. On the other side the configuration of resources belong to the model of the environment.
- Assumptions concerning the basic spatial representation – that means whether there is a 2d grid or a 3d continuous map – may belong to both depending on the degree of freedom that is provided by the simulation infrastructure. The interpretation of the granularity of the spatial representation (meter, kilometer, etc) is part of the model.

In addition to the agent system itself, all these assumptions and abstractions have to be justified for determining the validity of a multi-agent simulation. Concerning the infrastructure, this means that the modeler has to be aware why he is selecting a special kind of simulation infrastructure. If he is using a tool that is providing the simulation environment, he hopefully may assume that the infrastructure is working as specified.

2.3   Basic Categories of Multi-agent Simulations

Existing multi-agent models focus on different aspects of phenomena found in societies. These range from the development of dependence networks based on agents beliefs to emergent structures produced by a huge amount of massively interacting simple entities. Based on diverse domains and goals associated with particular multi-agent simulations, one may identify different types of them. Due to the huge amount of possible useful applications, this is just possible with fluent borderlines. Although these categories are in principle independent from the particular simulated environment the agents are living in, they nevertheless have important effects on the role and usage of the simulated environment.

Models for Prediction Versus Explanation. Simulation models in general are designed to answer questions about some real or hypothetic original system. These questions can be of either explanatory or predictive nature.

In explanatory simulation models the aim of the simulation study is to identify yet unknown relationships and interactions of the real world system. The hypothetic agent behavior reproduced in the simulation model should lead to some desired valid global behavior of the model. Thus, the goal is to design valid global model behavior by identifying a valid detailed model structure. Based on that, it is hoped to be possible to explain how the behavior of the real system is produced. Summarizing, in explanatory simulation one starts with a theory about the real world and tries to show the the plausibility of this theory using simulation.

In predictive simulation it is presumed that the knowledge about the system is available at the necessary level of detail. One wants to build a simulation model that enables to predict how the corresponding real world system will behave under certain conditions.

The consequences for the simulated environment are the same as for the agent system: Explanatory models are more abstract that predictive ones. That means, in the former the abstractions have to be controlled thoroughly so that they correctly fit to the agent behavior. The simulated environment thereby is not necessarily corresponding to the original environment in the same way the agents are corresponding to the original. The focus lies on the agents, the environment is just there to provide appropriate stimuli. On the other side, in predictive simulations the requirements concerning the details of the simulated environment are much harder. If predictive statements about the original produced by the model should be reasonable, the environmental model on its own should be able to produce correct predictions.

Behavior-Describing Versus Behavior-Generating Models. Another important distinction can be identified between *behavior-describing* and *behavior-generating* models of the agents. In behavior-describing agent models the agent can be modelled by specifying rules or scripts, etc. The modeler specifies the dynamics of the agent and its decision making directly e.g. using rules that determine the agents actions depending on its current state and perceptions. Activity diagrams may be used for structuring the rules allowing complex behavior models [3].

Behavior-generating agent models on the other hand are based on some kind of quality function or goal representation. The model provides an set of primitive actions and knowledge about the pre- and post-conditions of these actions. An agent is able to use some form of planning algorithm for determining the next action. Examples are models using extended AgentSpeak(L) [5].

In principle, there is a seamless transition from behavior-based to behavior-generating models. Some agent architectures that are based on skeletal-plan-like representations (like RAP [6] or PRS [7]) use some form of mixture. The potential behaviors are highly fixed by the plan representations, whereas the actual behavior of the agents is determined by algorithms (high-level rules) that select the appropriate plan skeleton and concretizes it according to the current situation.

Depending on the simulated environment, one of the both alternatives might seem more suitable: Behavior-describing methods are hard to handle if the environment is very rich and the agent has a very high degree of freedom in selecting the appropriate actions. In contrast to this, behavior generation may be unnecessarily complex in a model with fixed processes and few possible perceptions and decisions.

Experience shows that the selection of one form of agent architecture also requires different ways of dealing with the simulated environment. Describing models usually makes more assumptions concerning coupled dynamics between agents and the simulated environment. Agent-independent dynamics and agents decisions have to be synchronized carefully by the modeler. Otherwise a model easily becomes very complex when all possible environmental states have to be predicted and reactions specified in the behavior description. Therefore, stochastic dynamics of the "world entity" require more complex behavior descriptions.

Complex dynamics that are not foreseeable by the modeler are usually easier to deal with using a more complex agent architecture with behavior generation. The planning capabilities allow them to react to new situations, even if no agent behavior was explicitly specified for these situations. Agents may flexibly change their behavior if it seems appropriate to their goals.

3   Aspects of the Simulated Environment

The treatment of the simulated environment is essential for the overall model. This is discussed in the following in more detail. If the simulated environment is very reduced in the model, the complete environment of the multi-agent simulation, including the simulation infrastructure, nevertheless has to be tackled explicitly. However, this is not given here.

3.1   Role of the Simulated Environment for the Model

The simulated environment reproduces the environment of the original system. However, it does not need to possess a correspondence comparable to the agents, but may be modelled more or less abstract due to simulation efficiency but also due to the following functions that it may be responsible for.

The simulated environment forms an abstraction of the original environment of the agent system. It contains abstractions of all relevant active and passive elements in this environment. Thus, it forms the grounding and conceptual framework for the overall model abstraction. For example, in an abstract testbed used for studying different hypothesis about insect task allocation (see [8]) the simulated environment contains task objects with dynamic requirements that have to be worked on by the agents.

The simulated environment contains what the agents may perceive and manipulate. Thus, its richness and complexity determines the level of detail of the simulated multi-agent system. Consider for example a shopping model: Only if the simulated shops possess representations of properties like assortment or atmosphere, simulated agents are enabled to ground their shopping decision on that kind of information.

Thus, the simulated environment frames and constrains the behavior of the simulated agents. This is corresponding to the role of the environment in situated multi-agent systems. This issue is especially important in adaptive and evolutionary simulation. Agents may learn based on reward or similar feedback produced by the environment. In evolutionary simulations the selection is realized by the environment. Thus the direction of the adaptation process is given by the simulated environment.

Two of these aspects are now discussed in more detail:

3.2   The Right Level of Detail/Realism

In general the required level of detail for a simulation model is determined by the question that needs to be answered in the simulation study. Abstract questions may be answered by abstract simulation models that only require an abstract simulated environment. Questions that aim at predictions or are very concrete regarding some details of the original system, can only be answered by models that capture a certain level of detail. As the level of detail of the simulated environment determines the possible level of detail of the simulated multi-agent system, both, simulated environment and multi-agent system, become quite complex.

However, the problem with more realistic, detailed, and complex simulated environments and multi-agent systems – as with complex systems in general – is that they are hard to control and analyze. Complex relationships are controlled by using large numbers of model parameters related to the environment, the agent behavior, but also to the interaction between them. Examples are the movement speed of the simulated agents or thresholds of perceived values that are triggering certain behaviors. A valid configuration of these model parameter, i.e. a choice of parameter values that makes the overall simulation valid, can not determined a priori. As a result, calibration – that means the search for such a configuration – is essential, but can become very costly.

This fact makes the integration of real-world data into the design and calibration process very important. Parameter values may be set based on empirical data directly gained from the original system. Basically, this allows to keep control over complex simulation models by enabling to reduce and constraint the search space.

In general one may state that the design of a realistic environment is an especially important step in the simulation design process as the realism and validity of the environmental simulation constraints the validity of the rest of the simulation system, i.e. the agent simulation. No realistic agent simulation can be created without a realistic environmental simulation.

3.3   Evolutionary and Adaptive Multi-agent Simulation

As mentioned above, the particular model of the environment is especially important in simulations with adaptive agents or evolutionary simulation. Reward and feedback that the adaption process is based upon, are usually produced by the simulated environment. For example in a route choice model with agents that adapt their selection based on their experiences with their former decisions, the success of an agent is computed by the environment in the sense that the actual movement is executed in the simulated environment on its particular routes. An analogous situation can be identified in evolutionary simulations. Selection is normally realized by agents that are either not surviving long enough to reproduce or possess only limited chances for reproduction. This might be based on food availability and again based on the interaction with the environment. Thus, the environmental part of model is decisive for the direction of the adaptation process.

One might interpret an evolutionary simulation as an optimization problem with the simulated environment as its objective function. If this objective function has been chosen incorrectly, its attractor is not the desired attractor corresponding to the real world system and the optimization process will not yield the desired optimal setting: The complete evolution and adaption process centers around finding the best agent behavior for a given and possibly changing environment. Thus, as the adaption process is strongly related to the environmental properties, it is only possible to design a valid evolutionary process if the attractor of the simulation system, defined by the simulated environment, has been designed correctly. Otherwise the simulation system will evolve towards some agent behavior without correspondence to the original system. Then, nothing can be learned from the simulation about the real world system.

The consequence is that the simulated environment has to be tested very carefully to exclude artifacts in the results. That means, one has to make sure that the results of the adaptation process are not influenced by implementation details of this part of the model in an unintended way.

4   Characteristics and Categories of Simulated Environments

In this section characteristics of different types of simulated environments are presented. In general the most apparent property of a simulated environment is whether it is based on some spacial representation, namely a map. Different categories may be identified on this basis. Other dimensions that can be used as a categoric basis for discussion are its properties from the point of view of the agents, as given in [9]. Discreteness can also be seen from the modelling point of view relating to space and time. Another property may be whether the simulated environment is active or passive that means if it possesses some dynamics that is independent from the agents actions, e.g. some global temperature hat changes without influence of the simulated agents or if all changes in the environment are reactions triggered by the agents. One might also distinguish between simulated environments with state-like properties, containing passive resource objects or active entities in addition to the agents that are at the heart of the simulation study.

The following discussions are geared to the dimension of the used spacial framework in the simulated environment. After non-spacial simulated environ-

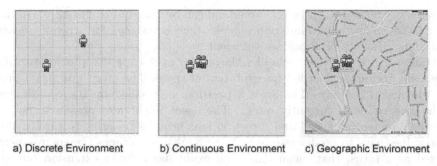

a) Discrete Environment   b) Continuous Environment   c) Geographic Environment

Fig. 2. Spacial representations with growing complexity

ments, several types of spacial representations starting with a very simple grid-based to more sophisticated ones are presented.

4.1   Non-spatial Environments

Locality and agent positions are not necessary depending on some notion of space. For instance simulated agents living in a simulated network are depending on the network topology. The spatial position of the hosting machine has no - or just little - effect on its behavior. In this case the network topology substitutes the map. The environmental model determines the topology, provides and limits communication of the agents.

Network structures – often without explicit representation of nodes and connections – can also be found in social models where an agent resembles a node and some relationship, e.g. acquaintance, can be seen as connection. Current prominent examples in this category are the so called small world networks [10] that form the basis not only for agent-based epidemic simulations. Another example is the simulation of a marketplace, where every agent has access to all offers. This simulated environment may provide tools for searching for certain products and for negotiation with suppliers, but has no internal structure.

As these examples show, there are also application domains where simulated agents are situated but not spatially positioned. This is especially true for simulation of software agents and abstract social science models. There is no need for specific frameworks provided by the simulation infrastructure, however tools for supporting message passing, addressing or searching for agents with particular properties may be helpful in certain simulation models.

Multi-agent simulation is a highly attractive method especially in biology as with the possibility of simulating individually distinct entities also heterogeneous space can be part of the model. In figure 2 different forms of maps are given. They are discussed in the following.

4.2   Discrete Spatial Environments

Most multi-agent simulation are using discrete maps as the basis for their simulated environment. This is simply due to the fact that the implementation of functionality related to space is simpler and can be done quite efficiently. On the other hand, in abstract simulation models there is no need for arbitrary exact positioning, discrete positions are sufficient.

Thus, agent simulation tools like Mason [11] or Ascape [12] provide two dimensional grid maps for the representation of space. The given grid has a limited dimension and size. The agent's position is specified by the coordinates of the grid cell it is currently set to. The agent might also possess some attributes representing speed and direction it is heading towards. Naturally also these values have to be discrete (e.g. N, S, E, W). Sometimes the environment is used as a torus, that means that the world has a finite extension but no borders. One can think of it like the opened surface of a donut. If a moving agent reaches an edge of the map, it continues its movement on the opposite edge.

Discrete environments are often associated with Cellular Automatons. Cellular Automatons were first introduced by Von Neumann [13] and are used for many microscopic models in traffic simulation, medicine, biology and social science. Every cell in a n-dimensional grid has a state and a rule set that updates this state depending on the states of the neighboring cells. In multi-agent simulation cellular automata can be used as more complex environmental model. A prominent example is the sugarscape model [14].

4.3   Continuous Spatial Environments

Continuous environments are less restrictive compared to discrete environments: They allow agents to be situated between the cells. The position of an agent is then described by coordinates of rational numbers. Truly continuous environments are not possible in computer simulation, since digital computing devices are finite and discrete in nature. Nevertheless, from the modelers point of view representing coordinates as a floating point numbers is as good as dealing with "continuous" environments. Another aspect of continuous environments is that agents usually are modelled with a certain size or shape. The direction of movement and speed may be represented on a more precise scale. This is not only important for more realistic modelling, but also for visualization because one cannot refer to a certain grid size. However, it makes implementation of such continuous maps more complex.

The main advantage of continuous space representations is that they allow the creation of more realistic simulation models as the original system mostly is also based on a continuous map. Modelers have less effort in proofing that the effects of discretion do not tamper the desired result. Finally, it should not be neglected that visualization and animation of continuous maps are more convincing.

4.4   Geographic Data for Environments

In some applications simple continuous spacial representations do not meet the requirements of simulation modelers. For example in microscopic traffic sim-

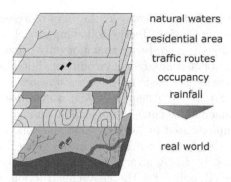

natural waters

residential area

traffic routes

occupancy

rainfall

real world

Fig. 3. Examples for thematic dimensions of a GIS [15]

ulations some form of road network can be used as the basis of the simulated environment. To represent such a structure using a plain continuous map is quite costly.

On the other side, real world data is stored in Geographic Information Systems (GIS) that provide means for representing structures with linear and plane shapes: so called vector data is based on a explicit representation of spatial shape objects like lines or shapes whereas raster data – the second data format used in Geographic Information Systems – associates data items directly with discrete (grid) positions.

For the representation of road networks vector data is highly appropriate. In addition to spatial information, data is grouped to thematic layers (see figure 3). Each layer is containing a certain type of objects, like roads, rivers or areas with certain utilization. These objects may be augmented with thematic (statements, attributes) and topological information (nodes, edges, areas).

For realistic simulations the use of such data is the optimum, as no abstraction between the real-world data and the one used in the model is necessary. Whereas raster data relates to grid environments, the use of a (vector-) GIS-based-environment in multi agent simulation means that agents and objects of the world may not just be associated with positions, but also with shapes or lines. Agents may be restricted to move on a road network instead of moving freely across the map. Algorithms for finding shortest paths to a destination and collision detection might be of interest. Currently, there are just a few tools supporting agent based simulation based on GIS data [10].

5   SeSAm

In contrast to the simulated environment that is model-specific, the simulation environment that provides the infrastructure for running a simulation should be provided by a modelling and simulation tool. As mentioned in the previous section, there are several tools that provide frameworks for specific spacial representations. As such a framework is independent from a particular model, it may be counted to the infrastructure. However, the map representation may be too inflexible for a certain application. In the following a tool for the development of multi-agent simulations is introduced that not only provides an explicit representation framework for a simulated environment, but also allows to change infrastructural components like basic map representations.

SeSAm (ShEll for Simulated Agent systeMs, www.simsesam.de) is an integrated tool for modelling and executing multi-agent simulations. The first prototype of SeSAm was implemented in LISP in 1995 and was specialized to biological simulations. Over the years SeSAm grew into a general purpose simulation tool and was redesigned in JAVA after the year 2000. Today, SeSAm provides powerful modelling functionality for the easy construction of complex models. Based on a high-level, partially declarative model representation it offers visual programming for all tasks from modelling to data gathering during simulation execution.

The basic element of all behavior descriptions in SeSAm are so called function primitives that can be combined to more abstract functions and used in higher-level behavior representations. These function primitive provide the interface between the declarative model representation and the executable JAVA program. In addition to the executable code every primitive requires an explicit description of its arguments, output, type and documentation. There is already a useful set of these basic functions available. This given set can be extended by the user.

The behavior of an agent is described using an activity graph (see figure 4 for a screenshot). These UML-like activity graphs are easy understandable. They basically consist of activities and transition rules. An activity contains a series of actions that is executed as long as the agent is in that activity. Firing rules may terminate one activity and activate the next activity.

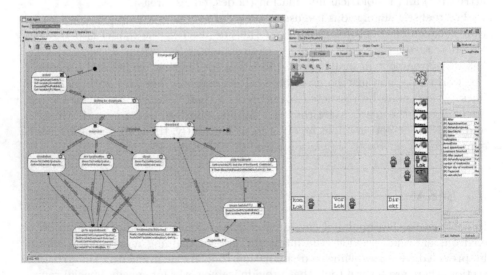

Fig. 4. Example of behavior modelling in SeSAm

The description of structure and dynamics is done on the level of agent, resource and world classes. Instances of those entities are configured and positioned in a "situation" that can be seen as a configuration. It may serve as a starting point for simulation execution. In a situation the simulated environment consisting of one world instance and potentially several resource instances is connected to the agent model done by bringing agent instances in relation to world and resources. After that, the actual simulation itself can be started.

The definition of a simulated environment in SeSAm consists of a particular world class and any number of agent and resource classes. The world as well as the agents are active entities. That means that also the dynamics of the world are described using activity graphs. In addition to that, a world may possess an map on that all other entities may be positioned or may position themselves.

The spacial representation framework that provides the structures for the map is based on a plugin concept. The default plugin associates a 2-dimensional continuous map with a world and provides relevant data structures for spacial information to other entities. The plugin also comes with specific primitive functions, e.g. for movement or perception. Based on that plugin concept different kinds of environmental representations can be integrated. Plugins have been developed for 3-dimensional maps as well as for vector data from Geographic Information Systems.

Thus, the infrastructure provided by SeSAm does not restrict the simulated environment. The framework for spacial representation may be exchanged to one that is appropriate for modelling the environment of the multi-agent system. The language for the environmental model is as powerful as the one for representing the agents enabling the modeler to design and implement an appropriate simulated environment for his simulated multi-agent system.

6 Application Examples

In this section examples of models from different application domains developed using SeSAm are presented. They show how different simulated environment may play different roles in the overall simulation model.

6.1 Biological Simulation

The first application example is a biological simulation: A simulation model of honey bees fostering their brood. The basic aim was the comparison of different task selection strategies. The brood model seems to be very apt for this aim as a restricted set of tasks has to be tackled and the success of a strategy is easily measured by the state and number of surviving brood. Although the simulated environment is based on a discrete map, the environmental model is very rich. It has not only to reproduce the physical dynamics of heat transfer in a sufficiently valid way for providing the basis for valid model of the heating task, it also has to contain other agents, namely the brood that has to be feeded and may suffer from bad provisioning and temperature.

In order to guarantee the survival of a bee hive, bees need to make sure that enough new bees are born to replace the worker bees that died by age or while carrying out some task. The honey bee brood nest lies in the center of the bee hive. It consists of a certain number of cells containing bee larvae. The bee queen moves around the brood nest and lays eggs into empty cells. During the first stage of growth the brood needs to be fed constantly. This is achieved by working bees bringing food to the individual cells. After this first stage the larvae containing cells are capped by the worker bees. It is critically important for their development that these capped larvae can develop at a constant temperature of about 35 degrees. To achieve this, the worker bees crawl into empty cells all over the brood nest and start to heat the cells by moving their flying muscles without actually fanning. The heat created at different points of the brood nest then disperses through the wax resulting in a comfortably warm brood area.

The SeSAm simulation model for reproducing this system consists of three important components. The simulation of the brood nest, the simulated brood agents, and the behavioral simulation of the worker bee agents fostering the brood. The actual multi-agent system for the research question are the working bees, the rest of the model can be identified as the simulated environment for it:

The real brood nest lies in the middle of the bee hive and is shaped like a lump. To simulate this nest a spacially explicit environmental model had to be used. As the brood nest consists of cells and bees are moving between cells a discrete spatial representation was decided for with bees moving from cell to cell. Here, a discrete grid could be used without loosing validity. Based on the comb structure the original 3D brood nest could be abstracted to a 2D spatial representation. Figure 5 shows a small part of the animation for the honey bee brood nest simulation.

In the context of temperature regulation the simulated environment plays an especially important role. In order to maintain an evenly temperatured brood

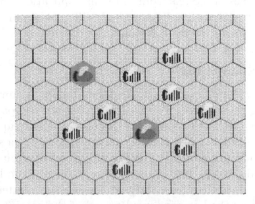

Fig. 5. Small section of the honey bee brood nest model animation

nest the bees heat single cells. This punctual heat is dispersed between the cells in a way determined by the properties of the wax and the way the brood nest is constructed. Only a realistic, valid environmental model of temperature dispersal in the honey bee brood nest will allow to reproduce realistic bee agent behavior. Thus, it is important to find the optimal level of detail for the environmental simulation. Based on particular measurements of the temperature dispersal in real bee comb with and without larvae, a physically correct model was developed and used in the simulated environment. It was also useful for determining parameters of the agent behavior, like maximum heat produced by a bee.

This example shows that the validity of the overall multi-agent simulation model completely depended on the validity of the environmental model which had to be defined and validated first.

6.2   Hospital Logistics Simulation

The second example shows that an equally detailed simulated environment does not need a map, but can also be developed without using explicit spacial representations:

The organization of patient's treatment is one of the most important management jobs in hospitals daily life. Patient schedules have effects on the load of resources (staff, devices) and the average patient stay time. They are therefore a very promising object for optimization. Different management actions can be taken, like the purchasing of additional devices, the reorganization of shifts or the introduction of a new scheduling strategy. In most cases reliable predictions about the effects of such strategies on the relevant output parameters cannot be done. Multi-agent simulation can help to get a better understanding about the effects and support decisions [17].

Basically a multi-agent simulation of this system can be realized in a non-spatial environment – like done in queueing network simulations. Patient agents follow a treatment process that is determined based on their disease. Functional units for diagnosis and treatment are also represented as agents and responsible for the execution of the medical actions.

In figure 6 an example simulation is shown. The picture depicts the situation of a clinic for radiation therapy. The spacial representation is just for visualization purposes and has no effect in the model. There are four units for radiation therapy as well as two units for initial examinations. These units provide a x-ray-device and a radiation simulator. When patients arrive at the hospital one of three possible treatment processes is randomly chosen and necessary tasks are scheduled. After scheduling the tasks have to be executed at the functional units. However, emergency events, breakdowns of devices and uncertainties in the duration of treatments might cause delays.

The basic functionality of the simulated environment is to represent and handle the process of new patients arrivals. Also "catastrophic" events like breakdowns are triggered by the simulated environment.

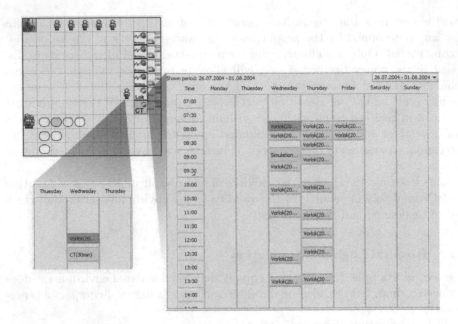

Fig. 6. SeSAm simulation of a radiation therapy clinic

Spatial information is negligible in this scenario because transfer and movement times are abstracted away, only waiting and actual treatment times are recorded. In a more detailed model also those spatial aspects can be integrated.

6.3   Microscopic Traffic Simulation

In contrast to the examples presented above, a sophisticated spatial representation is necessary for microscopic models of actual driving examining to the origin of traffic jams. As mentioned above, for such models real word data containing information about the road map should be used.

Based on the SeSAm-GIS connection, an agent-based traffic model was implemented that uses the Nagel-Schreckenberg model of car following behavior for simulating actual driving in a small road network [16].

The original Nagel-Schreckenberg model [18] is a 1-dimensional Cellular Automaton, where a road was cut down to discrete cells. It was also extended to road networks. The state of a cell represents the speed of the vehicle on that cell. One time step in the simulation corresponds to one second, a cell of the road network to 7,5m. Every vehicle-driver on the road has a maximum speed. Four rules determine the behavior of the vehicles. Three of them control acceleration and deceleration. The driver accelerates if there is enough space in front of the vehicle to speed up, decelerates if there is not enough distance. There is a certain probability for additionally decreasing the speed. The forth rule controls the actual movement. Thus, the speed is always calculated based on the current speed and the distance to the preceding vehicle. This simple traffic flow model is

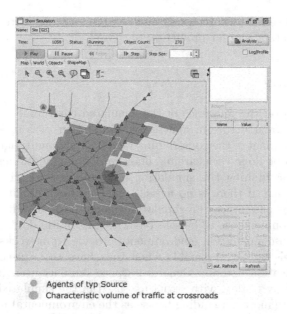

● Agents of typ Source
◐ Characteristic volume of traffic at crossroads

Fig. 7. Simulation of a traffic scenario based on real world road network data

able to reproduce real-world traffic phenomena like stop and go traffic or traffic jams without particular reasons like accidents or road works.

This basic model was extended to a multi-agent simulation model, where vehicles corresponded to simulated agents. Road network data was imported from a real world small city map. The behavior was basically the same as in the original model, except that there are some additional rules for finding the shortest path and deceleration in front of corners. Vehicle drivers have a punctual shape and are capable of moving just on roads. The roads are represented as line-shaped resources with attributes like maximum allowed velocity. The agents are generated at several source positions and leave the road network at designated goal positions. At crossings drivers always change the direction towards their individually assigned goal. Figure 7 shows a screenshot from an example simulation run.

The simulated environment consists here of the road network – the representation of inhabited areas is just for visualization purposes – that limits the movement of the agents. The dynamics of the simulated environment are associated with the generation of new agents at the source positions and the deletion at their goal. One may also imagine that dynamics may affect the structure and parameters of the road network, like accidents blocking roads or temporary speed limits.

Directly using vector data from GIS for representing the road network was advantages as real world could be imported and used in the simulation directly without any discretization step. The reality can be depicted in much more detail and simulation needs less abstraction and can therefore be more exact. That is an important prerequisite for prediction purposes.

7   Conclusion

In this contribution the relevance of the simulated environment in addition to the simulation infrastructure in multi-agent simulations was tackled. Since the simulated environment is the constraining factor for the multi-agent simulation, its design has to be done very careful. The simulation environment, namely the infrastructure for running the simulation, determines the structures that are possible at all – e.g. if there is no message passing functionality provided, the usage of message passing in the simulation model is hindered. Thus, also the simulation environment has to be selected with this in mind.

Special purpose simulation environments provide frameworks for rich environmental models but are inflexible when they have to be used beyond their envisioned application domain. General purpose simulation environments offer a more flexible way to deal with structures used in the simulated environment. However, they are more demanding to use as the environmental model is almost completely part of the simulation model that has to be developed and implemented by the modeler. To support the modeler, such tools should be open for extensions concerning environmental modelling. A possibility for this could be to provide plugins that define basic rules for the required scenario, thus making the generic tool "specialize-able".

References

1. Klügl, F., Oechslein, C., Puppe, F., Dornhaus, A.: Multi-agent modelling in comparison to standard modelling. Simulation News Europe **40** (2004) 3–9
2. Kuljis, J.: User interfaces and discrete event simulation models. Simulation Practice and Theory **1** (1994) 207–221
3. Klügl, F.: Multi-Agent Simulation – Concept, Tools, Application (in German). Addison Wesley, Munich (2001)
4. Uhrmacher, A.M.: Object-oriented and agent-oriented simulation: Implications for social science application. In Troitzsch, K.G., Mueller, U., Gilbert, G.N., Doran, J.E., eds.: Social Science Microsimulation. Springer (1996) 432–447
5. Rao, A.S.: Agentspeak(l): (bdi) agents speak out in a logical computable language. In de Velde, W.V., Perram, J., eds.: Seventh European Workshop on Modelling Autonomous Agents in a Multi-Agent World, Eindhoven, The Netherlands. Number 1038 in LNAI, Springer (1996) 42–55
6. Firby, J.: Adaptive Execution in Complex, Dynamic Domains. PhD thesis, Yale (1989)
7. Georgeff, M.P., Ingrand, F.F.: Decision making in an embedded reasoning system. In: Proc. of the IJCAI'89. (1989) 972–978
8. Klügl, F., Triebig, C., Dornhaus, A.: Studying task allocation mechanisms of social insects for engineering multi-agent systems. In Anderson, C., Balch, T., eds.: Mechanisms and Algorithms of Social Insects, Atlanta, 2003. (2003)

9. Russell, S., Norvig, P.: Artificial Intelligence - A Modern Approach. Prentice Hall (1995)
10. Milgram, S.: The small world problem. Psychology Today **60** (1967) 729–755
11. MASON: Mason. (http://cs.gmu.edu/ eclab/projects/mason/) (last visited 30.11.2004).
12. Parker, M.: What is ascape and why should you care? Journal of Artificial Societies and Social Simulation **4** (2001)
13. von Neumann, J.: The Theory of Self-reproducing Automata. Univ. of Illinois Press, Urbana, Illinois (1966)
14. Epstein, J.M., Axtrell, R.: Growing Artificial Societies. Social Science from the Bottom Up. MIT Press, Cambridge, MA (1996)
15. Bill, R.: Grundlagen der Geo-Informationssysteme Band 1 Hardware, Software und Daten. Wichmann (1999)
16. Schüle, M., Herrler, R., Klügl, F.: Coupling gis and multi-agent simulation – towards infrastructure for realistic simulation. In Lindemann, G., Denzinger, J., Timm, I.J., eds.: Multiagent System Technologies, Proceedings of the Second German Conference MATES 2004. Number 3187 in LNAI, Springer (2004) 228–242
17. Paulussen, T.O., Jennings, N.R., Decker, K.S., Heinzl:, A.: Distributed patient scheduling in hospitals. In Kohn, A., Gottlob, G., eds.: Proceedings of the Eighteenth International Joint Conference on Artificial Intelligence, Acapulco, Mexico. (2003)
18. Nagel, K., Rasmussen, S.: Traffic at the edge of chaos. In Brooks, R.A., Maes, P., eds.: Artificial Life IV, MIT-Press (1994) 222–235

Modelling Environments for Distributed Simulation

Michael Lees[1], Brian Logan[1], Rob Minson[2], Ton Oguara[2],
and Georgios Theodoropoulos[2]

[1] School of Computer Science and IT, University of Nottingham, UK
{mhl, bsl}@cs.nott.ac.uk
[2] School of Computer Science, University of Birmingham, UK
{txo, rzm, gkt}@cs.bham.ac.uk

Abstract. Decentralised, event-driven distributed simulation is particularly suitable for modelling systems with inherent asynchronous parallelism, such as agent-based systems. However the efficient simulation of multi-agent systems presents particular challenges which are not addressed by standard parallel discrete event simulation (PDES) models and techniques. PDES approaches based on the logical process paradigm assume a fixed decomposition into processes, each of which maintains its own portion of the state of the simulation. The interaction between the processes is fixed in advance and does not change during the simulation. In contrast, simulations of MAS typically have a large *shared* state, the agents' environment, which is only loosely associated with any particular process. In this paper, we present a model of the shared state of a distributed MAS simulation of situated agents. We consider the problems of efficient sensing, parallel actions and action conflicts, and present preliminary work on an approach to the simulation of the environment which addresses these issues.

1   Introduction

Simulation has traditionally played an important role in multi-agent system (MAS) research and development. It allows a degree of control over experimental conditions and facilitates the replication of results in a way that is difficult or impossible with a prototype or fielded system, freeing the agent designer or researcher to focus on key aspects of a system. As researchers have attempted to simulate larger and more complex MAS, distributed approaches to simulation have become more attractive [1, 2, 3]. Such approaches simplify the integration of heterogeneous agent simulators and exploit the natural parallelism of a MAS, allowing simulation components to be distributed so as to make best use of the available computational resources.

However the efficient simulation of multi-agent systems presents particular challenges which are not addressed by standard parallel discrete event simulation (PDES) models and techniques [4, 5]. While the modelling and simulation of agents, at least at a coarse grain, is relatively straightforward, it is harder to apply conventional PDES approaches to the simulation of the agents' environment. Parallel discrete event simulation approaches based on the logical process paradigm assume a fixed decomposition into processes, each of which maintains its own portion of the state of the simulation. The interaction between the processes is fixed in advance and does not change during

D. Weyns et al. (Eds.): E4MAS 2004, LNAI 3374, pp. 150–167, 2005.
© Springer-Verlag Berlin Heidelberg 2005

the simulation. In contrast, simulations of MAS typically have a large *shared* state, the agents' environment, which is only loosely associated with any particular process. At different times, different agents can access and update different parts of the shared state. The efficient simulation of the environment of a multi-agent system is therefore a key problem (perhaps even *the* key problem) in the distributed simulation of MAS.

In this paper, we present a model of the shared state of a distributed MAS simulation. We consider the problems of efficient sensing, parallel actions and action conflicts, and present preliminary work on an approach to the simulation of the environment which addresses these issues. The remainder of the paper is organised as follows. In section 2, we briefly outline a model of a MAS as a set of logical processes and explain why MAS simulations naturally result in a large shared state. In section 3 we present a model of the shared state as a global tuple space and describe how the agents' sensing and actions in the environment can be modelled as operations on the tuple space. In section 4 we describe an approach to the efficient distribution of the shared state and briefly describe a prototype implementation of this approach based on Communication Logical Processes. In section 5 we discuss related work and in section 6 we conclude with some remarks on the relationship between our approach and the requirements of distributed environments for MAS in general.

2   Modelling Multi-agent Systems

In this section, we outline our model of the agents and their environment.

We are primarily concerned with the simulation of *situated agents* [6], e.g., simulations of agents such as robots situated in a physical environment, or characters in a computer game or interactive entertainment situated in a virtual environment. The systems of interest typically involve large numbers (thousands or tens of thousands) of agents in complex environments, e.g., individual-based ecological modelling or simulations of massively multi-player online games, and the "agents" that we wish to simulate may be models of agents (e.g., DEVS models [7]), or they may be actual implemented agents in a simulated environment, or a mixture of the two. We therefore view the agents as 'black boxes' and focus on the interaction of the agents through the medium of their shared environment.

We adopt a standard parallel discrete event approach with optimistic synchronisation [4, 5]. Decentralised, event-driven distributed simulation is particularly suitable for modelling systems with inherent asynchronous parallelism, such as agent-based systems. This approach seeks to divide the simulation model into a network of concurrent *Logical Processes* (LPs), each maintaining and processing a disjoint portion of the state space of the system. The LPs run asynchronously and each has its own local notion of time within the simulation, referred to as its *Local Virtual Time* (LVT). State changes are modelled as timestamped events. From an LP's point of view, two types of events are distinguished: internal events which have a causal impact only on the state variables of the LP, and external events which may also have an impact on the states of other LPs. External events are typically modelled as timestamped messages exchanged between the LPs involved. In distributing the simulation across multiple processes, a key problem is ensuring that there are no causality violations. An LP is said to adhere to the *local causality constraint* (LCC) if it processes all events in nondecreasing time stamp order. If a message arrives in an LP's past (as determined by its LVT) it must rollback its state to the timestamp of the straggler event, and resume processing from that point. It must also cancel any messages it sent with timestamps greater than that of the straggler event, which may in turn initiate rollbacks on other LPs.

We model agents and their environment as Logical Processes. Each agent in the system is modelled as a single *Agent Logical Process* (ALP) and objects and processes within the agents' environment are modelled as one or more *Environment Logical Processes* (ELP)[1]. ALPs and ELPs are typically wrappers around existing simulation components. They map to and from the sensor and action interfaces of the agent and environment models to a common representation of the environment expressed in terms of objects and attributes, and also provide support for rollback processing.

In general, the agents' environment can be decomposed into ELPs in a number of different ways. For example, the blocks in a simple 'blocks world' environment could each be modelled as a separate ELP, as could the physics of stacking blocks etc. Alternatively, all the blocks could form part of a single 'blocks system' ELP. The appropriate 'grain size' of the simulation will depend both on the application and on practical considerations, such as the availability of existing simulation code. While there are obvious advantages in reusing part or all of an existing simulation, this can result in an inappropriate grain size which makes it difficult to parallelise the model. For example, modelling the environment as a single logical process can create a bottleneck in the simulation which degrades its performance.[2] The approach presented below is neutral with respect to the decomposition of the environment into processes.

Each ALP and ELP has both public data and private data. Private data is data which is not accessible to other LPs in the simulation, e.g., an agent's model of the environment, its current goals, plans etc. Public data is data which can, in principle, be accessed or updated by other LPs in the simulation, e.g., the colour, size, shape, position etc. of an object or agent. Public data is held in globally accessible locations or *state variables*, while private data is local to a particular LP. ALPs and ELPs interact via events, modelled as timestamped messages. The purpose of this interaction is to exchange information regarding the values of those shared state variables which define the agent's manifest environment and the interfaces between the ELPs.[3]

There are several ways in which this interaction could be managed. One approach would be to adopt a subscription-based approach to sensing, where the agent, via its sensors, implicitly indicates the kind of data it is interested in, and data which matches the subscription is sent to the agent whenever the environment changes. However there are a number of problems with this approach. If the agent senses less frequently than the environment changes, this needlessly propagates information to the agent. Moreover,

---

[1] For simplicity, we do not consider fine-grained modelling of processes within an agent, i.e., distributing the agent model across multiple LPs.

[2] Existing attempts to build distributed simulations of agent based systems have often adopted such a centralised approach in which the agents' environment forms part of a central time-driven simulation engine [8, 9, 1].

[3] In what follows we shall use the generic term 'LP' to refer to both ALPs and ELPs, since, unless otherwise noted, their behaviour is very similar.

with optimistic synchronisation, environmental updates propagated to the agent may be in its past or future. To receive only data with the "correct" timestamp, the agent's subscription must include the agent's LVT and the subscription must be continuously updated as the agent advances in time or rolls back. We therefore adopt a query based approach to sensing, and use other techniques (see below) to reduce the cost of querying the shared state.

In a conventional decentralised event-driven distributed simulation each LP maintains its own portion of the simulation state and LPs interact with each other in a small number of well defined ways. Even if the interactions are stochastic, the type of interaction and its possible outcomes are known in advance. The topology of the simulation is determined by the topology of the simulated system and its decomposition into LPs, and is largely static.

In contrast, the interaction of agents in a multi-agent system is often hard to predict in advance. Different kinds of agent have differing degrees of access to different parts of the environment at different times. The degree of access is dependent on the range of the agent's sensors (read access) and the actions it can perform (write access). Moreover, in many cases, an agent can effectively change the topology of the environment, for example, by moving from one part of the environment to another.[4] For example, if an agent is "mobile", then what it can sense at different times is a function of the actions it performed in the past which is in turn a function of what it sensed in the past. As a result, it is difficult to predict which state variables it can or will access without running the simulation.

It is therefore difficult to determine an appropriate topology for a MAS simulation *a priori*. As a result, MAS simulations typically require a (very) large set of shared variables which could, in principle, be accessed or updated by the agents (if they were in the right position at the right time etc.).

3   Modelling the Shared State

We model the state of the simulation in terms of objects and attributes. We assume each object in the simulation has a type, and each object type is associated with a number of attributes. For example, a simple Tileworld [10] simulation might contain object types such as *tile* and *hole* and attributes *x-position*, *y-position* etc. The simulation consists of a variable number of objects whose state is defined by the value of their attributes. Events generated by LPs read and write attribute values. Each attribute has a timestamp which indicates the time at which the attribute acquired the value. The values of attributes can be set independently of each other and at different times, i.e., updates to the environment do not have to specify values for all the attributes of an object. The global state of the simulation is split into the shared state: i.e., those attributes which are accessible to more than one LP, and the local state of each LP (which for ease of exposition we assume to be also modelled in terms of objects and attributes).

---

[4] It may be the case that, at any particular time, there are parts of the environment that are not accessible to any agent. However, if there is no sequence of actions that any agent can perform from the initial state which makes some data accessible, then this data does not form part of the shared state as defined here.

We represent the simulation state as a set of tuple spaces. All LPs can access a global tuple space containing the shared state of the simulation. The global tuple space consists of a set of 6-tuples:

$$< object\text{-}type, object\text{-}id, attribute\text{-}type, attribute\text{-}id, value, timestamp > .$$

For example, the fact that a tile in the Tileworld has an x-position of 5 at time 25 might be represented

$$< tile, tile101, x\text{-}position, 101001, 5, 25 > .$$

As the simulation progresses, new tuples are added to the shared state, either because a new object (and its corresponding attributes and values) has been created, or because one of the LPs comprising the simulation has changed the value of an attribute of an object. Note that the shared state may contain different values for the same attribute so long as these have different timestamps. In addition, each LP has its own private tuple space containing the private state of the LP.

LPs can perform a number of operations on the global tuple space:

request the value(s) of one or more attributes with a given timestamp;
add the value(s) of one or more attributes at a given timestamp; and
remove one or more attributes from a given timestamp.

add and *remove* operations are non-blocking. A *request* blocks until the requested tuples are returned. Operations can also give rise to 'exceptions' which indicate that it was impossible to complete the requested operation on the shared state. All operations occur asynchronously and at the specified simulation time. However problems can arise when an operation is performed in real time after another operation on the same attribute which has a later timestamp, resulting in further processing of the global tuple space and the private tuple space of one or more LPs. Such causality violations are a standard problem with optimistic synchronisation approaches and our solution is discussed in more detail below. The operations are atomic and may be arbitrarily interleaved. As a convenience, the operations accept multiple arguments, but the processing of arguments may be interleaved with other operations. As we will show, so long as the processing of each argument is atomic, correct behaviour is guaranteed.

In the remainder of this section, we consider each operation in turn and briefly describe their arguments, return values, exceptions and any side-effects on the shared state and the state of other LPs.

3.1   Requests

For an LP to sense the world it firstly constructs a *state query*. The state query consists of a query id and a set of query tuples. A query tuple is either a range query (query by attribute value) or an id query (query by attribute id).

A *range query* is a list of 4-tuples of the form:

$$< object\text{-}type, attribute\text{-}type, value\text{-}range, timestamp > .$$

The *value-range* indicates the attribute values which are of interest (i.e., that match the query). Range queries allow sensing of the environment. For example, to find the x-positions of all tiles within 5 squares of an agent at time 50, we could use the range query

$$< \text{\textit{tile}, x-position, } a_x - 5 \leq x \leq a_x + 5, 50 >,$$

where a_x is the *x-position* of the agent at time 50.

An id query is a list of 2-tuples of the form:

$$< \text{\textit{attribute-id, timestamp}} > .$$

Id queries allow query by reference, for example it allows an LP to obtain the current value of one of its own public attributes or the current value of an attribute returned by a range query. They are provided as an optimisation for those cases where the attribute in question is guaranteed to persist until after the timestamp of the query.

Requests can give rise to a (possibly empty) set of tuples (in the case of range queries), or, in the case of an attribute query, a single tuple or a "no such attribute" exception. The tuple(s) contain the value(s) of the requested state variable(s) which were valid at the time denoted by the request timestamp. If there is no tuple with a timestamp equal to that of the request, for example, if the request timestamp lies between the timestamps of two tuples or the query timestamp is greater than the timestamp of any matching tuple, the request returns the tuple with the greatest timestamp prior to the timestamp of the request. For example, if agent 1 has an *x-position* of 10 at time 50, evaluating the range query above against the tuples

$$< \text{\textit{tile}, tile101, x-position, 101001, 6, 40} >$$
$$< \text{\textit{tile}, tile101, x-position, 101001, 7, 52} >$$

would return the tuple

$$< \text{\textit{tile}, tile101, x-position, 101001, 6, 40} > .$$

3.2   Add

When an LP creates a new object in the simulation or updates an attribute of an existing object, it adds a new tuple to the shared state with the new value and timestamp, indicating the simulation time at which the object was created or the attribute acquired the specified value. Add operations are non blocking and do not return a result. However they may give rise to an exception if objects of the specified *object-type* can't have attributes of the specified *attribute-type*. For simplicity, we assume that objects are only ever created or deleted in their entirety, i.e., we cannot create an object without specifying all values for all its attributes. Adding the first attribute to an object instance implicitly creates the object in the shared state.

Assuming agents execute a sense, think, act cycle, an update will occur after the range query *request*(s) generated by sensing. The agent (or ELP) will therefore have a list of the sensed attributes and their ids, which can be used to construct the new tuple. We assume that there is a delay between an agent's sensing and action. In general, it is impossible for an LP to know that the state of the environment that led to an *add* operation still holds when the operation is performed. We therefore allow *add* operations to be guarded. A *guard* is a predicate on the shared state in the form of a list of tuples which must be true (i.e., the attributes must have the specified values at the timestamp of the *add*) for the operation to be performed. A guard is effectively the precondition for the successful execution of an action in the environment. If the guard evaluates to false, the *add* operation is not performed (with the exception that we ignore violations of the precondition due to add operations performed by the same agent at the same timestamp). For example, to prevent two (or more) agents pushing the same tile at the same time in Tileworld, we can require that the tile is still where the agent sensed it (e.g., directly in front of the agent) at the time of a push action before allowing the agent to update the position of the tile.

We distinguish different categories of attributes depending on the types of updates they admit. *Static attributes* are set once, e.g., when an object is created, and can't be changed during the simulation. Attributes which can be updated at most once at a given timestamp are termed *mutually exclusive attributes*. For example, in Tileworld, we may wish to prohibit two agents picking up a tile at the same time. *Cumulative attributes* can be updated multiple times by different LPs at the same timestamp. For example, in the Tileworld, several agents may be able to drop a tile into a hole at the "same" time, with each operation decreasing the depth of the hole by one. All updates of static attributes are ignored. If two or more LPs attempt to perform conflicting updates, i.e., attempt to specify different values for a mutually exclusive attribute at a given timestamp, we apply the update of the LP with the highest rank. The *rank* of an LP determines it's priority when attribute updates conflict. Ranks may reflect some property of the LP which is relevant to the simulation, but in general are simply a way of ensuring repeatability. If both LPs have the same rank then we choose an update arbitrarily (saving the random seed to preserve repeatability). If the attribute has already been updated at this timestamp by an LP with lower rank, this value is over-written and any LPs which read the previous value are rolled back (see below).

3.3   Remove

Removing an attribute of an object in effect deletes the attribute from the specified time forward. Subsequent request and add operations on the attribute with timestamps prior to the specified timestamp proceed as normal. Range queries with timestamps later than the specified timestamp give rise an empty list of result tuples. Attempting to add a new attribute with a timestamp greater than the specified timestamp has no effect (i.e., it is not possible to recreate an object id after it has been removed from the simulation). As with creation, we assume that objects are only ever deleted in their entirety, with all attributes being deleted at the same timestamp.

3.4   Rollbacks

Some sequences of operations by the LPs give rise to further processing of the shared state and the private state of one or more LPs.

An add or remove operation with timestamp t which is processed in real time after a request with timestamp t', where $t' > t$ invalidates the request operation, and triggers a rollback on all LPs which read the previous (interpolated) value of the attribute. A *rollback* indicates that the set of tuples returned in response to the request was incorrect, and that the LP should rollback its processing to the timestamp of the request and restart. Rolling back an LP removes all tuples from the LP's private tuple space which have a timestamp $> t'$ and resets the LP's LVT to t'. The effect is as if the LP had just returned from the original request operation (at timestamp t'), but this time with the 'correct' value of the attribute. For example, if agent 2 moves tile101 at time 47 so that it's *x-position* is now 5 but the tuple recording the update is not added to the global tuple space until after the range query by agent 1 in section 3.1 has been performed, then agent 1 must be rolled back to time 50 and restarted, returning from the *request* with the tuple

$$< tile, \text{tile}101, x\text{-}position, 101001, 5, 47 > .$$

A subsequent add operation with timestamp t'', where $t'' < t < t'$ can of course cause further rollbacks on the LP. Rolling back an LP also cancels any add operations on the shared state performed by the LP which have a timestamp $> t'$. This may in turn invalidate requests made by other LPs, requiring them to rollback too.

Note that the presence of rollback obviates the need for coarse-grain atomic operations, i.e., each tuple argument to an add operation can be processed independently of any others and may be arbitrarily interleaved with other operations such as request operations.[5] It is therefore possible for an LP to "see" an inconsistent version of the shared state or for the guard conditions of an add operation to evaluate to true for some orderings of operations on the shared state and false for others. When the updates are finally made, the inconsistency will be detected and any affected LPs rolled back.

4   Distributing the Shared State

A naive implementation of the shared state, e.g., in which the shared state is maintained by a single process, is a potential bottleneck in a MAS simulation. In this section we present an approach to the efficient distribution of the shared state.

The shared state of the simulation is stored in *state variables*. Each state variable corresponds to a set of tuples, namely those that have the same *object-type*, *object-id*, *attribute-type* and *attribute-id*.[6] We assume that each LP is capable of generating and responding to a finite number of event types, and a specification of the possible input and output event types forms the interface between the LPs. Different types of events will typically have different effects on the shared state, and, in general, events of a given type will affect only certain types of state variables (all other things being equal). For example, in [11], we showed that for a simple predator and prey simulation, the probability of a given state variable being accessed by more than 3 agents was fairly small, and agents tend to access the same state over time.

Another way of expressing this is to say that different types of event have different *spheres of influence* within the shared state. 'Sphere' is used here metaphorically, to indicate those parts of the shared state immediately affected by an instance of an event of a particular type with a given timestamp. More precisely, we define the 'sphere of influence' of an event as the set of state variables read or updated as a consequence of the event.

---

[5] While this isn't a correctness issue, it may be an efficiency issue.

[6] In practice, not all tuples need to be stored in state variables, e.g., if a tuple has a timestamp lower the LVT of any LP it is inaccessible within the simulation and can be garbage collected.

We can use the spheres of influence of the events generated by each LP to derive an idealised decomposition of the shared state into logical processes (see [11] for details). We define the sphere of influence of an LP p_i over the time interval $[t_1, t_2]$, $s(p_i)$, as the union of the spheres of influence of the events generated by the LP over the interval. Intersecting the spheres of influence for each event generated by the LP gives a partial order over sets of state variables for the LP over the interval $[t_1, t_2]$, in which those sets of variables which have been accessed by the largest number of events come first, followed by those less frequently accessed, and so on. The rank of a variable v_j for LP p_i over the interval $[t_1, t_2]$, $r(v_j, p_i)$ is the number of events in whose sphere of influence v_j lies.

Intersecting the spheres of influence for each LP gives a partial order over sets of state variables, the least elements of which are those sets of state variables which have been accessed by the largest groups of LPs over the interval $[t_1, t_2]$. This partial order can be seen as a measure of the difficulty of associating variables with a particular ALP or ELP: the state variables which are members of the sets which are first in the order are accessed by the largest number of ALPs and/or ELPs, whereas those sets of state variables which come last are accessed by only a single LP. (Assuming that all variables have the same rank.)

For example, suppose there are three ALPs, a_1, a_2 and a_3, and five variables, $v_1, \ldots, v_5$. The first ALP generates events which read and update only the variables v_1 and v_2; its sphere of influence therefore is $\{v_1, v_2\}$. Similarly, let the sphere of influence of a_2 be $\{v_2, v_3\}$ and the sphere of influence of a_3 be $\{v_4, v_5\}$. The variable v_2 is accessed by two agents, hence $\{v_2\}$ is the least in the ordering, followed by $\{v_1\}$, $\{v_3\}$ and $\{v_4, v_5\}$.

To minimise the computational and communication loads, any approach to the decomposition of the shared state into logical processes should, insofar as is possible, reflect this ordering and grouping of variables. In the example above, we would expect the state to be partitioned into $\{v_1\}$, $\{v_3\}$, $\{v_4, v_5\}$ and $\{v_2\}$. $\{v_1\}$, $\{v_3\}$ and $\{v_4, v_5\}$ can be located close (in a computational sense) to the ALPs in whose sphere of influence the variables lie, i.e., a_1, a_2 and a_3 respectively. $\{v_2\}$ is shared by a_1 and a_2 and should be allocated to an LP which is equidistant (in a computational sense) from a_1 and a_2. However, any implementation can only approximate this idealised decomposition, since calculating it requires information about the global environment, and obtaining this information in a distributed environment is costly. Moreover, this ordering will change with time, as the state of the environment and the relative number of events of each type produced by the LPs changes.

In the remainder of this section, we describe a prototype implementation of these ideas which distributes the state according to the spheres of influence of the LPs in the simulation. The partitioning of the shared state is performed dynamically, in response to the events generated by the ALPs and ELPs during the simulation.

4.1   CLPs

The decomposition of the state is achieved by means of an additional set of Logical Processes, namely *Communication Logical Processes* (CLPs). The CLPs form a complete binary tree with the ALPs and ELPs as the leaves and each CLP maintains a portion of the state which is associated with the ALPs/ELPs which are below it in the tree (see Figure 1).

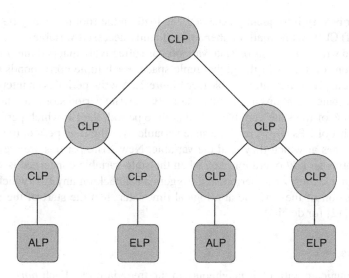

Fig. 1. The tree of CLPs

At any given point in the simulation, each CLP maintains a disjoint subset of the state variables and the interaction of ALPs and ELPs is via the variables maintained by the CLPs. In general, different CLPs will maintain different numbers of state variables. The aim is to minimise both computational and communication loads. Frequently accessed data should therefore be maintained by CLPs close to the ALPs which access it. The tree of CLPs provides a large number of local caches for data accessed by a single agent small groups of agents. Less frequently accessed data can be stored further away. In the limit, the root node may hold, e.g., 90% of the shared state (swapped out) — so long as

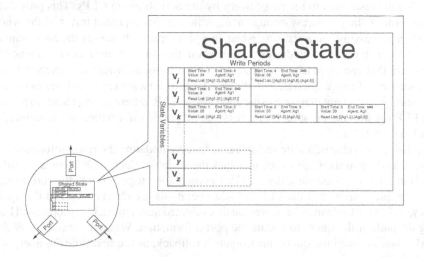

Fig. 2. The structure of a CLP

this is never or very infrequently accessed, the load on the root node may be similar to that on (leaf) CLPs with small numbers of frequently accessed variables.

Read and write operations on state variables are effectively mapped into *request* and *add* operations on tuples in the global tuple space. Each tuple corresponds to a *write period* of the appropriate state variable (see Figure 2). A write period is an interval during which an attribute maintains a particular value. Each write period stores its start and end time, the value of the state variable over that time period, the LP which performed the write and a list of LPs which read the state variable over the time period, together with the logical times at which they read the variable. New write periods are created when an LP performs an *add* operation, i.e., when the state variable concerned is written to. This splits an existing write period, and triggers a rollback on any LPs which read the previous version of the variable at a logical time later than the start of the new write period (see [12] for details).

4.2   Ports

CLPs communicate with their neighbours in the tree via ports. Each *port* holds information about the ranges of attribute values maintained by CLPs beyond the port in the form of 4-tuples:

$$< object\text{-}type, \ attribute\text{-}type, \ value\text{-}range \ timestamp\text{-}range > .$$

For example, in a Tileworld simulation, a port tagged with *object-type tile, attribute-type x-position value-range* 10–20 and *timestamp-range* 50–100 would indicate that state variables holding x positions of tiles with values in the range 10 to 20 and timestamps between 50 and 100 are held in CLPs beyond this port. Initially, the *value-range* for each object and attribute type at each port is "all values" for all timestamp ranges. As range queries are processed (initially by forwarding the query to all CLPs in the tree), a CLP acquires information about the kinds of attributes that lie beyond each port by analysing the responses to the range query by the neighbouring CLPs. This provides a simple form of 'lazy' interest management, which avoids repeated traversal the whole tree when processing *requests*, e.g., when an agent repeatedly senses the environment. In addition, each port also holds information about the attribute instances maintained by other CLPs that can be reached via the port. This routing information is cached during the processing of range queries, and allows a CLP to forward reads and writes of state variables that it does not maintain to the appropriate CLP. Where the port leads to an ALP or an ELP, the port information is empty (since all public information in the simulation is held in the CLPs).

Updating the value of a state variable may involve updating the range information of the ports leading to the CLP which manages the variable. Each CLP keeps a record of all queries it has received since the last GVT computation together with the port through which the query arrived at the CLP. All add operations are checked against this query history, and, if the tuple matches a previously evaluated query, the add is propagated back along the path of the query to update the port information. When the traversal reaches the ALP that initiated the query this triggers a rollback, as the first time the query was evaluated, it returned too few tuples.[7] Conversely, if a tuple matches no query in the query record, then no ALP has ever queried this attribute value at this timestamp, and there is no need to propagate the tuple beyond the current CLP.

4.3   Load Balancing

As well as storing state variables and enabling communication via ports, the CLPs also facilitate load balancing. As the total number and distribution of instances of each event type generated by an ALP/ELP varies, so the partial order over the spheres of influence changes, and the contents of the CLPs must change accordingly to reflect the ALPs/ELPs' current behaviour and keep the computational and communication loads balanced. This may be achieved in two ways, namely by changing the position of the ALPs/ELPs, and by moving the state variables from one CLP to another. In general, it is easier to migrate the shared state than the agents, and our strategy is to bring the environment close to the agents (in a computational sense).

To achieve this we have developed a load balancing scheme in which the cost of accessing state variables maintained at each CLP is used in making load management decisions. We define the cost of accessing a state variable v_j by an ALP/ELP p_i as the number of times v_j was accessed by p_i times the number of CLPs that must be traversed to reach v_j during the time interval $[t_1, t_2]$. The access cost for a CLP is therefore:

$$\sum_j \sum_i (r(v_j, p_i) \times l(v_j, p_i))$$

where $r(v_j, p_i)$ is the number of accesses by each ALP/ELP p_i to each variable v_j maintained by the CLP, and $l(v_j, p_i)$ is the number of CLPs traversed to reach v_j from p_i. Periodically, each CLP chooses a set of state variables it maintains, which, if migrated to a neighbouring CLP, would reduce the total access cost at the originating CLP. This simple load shedding scheme is complemented by a "reverse migration" phase which ensures that the load on any single CLP does not exceed a maximum value.

State variables are considered for migration when their access cost over the last period is greater than a preset threshold value. (With a cost threshold of zero, all variables maintained at the CLP are potential migration candidates.) Once the set of migration candidates has been determined, the CLP chooses to which of the neighbouring CLPs each migration candidate should be pushed (if any). For a variable to be pushed to a neighbouring CLP, the number of accesses to the state variable arriving through the port leading to the neighbouring CLP must exceed the total number of accesses to the variable arriving through other ports by a predetermined access threshold. To avoid the oscillation of a state variable between the two CLPs, the CLP initiating the load balancing process must check that the cost of accessing a state variable at its new location will be reduced (assuming that the pattern of accesses in the future is similar to that in the present), before pushing the load.

A state variable which satisfies both these conditions is migrated to the CLP responsible for the majority of the accesses to the variable over the last period. This simple

---

[7] Note that remove operations do not require special processing: the removed tuple must have been read by the query and the reading ALP is recorded in the write period.

strategy guarantees that the computational load on the "pushing" CLP and the overall communication load on the system will be lower following migration. However it can result in excessive computational loads on the "receiving" CLPs. To avoid this, we allow the receiving CLP to "swap" load with the pushing CLP. If the difference between the computational load of the pushing and receiving CLPs is greater than a predetermined load threshold, the receiving CLP may chose to swap some state variables with the pushing CLP. However, the receiving CLP will only chose to a swap state variable if doing so will reduce the cost of accessing that variable. A state variable is selected for swapping if and only if the majority of its accesses are through the port from which the pushed load was received. We use a swap load selection criterion in which the difference between the swap load (total access on the selected swappable variables) and the initial push load is less than or equal to the load threshold.

When load balancing is performed, the range information for the port through which the state is migrated must be updated to record the fact that attribute values held in the pushed variables are now accessible via the port. In addition, for the receiving CLP to correctly process new tuples in future, it must know what assumptions other CLPs would otherwise make about its contents based on previous queries. Any queries which match the state being pushed must therefore be copied from the pushing CLP to the receiving CLP.

5   Related Work

The model of the shared state presented above has some similarities with tuple space-based approaches [13]. For example, the *add* operator is similar to the *out* operator and the *request* and *remove* operators are similar to non-blocking *rdp* and *inp* operators. There has also been considerable work on distributed tuple spaces, for example systems such as LIME [14] and EgoSpaces [15], support distribution and the propagation of tuples from one tuple space to another.

However there are important differences. In Linda, matching is only on the position and type of a field (though some tuple space approaches, e.g., [16, 14, 15], support simple range matching in templates). Nor is it possible to guard an *out* operation, or easily construct such an atomic operation from the existing primitives. The key difference, however, is the model of time. In PDES, operations occur asynchronously but at a specific virtual time. As a result, we have to deal with conflicting updates with the same timestamp. We also have to manage the relationship between virtual and real time, for example, recording which request operations have been performed so that we can detect straggler updates and rollback. In contrast, coordination languages don't have an explicit model of time built into the semantics. Some implementations, e.g., [16, 17], support leases and/or transactions, but these are insufficient to implement guarded updates and rollback. In [18] a framework is proposed which allows, e.g., timestamping, rollback, and atomic transactions (as user-defined operations), but as far as we are aware, no distributed implementation exists.

In addition to the differences in the operations supported by existing tuple space models, scalability is also an issue. For example, LIME uses a subscription-like model to implement query operations on (remote) tuple spaces, in which the middleware registers a 'weak reaction' on a remote tuple space which is triggered when a tuple matching a pattern is added to the remote tuple space. However this approach potentially requires a weak reaction to be registered with every remote tuple space for every query. In EgoSpaces, which in part builds on the work on LIME, 'network constraints' limit consideration to "nearby" tuple spaces, i.e., to a subnet of the network. While such a network metric has a natural interpretation in the ad hoc mobile environments for which EgoSpaces was developed, there is no obvious corresponding metric in a MAS simulation, and it is not clear that the LIME/EgoSpaces model would scale to the very large numbers of tuple spaces required for a large MAS simulation, where, in principle, any agent may sense and update any part of its environment.

The approach described above also has some similarities with the ant algorithm approach outlined in [19] and with the TOTA middleware described in [20]. In [19] templates and tuples are modelled as ants which search a landscape of tuple servers for matching tuples or templates respectively, leaving trails to the locations for successful matches. In TOTA, the propagation of tuples from tuple space to tuple space across a network is determined by propagation rules which form part of the tuple's definition. This approach is very flexible and can be used to implement some of the features described above. For example, in TOTA, tuples can be used to create a routing overlay structure in a way somewhat similar to the caching of port information by a CLP during the processing of a range query. However, in TOTA, routing has to be programmed at the user level using propagation rules, and TOTA provides no direct support for guarded updates, virtual time or rollback.

In the simulation community, the efficient distribution of updates has received more attention, particularly in the context of large scale real-time simulations where it is termed *Interest Management*. Interest Management techniques utilise filtering mechanisms based on *interest expressions* (IEs) to provide the processes in the simulation with only that subset of information which is relevant to them (e.g., based on their location or other application-specific attributes). Special entities in the simulation, referred to as *Interest Managers*, are responsible for filtering generated data and forwarding it to the interested processes based on their IEs [21].

Various Interest Management schemes have been devised, utilising different communication models and filtering schemes. In most existing systems, Interest Management is realised via the use of IP multicast addressing, whereby data is sent to a selected subnet of all potential receivers. A multicast group is defined for each message type, grid cell (spatial location) or region in a multidimensional parameter space in the simulation. Typically, the definition of the multicast groups of receivers is static, based on a priori knowledge of communication patterns between the processes in the simulation [22, 23, 24, 25, 26]. For example, the High Level Architecture (HLA) utilises the *routing space* construct, a multi-dimensional coordinate system whereby simulation federates express their interest in receiving data (subscription regions) or declare their responsibility for publishing data (update regions) [27]. In existing HLA implementations, the routing space is subdivided into a predefined array of fixed size cells and each grid cell is assigned a multicast group which remains fixed throughout the simulation; a process joins those multicast groups whose associated grid cells overlap the process subscription region.

Static, grid-based Interest Management schemes have the disadvantage that they do not adapt to the dynamic changes in the communication patterns between the processes during the simulation and are therefore incapable of balancing the communication and computational load, with the result that performance is often poor. Furthermore, in order to filter out all irrelevant data, grid-based filtering requires a reduced cell size, which in turn implies an increase in the number of multicast groups, a limited resource with high management overhead. Some systems, such as JPSD [24] and STOW-E [28] allowed a degree of dynamism in their filtering schemes, and, more recently, there have been attempts to define alternative dynamic schemes for Interest Management concentrating mainly on the dynamic configuration of multicast groups within the context of HLA. For example, Berrached et al. [29] examine hierarchical grid implementations and a hybrid grid/clustering scheme of update regions to dynamically reconfigure multicast groups while Morse et al. [30] report on preliminary investigations on a dynamic algorithm for dynamic multicast grouping for HLA. The Joint MEASURE system [31, 32, 33] is implemented on top of HLA and utilises event distribution and predictive encounter controllers to efficiently manage interactions among entities. However, despite these efforts, the problem of dynamic interest management remains largely unsolved.

In contrast, our approach is not confined to grids and rectangular regions of multi-dimensional parameter space and does not rely on the support provided by the TCP/IP protocols. Rather, the shared state is distributed dynamically based on the spheres of influence of the ALPs and ELPs in the simulation. In addition, our approach aims to exploit this decomposition in order to perform load balancing. Although load balancing has been studied extensively in the context of conventional distributed simulations [34, 35, 36, 37, 38, 39], it has received very little attention in relation to Interest Management, and work in this area to date is only preliminary [21, 40, 41, 42].

6   Conclusion and Further Work

In this paper, we have presented a model of the environment of a multi-agent system and an approach to the distributed simulation of MAS environments based on this model. Our model addresses the problems of efficient sensing, parallel actions and action conflicts, and the efficient distribution of the resulting shared state of the simulation. The work reported is still at a preliminary stage. To date, we have implemented the core of the CLPs including the rollback mechanism and calculation of virtual time [43] and load balancing [44] and are currently working on the implementation of interest management. Initial experiments with the rollback mechanism are encouraging, and show a reduction in the number of rollbacks compared to other approaches in the literature which rollback on every straggler event [12].

In the short term, our focus will be on completing the implementation and evaluating its performance relative to conventional PDES approaches. However in the longer term, it would be interesting to explore the application of the ideas described above to MAS environments in general. With the exception of our model of time (which is local to the agent), the concerns which we address, i.e., the tuple space-like model of the environment state, the operations we can perform on it (and the associated issues of simultaneity and guarded updates) and its efficient distribution, are relevant to environments for MAS in general. Much of the work on modelling of state and action and, at the implementation level, on distribution and routing could potentially carry over to the modelling and implementation of (non-simulated) environments.

Acknowledgements

This work is part of the PDES-MAS project[8] and is supported by EPSRC research grant No. GR/R45338/01.

References

1. Anderson, J.: A generic distributed simulation system for intelligent agent design and evaluation. In Sarjoughian, H.S., Cellier, F.E., Marefat, M.M., Rozenblit, J.W., eds.: Proceedings of the Tenth Conference on AI, Simulation and Planning, AIS-2000, Society for Computer Simulation International (2000) 36–44
2. Schattenberg, B., Uhrmacher, A.M.: Planning agents in JAMES. Proceedings of the IEEE **89** (2001) 158–173
3. Gasser, L., Kakugawa, K.: MACE3J: Fast flexible distributed simulation of large, large-grain multi-agent systems. In: Proceedings of AAMAS-2002, Bologna (2002)
4. Ferscha, A., Tripathi, S.K.: Parallel and distributed simulation of discrete event systems. Technical Report CS.TR.3336, University of Maryland (1994)
5. Fujimoto, R.: Parallel discrete event simulation. Communications of the ACM **33** (1990) 31–53
6. Ferber, J.: Multi-Agent Systems. Addison Wesley Longman (1999)
7. Zeigler, B.P., Praehofer, H., Kim, T.G.: Theory of Modeling and Simulation. 2nd edn. Academic Press (2000)
8. Baxter, J., Hepplewhite, R.T.: Broad agents for intelligent battlefield simulation. In: Proceedings of the 6th Computer Generated Forces and Behavioural Representation, Institute of Simulation and Training (1996)
9. Vincent, R., Horling, B., Wagner, T., Lesser, V.: Survivability simulator for multi-agent adaptive coordination. In: Proceedings of the International Conference on Web-Based Modeling and Simulation 1998 (WMC'98). (1998)
10. Pollack, M.E., Ringuette, M.: Introducing the Tileworld: Experimentally evaluating agent architectures. In: National Conference on Artificial Intelligence. (1990) 183–189
11. Logan, B., Theodoropoulos, G.: The distributed simulation of multi-agent systems. Proceedings of the IEEE **89** (2001) 174–186
12. Lees, M., Logan, B., Theodoropoulos, G.: Time windows in multi-agent distributed simulation. In: Proceedings of the 5th EUROSIM Congress on Modelling and Simulation (EuroSim'04). (2004)
13. Carriero, N., Gelernter, D.: Linda in context. Communications of the ACM **32** (1989) 444–458
14. Murphy, A.L., Picco, G.P., Roman, G.C.: Lime: A middleware for physical and logical mobility. In: Proceedings of the the 21st International Conference on Distributed Computing Systems (ICDCS 2001), IEEE Computer Society (2001) 524–533
15. Julien, C., Roman, G.C.: Egocentric context-aware programming in ad hoc mobile environments. SIGSOFT Softw. Eng. Notes **27** (2002) 21–30

---

[8] http://www.cs.bham.ac.uk/research/pdesmas

16. Wyckoff, P., McLaughry, S.W., Lehman, T.J., Ford, D.A.: T Spaces. IBM Systems Journal **37** (1998) 454–474
17. Sun Microsystems: JavaSpaces service specification v1.1. http://www.sun.com/software/jini/specs/js1_1.pdf (2000) (verified 01/04/2004).
18. Merrick, I., Wood, A.: Coordination with scopes. In: Proceedings of the 2000 ACM Symposium on Applied Computing, ACM Press (2000) 210–217
19. Menezes, R., Tolksdorf, R.: A new approach to scalable lind-sysatems based on swarms. In: Proceedings of the 2003 ACM Symposium on Applied Computing, ACM Press (2003) 375–379
20. Mamei, M., Zambonelli, F., Leonardi, L.: Tuples on the air: A middleware for context-aware computing in dynamic networks (2003)
21. Morse, K.L.: Interest management in large-scale distributed simulations. Technical Report ICS-TR-96-27 (1996)
22. Smith, J., Russo, K., Schuette, L.: Prototype multicast IP implementation in ModSAF. In: Proceedings of the Twelfth Workshop on Standards for the Interoperability of Distributed Simulations. (1995) 175–178
23. Mastaglio, T.W., Callahan, R.: A large-scale complex virtual environment for team training. IEEE Computer **28** (1995) 49–56
24. Macedonia, M., Zyda, M., Pratt, D., Barham, P.: Exploiting reality with multicast groups: a network architecture for large-scale virtual environments. In: Virtual Reality Annual International Symposium. (1995) 2–10
25. Calvin, J.O., Chiang, C.J., Van Hook, D.J.: Data subscription. In: Proceedings of the Twelfth Workshop on Standards for the Interoperability of Distributed Simulations. (1995) 807–813
26. Steinman, J.S., Weiland, F.: Parallel proximity detection and the distribution list algorithm. In: Proceedings of the 1994 Workshop on Parallel and Distributed Simulation. (1994) 3–11
27. Defence Modeling and Simulation Office: High Level Architecture RTI Interface Specification, Version 1.3. (1998)
28. Van Hook, D., Calvin, J., Newton, M., Fusco, D.: An approach to DIS scaleability. In: Proceedings of the 11th Workshop on Standards for the Interoperability of Distributed Simulations. (1994) 347–356
29. Berrached, A., Beheshti, M., Sirisaengtaksin, O., de Korvin, A.: Alternative approaches to multicast group allocation in HLA data distribution. In: Proceedings of the 1998 Spring Simulation Interoperability Workshop. (1998)
30. Morse, K.L., Bic, L., Dillencourt, M., Tsai, K.: Multicast grouping for dynamic data distribution management. In: Proceedings of the 31st Society for Computer Simulation Conference (SCSC '99). (1999)
31. Hall, S.B., Zeigler, B.P., Sarjoughian, H.: Joint MEASURE: Distributed simulation issues in a mission effectiveness analytic simulator. In: Proceedings of the Simulation Interoperability Workshop, Orlando, FL (1999)
32. Hall, S.B.: Using Joint MEASURE to study tradeoffs between network traffic reduction and fidelity of HLA compliant pursuer/evader simulations. In: Proceedings of the Summer Simulation Conference, Vancouver, Canada, Society for Computer Simulation (2000)
33. Sarjoughian, H.S., Zeigler, B.P., Hall, S.B.: A layered modeling and simulation architecture for agent-based system development. Proceedings of the IEEE (2000)
34. Burdorf, C., Marti, J.: Load balancing strategies for Time Warp on multi-user workstations. The Computer Journal **36** (1993) 168–176
35. Glazer, D.W., Tropper, C.: On process migration and load balancing in Time-Warp. IEEE Transactions on Parallel and Distributed Systems **3** (1993) 318–327
36. Goldberg, A.: Virtual time synchronisation of replicated processes. In: Proceedings of 6th Workshop on Parallel and Distributed Simulation, Society for Computer Simulation, Society for Computer Simulation (1992) 107–116

37. Reiher, P.L., Jefferson, D.: Dynamic load management in the Time-Warp operating system. Transactions of the Society for Computer Simulation **7** (1990) 91–120
38. Schlagenhaft, R., Ruhwandl, M., Sporrer, C., Bauer, H.: Dynamic load balancing of a multi-cluster simulation on a network of workstations. In: Proceedings of 9th Workshop on Parallel and Distributed Simulation, Society for Computer Simulation, Society for Computer Simulation (1995) 175–180
39. Carothers, C., Fujimoto, R.: Background execution of Time-Warp programs. In: Proceedings of 10th Workshop on Parallel and Distributed Simulation, Society for Computer Simulation, Society for Computer Simulation (1996)
40. Messina, P., Davis, D., Brunette, S., Gottshock, T., Curkendall, D., Ekroot, L., Miller, C., Plesea, L., Craymer, L., Siegel, H., Lawson, C., Fusco, D., Owen, W.: Synthetic forces express: A new initiative in scalable computing for military simulation. In: Proceedings of the 1997 Spring Simulation Interoperability Workshop, IST (1997)
41. White, E., Myjak, M.: A conceptual model for simulation load balancing. In: Proceedings of the 1998 Spring Simulation Interoperability Workshop. (1998)
42. Myjak, M., Sharp, S., Shu, W., Riehl, J., Berkley, D., Nguyen, P., Camplin, S., Roche, M.: Implementing object transfer in the HLA. Technical report (1999)
43. Lees, M., Logan, B., Theodoropoulos, G.: Adaptive optimistic synchronisation for multi-agent simulation. In Al-Dabass, D., ed.: Proceedings of the 17th European Simulation Multiconference (ESM 2003), Delft, Society for Modelling and Simulation International and Arbeitsgemeinschaft Simulation, Society for Modelling and Simulation International (2003) 77–82
44. Oguara, T.: Load balancing in distributed simulation of agents. Thesis Report 5, School of Computer Science, University of Birmimgham (2004)

Supporting Context-Aware Interaction in Dynamic Multi-agent Systems

Christine Julien[1] and Gruia-Catalin Roman[2]

[1] Department of Electrical and Computer Engineering,
The University of Texas at Austin
c.julien@mail.utexas.edu
[2] Department of Computer Science and Engineering,
Washington University in Saint Louis
roman@wustl.edu

Abstract. The increasing ubiquity of mobile computing devices has made mobile ad hoc networks an everyday occurrence. Applications in these networks are commonly structured as a logical network of mobile agents that coordinate with each other to achieve their goals. In these highly dynamic multi-agent systems, the multitude of devices provides a varied and rapidly changing context in which agents must learn to operate. Successful end-user applications will not only learn to handle dynamic conditions, but will take advantage of the wide variety of available information and resources. Any environment that supports agents and their interactions must facilitate flexible communication mechanisms. Such protocols for enabling an application agents task of gathering contextual information must function in a timely and adaptive fashion. This paper presents a protocol for mediating these context-based interactions among mobile agents. We present an implementation and show how it facilitates information exchange among mobile application agents. We also provide an analysis of the tradeoffs between consistency and range of context definitions in highly dynamic ad hoc networks.

1 Introduction

In large-scale multi agent systems, an application agent must adapt its behavior to a constantly changing environment defined by a multitude of mobile computing devices supporting a variety of other application agents and services. Mobile networks form opportunistically and change rapidly in response to the movement of the devices and agents that define the network. To communicate, applications in such a network commonly use ad hoc routing protocols (e.g., DSDV [1], DSR [2], AODV [3]) that deliver messages between a known source and destination using intermediate devices as routers. Ad hoc multicast routing protocols require devices to register as receivers for a specific multicast address. The network maintains a multicast tree [4,5] or mesh [6,7] for delivering messages to registered receivers.

D. Weyns et al. (Eds.): E4MAS 2004, LNAI 3374, pp. 168–189, 2005.

Directly applying these routing techniques to gathering the context information needed by a particular application agent (or just "agent") poses several drawbacks. In both unicast and multicast routing, the paths along which messages are delivered may extend across the entire network. As the ubiquity of mobile devices increases, mobile networks may grow very large, have large network diameters, and support increasing numbers of coordinating agents. Consider a network composed of cars on a highway. Cars may be transitively connected for hundreds of miles, but it is generally not necessary or desirable for an application to communicate at great distances. Each car may support several agents, but many application agents require only local interactions, e.g., an agent may be responsible for gathering local traffic information for a particular driver. In addition, for traditional routing protocols to function, senders and receivers require explicit knowledge of each other. Often, however, an application has no a priori knowledge about the agents and services with which it will want to interact, since components in the networks move at will, and agents or services that are encountered once may never be encountered again. Supporting context-aware agents in this unpredictable environment requires reevaluating what application agents need from underlying protocols and providing solutions tailored to these needs.

Emerging applications for this environment (like the traffic example above) focus on using application agents to provide context information to the user. This context can be defined by physical properties of the device (heretofore referred to as a "node") or other devices in the environment and by information or services available on them. For example, a context-aware tour guide [8, 9] may interact with nearby kiosks to display locally relevant tourist information. Cars on a highway may interact to gather traffic information about their intended routes. In any of these cases, application agents cooperate to gather the information presented to the user. This information defines the operating context of the application, which differs for each application. The scope of interaction is driven by the instantaneous needs of applications, which change over time.

We focus on providing a protocol to support an agent's ability to specify what context information it needs from its environment and to gather that information in a manner that adapts to environmental changes. Because the network is constantly being reshaped, an agent's requests must be evaluated in a timely fashion to ensure the freshness of the information. Previous work resulted in the Content-Based Multicast model (CBM) [10], which focuses on disseminating information collected by sensors. In general, this model is tailored for distributing information about a (possibly mobile) threat to interested parties. The dissemination pattern in CBM is based on the relative movement patterns of the threat being sensed and the interested parties. Mobile nodes that sense the presence of a threat push information about the threat in the direction of its movement. At the same time, mobile components pull information about threats present in their direction of travel. This combination of both push and pull actions allows this multicast protocol to adjust to dynamic components with varying speeds.

While the CBM model addresses needs of context aware applications, it is tailored to a specific class of context-aware applications. It is a protocol tailored to dissemination of mobile threats to mobile parties. Our approach focuses on a more general treatment of context that caters to the varying and unpredictable needs of applications in heterogeneous mobile networks. While traditional approaches to context-aware computing either deal with specific types of context [10, 11] or only context that is sensed by the local node [8, 9, 11, 12], we extend the notion of context to include information available in a region of the network surrounding the node where the requesting agent resides. The protocol constructs and dynamically maintains a tree over a subnet of neighboring nodes and links whose attributes contribute to an application agent's specific definition of context. Here we present the first protocol implementing the *Network Abstractions* model [13]. We explore the protocol in detail, focusing on its practicality, implementation, and performance in an effort to quantify the guarantees that can be associated with extended contexts in dynamic mobile networks.

Given our approach, the *environment* of an agent is defined by the world surrounding the agent and the capabilities the surroundings contain. This includes the ability to communicate with other agents on other network nodes and the ability to access data owned by the agents. The *context* of an agent is more specific and is defined as exactly the data that the agent is interested in (for the purpose of its application) at a particular moment in time. What is defined to be part of the context at any time is influenced by the agent's environment.

The remainder of this paper is organized as follows. Section 2 provides an overview of the Network Abstractions model and protocol. Section 3 discusses our implementation. Section 4 provides an analysis of the model through simulation. Conclusions appear in Section 5.

2   Network Abstractions Overview

Today's dynamic mobile networks contain many nodes and links with varying properties which define the context for any individual agent in the network. The behavior of an adaptive agent depends on this continuously changing context. This context definition is broader than traditional definitions that include only local information. This has the potential to greatly increase the amount of context information available, and so an application agent desires the ability to precisely specify its context based on the properties of nodes and links in the network. For example, a network on a highway might extend for hundreds of miles, but an agent operating on behalf of a driver may be interested only in gas stations within five miles. Our approach allows the corresponding agent's context specification to remain as general and flexible as possible while ensuring the feasibility of the protocol to dynamically compute the context. The *Network Abstractions* model provides an agent on a particular node, called the reference, the ability to specify a context that spans a subset of the network.

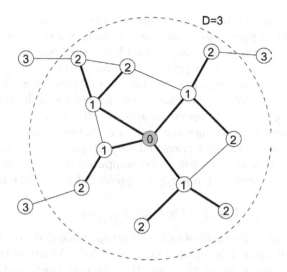

Fig. 1. A Network Abstraction defined to include all nodes within three hops of the reference (shown in gray)

2.1   Model Overview

As discussed previously, an adaptive application in a mobile network operates optimally only over a context tailored to its specific needs. The Network Abstractions model views this context as a subnet surrounding the application agent. Consider the example network shown in Fig. 1. In this network, the reference node where the agent is running is shown in gray. The links shown are available communication links. This figure represents the agent's definition of a context that includes all nodes within fewer than three hops. The number inside each node is its shortest distance from the reference in terms of number of hops. The dashed line labeled "D=3" represents the agent's bound on the context (three hops), while the darkened links indicate paths in a tree that define the context. By defining such a context, the agent has restricted its operation to a subnet of the network that is locally relevant to its desired functionality.

This example uses a simple definition of "distance" (number of hops), but this approach can be generalized to include distance definitions tailored to unique applications. We will provide examples of more sophisticated distance metrics later in this section. In general, after providing its application-specific definition of distance and the maximum allowable distance, the reference agent would like a list of nodes such that:

> Given a node α and a positive D, find the set of all nodes Q_α such that all nodes in Q_α are reachable from α, and for all nodes β in Q_α, the cost of the shortest path from α to β is less than D.

In the Network Abstractions model, an agent specifies its distance metric with two components. The first defines the weight of a link in the network. This can be computed using information available to the two nodes connected by the link. The second component is a cost function evaluated over a series of weights. In the hop count example, the weight of all links is defined to be one, while the cost function simply adds the weights of links along the path.

The weight on a link, w_{ij}, is a combination of properties of the link (e.g., latency, bandwidth, or physical distance) and properties of the two nodes (i and j) it connects (e.g., available power, location, or direction).

The cost function determines the cost of a particular path in the network, defined by the series of nodes traversed by the path. Cost functions are defined recursively; this allows them to be computed in a distributed fashion. A path from reference node 0 to node k is represented as P_k. The cost function is defined as:

$$f_0(P_k) = Cost(f_0(P_{k-1}), w_{k-1,k})$$

where *Cost* indicates the agent-specified function evaluated over the cost at the previous hop and the weight of the most recent link. As will become evident in the upcoming examples, we must require that the cost function strictly increases with the number of hops from the reference node. Recursive evaluation of this cost function over a network path determines its cost. In a real network, multiple paths may exist between two nodes. Therefore, as shown by the darkened links in Fig. 1, we build a tree rooted at the reference node that includes only the lowest cost path to each node in the network.

An agent exploits the availability of the cost function and its associated properties to limit the scope of the context computation by providing a bound on the maximum allowable cost. Nodes to which the cost is less than the bound are included in the context. This allows the computation to avoid touching nodes outside its context bound.

2.2   Example Metrics

Next we examine some example distance metrics. First we provide a metric that uses a more sophisticated weight definition, then show a more complicated cost function.

Network Latency. Consider an application in which field researchers share sensor data and video feeds. The context requirements for each researcher's tasks will likely be different. The Network Abstractions model allows the agents running on behalf of each researcher to tailor their context definitions to the researcher's needs by defining a weight for each network link. Because we are sending video, we want a link's weight to account for the node-to-node latency:

$$w_{ij} = \frac{node\ latency_i}{2} + \frac{node\ latency_j}{2} + link\ latency_{ij}.$$

where the first two components define the average time between when the node receives a packet and when it propagates the packet. We use only half of this number; otherwise we would count the node's latency twice if the node is in the middle of the path. This latency value will suffice under the assumption that a node's incoming latency is approximately equivalent to the node's outgoing latency. The third component of w_{ij} is the time required for a message to travel between two nodes.

The application agent also provides a cost function; a simple one to use with this weight definition is the same as in the hop count example:

$$f_0(P_k) = f_0(P_{k-1}) + w_{k-1,k},$$

where the cost of the path from node 0 (the reference) to node k along path P_k is the sum of the cost to the previous node plus the weight of the new link. A bound on this cost function is defined by a bound on the total allowed latency.

Physical Distance. Next we present a general-purpose metric based on physical distance. Agents running on cars traveling on a highway collect information about weather conditions, highway exits, accidents, traffic patterns, etc. As a car moves, its agent wants to operate over the information that will affect the driver's immediate route, so the data should be restricted to information within a certain physical distance (e.g., within a mile).

The agent's calculated context should be based on the physical distance between the reference node and other nodes. For this example, a link's weight reflects the distance vector between two connected nodes, accounting for both the displacement and the direction of displacement between the two nodes:

$$w_{ij} = \mathbf{IJ}$$

Fig. 2a shows an example network where specifying distance alone causes an agent's context to not be easily bounded. This results from the fact that a cost function based on distance alone is not strictly increasing as the number of hops from the reference node grows. To overcome this problem, the car agent's cost function should be based on a combination of the distance vector *and* a hop count. The cost function's value (ν) at a given node consists of three values:

$$\nu = (maxD, C, \mathbf{V})$$

The first value, $maxD$, stores the maximum distance seen on this path. This may or may not be the magnitude of the distance vector from the reference to this node. The second value, C, keeps the number of consecutive hops for which $maxD$ did not increase. The final value, $\mathbf{V}$, is the distance vector from the reference nods to this node. Through the remainder of this description, we will refer to these value using a "." notation (e.g., $\nu.maxD$ refers to the $maxD$ component of the cost function value ν).

Specifying a bound for this cost function requires bounding both $maxD$ and C. A node is in the context only if both its $maxD$ and C are less than the bound's values. Neither the value of $maxD$ nor the value of C can ever decrease, and, if one value remains constant for any hop, the other is guaranteed to increase.

Fig. 2d shows the cost function. In the first case, the new magnitude of the vector from the reference node to this node is larger than the current value of

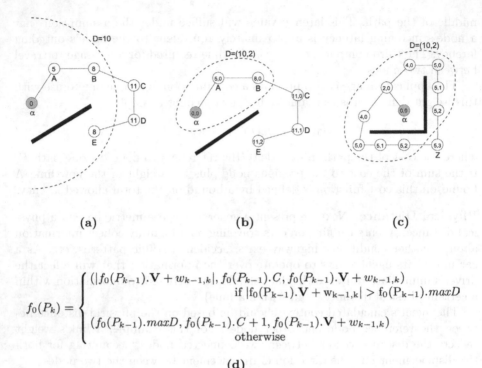

(a)   (b)   (c)

$$f_0(P_k) = \begin{cases} (|f_0(P_{k-1}).\mathbf{V} + w_{k-1,k}|, f_0(P_{k-1}).C, f_0(P_{k-1}).\mathbf{V} + w_{k-1,k}) \\ \qquad \text{if } |f_0(P_{k-1}).\mathbf{V} + w_{k-1,k}| > f_0(P_{k-1}).maxD \\[2ex] (f_0(P_{k-1}).maxD, f_0(P_{k-1}).C + 1, f_0(P_{k-1}).\mathbf{V} + w_{k-1,k}) \\ \qquad \text{otherwise} \end{cases}$$

(d)

Fig. 2. (a) Physical distance only; (b) Physical distance with hop count, restricted due to distance; (c) Physical distance with hop count, restricted due to hop count; (d) The correct cost function

$maxD$; $maxD$ is reset to the magnitude of the vector from the reference to this node, C remains the same, and the distance vector to this node is stored. In the second case, $maxD$ is the same for this node as the previous node; $maxD$ remains the same, C is incremented by one, and the distance vector to this node is stored.

Fig. 2b shows the same nodes as Fig. 2a using this new cost function. The agent specified bound shown in Fig. 2b is $D = (10, 2)$ where 10 is the bound on $maxD$ and 2 is the bound on C. This cost function can be correctly bounded, and no nodes that should qualify are missed. Fig. 2c shows the same cost function applied to a different network. In this case, while the paths never left the area within distance 10, node Z still falls outside the context because the maximum distance remained the same for more than two hops.

2.3   Protocol Overview

An agent desires the guarantee that any message it sends will be received only by nodes within its context *and* that it is received by all nodes within its context. Our protocol builds a tree over the network based on an application agent's specification, defining a single route from the reference node to all other nodes in the context. In this section, we provide an overview of the protocol in preparation for a discussion of its implementation and analysis. More details of the protocol can be found in [13] and [14].

In general, the protocol can be divided into two components. The first deals with the dissemination of an agent's one-time queries on its context. Such queries may require replies from context members, but the context that is built need not be maintained. This lack of maintenance is beneficial when an agent's operation over its context occurs in a periodic polling fashion, because it reduces the overhead needed to maintain the context in a highly dynamic network. The second portion of the protocol deals with maintaining the context when the agent needs continuous information. Due to the maintenance cost involved, ideal interactions would extend one-time queries to larger contexts (e.g., poll for traffic conditions for the next five miles), but only maintain smaller contexts (e.g., react to cars within potential collision range of my car).

Assumptions. The protocol assumes a message passing mechanism that guarantees reliable delivery with associated acknowledgements. The protocol also assumes that when a link disappears, both nodes that were connected by the link can detect the disconnection. The protocol requires that all configuration changes and an agent's issuance of queries over the context are serializable with respect to each other. A configuration change is defined as the change in the value of the distance metric at a given link and the propagation of those changes through the tree structure. Finally, we assume that the underlying system maintains the weights on links in the network by responding to changes in the contextual information required by application agents.

The Query Component. The protocol is on-demand in that a tree is built only when an agent sends a data query. Piggy-backed on this data message are the context specification and the information necessary for its computation. Specifically, the query contains the context's definition of link weight, the cost function, and the bound. The protocol uses this information to determine which nodes should receive this message.

Tree Building. Because any information required for computing an agent's context arrives in a query, nodes need not keep information about the system's global state. An agent with a data query to send bundles the context specification with the query and hands it to the protocol implementation which in turn determines which of the reference node's neighbors are within the context and sends them the query. Due to the wireless nature of the network, this can be accomplished via one message transmission broadcast to all the neighbors; those not in the context disregard the message. Neighbors in the context determine if any of their neighbors are also in the context and, if so, rebroadcast the message. In the course of query propagation, every context member remembers the previous hop in its shortest path back to the reference node. A node only rebroadcasts a duplicate message if its cost has decreased since this may cause inclusion of additional nodes in the context. When the query reaches the bound, it will not be forwarded on; the query distribution stabilizes when every node in the context knows its shortest path to the reference node. Each node that receives the context message for the first time also passes the application level information carried with the query to the designated application agent(s) running on the node.

Tree Maintenance. As discussed above, contexts over which an agent issues persistent queries require maintenance. One example of an application that needs such a persistent query is one in which the application agent wishes to notify the driver of the car if any other cars come within a potential collision radius. The protocol for maintaining the context builds on the one-time query protocol above. Ultimately, the entire protocol is an extension of a distance-vector protocol with modifications for managing the distance metric and bound. To achieve context maintenance, nodes within the context must react to changes that affect their cost. The new cost may push the node (or other downstream nodes) out of the context or pull them in. Because all needed information is stored within the nodes in the context, the reference node need not participate in this maintenance; instead it is a local adjustment to a local change. Due to the nature of distance vector routing, this protocol suffers from the count-to-infinity problem, where, upon loss of a link, two nodes both believe their route back to the reference node is through each other. Under the assumption that maintained contexts will be small, this problem can be overcome by maintaining the entire routing path.

2.4   Practical Research Issues

In the remainder of this paper, we present an implementation and analysis of the protocol described above. The particular reference implementation discussed allows us to explore the range of distance metrics and cost functions application agents can use and to build an extensive software system for operating over contexts in a dynamic mobile environment. We also provide an analysis of the protocol over a simple metric (the hop count example discussed previously) used to examine the feasibility of the consistency assumptions we make and to study the performance of the protocol in a variety of networks. Specifically, we test the limits of the network changes our protocol can handle and measure the correctness of the context building mechanisms.

3   Implementation

Our implementation is written entirely in Java. This decision is driven by the fact that we aim to ease application development, which means placing control over the context in the hands of novice programmers. We feel that by using Java to provide interfaces to application programmers, we can leverage its object-oriented abstractions to ease the programming task. It is also imperative that we provide a flexible protocol that an application developer can tailor to its

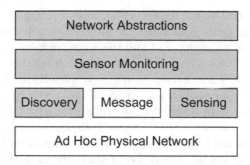

Fig. 3. Architecture of a system using Network Abstractions. In this figure, the gray components are provided as part of our infrastructure; the white components we assume to exist. *Message* refers to a message passing mechanism. *Discovery* refers to our neighbor discovery protocol. *Sensing* refers to a low-level sensing component that communicates with sensors on this local host. *Sensor Monitoring* allows this host to interact not only with its sensors, but the sensors on its direct neighbors. Finally, *Network Abstractions* refers to the protocol that is the focus of this paper

needs. Thus, application agents can define individualized distance metrics and add new environmental monitors to the system to increase the flexibility of link weight definitions.

The implementation allows issuance of both one-time and persistent queries and maintains contexts which have persistent queries. We include built-in metrics (e.g., hop count) but also provide a general framework for defining new metrics. Our implementation uses the support of two additional packages; one for neighbor discovery and one for environmental monitoring. We describe these two packages briefly before detailing the protocol implementation.

3.1   Support Packages

Fig. 3 shows the overall architecture of a system utilizing the Network Abstractions protocol we will describe. The Network Abstractions protocol assumes a physical network and a message passing mechanism to exist. It also relies on two additional packages: a neighbor discovery protocol and an environmental monitoring component comprising both local sensing and neighborhood sensor monitoring.

Neighbor Discovery. A node in our protocol receives knowledge of its neighbors from a discovery service. This service uses a periodic beaconing mechanism and can be parameterized with policies for neighbor addition and removal (e.g., a neighbor is only added when its beacon has been heard for two consecutive beacon periods, and a neighbor is removed when it has not been heard from for 10 seconds).

Environmental Monitoring. Our protocol relies on the availability of context information from the environment. To perform this context-sensing service in mobile ad hoc networks, we use the CONSUL monitoring package [15]. As shown in Fig. 3, two components contribute to providing environmental monitoring functionality: the sensing component and the sensor monitoring component. The sensing component allows software to interface with sensing devices connected to a host. Each device has a corresponding piece of software (a *monitor*) within the CONSUL service. An application (or in this case, the Network Abstractions protocol) can interact with a monitor by polling for its value or by reacting to changes in its value. The sensor monitoring component maintains a registry of monitors available on the local hosts (*local monitors*) and on hosts found by the discovery package (*remote monitors*). Local monitors make the services available on a host accessible to applications on that host. To gain access to local monitors, the application provides the name of the monitor (e.g., "location") to the registry. To monitor context information on remote hosts (i.e., on neighboring hosts), the registry creates local proxies that connect to and interact with monitor components on the remote devices. To access remote monitors, the application provides the ID of the remote host (which can be retrieved from the discovery package) and the name of the monitor. The behavior of this package is similar to that provided by the Context Toolkit [16]. Instead of gathering information directly from hosts an arbitrary distance away, however, we focus on gathering context information only about the links that connect a node to its neighbors as defined by the discovery package. This allows the CONSUL package to not rely on any centralized infrastructure or even any a priori knowledge, making it highly applicable to dynamic ad hoc networks.

3.2   Network Abstractions Protocol Implementation

Before defining a context, an agent must build a distance metric. This requires developing an object that adheres to a well defined metric interface and includes two methods. The first determines the weights on links to neighbors using monitors available on the local host and its neighbors. Because this link weight definition is a Java method in the base class that is overridden by the application agent's subclass, it can include arbitrary code. The second method determines the cost of a path, given a previous cost and a next hop weight. Again, because this can include any code, the cost function definition can be tailored to the application's needs.

While some application programmers enjoy the flexibility this open interface provides them, the complexity increases the development burden, especially for those programmers unfamiliar with the inner workings of the Network Abstractions protocol. To further ease the use of the protocol, we provide several build in distance metrics and cost functions. These include commonly used metrics, e.g., a cost function based on hop count and a cost function based on physical distance.

An agent defines a context by providing the aforementioned distance metric and a bound. Until a query is registered on the context, however, the protocol simply stores the information locally. It returns to the application agent a handle to the defined context.

To send a one-time query, the application passes a data packet to the protocol with a handle to a context. The protocol layer uses information provided by the neighbor discovery and environmental monitoring services to determine which neighbors must receive the message, if any. If neighbors exist that are within the context's bound, the local host packages the application agent's data with the context information and broadcasts the entire packet to its qualifying neighbors.

Upon receiving a one-time context query, the receiving host stores the previous hop, and repeats the propagation step, forwarding the packet to any of its neighbors within the bound. It also passes the packet's data portion to application level listeners registered to receive it. These listeners are registered by agents or services running on the receiving host that can respond to the sending agent. If this same query (identified by a sequence number) is received from another source, the new information is remembered and propagated only if the cost of the new path is less than the previous cost.

An agent or service on a host receiving a query can reply to a data packet. The protocol uses the stored previous hop information to route the reply back to the reference host and ultimately the sending agent. Because this reply is asynchronous and the context for a one-time query is not maintained, it is possible that the route no longer exists. In these cases, the reply is dropped. To provide a stronger guarantee on a reply's return, an agent should use a persistent query which forces the protocol to maintain the context.

The structure of a persistent query differs slightly from a one-time query in that it must include the entire path. This information is used to overcome the count-to-infinity problem encountered in distance vector protocols. The distribution of the query is the same as above, but the actions taken upon query reception vary slightly. The receiving host must remember the entire path back to the reference host. When the same query arrives on multiple paths, the host remembers every qualifying path. If the currently used path breaks, the protocol can replace it with a viable path. To keep both the current path and the list of possible paths consistent, the protocol monitors the aspects of the context that contribute to distance definition; if these values change, the cost at this host or its neighbors could also change. For example, to maintain a context built around physical distance, the protocol must monitor the physical location of this host and the physical locations of all neighbors also in the same context. This is accomplished through the local and remote monitors of the environmental monitoring package. The protocol reacts to these changes and updates its cost information locally. It also propagates these changes to affected neighbors. Therefore local changes to the metric do not affect the entire context; instead they only affect nodes from the point of change out to the bound. Before replacing a path, the protocol checks that the new path is loop-free.

Replies to persistent queries propagate back towards the reference host along the paths maintained by the protocol. A query is not guaranteed to reach the reference. Our practical experience shows, however, that, in reasonably sized networks with a fair amount of mobility, the delivery assumption is likely to hold. Section 4 provides an empirical evaluation of this assumption.

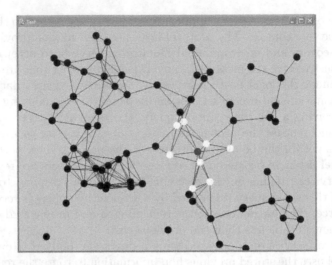

Fig. 4. Screen capture of demonstration system

3.3   Demonstration System

Fig. 4 shows a screen capture of our demonstration system. In this example, each circle depicts a single host running an instance of the protocol. Even though, in this case, all of the code runs on one machine, the demonstration system uses the network for communication, which allows this system to display information gathered from actual mobile hosts. This figure shows a single context defined by an agent on the reference host (the gray host in the center of the white hosts). This context is simple; it includes all hosts within one hop. When a host moves within the context's bound, it receives a query registered on the context that causes the node to turn its displayed circle white. When the node moves out of the context, the persistent query is removed, and the pictured node turns itself black. The demonstration system allows simulation of a variety of mobility models, including a Markov model, a random waypoint model [17], and a highway model. It is useful to developers who wish to visualize the behavior of their context definitions (distance metrics and cost functions) before deploying an application in the real world.

3.4   Example Usage

The protocol implementation described here is currently in use to support the ongoing implementation of a middleware model for ad hoc mobile computing. In this system, called EgoSpaces [18], application agents operate over projections (*views*) of the data available in the world. EgoSpaces addresses the specific needs of individual application agents, allowing them to define what data is to be included in a view by constraining properties of the data items, the agents that own the data, the hosts on which those agents are running, and attributes of the ad hoc network. This protocol provides the latter in a flexible manner, and

EgoSpaces uses the Network Abstractions protocol to deliver all communication among agents.

4 Analysis and Experimental Results

The previous sections have overviewed the Network Abstractions protocol and its implementation. In this section, we further motivate the use of this package by developers of mobile agent systems by providing some performance measurements. Ideally, a suite of such measurements will be used by application developers in determining which context definitions are appropriate for different needs or situations.

To examine the practicality of defining contexts on real mobile ad hoc networks, we used the ns-2 network simulator, version 2.26. This section provides simulation results for context dissemination. These simulations are a first step in analyzing the practicality of the protocol we have implemented. Not only do they serve to show that it is beneficial to define contexts in the manner described in ad hoc networks, the measurements also provide information to application programmers about what types or sizes of contexts should be used under given mobility conditions or to achieve required guarantees. All of the simulations we describe in this section implement a context defined by the number of hops from the reference node. Because this is the simplest type of context to define using the Network Abstractions protocol, this provides a baseline against which we can compare simulations of more complex or computationally difficult definitions. Before providing the experimental results, we detail the simulation settings and parameters we used.

4.1 Simulation Settings

We generated random 100 node ad hoc networks that use the random waypoint mobility model [17]. The simulation is restricted to a $1000 \times 1000 m^2$ space. We vary the network density (measured in average number of neighbors) by varying the transmission range. We measured the average number of neighbors over our simulation runs for each transmission range we used; these averages are shown in Fig. 5. While the random waypoint mobility model suffers from "density waves" as described in [19], it does not adversely affect our simulations. An average of 1.09 neighbors (e.g., $50m$ transmission range) represents an almost disconnected network, while an average of 23.89 neighbors (i.e. $250m$ transmission range) is extremely dense. While the optimal number of neighbors for a static ad hoc network was shown to be the "magic number" six [20], more recent work [19]

Range (m)	50	75	100	125	150	175	200	225	250
Neighbors	1.09	2.47	4.21	6.38	9.18	12.30	15.51	19.47	23.89

Fig. 5. Average number of neighbors for varying transmission ranges

shows that the optimal number of neighbors in mobile ad hoc networks varies with the degree of mobility and mobility model. The extreme densities in our simulations lie well above the optimum for our mobility degrees.

In our simulations, we used the MAC 802.11 standard [21] implementation built in to ns-2. Our protocol sends only broadcast packets, for which MAC 802.11 uses Carrier Sense Multiple Access with Collision Avoidance (CSMA/CA)[1]. This broadcast mechanism is not reliable, and we will measure our protocol's reliability over this broadcast scheme in our simulations. We implemented a simple "routing protocol" on top of the MAC layer that, when it receives a packet to send simply broadcasts it once but does not repeat it.

We also tested our protocol over a variety of mobility scenarios using the random waypoint mobility model with a $0s$ pause time. In the least dynamic scenarios, we use a fixed speed of $1m/s$ for each mobile node. We vary the maximum speed up to $20m/s$ while holding a fixed minimum speed of $1m/s$ to avoid the speed degradation described in [22].

4.2   Simulation Results for Context Query Dissemination

The results presented evaluate our protocol for three metrics in a variety of settings. The first metric measures the context's consistency, i.e., the percentage of nodes receiving a context notification given the nodes that were actually within the context when the query was issued. The second metric measures the context notification's settling time, i.e., the time that passes between the reference host's issuance of a context query and the time that every node in the context that will receive the query has received it. The third metric evaluates the protocol's efficiency through the rate of "useful broadcasts", i.e., the percentage of broadcast transmissions that reached nodes that had not yet received the context query.

The first set of results compare context definitions of varying sizes, specifically, definitions of one, two, three, and four hop contexts. We then evaluate our protocol's performance as network load increases, specifically as multiple nodes define contexts simultaneously. Unless otherwise specified, nodes move with a $20m/s$ maximum speed.

Increased Size of Logical Context Decreases Consistency. In comparing contexts of varying sizes, we found that as the size increases, the consistency of the context decreases. Results for different context sizes are shown in Fig. 6. These results show a single context definition on our 100 node network. The protocol can provide localized contexts (e.g., one or two hops) with near 100% consistency. With broader context definitions, the percentage of the context notified drops to as low as 94%. The disparity between large and small context definitions becomes most apparent with increasing network density. At large

---

[1] In CSMA/CA a node ready to send senses the medium for activity and uses a back off timer to wait if the medium is busy. When the node senses a clear medium, it broadcasts the packet but waits for no acknowledgements.

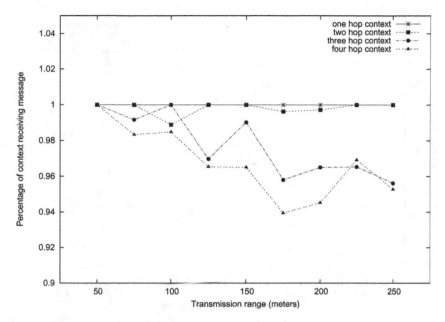

Fig. 6. Percentage of context members receiving the message for contexts of varying sizes

densities, the extended contexts contain almost the entire network, e.g., at a transmission range of $175m$, a four hop context contains $\sim 80\%$ of the network's nodes. In addition, the number of neighbors is 12.3, leading to network congestion when many neighboring nodes rebroadcast. This finding lends credence to the idea that applications should define contexts which require guarantees (e.g., collision detection) as more localized, while contexts that can tolerate some inconsistency (e.g., traffic information collection) can cover a larger region.

Larger Contexts Take Longer to Settle. As the size of the defined context increases, more time is required to notify all the context members. For a two hop context with a reasonable density (9.18 neighbors at $150m$ transmission range), the maximum time to notify a context member was $20.12ms$. Results for this measurement are shown in Fig. 7 The settling times for different sized networks eventually become similar as network density increases. This is due to the fact that even though the context is defined to be four hops, all nodes are within two hops of each other, effectively rendering a four hop context definition a two hop context.

Efficiency Decreases Almost Linearly with Increasing Density. Fig. 8 shows the protocol's efficiency versus density for different sized contexts. First, notice that the efficiency for a one hop network is always 100% because only one broadcast (the initial one) is ever sent. For larger contexts, the efficiency is lower and decreases with increasing density. Most of the lower efficiency and the descending nature of the curve results from the fact that rebroadcasting neighbors

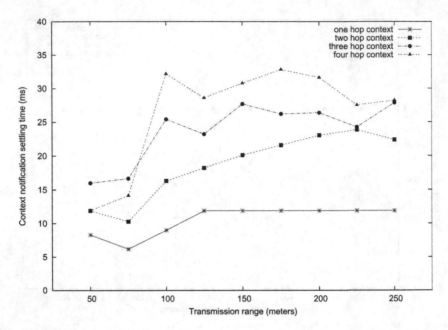

Fig. 7. Maximum time for last context recipient to receive notification for contexts of varying sizes

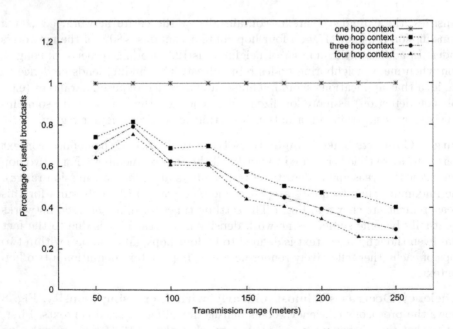

Fig. 8. Percentage of broadcasts that reached new context members for contexts of varying sizes

are likely to reach the same set of additional nodes. This becomes increasingly the case as the density of the network increases. Even at high densities, however, a good number ($> 20\%$) of the broadcasts reach additional context members.

This drop in efficiency as the density increases (as well as the corresponding drop in context consistency) is caused in part by a "broadcast storm," a commonly known problem well defined even in ad hoc networks. Previous work [23] has quantified the additional coverage a broadcast gains in mobile ad hoc networks. Several alternative broadcasting mechanisms have been proposed, many of which are compared in [24]. Integrating these or similar intelligent broadcast mechanisms may increase the resulting consistency and efficiency of context notification.

Increased Network Load Decreases Consistency. The remainder of the analysis focuses on an increasing load in the network, caused by multiple simultaneous context definitions by multiple nodes in the network. In all cases, the multiple registrations were issued at randomly distributed times within a $100ms$ window. We show only results for four hop contexts; results for smaller contexts are discussed in comparison. As Fig. 9 shows, five context definitions have no significant impact on the consistency as compared to a single definition. This is due to the fact that, on average, the different contexts issue queries after other queries have had time to settle. For ten definitions, the atomicity starts to decrease, bottoming out at $\sim 80\%$ at a $200m$ transmission range. With more

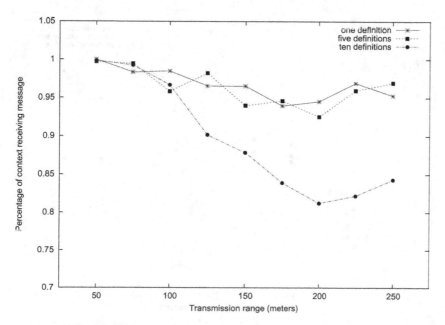

Fig. 9. Percentage of context members receiving context messages for varying network loads

registrations, especially at the larger densities, the different context messages interfere with each other. This has two ramifications. The first is that the broadcast messages collide and are never delivered. The second results from the fact that MAC 802.11 uses CSMA/CA. Because the medium is busier (more neighboring nodes are broadcasting), nodes are more likely to back off and wait their turn to transmit. During this extended waiting time, the context members are moving (at a maximum speed of $20m/s$). By the time the medium is available, context members that were in the context initially have moved out of it and will not be notified. These effects decrease significantly with smaller context sizes, e.g., at a transmission rate of $175m$, ten definitions on a two hop context can be delivered with ~97% consistency, and twenty can be delivered with ~89.5% consistency.

Extensions to this protocol may be able to start to handle the negative effect that increased network load has on the atomicity metric. These extensions could include reusing information available about already constructed contexts to limit the amount of work required to construct another context for a new agent. Also, one-time context distributions may be able to use information stored on nodes servicing persistent queries over maintained contexts.

Increased Network Load Increases Settling Time at High Densities.
Given the previous results, it is not surprising that increasing the network load to five context definitions does not increase settling time. As shown in Fig. 10,

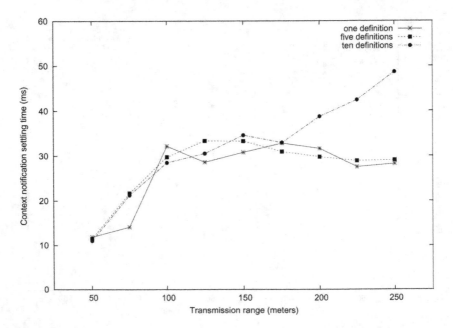

Fig. 10. Maximum time for last context recipient to receive notification for varying network loads

however, increasing the network load to ten definitions increases settling times of networks with high densities. Again, when the network density is large and multiple nodes are building contexts, the dispersions of their contexts queries interfere with each other, causing the broadcasting nodes to use their back off timers. This increased back off causes a longer delay in the delivery of context messages, especially to outlying context members.

We do not present any results for efficiency with changing network load, since network load seems to have no real effect on the percentage of useful broadcasts.

Changing Speed Has No Impact on Context Notification. In our analysis of this protocol over a variety of network speeds, we found that the dissemination of context messages is not greatly affected by the speed of the nodes. This is because the queries are only being sent out, and replies are not attempted. Were we to provide results for reply transmission back to the reference host, we would see that the routes are less likely to hold up for the scenarios with higher node speeds. This concern is addressed by the maintenance protocol, but simulation results for this portion of the protocol are outside the scope of this paper.

5   Conclusions

The ideas behind this work are rooted in the notion that communication in multi-agent systems for mobile ad hoc networks is an essential component of any environment supporting the execution of such agents. These types of systems are open, decentralized environments in which no centralized authority can control who enters into communication range or even mediate communication among agents who do manage to connect. The agents themselves are often quite autonomous, each with its own independent task and goals to meet. This paper demonstrates the feasibility of the Network Abstractions protocol to specifically support the communication needs of such agents. While the protocol was presented and has been used within the context of mobile ad hoc networks, it can extend to other genres of multi-agent systems in which the communication requirements of the agents can be expressed in some form of a strictly increasing distance metric. The dynamic nature of the protocol allows it to adapt to the openness and unpredictability of a variety of multi-agent environments. In the Network Abstractions protocol, the notion of an agent's *context* is broadened to include, in principle all available information, yet it can be conveniently limited in scope to a neighborhood whose size and scope is determined by the specific needs of a particular application agent as it changes over time.

This work implements and analyzes a protocol for providing contexts in mobile ad hoc networks. The protocol provides a flexible interface that gives the application agent explicit control over the expense of its operation while maintaining ease of programming by making the definition of sophisticated contexts simple. This protocol generalized the notion of "distance" to account for any properties, allowing an application agent to adjust its context definitions to account for its instantaneous needs or environment. Most importantly, the protocol explicitly bounds the computation of the agent's context to exactly what the application needs. In general, in an ad hoc network, these interactions will be localized in the neighborhood surrounding the host of interest, and therefore the agent's operations do not affect distant nodes. This bounding allows the agent to tailor its context definitions based on its needed guarantees. The protocol has been integrated with EgoSpaces, a middleware system for mediating coordination among distributed agents in mobile ad hoc networks. This, coupled with extensions to the analysis presented in this paper will provide further evaluation and feedback for protocol refinement and extension.

Acknowledgements

This research was supported in part by the Office of Naval Research MURI Research Contract No. N00014-02-1-0715. Any opinions, findings, and conclusions or recommendations expressed in this paper are those of the authors and do not necessarily reflect the views of the Office of Naval Research. The authors would also like to thank Qingfeng Huang for his work on the initial model, implementation of mobility models, and simulation advice.

References

1. Perkins, C., Bhagwat, P.: Highly dynamic Destination-Sequenced Distance-Vector routing (DSDV) for mobile computers. In: ACM SIGCOMM Conference on Communications Architectures, Protocols and Applications. (1994) 234–244
2. Broch, J., Johnson, D.B., Maltz, D.A.: The dynamic source routing protocol for mobile ad hoc networks. Internet Draft (1998) IETF Mobile Ad Hoc Networking Working Group.
3. Perkins, C., Royer, E.: Ad hoc on-demand distance vector routing. In: Proceedings of the 2nd IEEE Workshop on Mobile Computing Systems and Applications. (1999) 90–100
4. Chiang, C., Gerla, M., Zhang, L.: Adaptive shared tree multicast in mobile wireless networks. In: Proceedings of GLOBECOM. (1998) 1817–1822
5. Gupta, S., Srimani, P.: An adaptive protocol for reliable multicast in mobile multihop radio networks. In: IEEE Workshop on Mobile Computing Systems and Applications. (1999) 111–122
6. Bae, S., Lee, S.J., Su, W., Gerla, M.: The design, implementation, and performance evaluation of the On-Demand Multicast Routing Protocol in multihop wireless networks. IEEE Network, Special Issue on Multicasting Empowering the Next Generation Internet 14 (2000) 70–77
7. Madruga, E., Garcia-Luna-Aceves, J.: Scalable multicasting: The core assisted mesh protocol. ACM/Baltzer Mobile Networks and Applications, Special Issue on Management of Mobility 6 (1999) 151–165
8. Abowd, G., Atkeson, C., Hong, J., Long, S., Kooper, R., Pinkerton, M.: Cyberguide: A mobile context-aware tour guide. ACM Wireless Networks 3 (1997) 421–433

9. Cheverst, K., Davies, N., Mitchell, K., Friday, A., Efstratiou, C.: Experiences of developing and deploying a context-aware tourist guide: The GUIDE project. In: Proceedings of the International Converence on Mobile Computing and Networking (MobiCom). (2000) 20–31

10. Zhou, H., Singh, S.: Content based multicast (CBM) in ad hoc networks. In: Proceedings of International Symposium on Mobile Ad Hoc Networking and Computing (MobiHoc). (2000) 51–60

11. Pascoe, J.: Adding generic contextual capabilities to wearable computers. In: Proceedings of the 2nd International Symposium on Wearable Computers. (1998) 92–99

12. Rhodes, B.: The wearable remembrance agent: A system for augmented memory. In: Proceedings of the 1st International Symposium on Wearable Computers. (1997) 123–128

13. Roman, G.C., Julien, C., Huang, Q.: Network abstractions for context-aware mobile computing. In: Proceedings of the 24th International Conference on Software Engineering. (2002) 363–373

14. Julien, C., Roman, G.C., Huang, Q.: Network abstractions for simplifying mobile application development. Technical Report WUCSE-04-37, Washington University (2004)

15. Hackmann, G., Julien, C., Payton, J., Roman, G.C.: Supporting generalized context interactions. In: Proceedings of the 4th International Workshop on Software Engineering for Middleware. (2004)

16. Dey, A.K., Salber, D., Abowd, G.D.: A conceptual framework and a toolkit for supporting the rapid prototyping of context-aware applications. Human Computer Interaction 16 (2001) 97–166

17. Broch, J., Maltz, D., Johnson, D., Hu, Y.C., Jetcheva, J.: A performance comparison of multi-hop wireless ad hoc network routing protocols. In: Proceedings of the International Converence on Mobile Computing and Networking (MobiCom). (1998) 85–97

18. Julien, C., Roman, G.C.: Egocentric context-aware programming in ad hoc mobile environments. In: Proceedings of the 10th International Symposium on the Foundations of Software Engineering. (2002) 21–30

19. Royer, E., Melliar-Smith, P., Moser, L.: An analysis of the optimum node density for ad hoc mobile networks. In: Proceedings of the IEEE Conference on Communications. (2001) 857–861

20. Kleinrock, L., Silvester, J.: Optimum transmission radii in packet radio networks or why six is a magic number. In: Proceedimgs of the IEEE National. Telecommunications Conference. (1978) 4.3.1–4.3.5

21. IEEE Standards Department: Wireless LAN medium access control (MAC) and physical layer (PHY) specifications. IEEE standard 802.11 1999 (1999)

22. Yoon, J., Liu, M., Noble, B.: Random waypoint considered harmful. In: Proceedings of INFOCOM. (2003) 1312–1321

23. Ni, S.Y., Tseng, Y.C., Chen, Y.S., Sheu, J.P.: The broadcast storm problem in a mobile ad hoc network. In: Proc. of MobiCom. (1999) 151–162

24. Williams, B., Camp, T.: Comparison of broadcasting techniques for mobile ad hoc networks. In: Proc. of MobiHoc. (2002) 194–205

Environment-Based Coordination Through Coordination Artifacts

Alessandro Ricci, Mirko Viroli, and Andrea Omicini

DEIS, Università di Bologna, via Venezia 52, 47023 Cesena, Italy
{aricci, mviroli, aomicini}@deis.unibo.it

Abstract. In the context of human organisations, environment plays a fundamental role for supporting cooperative work and, more generally, complex coordination activities. Support is realised through services, tools, *artifacts* shared and exploited by the collectivity of individuals for achieving individual as well as global objectives.

The conceptual framework of *coordination artifacts* is meant to bring the same sort of approach to multiagent systems (MAS). Coordination artifacts are the entities used to instrument the environment so as to fruitfully support cooperative and social activities of agent ensembles. Here, infrastructures play a key role by providing services for artifact use and management.

In this work we describe this framework, by defining a model for the coordination artifact abstraction, and discussing the infrastructures and technologies currently available for engineering MAS application with coordination artifacts.

1 Introduction

Direct interaction and explicit communication are not always the best approaches to achieve coherent systemic behaviour in the context of MAS and agent societies. This is quite evident when taking into account the main approaches dealing with environment-based coordination such as stigmergy and, more generally, mediated interaction frameworks and infrastructures based on forms of coordination / cooperation without direct communication [1, 2, 3, 4, 5, 6].

Mediated interaction and environment-based coordination are highly debated also in other research fields outside MAS and CS, where collaborative and cooperative activities are studied in complex social contexts: notable examples are CSCW and HCI [7], recently focussing on cognitive and social theories which explicitly take into account the role of environment in coordination, such as Distributed Cognition [8] and Activity Theory [9]. There, a relevant issue is to understand what makes an environment a good place for actors to work together:

How (if) the agent environment can be designed to suitably support the social (coordination / cooperation / competition) activities of a dynamic set of heterogeneous agents?

This question can be considered of primary importance also in MAS, and it involves issues that are not fully considered by current approaches dealing with coordination through the environment. In particular:

D. Weyns et al. (Eds.): E4MAS 2004, LNAI 3374, pp. 190–214, 2005.

"Not only ants" — Approaches dealing with environment based coordination typically consider *reactive* agents, either embedding all the intelligence into the environment or obtaining it as emergent phenomenon (well known examples are stigmergy coordination and swarm intelligence [1, 5, 4]). Here instead we are interested on the one side to devise out environmental support useful meant to amplify the intelligence of individual agents, possibly exploiting their cognitive capabilities. On the other side, we are interested in considering intelligence not only as an emergent phenomenon, but promoting the engineering of intelligence by designing and building suitable environmental abstractions.

"Not only special-purpose coordination" — Existing environment-based approach to coordination – such as stigmergy – typically provide solutions only to specific coordination problems, without the abstraction required to use and systematise coordination in the wide range of social activities. Here instead we are interested in conceiving general purpose environment supports that could be suitably specialised and dynamically configured / tuned for addressing specific and heterogeneous coordination activities.

"Toward engineering" — Frequently, investigations in literature only concern simulation and abstract models (a notable example can be found in [6], where a model for situated MAS is provided for the engineering of systems). Here we are interested instead in methodologies and infrastructures, i.e. in identifying models, languages, architectures and middleware technologies to be exploited at the design stage in agent oriented software engineering, as well as for development and online management of MAS.

In this paper we describe the conceptual and engineering framework based on the notion of *coordination artifact*, which aims at addressing the above issues. Our framework provides a systematic view of environment-based coordination for general coordination problems, and extends the scope of applicability to heterogeneous, *cognitive / intelligent* agents. Coordination artifacts are runtime abstractions encapsulating and providing coordination services, to be exploited by agents within a given social context. They can be exploited then as basic building blocks for designing and developing suitable working environments for heterogeneous multi-agent systems, supporting their coordination for collaboration or competition.

The remainder of the paper is organised as follows. section 2 recalls the conceptual framework inspired by Activity Theory, as a background for the approach described in the paper, focussing on the importance of the environment in supporting social activities. section 3 presents in detail the coordination artifact abstraction, along with its main properties. section 4 sketches the features of formal models which can be suitably used to rigorously define coordination artifacts, their behaviour and properties. section 5 discusses the impact of the framework of MAS engineering, and section 6 discusses TuCSoN as a model / infrastructure / technology supporting the main features of the coordination artifact approach. Finally, related work and conclusion are presented in section 7 and section 8, respectively.

2   Environment as Context of Social Activities: The Activity Theory Perspective

Environment support for both the analysis and the development of activities in complex systems – such as human society – is among the main issues studied by socio-psychological approaches such as Activity Theory (AT) and Distributed Cognition.

Activity Theory, defined also Cultural-Historical Activity Theory (CHAT), is a social psychological theory born in the context of Soviet Psychology (SP) from the work of Lev Vygotsky (1926–62), rooted in the dialectic materialism of Marx and Engels [10]. Originated as a part of the attempt to produce a Marxist Psychology, AT has been developed and evolved in the Soviet Union by Vygotsky's students – Alexey Leontiev in particular – for the first half of the 20th century. Then, in the second half it has been spread also outside Soviet Union, first in Scandinavia and in Germany and then – at the end of the 1990s – in United States. Nowadays it has been applied also in the context of computer science related fields, such as Computer Supported Cooperative Work (CSCW) and Human Computer Interaction (HCI) (see [9] for a survey).

AT is a very general framework for conceptualising human activities – how people learn and society evolves – based on the concept of human *activity* as the fundamental unit of analysis. The approach was developed in contrast to purely cognitive approaches which were dominating the first years of the 20th century: according to them, human individual and social activities could be analysed and understood focussing only on the internal (mentalistic) representation of the individuals, in other words on the individual information-processing capabilities. On the contrary, the basic inspiration principle of AT is the *principle of unity and inseparability of consciousness (human mind) and activity*: human mind comes to exist, develops, and can only be understood within the context of a meaningful, goal-oriented, and socially determined interaction between human beings and their material environment. Then, a fundamental aspect for AT has been from the beginning the *interaction* between the individuals and the *environment* where they live, in other words their *context*. After an initial focus on the activity of the individuals, the AT research has evolved toward the study of human collective work and social activities, then facing issues such as the coordination and organisation of activities in human society.

Here the investigation of AT is of particular relevance important because it remarks the fundamental role of the environment in the development of complex systems. According to AT any activity carried on by one or more components of a systems – individually or cooperatively – cannot be conceived or understood without considering the tools or *artifacts* mediating the actions and interactions of the components. Artifacts on the one side mediate the interaction between individual components and their environment (including the other components), on the other side embody the part of the environment that can be designed and controlled to support components' activities. Moreover, as an observable part of the environment, artifacts can be monitored along the development of the activities to evaluate overall system performance and keep track of system history. In other words, mediating artifacts become first class entities for both the analysis and synthesis of individual as well as cooperative working activities inside complex systems.

The complexity of the activities of the social systems focussed by AT can be found nowadays in MAS and agent societies. With analogous consideration, we consider fundamental to frame the role of the environment for the analysis and synthesis of social activities inside MAS, and in particular of the artifacts mediating such activities. Among them we can include disembodied artifacts, such as communication languages [11], ontologies, protocols, but also embodied ones, such as the pheromone infrastructure [12] in the context of stigmergy coordination, or Institution middleware in electronic Institution approaches [13]. In this work we describe the framework of *coordination artifacts* as an approach to systematise this vision and making it effective for the engineering of systems as MASs, from design to development and runtime, including their dynamic observation and management.

3   The Coordination Artifact Abstraction

Coordination artifacts can be conceived as persistent entities specialised in providing a coordination service in a MAS [14, 15]. The term coordination should be here understood in its most general acceptation, as the management of dependencies among separate activities [16], shaping and constraining the (agent) interaction space [3]. Coordination artifacts are *infrastructure* abstractions meant to improve coordination activities automation; they can be considered then as basic building blocks for creating effective shared collaborative working environments, alleviating the coordination burden for the involved agents. Human society is full of entities like coordination artifacts, engineered by humans in order to support and automate coordination activities: well-known examples are street semaphores, blackboards, queuing tools at the supermarkets, maps, synchronisers and so on.

Basically, a coordination artifact *(i)* entails a form of mediation among the agents using it, and *(ii)* embeds and enact effectively some coordination policy. Accordingly, two basic aims can be identified: *(i) constructive*, as an abstraction essential for creating and composing social activities, *(ii) normative*, as an abstraction essential for ruling social activities.

Also taking inspiration from our society, we can then devise a basic abstract model, where a coordination artifact features:

- a *usage interface*, defined in terms of a set of *operations*. Agents *use* coordination artifacts by executing operations provided by the artifact, and by eventually perceiving information about the operation completion. Notice that due to the nature of coordination artifacts and their interaction schema, agent actions executing operations are more similar to *physical acts* rather than *communicative acts* – which makes our approach sensibly different from direct, ACL based interaction [17];
- a set of *operating instructions*. This information describe (formally) how to use the artifact in order to exploit its coordination service. For instance, operating instructions might specify the protocol of interactions to be used, and the mentalistic semantics of actions and perceptions [18];
- a *coordination behaviour specification*. This information describe (formally) the coordinating behaviour of the artifact, in terms of coordination rules required for enacting the coordination service.

In particular, taking the agent viewpoint, to exploit a coordination artifact simply means to follow its operating instructions, on a step-by-step basis. It is worth noting that, since a considerable coordination burden can be charged upon the artifact and be hidden from the agents, operating instructions are generally quite simple when compared to the interactive behaviour required in the case of direct communication (protocols). Hence, our approach to interaction can be fruitfully leveraged by intelligent agents, which can exploit an artifact through its operating instructions so as to take part to complex coordination scenarios.

A simple but effective example of coordination artifact is a *task scheduler* in co-operative working environments, which can be found in concurrent systems as well as in human society. The coordination problem concerns ruling the order of execution of a dynamic set of tasks taken in charge by some agents, according to some scheduling policy. A coordination artifact can be designed to provide such a scheduling service. A possible usage interface would consist – for instance – in two basic operations[1]:

- *taskStart(-Token)*, to manifest its intent to start executing the task. The completion of the operation means that the agent can start the task according to the scheduling policy of the artifact. A token is returned to the agent for identifying its activity;
- *taskCompleted(+Token)*, to signal the completion of the task.

Operating instructions simply consist in: first, invoking the *taskStart* operation to manifest the intention to start a task; then, invoking *taskCompleted* to signal the completion of the task. The coordinating behaviour of the artifact concerns the enactment of the scheduling policy, FIFO-based for instance, queueing requests and serving them according their position in the queue.

3.1   Main Properties

The basic properties of the agent abstraction have been extensively described in literature, in terms of autonomy, pro-activeness, reactivity, social ability and so on [19]. Analogously, here we focus on the main features that characterise coordination artifacts, which are indeed different.

Specialisation — Coordination artifacts are specialised in automating coordination activities. For this purpose, they typically adopt a computational model suitable for effective and efficient interaction management, whose semantics can be easily expressed with concurrency frameworks such as process algebra [20], Petri nets [21], Chemical Abstract Machines [22].

Encapsulation: Abstraction and Reuse — Coordination artifacts encapsulate a coordination service, allowing user agents to abstract from how the service is implemented. As such, a coordination artifact is perceived as an individual entity, but actually it can be distributed on different nodes of the MAS infrastructure, depending on its specific model and implementation. Encapsulation is the key to achieve reuse of coordination. Agent society engineers can create and exploit handbooks or catalogs of coordination artifacts, embodying the solutions to general coordination problems in organisations. Finally, a coordination artifact provides a certain *quality of co-ordination*, in particular in terms of the scalability with respect to the dimensions

---

[1] The basic Prolog notation is adopted for describing argument of operations: + means an output argument, - an input argument, ? an input / output argument.

identified by Durfee in [23], which are related to performance, robustness, reliability, and so on. The description of such dimensions is important to identify the range of applicability of the artifact in the engineering of agent societies.

Malleability — Coordination artifacts are meant to support coordination in open agent systems, characterised by unpredictable events and dynamism. For this purpsose, their coordination behaviour can be adapted and changed dynamically, either *(i)* by engineers (humans) willing to sustain the MAS behaviour, or *(ii)* by agents responsible of managing the coordination artifact, with the goal of flexibly facing possible coordination breakdowns or improving the coordination service provided.

Inspectability and controllability — A coordination artifact typically supports different level of inspectability: *(i)* inspectability of its operating instructions and coordination behaviour specification, in order to let user agents to be aware of how to use it or what coordination service it provides; *(ii)* inspectability of its dynamic state and coordination behaviour, in order to support testing and diagnosing (debugging) stages for the engineers and agents responsible of its management. Controllability is also fundamental for runtime management of a coordination artifact, by making it possible to freeze its behaviour, to trace it, supporting step-by-step execution while watching its state, to restart it, and so on. So, from an operational point of view, a coordination artifact can be understood as a sort of *virtual machine of coordination*, executing some form of coordination specification, fully inspectable and controllable by coordination artifact administrators [24].

Summing up, coordination artifacts are conceived to be engineering abstractions used for designing, building and supporting at runtime coordination in agent societies, suitably instrumenting their dynamic working environment. Also, they can be useful to support forms of scientific investigation of collective behaviours. As mediating entities, coordination artifacts typically reify and manage agent communication events; accordingly, they can be used to trace and log the overall interaction behaviour of the agent societies exploiting them. Thus, they can act as kinds of *social memory*, which can then be inspected for possible scientific analysis about global behaviours.

3.2   Artifacts as First Class Citizens of MAS

How to model the coordination artifact abstraction in MAS? Given the features described previously, it is evident that the agent notion do not fit: properties such as inspectability, controllability, malleability are extraneous (and to some extent in contrast) to agents, and viceversa, autonomy, proactiveness, and rationality are extraneous to coordination artifacts. Coordination artifacts are do not have goals to be achieved autonomously, interacting with other artifacts: instead, they can are objects that can be shared and used to achieve some collective goals, as a kind of *glue* among the agents exploiting them.

Moreover, the inter-agent and agent-artifacts models of interaction are profoundly different: agents *have no interfaces*, in the sense that they are not used by other agents through operations. Coordination artifacts are environment resources, which agents use, instead of communicating with them according to an high-level ACL. So, the agent abstraction is not the fittest one in order to understand, model, and engineer a coordination artifact behaviour.

For this reason, it is reasonable to introduce coordination artifacts in MASs as first class entities, as a part of the MAS resource environment. Using agents to model coordination artifacts – shaping their structure and behaviour in order to emulate the properties discussed previously – leads to an *abstraction gap* which makes the engineering of systems problematic as far as they grow in complexity. Our motto here for governing such complexity is *keep the abstraction alive*: i.e. consider the abstractions used at the design stage as first class ones also at the development stage and at runtime, enabling their identification, observation, control and testing at any stage of the engineering process. In order to support this vision, we consider fundamental on the one side to adopt formal models capturing essential aspects of coordination artifacts, so as to promote their correct specification, behaviour runtime controllability and testing. On the other side, to design and build suitable infrastructures providing services for coordination artifact organisation, use and dynamic management. The former aspect will be discussed more in detail in section 4, while the latter is discussed in section 6.

4   Formal Models for Coordination Artifacts

The ontological difference between the coordination artifact and the agent abstraction is reflected also by the formal models that we can adopt to define the structure and behaviour of a coordination artifact. To emphasise this point, in this section we provide a formal model of the behaviour of coordination artifacts, taking into account its three basic ingredients: *(i)* the concepts of actions and perceptions — that is, the usage interface —, which characterise agent interactions with artifacts; *(ii)* the usage instructions associated to each agent, which can be used to enforce agent correct behaviours and to promote its rational exploitation of artifacts; and *(iii)* the coordination policy that the artifact realises, defining the task actually automatised. Since we argue that coordination artifacts are not suitably modelled and engineered as cognitive entities like agents, we do not describe their behaviour in terms of mentalistic properties. In fact, the formal framework of modal logics for mentalistic properties appears to be useful as a tool to model complex, often intrinsically unpredictable systems, whose behaviour is hardly understood in terms of their design [25]. Rather, we here promote the idea that coordination artifacts are designed so as to encapsulate well-designed coordination tasks, and to accordingly feature predictable behaviour. We hence rely on a formal description based on operational semantics, which — by definition — can be directly exploited to devise a correct implementation [26]. In particular, as far as interaction and coordination are concerned, we find it useful to leverage the formal framework of concurrency theory and process algebraic approaches (such as in CCS [27]). The application of such languages and tools to the MAS field is not completely new but it is still under development [28, 29] — with the application presented here being a new interesting example. Here, a coordination artifact is a tuple $\langle \alpha, \beta, \rho, \delta, \longrightarrow_\sigma \rangle$. α is a meta-variable ranging over the operations allowed by the coordination artifact, namely, identifying the actions the agent can execute on it. β is the meta-variable ranging over perceptions of action completion, which may possibly contain some information about the outcome of the action. Correspondingly, the set L of interactions between agents and the coordination artifact, ranged over by l, is defined by the syntax

$$l ::= id!\alpha \mid id?\alpha\beta$$

where $id!\alpha$ represents agent id executing action α, and $id?\alpha\beta$ represents agent id perceiving the completion β to action α. ρ is a function associating to each agent identifier id the usage instruction I he has to follow, here expressed as the protocol of admissible actions and perceptions for that agent. Following the approach described in [18], instructions can be defined by exploiting typical process algebraic operators, e.g. by the syntax:

$$I ::= 0 \mid !\alpha.I \mid ?\beta.I \mid I + I \mid I \| I \mid \mathcal{D}$$

Here, 0 is the void instruction, $!\alpha.I$ is the execution of action α followed by continuation I, $?\beta.I$ is the perception of a completion β followed by continuation I, operator "$+$" is used for choice between instructions, "$\|$" for parallel (concurrent) composition of instructions, and $\mathcal{D}$ is the invocation of a recursive definition. When an action / perception continuation is 0, it is usually omitted, writing e.g. α in place of $\alpha.0$ with no risk of ambiguity (as in CCS). As an example, the definition $I_X :=!a.((?b.I_X)+?c)$ means that the agent is initially allowed to execute action a, and later perceives either completion b or c: while c involves termination of the instructions, b causes the whole instructions to be allowed again, through the recursive call to I_X. This is a typical schema for an agent repeatedly asking information through the artifact until the protocol is shut down. An operational semantics can be defined for this language, based on a transition relation $\longrightarrow_I$, where notation $I \xrightarrow{!\alpha}_I I'$ means that instructions (state) I moves to I' by the execution of action α, and $I \xrightarrow{?\alpha\beta} I'$ that I moves to I' as action α completes with perception β. The details of that semantics are not particularly relevant here, for the meaning of the above algebraic operators is quite standard and plays no significant role in the following. Therefore, operational rules are avoided for the sake of brevity: the interested reader can refer to [18] for their presentation. Meta-variable δ ranges over the data reified into the coordination artifact to keep track of the state of the coordination task. Correspondingly, we let meta-variable σ range over the set Σ of states of the coordination artifact, which is defined as:

$$\sigma ::= 0 \mid \delta \mid l \mid (\sigma \| \sigma)$$

Operator $\|$ is characterised by the following congruence rules:

$$\sigma \| 0 \equiv \sigma \quad \sigma \| \sigma' \equiv \sigma' \| \sigma \quad \sigma \| (\sigma' \| \sigma'') \equiv (\sigma \| \sigma') \| \sigma''$$

Thus, elements σ can be expressed as $\delta_1 \| \dots \| \delta_n \| l_1 \| \dots \| l_k$, and are easily understood as parallel compositions of elements δ and interactions l — the latter used to represent pending actions waiting to be executed and pending completions waiting to be perceived. State changes as interactions occur: the dynamics is modelled by the transition relation $\longrightarrow_\sigma \subseteq \Sigma \times \Sigma$, representing the fact that a state σ may eventually move to another σ', which typically happens when a new pending action has to be computed. So, while α and β shape the interactions allowed by the coordination artifact, ρ defines the protocols allowed to the agents, while δ and $\longrightarrow_\sigma$ define the actual coordination task. Given the tuple $\langle \alpha, \beta, \rho, \delta, \longrightarrow_\sigma \rangle$, the (interactive) behaviour of a coordination artifact is described by a transition system $\langle C, \longrightarrow, L \cup \{\tau\} \rangle$. C is the set of configurations of the coordination artifact, which are of the kind $\rho \otimes \sigma$ namely, the composition of a function ρ associating to each agent the instructions it currently has to follow, and the current state of the artifact σ. The transition relation $\longrightarrow \subseteq C \times (L \cup \{\tau\}) \times C$ is then defined by the rules:

$$\frac{\rho(id) \xrightarrow{!\alpha}_I I}{\rho \otimes \sigma \xrightarrow{id!\alpha} \rho[id \mapsto I] \otimes \sigma \,\|\, id!\alpha} \quad \text{[ACT]}$$

$$\frac{\rho(id) \xrightarrow{?\alpha\beta}_I I}{\rho \otimes \sigma \,\|\, id?\alpha\beta \xrightarrow{id?\alpha\beta} \rho[id \mapsto I] \otimes \sigma} \quad \text{[COMP]}$$

$$\frac{\sigma \rightarrow_\sigma \sigma'}{\rho \otimes \sigma \xrightarrow{\tau} \rho \otimes \sigma'} \quad \text{[COORD]}$$

The first rule handles a new action α executed by agent id to the coordination artifact. This is allowed only if the associated instructions $\rho(id)$ admit the transition towards some instructions I, in which case such instructions become the new instructions associated to id — ρ moves to $\rho[id \mapsto I]$ — and interaction $id!\alpha$ is reified in the state σ. In a similar way, the second rule deals with completion β to action α: when this is reified in the state σ and the instructions admit its perception, the completion is actually executed, and the ρ function is updated. Finally the third rule deals with the actual coordination task realised inside the artifact: simply, when transition relation $\longrightarrow_\sigma$ enables a transition for the state σ this can be applied to the current configuration and becomes a silent transition for the whole coordination artifact. So, while the first two rules handle agent interactions according to the operating instructions, the last rule encapsulates the core behaviour of the coordination artifact: the coordination task by which the interaction of agents is governed. Notice that in this formalisation we reify the current state of instructions for each role — namely, the role function — along with the coordination artifact state σ. This choice should amount to the idea that the MAS infrastructure handling the coordination artifact is in charge of keeping track of the dynamic evolution of such a function, most likely to enforce the compliance of each agent interactive behaviour with respect to the associated operating instructions. In general, however, each MAS infrastructure can support such an enforcement in different ways. On the one hand, the coordination artifacts provided could support this built-in ability: in this case operating instructions are not only a design-tool for the artifact, but really make into its actual run-time behaviour. On the other hand, because of many reasons including effectiveness and security, the MAS infrastructure could rely on different run-time (infrustructural) abstractions in charge of enforcing correct agent behaviours. This is the case for instance of TuCSoN [30] described in section 6, where the Agent Coordination Context notion is used to encapsulate, enable, and — most relevant here — enact agent interactions with the environment, and with coordination artifacts in particular.

5   Engineering Social Activities

The introduction of coordination artifacts impacts on the methodology adopted for engineering social activities in agent societies. Taking inspiration from Activity Theory,

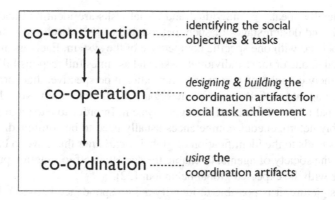

Fig. 1. Levels of a social activities

we can identify three different stages characterising any social activities supported by coordination artifact (see Fig. 1):

Co-construction — In this stage, engineers and scientists understand and reason about the social objectives of the society, and define a model of the social tasks required to achieve them. This implies understanding the shape of the agent interaction space, by eventually identifying also the dependencies that need to be managed (dependency detection is a fundamental aspect of coordination, according to the theory of coordination [16] and to cognitive theories of agent societies [31]).

Co-operation — In this stage, society engineers – and eventually intelligent agents – design and build the coordination artifacts according to the objective identified in the previous stage (co-construction). This implies understanding how to manage the dependencies previously identified, and defining a coordinating behaviour useful for the purpose. A model of coordination artifact must be chosen, according to its ability of embedding and enacting such a coordinating behaviour.

Co-ordination — In this stage, coordination artifacts are exploited, supporting the execution of the social activity. Here, the focus is on the efficient execution and automation of the coordination activities.

As in the case of AT, the three levels are distinct analytical moments that can be applied continuously, since a social activity is considered to be always under development, given the intrinsic openness of the environment and the dynamism of organisations.

5.1   Activity Levels as Engineering Stages

It is not without reason that Activity Theory is primarily used as an analytical tool for understanding collaborative work in complex organisational contexts, and as a design tool to improve them. In such contexts, AT makes it possible to face the social complexity first by separating individual and collective activities, then by identifying and designing the artifacts required to support both of them.

Along this line, we can devise a correspondence between the three collaborative stages in Fig. 1, and the engineering stages as typically found in (agent-oriented) software engineering methodologies, i.e., analysis, design, development and deployment /

runtime. Generally speaking, individual and social tasks are identified and described in the analysis and design stages of such methodologies [32]. Each individual tasks is typically associated with one specific competence of the system. Each agent in the system is assigned to one or more individual tasks, and assumes full responsibility for their correct and timely completion. From an organisational perspective, this corresponds to assigning each agent a specific role in the organisation. Conversely, social tasks represent the global responsibilities of the agent system. In order to carry out such tasks, several possibly heterogeneous competences usually need to be combined. The design of social tasks leads to the identification of global *social laws* that have to be respected / enforced by the society of agents, to enable the society itself to function properly and in accordance with the expected global behaviour [32].

Given this picture, it is possible to identify a correspondence between the analysis stage (where individual and social tasks are identified) and the co-construction level, where the social objectives of the activities are shaped. Then, the identification of the social laws required to achieve the social tasks can be seen as a first step in the co-operation level. This level roughly corresponds to the design and development stages of the engineering process: coordination artifacts are the abstractions which make it possible to design and develop social tasks. At the co-operation level such artifacts are designed and developed to embody and enact – as governing abstractions provided by the infrastructure – the social laws and norms previously identified. Finally, the deployment and runtime stages correspond to the co-ordination level, when the coordination artifacts are instantiated and exploited.

The dynamism among the levels, that are compared here to the engineering stages of a system, promote then a new approach in the engineering of systems that we can call here *online engineering*: coordination artifacts can be re-designed, manipulated, tested, debugged, analysed dynamically, at runtime. In order to support online engineering methodology two aspects are essential: first, working with abstractions featuring suitable properties such as inspectability, controllability and malleability, which are necessary for their online analysis and synthesis; second, designing and building infrastructures that – as mentioned in previous section – keep the abstractions alive, with services enabling their access and exploitation – supporting the co-ordination stage –, and tools for their manipulation (inspection, control, adaptation) – supporting the co-operation stage. In section 6 a concrete example of such an infrastructure – TuCSoN – is described.

5.2   Bridging the Gap Between Subjective and Objective Coordination

The three scientific and engineering levels of the social activities make it possible to frame explicitly the role of *subjective* and *objective* coordination inside the systems, and to bridge the gap between them. The distinction between subjective and objective approaches has been recognised as fundamental to characterise the role of the environment in the engineering of social aspects in multi-agent systems [33, 34]. Generally speaking, in subjective approaches agents coordinate with each other by observing and reasoning subjectively on the environment and acting consequently, in order to achieve collective goals: coordination is then interpreted as an individual, psychological activity trying to achieve its own subjective goals in the context of a multi-component system. In objective approaches instead the environment is considered as an active part of the coordination process, driving agent interactions toward the achievement of the global objectives: co-ordination is basically regarded as a normative activity performed by some parts of a multi-component system on behalf of the system designer – typically, by a coordination medium provided by an infrastructure. The first approach seems to better suit systems whose components exhibit a high degree of autonomy (intelligent agents being the most obvious example), whereas the second fits well application scenarios involving a finer component granularity (as typical in the case of mobile agents). The engineering of com-plex applications call for bridging the gap between subjective and objective approaches [33, 17]: on the one side, the flexibility typically characterising subjective approaches is required to face openness of complex coordination activities, reacting to unpredictable events and change of strategies and goals. On the other side, the engineering attitude on coordination which characterises objective approaches is required to automate the coordination process, scaling up with its complexity.

Adopting the framework of coordination artifacts, it is possible then to frame sub-jective and objective coordination in the same methodological context [14]. In the co-ordination stage we can clearly see the level of objective coordination: coordination arti-facts are exploited in order to maximise the automation and performance of coordination activities, with no need of complex negotiation protocols between the participants. In-stead, co-operation is typically the stage where the subjective approaches are necessary, because they account for reasoning about the features of the coordination artifacts that can be used to achieve the system goals and properties identified at the co-construction stage.

The dynamism between the levels is the key to frame both subjective and objective coordination in the same context. This is captured by two basic transitions, the *reflection* and the *reification* of coordination, which must be supported dynamically during system execution:

Reification — In this transition, coordination laws designed and developed at the co-operation stage are reified or *objectified* in coordination artifacts: intelligent agents forge the behaviour of coordination artifacts in order to reflect the social rules estab-lished in the co-operation stage, to be used as artifacts in the co-ordination stage. It is worth noting that coordination artifacts are meant to embed not only rules promot-ing cooperation among agents, but in general laws to rule their interaction. These interaction rules are useful to represent also norms and environment constraints, either mediating agent competitive (non cooperative) behaviour, or harnessing self-interested agent behaviours so as to achieve global MAS goals without affecting agent autonomy.

Reflection — In this transition, the behaviour of the coordination artifacts deployed at the co-ordination stage is inspected and possibly understood. Agents (as well as engineers) can retrieve the coordination laws underlying artifact behaviour, and relate them to the history of MAS evolution, in order to either evolve them according to changes in coordination policies or in environmental conditions, or learn how to exploit the artifacts in a more effective and efficient way.

Coordination artifacts become then fundamental for dynamically balancing subjec-tive and objective coordination, allowing the distribution of the coordination burden between artifacts and agents to be defined at runtime. The capability of balancing task automation and cooperation in a flexible way is among the most important requirements for state-of-the-art systems for workflow management, supply chain management, and CSCW [35, 36]. The ability to change the "engineering point" of coordination dynamically is also of special importance for open MAS, where the environment can unpredictably change, and the overall structure and functionality of the system may evolve in time [37].

The above considerations lead to some additional requirements for coordination infrastructures. In particular, in order to support these capabilities, coordination infrastructures should provide the means (languages and tools) for enabling coordination reflection (objective-to-subjective transition), to inspect the coordination laws defining coordination artifact behaviour, and coordination reification (subjective-to-objective transition), defining and programming the behaviour of the coordination artifacts. TuCSoN – introduced in section 6 – is an example of infrastructure supporting most of such requirements.

5.3   The Organisation Perspective: Structuring the Working Environment

Coordination artifacts can be suitably used in a structured and ruled organisation. Coordination artifacts become the entities around which the social activities are built, inducing a natural form of organisation structuring and modelling. By abstracting from details, several independent collaborative and cooperative activities are carried over inside an organisation, each one charged upon a group of agents and a suitable coordination artifact. The group of agents can be thought as a sort of *society* (permanent or temporal) with a specific objective, which is reflected by the structure and behaviour of the coordination artifact. An organisation can be conceived then as a static as well as dynamic set of societies, composed by agents playing some *roles*, characterised by different ways of using the coordination artifact. Organisational models based on the notion of role are pervasive in computer science as well as in the context of human organisation theories, impacting also on security and coordination aspects; role-based access control (RBAC) architectures – well-known in state of the art of security in information systems [38] – have been recently introduced also in MAS to capture such aspects, framing organisation, security and coordination in the same model [39].

Following the organisation perspective, coordination artifacts are the key to shape agent working environment, as *(i)* tools for pure coordination, and *(ii)* interfaces mediating agent access to the resources and the services provided by the environment itself. As mediating interfaces, coordination artifacts can encapsulate the policies for resource management, involving the coordination of both the users and the resources or the providers of the services.

The two issues above point out the fundamental role of artifacts in the design and construction of an effective working environment, supporting agent activity toward the achievement of their individual and social tasks. This is particularly relevant in the context of cognitive theories applied for CSCW, such as Distributed Cognition [8]. In the design and construction of a good working environment for the organisation the tension between subjective and objective approaches emerges again in terms of the dichotomy between *flexibility* – the capability of individuals of adapting to contingent situation – and *automation* – the capability of making fluid the execution of activities. On the one side, given the complexity and the openness of agent organisations, a working environment keeps on evolving and requires flexibility in order to allow for supporting changes and adaptations. The lack of flexibility dramatically impacts on all system activities. On the other side, a good working environment should assist workers as much as possible in their coordination, providing services to alleviate their coordination burden and let them focus on their individual work. The lack of system coordination typically makes organisations unable to govern the complexity of the activities: the end result is typically a weak control of activities, and poor performances in their execution.

6   Toward Infrastructures for Coordination Artifacts

Coordination artifact infrastructures provide services for their access and use, effectively supporting the co-operation and co-ordination levels and the reflection / reification transitions. Services range from artifacts creation, to inspection of their state and dynamic adaptation of their coordinating behaviour.

In the overall, coordination artifacts can be seen then a fundamental abstraction for realising *governing* infrastructures [33], i.e. infrastructure providing flexible and robust abstractions to model and shape the agent interaction space, in accordance with the social and normative objectives of systems. Infrastructures also represent an effective approach to the general problem of formalisability of complex systems, which may come either for pragmatical or theoretical issues. By their very nature, infrastructures intrinsically encapsulate key portions of systems — often in charge of the critical system behaviour. In this case, governing infrastructure encapsulate agent interaction and coordination through coordination artifacts. As a result, providing well-specified infrastructures, and in particular formally-defined coordination artifacts (as seen in section 4) promotes the discovery and proof of critical system properties. Most notably, a system property can be assessed at design-time through the formal definition of some design abstraction. Then, by ensuring compliance of the corresponding run-time abstraction provided by the infrastructure, such a property can be enforced at execution time and be automatically verified for any system based on the infrastructure [40].

6.1   TuCSoN Coordination Infrastructure

TuCSoN [41] is a coordination infrastructure for MAS whose model brings the main principles that characterise the coordination artifact framework[2].

The infrastructure enables agent interaction and coordination by means of *tuple centres*, which here can be considered as a kind of coordination artifacts. Technically, tuple centres are *programmable tuple spaces* – sort of reactive, logic-based blackboards that agents access associatively by writing, reading, and consuming *tuples* – ordered collections of heterogeneous information chunks – via simple communication operations (*out*, *rd*, *in*, *inp*, *rdp*) [24]. While the behaviour of a tuple space in response to communication events is fixed, the behaviour of a tuple centre can be tailored to the application needs by defining a set of *specification tuples* expressed in the ReSpecT language, which define

---

[2] The TuCSoN technology is available as an open source project at the TuCSoN web site
http://tucson.sourceforge.net

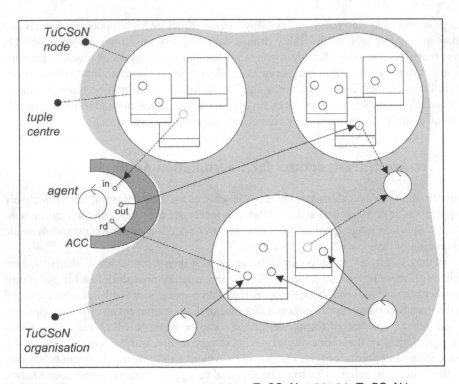

Fig. 2. Overview of a multi-agent system exploiting TuCSoN. A MAS in TuCSoN is composed by a dynamic set of agents (represented in the figure by a circle with an arrow) and tuple centres (represented by a box with a line in the bottom), hosted by the nodes of the infrastructure. Each agent can access and exploit the tuple centres by means of its ACC (represented by a semi-circle), which enables and mediates agent actions on the environment. In the TuCSoN case such operations are the basic coordination primitives on the tuple centres

how a tuple centre should react to incoming / outgoing communication events. So, unlike from tuple spaces, tuple centres can be programmed with reactions so as to encapsulate coordination laws directly in the coordination media.

From the topology point of view, TuCSoN coordination artifacts are collected in infrastructure nodes (see Fig. 2), distributed over the network, organised into articulated domains [42]. A domain is characterised by a *gateway* node and a set of nodes called *places*. Briefly, a place is meant to host tuple centres for the specific applications / systems, while the gateway node is meant to host tuple centres used for domain administration, keeping information on the places. A place can belong to different domains, and can be itself a gateway for a sub-domain.

So, tuple centres can be conceived as general-purpose coordination artifacts, which can be customised (programmed, tuned) dynamically to entail a specific coordinating behaviour. Generally speaking, tuple centres exhibit the properties that characterise coordination artifacts: they provide different levels of inspectability – both the communication and the coordination state can be inspected at runtime –, different levels of malleability and controllability – both by changing dynamically their coordinating behaviour and by controlling its execution by means of proper infrastructure tools [43]. Also, we can identify the basic elements that characterise the abstract model of coordination artifacts: the usage interface is composed by the basic coordination primitives plus the primitives to inspect and change tuple centre behaviour (*set_spec* and *get_spec*). The coordination behaviour specification is given by the ReSpecT specification. The notion of operating instructions is not directly supported in tuple centres, even if the ReSpecT specification tuples implicitly contain a description of how to exploit the tuple centre in order to obtain the coordinating service.

Actually, in TuCSoN operating instructions are supported instead by another infrastructural first class abstraction, the *Agent Coordination Context* (ACC), which has recently extended the basic TuCSoN model to face also organisation and security issues in synergy with coordination [44, 30]. Roughly speaking, in TuCSoN an ACC is an runtime and stateful interface released to an agent to execute operations on the tuple centres of a specific organisation. More generally, an ACC is a sort of interface provided to the agent by the infrastructure to make it interact within a certain organisation environment. A fundamental aspect is that an ACC is a *ruled* interface: it encapsulates and enforces some security and organisation policies which define and constrain the space of the agent allowed actions and protocols, according to the role(s) the agent is actively playing inside the organisation. Also an ACC embodies the notion of *work session* of an agent inside an organisation: an agent aiming at participating to the activities of an organisation – i.e. accessing its tuple centres – must first request an ACC. If the request is compatible with the organisation rules, an ACC properly configured with role policies is released to the agent, which can then start working and interacting with tuple centres. So, if tuple centres can be considered coordination artifacts encapsulating and applying global coordination laws, ACCs can be framed as mediating artifacts embedding and enforcing local rules.

Finally, a key role in TuCSoN infrastructure is played by tools – which are essential for supporting online engineering methodology. In particular, the *Inspector* tool – available with TuCSoN technology – makes it possible to dynamically inspect and control both the communication and coordination state of a tuple centre, including also the possibility of tracing its coordinating behaviour [43]. Using an Inspector, engineers and scientist can then observe, analyse, and control the runtime behaviour of a society of agents by suitably inspecting and controlling the tuple centres used by the society.

6.2   Examples of Coordination Artifacts in TuCSoN

Coordination artifacts can be considered as units of reuse for engineering cooperative working environments: as agents encapsulate skills and competences concerning the execution of some task, the achievement of some goal or the solution of some problem, coordination artifacts encapsulate strategies, knowledge and experiences for constructing and ruling social activities.

In the following we describe some types of coordination artifacts commonly used in the engineering of systems, implemented on top of TuCSoN. The properties of inspectability, controllability and malleability of tuple centres should be considered in the background of all the examples: they are the key to conceive scenarios where the cooperative working environment can be analysed and improved at runtime, by inspecting and adapting the coordinating behaviour of its coordination artifacts.

Coordination Artifacts for Communication. A common form of coordination artifacts is used to provide communication services, enabling the exchange of information among agents in open and dynamic contexts which require a certain level of uncoupling among the participants. In particular, coordination artifacts can be adopted to support communication even if participants do know each other (identity uncoplying), if they are not simultaneously taking part to the interaction (temporal uncoupling), if they do not belong to the same spatial context or they ignore their mutual position (spatial uncoupling).

A *mailbox* for instance can be adopted as an artifact supporting temporal and spatial uncoupling among multiple senders and typically a single receiver, with some kind of policy – e.g. FIFO – for storing and accessing the messages. Fig. 3 shows a tuple centre – called mailbox – instrumented to provide the services of a mailbox. The usage interface accounts for an operation to insert new messages (by inserting a msg tuple), to retrieve last message (by retrieving the tuple last_msg), and to read the number of messages available (by reading the tuple num_messages). The tuple centre is programmed so as to realise a FIFO policy for managing messages: the ReSpecT specification defining tuple centre behaviour (shown in Fig. 3) basically indexes the messages as soon as they are inserted in the mailbox, keeping track of the index of the first and last message, and then using it to get last one on request. This policy could be adapted dynamically according to the need, for instance adopting a strategy based on priorities or establishing a maximum number of messages which can be stored in the mailbox.

Blackboards are another kind of well-known coordination artifacts, as shared spaces of evolving knowledge where participants insert and access / retrieve information associatively. With respect to the original model developed in the context of DAI [45], here control is distributed and encapsulated within agents, while the blackboard can be programmed to have a reactive behaviour to manipulate knowledge according to social rules shared and acknowledged by the agents. Tuple centres directly maps the notion of blackboard: the coordination primitives are meta-predicates to insert, inspect and retrieve knowledge in terms of logic tuples, forming a theory of communication. ReSpecT specification tuples represent the reactive rules which manipulate the theory of communication as a theory of coordination.

Coordination Artifacts for Knowledge Mediation. Coordination artifacts can be exploited to entail automated forms of knowledge mediation for managing heterogeneity in open environments. As an example, we consider a tuple centre mediating the interaction between agents providing some services or information, and agents looking for such services or related. As an abstract case, we suppose that an agent A needs to know information pq(X,Y). According to some social knowledge – which is unknown to agent A – the information can be constructed by aggregating knowledge represented by tuple p(X) and q(Y), provided by other agents working as knowledge sources. The tuple centre can be suitably programmed then to act as knowledge mediator, applying the rules to construct the information pq from p and q:

```
reaction(rdp(pq(X,Y)), (
     pre, rd_r(p(X)), rd_r(q(Y)), out_r(pq(X,Y)) )).

reaction(rdp(pq(X,Y)), (
     post, in_r(pq(X,Y)) )).
```

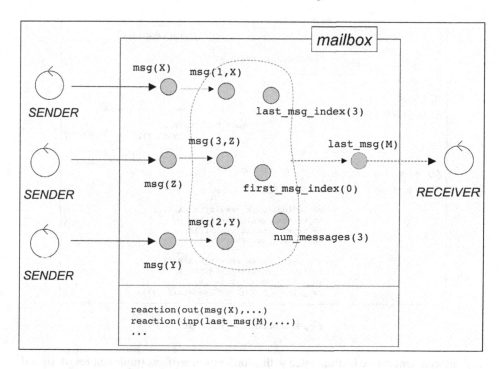

```
reaction(out(msg(M)),(
  in_r(msg(M)),
  in_r(num_messages(N)), N1 is N + 1, out_r(num_messages(N1)),
  in_r(last_msg_index(I)), I1 is I + 1,
out_r(last_msg_index(I1)),
  out_r(msg(I1,M)) )).

reaction(inp(last_msg(M)),( pre,
  in_r(first_msg_index(I)), rd_r(last_msg_index(N)), I < N,
  I1 is I + 1, out_r(first_msg_index(I1)),
  in_r(msg(I1,M)), out_r(last_msg(M)) )).

reaction(inp(last_msg(M)),( post, success,
  in_r(num_messages(N)),N1 is N - 1,out_r(num_messages(N1)) )).
```

Fig. 3. Mailbox tuple centre *(Top)* and its coordinating behaviour in ReSpecT Ê*(Bottom)*

Whenever a request for reading information pq is executed, the information is constructed dynamically by reading the content of the tuples p and q and inserted as a new pq tuple in the tuple set to satisfy the request. The request fails if the information cannot be constructed, because of the absence of p or q.

Coordination Artifacts for Resource Sharing. Resource and task sharing are among the most common coordination problems in distributed and concurrent systems. A work-

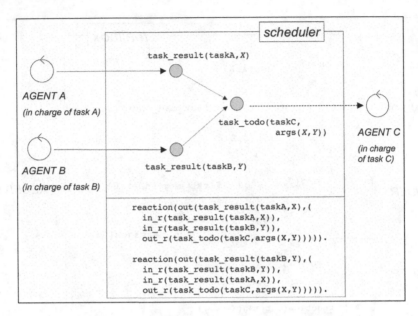

Fig. 4. Scheduler tuple centre

ing environment can be instrumented with coordination artifacts (tuple centres) designed and programmed to provide some form of access policy in task or resource access, embodying mechanisms and synchronisation strategies well-known in concurrent systems, such as semaphores, synchronisation barries, monitors, etc.

As a simple example, we consider here a tuple centre used to act as a semaphore. The P operation provided by a semaphore used to request and obtain access to the resource can be realised by means on an in(sem) operation, i.e. retrieving a tuple sem from the tuple centre; dually, the V operation used to manifest the release of the resource can be realised by inserting back the tuple in the tuple set, by means of an out(sem). To obtain the coordinating behaviour of a semaphore it is not necessary to program the tuple centre, since the basic form of synchronisation directly provided by the *in* and *out* coordination primitives is sufficient for the purpose. Programming the tuple centre would instead be needed to obtain a more articulated and robust solution, for instance allowing multiple agents to acquire the semaphore simultaneously.

Coordination Artifacts for Workflow Management. Workflow management concerns the automated integration and coordination of heterogeneous and independent activities involved in the same global business process. Among the others it includes activity scheduling and synchronisation, information and control flow management, exception management, and so on. Currently, in the context of service-oriented architectures – in particular Web Services – workflow management is also called *orchestration* [46].

Typically, special purpose languages – XPDL, BPEL are examples – can be used to define the workflow specification; their specification is executed by the *workflow engine*, the core component of Workflow Management Systems. A workflow engine – also called orchestration engine – can be framed here as a general purpose coordination artifact, which is dynamically programmed to enact a coordinating behaviour according to the workflow specification.

In the context of MASs, a tuple centre then can be programmed to provide the services from a simple task scheduler up to a full-fledged general purpose workflow engine. As an example, here we consider the realisation of a simple scheduler of three activities – A, B and C – coordinated according a join pattern: task C can only start when both tasks A and B have been completed. Tasks are executed by independent agents, typically unaware of the global workflow and focussed on the achievement of their specific job. The tuple centre `scheduler` shown in Fig. 4 is an example of a coordination artifact providing such a scheduling service. The operation of the usage interface can be:

- `in(task_todo(+TaskName,-TaskInfo))`, for taking in charge the execution of a task. The presence of a tuple `task_todo` manifests the fact that a specific task has to be done, according to current workflow.
- `out(task_result(+TaskName,+TaskResult))`, for communicating the result of the execution of a task, signaling its completion.

In the example, *TaskName* can be `taskA`, `taskB` or `taskC`. The operating instructions of this coordination artifact to be followed by agents in charge of task execution would consist first in getting information about task, then in providing the result. Fig. 4 shows also the **ReSpecT** specification realising the scheduling behaviour: basically, a suitable `task_todo` tuple is automatically generated in the tuple set as soon as the results of the execution of both tasks A and B are available.

In [47] the architecture of a workflow management system based on **TuCSoN** is described, with tuple centres used as general purpose workflow engines.

7   Related Work

The coordination artifact framework discussed in this paper has been mostly inspired on the one side directly by Activity Theory studies, and on the other side by the research work developed in the context of coordination models, languages and architectures, developed mainly in the field of concurrent systems [48, 49]. In particular the notion of coordination artifact is strictly related to the *programmable coordination medium* abstraction defined in [50], on which the tuple centre model is based. According to the frequently adopted meta-model described in [51], a coordination model can be described by identifying the *coordinables* – the entities participating to coordination activities –, and the *coordination media* – the entities enabling and managing agent communication according to some coordination laws defining the semantics of the coordination activities. Programmable coordination media extend the basic notion of coordination medium by making its behaviour programmable with some specific language, so as to flexibly specify the coordination rules according to the need. So, programmable coordination media share some properties which characterise coordination artifacts, such as encapsulation of coordination and malleability of the behaviour. Instead, differently from programmable coordination media and coordination media in general, coordination artifacts do not manage necessarily communication among agents, but – more generally – interactions caused by the execution of operations provided by the usage interface. Also, the coordination artifact framework introduces some structural properties – such as operating instructions – which are new with respect to the classic coordination meta-model, and which are indeed important in the context of open agent societies.

The design and exploitation of cooperative working environment and related infrastructures for supporting coordination activities are central themes in the context of CSCW [7]. Here, the expressiveness and effectiveness of coordination through mechanisms mediating human interaction have been clearly remarked, and related models, languages and infrastructures have been developed [52, 53]. Coordination artifacts feature some of the basic properties of *coordinative artifacts* defined in such contexts [7] – in particular the properties concerning malleability and linkability –, contextualising and extending them for the MAS context. Operating instructions, for instance, are part of the extension.

Finally, the coordination artifact framework can be exploited as an analytical tool for describing existing coordination approaches based on some form of mediated interaction and environment-based coordination. For instance, the environment provided by the pheromone infrastructure in [12] supporting stigmergy coordination can be interpreted as a coordination artifact exploited by ants to coordinate: as such, it provides operations for depositing and sensing pheromones, and the coordinating behaviour is given by the environmental laws ruling the diffusion, aggregation and evaporation of pheromones. Analogously, the *field* abstraction in the co-field approach [54] – a recent approach for engineering of swarm intelligent systems – can be seen as a coordination artifact, mediating mobile agents interaction and supporting their coordinated navigation inside some kind of space. Also some coordination approaches developed in the context of intelligent / cognitive agents can be framed in terms of coordination artifacts. An example is the TEAMCORE model / infrastructure [55], which provides a coordination support to teams composed by heterogeneous agents – including agents with no teamwork capabilities. Here, each agent of a team is provided with a STEAM module, a sort of a proxy of the TEAMCORE infrastructure which mediate agent interactions and generate suitable communication actions according to a global plan specification. A STEAM module can be then understood as a coordination artifact, whose coordinating behaviour is essential for the achievement of the team goals.

8   Conclusion

In the context of human activities and CSCW Activity Theory and Distributed Cognition remark the importance of the environment – and in particular of the tools available in the environment – for governing the complexity of cooperative / social work, in particular for its analysis and construction. Analogously, the framework of coordination artifacts aims at providing an engineering key for instrumenting a MAS working environment with first class abstractions which could help agents of a MAS to cooperate and coordinate. Such first class abstractions are meant to be exploited in the various stage of the engineering process in agent-oriented software engineering methodologies: at the design stage, as modelling entities for designing social activities; at development and runtime stage, as runtime abstractions – supported by suitable infrastructures – to be used by agents to execute the social activities; and at runtime stage also for online engineering of systems, as inspectable, malleable abstractions which can be dynamically observed, controlled, adapted – by human as well as by intelligent agents – to support online debugging and evolution of the activities.

Several issues will be subject of investigation in future work. Among the other: *(i)* the extension of an existing methodology – SODA [56] – with the coordination artifact framework, in particular identifying the role of the co-construction / co-operation / co-ordination stages, essential for supporting the online engineering approach; *(ii)* the extension of TuCSoN infrastructure model, design and technology, so as to fully support the coordination artifact vision, in particular framing and implementing the notion of operating instructions for tuple centres; *(iii)* the (offline and online) verification of formal properties of coordination activities, exploiting the well-founded formal semantics of TuCSoN coordination artifacts, i.e. tuple centres; and finally, *(iv)* the benefits and effectiveness of the framework in engineering real-world systems, exploiting TuCSoN as the basic infrastructure technology.

References

1. Parunak, H.V.D., Brueckner, S., Fleischer, M., Odell, J.: A preliminary taxonomy of multi-agent interactions. In: 2nd International Joint conference on Autonomous Agents and Multi-agent Systems (AAMAS 2002), ACM Press (2003) 1090–1091
2. Fenster, M., Kraus, S., Rosenschein, J.S.: Coordination without communication: Experimental validation of focal point techniques. In: 1st International Conference on Multi-Agent Systems (ICMAS'95), AAAI (1995) 102–108
3. Ciancarini, P., Omicini, A., Zambonelli, F.: Multiagent system engineering: The coordination viewpoint. In Jennings, N.R., Lespérance, Y., eds.: Intelligent Agents VI. Agent Theories, Architectures, and Languages. Volume 1757 of LNAI., Springer-Verlag (2000) 250–259
4. Bonabeau, E., Dorigo, M., Theraulaz, G.: Swarm Intelligence: From Natural to Artificial Systems. Oxford University Press (1999)
5. Steels, L.: The artificial life roots of Artificial Intelligence. Artificial Life Journal 1 (1994) 89–125
6. Ferber, J., Müller, J.P.: Influences and reaction: a model of situated multiagent systems. In: 2nd International Conference on Multi-Agent Systems (ICMAS'96). (1996)
7. Schmidt, K., Simone, C.: Coordination mechanisms: Towards a conceptual foundation of CSCW systems design. International Journal of Computer Supported Cooperative Work (CSCW) 5 (1996) 155–200
8. Kirsh, D.: Distributed cognition, coordination and environment design. In: European conference on Cognitive Science. (1999) 1–11
9. Nardi, B.A.: Context and Consciousness: Activity Theory and Human-Computer Interaction. MIT Press (1996)
10. Vygotsky, L.S.: Mind and Society. Harvard University Press (1978)
11. Cost, S.R., Labrou, Y., Finin, T.: Coordinating agents using agent communication languages conversations. [57] chapter 7 183–196
12. Parunak, H.V.D., Brueckner, S., Sauter, J.: Digital pheromone mechanisms for coordination of unmanned vehicles. In: 1st International Joint Conference on Autonomous Agents and Multiagent Systems AAMAS'02, ACM Press (2002) 449–450

13. Esteva, M., Rosell, B., Rodríguez-Aguilar, J.A., Arcos, J.L.: Ameli: An agent-based middle-ware for electronic institutions. In Jennings, N.R., Sierra, C., Sonenberg, L., Tambe, M., eds.: 3rd international Joint Conference on Autonomous Agents and Multiagent Systems (AAMAS 2004). Volume 1., New York, USA, ACM (2004) 236–243
14. Ricci, A., Omicini, A., Denti, E.: Activity Theory as a framework for MAS coordination. In Petta, P., Tolksdorf, R., Zambonelli, F., eds.: Engineering Societies in the Agents World III. Volume 2577 of LNCS. Springer-Verlag (2003) 96–110
15. Omicini, A., Ricci, A., Viroli, M., Castelfranchi, C., Tummolini, L.: Coordination artifacts: Environment-based coordination for intelligent agents. In Jennings, N.R., Sierra, C., Sonenberg, L., Tambe, M., eds.: 3rd International Joint Conference on Autonomous Agents and Multiagent Systems (AAMAS 2004). Volume 1., New York, USA, ACM (2004) 286–293
16. Malone, T., Crowston, K.: The interdisciplinary study of coordination. ACM Computing Surveys **26** (1994) 87–119
17. Omicini, A., Ricci, A., Viroli, M., Cioffi, M., Rimassa, G.: Multi-agent infrastructures for objective and subjective coordination. Applied Artificial Intelligence **18** (2004) 815–831 Special Issue: Best papers from EUMAS 2003: The 1st European Workshop on Multi-agent Systems.
18. Viroli, M., Ricci, A.: Instructions-based semantics of agent mediated interaction. In Jennings, N.R., Sierra, C., Sonenberg, L., Tambe, M., eds.: 3rd International Joint Conference on Autonomous Agents and Multiagent Systems (AAMAS 2004). Volume 1., New York, USA, ACM (2004) 286–293
19. Wooldridge, M.J., Jennings, N.R.: Intelligent agents: Theory and practice. The Knowledge Engineering Review **10** (1995) 115–152
20. Bergstra, J.A., Ponse, A., Smolka, S.A., eds.: Handbook of Process Algebra. North-Holland, Amsterdam, London, New York, Oxford, Paris, Shannon and Tokyo (2001)
21. Petri, C.A.: Kommunikation mit Automaten. PhD thesis, Institut für Instrumentelle Mathematik, University of Bonn, Bonn, Germany (1962)
22. Berry, G., Boudol, G.: The chemical abstract machine. In: 17th ACM SIGPLAN-SIGACT symposium on Principles of programming languages, ACM Press (1990) 81–94
23. Durfee, E.H.: Scaling up agent coordination strategies. IEEE Computer **34** (2001)
24. Omicini, A., Denti, E.: From tuple spaces to tuple centres. Science of Computer Programming **41** (2001) 277–294
25. Dennett, D.: The Intentional Stance. Bradford Books/MIT Press, Cambridge, MA (1987)
26. Broy, M., Olderog, E.R.: Trace-oriented models of concurrency. In: Handbook of Process Algebra. North-Holland (2001) 101–195
27. Milner, R.: Communication and Concurrency. Prentice Hall (1989)
28. Kinny, D., ed.: The Psi Calculus: An Algebraic Agent Language. In Kinny, D., ed.: Intelligent Agents VIII, 8th International Workshop, ATAL 2001 Seattle, WA, USA, August 1-3, 2001, Revised Papers. Volume 2333 of Lecture Notes in Computer Science., Springer (2002)
29. van Eijk, R.M., de Boer, F.S., van der Hoek, W., Meyer, J.J.C.: A verification framework for agent communication. Autonomous Agents and Multi-Agent Systems **2** (2003) 185–219
30. Ricci, A., Viroli, M., Omicini, A.: Agent coordination context: From theory to practice. In Trappl, R., ed.: Cybernetics and Systems 2004. Volume 2., Vienna, Austria, Austrian Society for Cybernetic Studies (2004) 618–623 17th European Meeting on Cybernetics and Systems Research (EMCSR 2004), Vienna, Austria, 13–16 April 2004. Proceedings.
31. Conte, R., Castelfranchi, C.: Cognitive and Social Action. University College London (1995)
32. Zambonelli, F., Jennings, N.R., Omicini, A., Wooldridge, M.: Agent-oriented software engineering for internet applications. [57] chapter 13 369–398

33. Omicini, A., Ossowski, S.: Objective versus subjective coordination in the engineering of agent systems. In Klusch, M., Bergamaschi, S., Edwards, P., Petta, P., eds.: Intelligent Information Agents: An AgentLink Perspective. Volume 2586 of LNAI: State-of-the-Art Survey. Springer-Verlag (2003) 179–202

34. Schumacher, M.: Objective Coordination in Multi-Agent System Engineering – Design and Implementation. Volume 2039 of LNAI. Springer-Verlag (2001)

35. Dayal, U., Hsu, M., Rivka, L.: Business process coordination: State of the art, trends and open issues. In: 27th VLDB Conference, Rome, Italy (2001)

36. Nutt, G.: The evolution toward flexible workflow systems. Distributed Systems Engineering **3** (1996) 276–294

37. Omicini, A., Ossowski, S., Ricci, A.: Coordination infrastructures in the engineering of multiagent systems. In Bergenti, F., Gleizes, M.P., Zambonelli, F., eds.: Methodologies and Software Engineering for Agent Systems: The Agent-Oriented Software Engineering Handbook. Kluwer Academic Publishers (2004) 273–296

38. Sandhu, R., Coyne, E.J., Feinstein, H.L., Youman, C.E.: Role-based control models. IEEE Computer **29** (1996) 38–47

39. Ricci, A., Viroli, M., Omicini, A.: Role-Based Access Control in MAS using Agent Coordination Contexts. In Dignum, V., Corkill, D., Jonker, C., Dignum, F., eds.: 1st International Workshop "Agent Organizations: Theory and Practice" (AOTP'04), AAAI-04, San José, CA, USA, AAAI Press (2004) 15–22 Proceedings.

40. Omicini, A., Ricci, A., Viroli, M.: Formal specification and enactment of security policies through Agent Coordination Contexts. In Focardi, R., Zavattaro, G., eds.: Security Issues in Coordination Models, Languages and Systems. Volume 85(3) of Electronic Notes in Theoretical Computer Science. Elsevier Science B. V. (2003)

41. Omicini, A., Zambonelli, F.: Coordination for Internet application development. Autonomous Agents and Multi-Agent Systems **2** (1999) 251–269

42. Cremonini, M., Omicini, A., Zambonelli, F.: Multi-agent systems on the Internet: Extending the scope of coordination towards security and topology. In Garijo, F.J., Boman, M., eds.: Multi-Agent Systems Engineering. Volume 1647 of LNAI., Springer-Verlag (1999) 77–88 9th European Workshop on Modelling Autonomous Agents in a Multi-Agent World (MAA-MAW'99), Valencia (E), 30 June – 2 July 1999, Proceedings.

43. Denti, E., Omicini, A., Ricci, A.: Coordination tools for MAS development and deployment. Applied Artificial Intelligence **16** (2002) 721–752 Special Issue: Engineering Agent Systems – Best of "From Agent Theory to Agent Implementation (AT2AI-3)".

44. Omicini, A., Ricci, A.: MAS organisation within a coordination infrastructure: Experiments in TuCSoN. In Omicini, A., Petta, P., Pitt, J., eds.: Engineering Societies in the Agents World IV. Volume 3071 of LNAI. Springer-Verlag (2004) 200–217 4th International Workshop (ESAW 2003), London, UK, 29–31 October 2003. Revised Selected and Invited Papers.

45. Corkill, D.: Blackboard systems. Journal of AI Expert **9** (1991) 40–47

46. Peltz, C.: Web services orchestration and choreography. IEEE Computer **36** (2003) 46–52

47. Ricci, A., Omicini, A., Denti, E.: Virtual enterprises and workflow management as agent coordination issues. International Journal of Cooperative Information Systems **11** (2002) 355–379 Special Issue: Cooperative Information Agents – Best Papers of CIA 2001.

48. Papadopoulos, G.A.: Models and technologies for the coordination of Internet agents: A survey. In Omicini, A., Zambonelli, F., Klusch, M., Tolksdorf, R., eds.: Coordination of Internet Agents: Models, Technologies, and Applications. Springer-Verlag (2001) 25–56

49. Papadopoulos, G.A., Arbab, F.: Coordination models and languages. Advances in Computers **46** (1998) 329–400

50. Denti, E., Natali, A., Omicini, A.: Programmable coordination media. In Garlan, D., Le Métayer, D., eds.: Coordination Languages and Models – Proceedings of the 2nd International Conference (COORDINATION'97). Volume 1282 of LNCS., Berlin (D), Springer-Verlag (1997) 274–288
51. Ciancarini, P.: Coordination models and languages as software integrators. ACM Computing Surveys **28** (1996) 300–302
52. Cortes, M.: A coordination language for building collaborative applications. International Journal of Computer Supported Cooperative Work (CSCW) **9** (2000) 5–31
53. Agostini, A., De Michelis, G., Grasso, M.A.: Rethinking CSCW systems: The architecture of MILANO. In: European Conference on Computer Supported Cooperative Work (ECSCW), Kluwer (1997)
54. Mamei, M., Zambonelli, F., Leonardi, L.: Co-fields: Towards a unifying approach to the engineering of swarm intelligent systems. In Petta, P., Tolksdorf, R., Zambonelli, F., eds.: Engineering Societies in the Agents World III. Volume 2577 of LNCS. Springer-Verlag (2003) 68–81
55. Pynadath, D.V., Tambe, M.: Automated teamwork among heterogeneous software agents and humans. Journal of Autonomous Agents and Multi-Agent Systems (JAAMAS) (2003) 71–100
56. Omicini, A.: SODA: Societies and infrastructures in the analysis and design of agent-based systems. In Ciancarini, P., Wooldridge, M.J., eds.: Agent-Oriented Software Engineering. Volume 1957 of LNCS., Springer-Verlag (2001) 185–193
57. Omicini, A., Zambonelli, F., Klusch, M., Tolksdorf, R., eds.: Coordination of Internet Agents: Models, Technologies, and Applications. Springer-Verlag (2001)

"Exhibitionists" and "Voyeurs" Do It Better: A Shared Environment for Flexible Coordination with Tacit Messages

Luca Tummolini[1], Cristiano Castelfranchi[1], Alessandro Ricci[2],
Mirko Viroli[2], and Andrea Omicini[2]

[1] Institute of Cognitive Sciences and Technologies, CNR
viale Marx 15, 00137 Roma, Italy
{tummoli, castel}@ip.rm.cnr.it
[2] DEIS, Università degli Studi di Bologna,
via Venezia 52, 47023 Cesena, Italy
{aricci, mviroli, aomicini}@deis.unibo.it

Abstract. Coordination between multiple autonomous agents is a major issue for open multi-agent systems. This paper proposes the notion of *Behavioural Implicit Communication* (BIC) originally devised in human and animal societies as a new and critical coordination mechanism also for artificial agents. BIC is a parasitical form of communication that exploits both some environmental properties and the agents' capacity to interpret their actions. In this paper we abstract from the agents' architecture to focus on the interaction mediated by the environment. Observability of the environment – and in particular of agents' actions – is crucial for implementing BIC-based form of coordination in artificial societies. Accordingly in this paper we introduce an abstract model of environment providing services to enhance observation power of agents, enabling BIC and other form of observation-based coordination. Also, we describe a typology of environments and examples of observation based coordination with and without implicit communication.

1 Introduction

In this paper we advance the notion of *Behavioural Implicit Communication* (BIC) as a kind of communication that does not involve specific codified actions aimed only at communication [1]. We have BIC when usual practical actions are *contextually used* as messages for communicating. We argue that providing agents with an environment enabling BIC eases coordination achievement [2] *also* because it can enable a more flexible form of communication between agents.

BIC is a critical coordination mechanism that is mainly responsible for the overall social order of human societies. A sub-category of BIC, commonly known as *stigmergy* [3], is shared also with animal societies, and is widely considered as a necessary means to achieve coordination without a central control. Stigmergy has been proposed also as a model of decentralised coordination for Multi-Agent Systems [4], and it is usually characterised as a form of communication mediated

D. Weyns et al. (Eds.): E4MAS 2004, LNAI 3374, pp. 215–231, 2005.

by the environment which simply needs ant-like agents. BIC is proposed as a general framework able to provide a more comprehensive theory that covers also intentional BDI agents.

This paper focuses on the basic properties / services which can be used to instrument an agent (working) environment so as to support BIC and other observation-based forms of coordination. In other words we are looking for an abstract model of environment which could provide a systematic support to BIC, which could be exploited by MAS for their heterogeneous cooperative activities. In this paper a formal specification of such a model will be provided, so as to (i) making unambiguous the description of observation-form of coordination, (ii) making easier its engineering on top of MAS infrastructure, (iii) enabling form of automated reasoning on the dynamic behaviour of the MAS exploiting the services provided by the environment.

Approaches to coordination have been recently classified in two main categories: subjective and objective coordination [5, 6]. Subjective approaches rely on the viewpoint of the individual agent that can "perceive" and understand the actions of its peers. For instance, agents can agree on a coordinated plan thanks to explicit communication [7] or plan recognition [8, 9]. However, what does it mean in this approaches that an agent can "perceive" or "observe" another agent? Do perception and observation always imply a form of communication between the two agents? On the other hand, objective approaches are mainly concerned with the viewpoint of an observer that is external to the agents. According to this interpretation, coordination is instilled in multi-agent systems by means of *ad hoc* abstractions, often termed as *coordination artifacts* [10], that mediate agent interactions. Coordination artifacts globally affect the behaviour of a multi-agent system, and are typically provided by agent coordination infrastructures [11, 12] that shape the environment where agents live and interact.

The remainder of the paper is structured as follows. In Section 2 we summarise what Behavioural Implicit Communication is, and why it is relevant for coordination in a multi-agent system. Section 3 focuses on the role of the environmental properties that can enable BIC, in particular the capacity of the environment to affect the observability of agents' actions: we advance a notion of *shared environment* and formalise a first typology. In Section 4 we provide a formal characterisation for multi-agent systems based on the notion of shared environment and BIC, and in Section 5 we show its usefulness in modelling properties of BIC and other scenarios. Section 6 describes how forms of observation-based coordination can be realised by exploiting the observability features provided by shared environments. Finally, Section 7 concludes trying to identify a path toward a future implementation of the shared environment.

2   Behavioural Implicit Communication for Coordination

2.1   Interaction Is not Always Communication

There is a sense in which the famous claim of the Palo Alto psychotherapy school "any behaviour is communication" [13] is true: in artificial multi-agent system, interaction with other agents or with the environment is usually implemented in terms of a message passing protocol, typically "wrapping" non-agent environmental resources to shape them as agents. Even the only widespread standards for agent technologies, provided by FIPA, currently account for speech acts only, neglecting in practice physical acts of any form [14].

However, interaction via messages is not the only viable solution to achieve coordination. As a more powerful framework, indirect interaction has been proposed [15] as a way to implement *stigmergy* for MAS societies. Decentralised coordination would be achieved thanks to interaction via persistent observable state changes. Indirect interaction is modelled on the pheromone metaphor: to find the shortest way to reach food ants mark their trail with a pheromone that is attractive for other ants [16]. However from a functional perspective, even a pheromone is a message, like one written on a blackboard. Everyone autonomously accessing the blackboard can read the message and act upon it.

While we will also argue for having persistence and observability of changes in the agents' environment as necessary requirements for having global coordination, we strive for a coordination mechanism which does not rely only on explicit codified communication. In fact not all kinds of communication exploit codified (and hence rigid) actions. Our claim is that human and animals are able to communicate also without a *predefined* conventional language, and this capacity should be also instilled into artificial agents.

In order to distinguish it from mere interaction, we define communication as a process where information arriving from agent X (Sender) to agent Y (Receiver) is *aimed at* informing Y. X's behaviour has the goal or the function of informing Y. X is executing a certain action "in order" to have other agents receiving a message and updating their beliefs or epistemic state. Communication is an intentional or functional notion in the sense that it is always goal oriented such that a behaviour is selected also for its communicative effect.[1]

While we agree with [17] that coordination can be seen as a causal process of correlation between agents' actions always involving an information flow between an agent and its environment, we do not consider always this flow as a process of communication. Consider a case where an hostile agent, whose actions are "observable", is entering a MAS. If another agent becomes aware of his presence and can observe him, should we say that the hostile agent is communicating his position? Or, differently, is the escaping prey communicating to the predator her movements?

---

[1] An agent's behaviour can be goal oriented for different reasons. An intentional agent (i.e. a BDI agent) is a goal governed agent (the goal is internally represented) which instantiates a communicative plan to reach the goal that another agent is informed about something. However also simple reactive agents (i.e. insect-like) can act purposively (hence can communicate) if their behaviour has been shaped by natural or artificial selection, by reinforcement learning or by design (in the interest of the agent itself). In these latter cases the behaviour has the *function* of communicating in the sense that it has been selected *because of* a certain communicative effect.

When reasoning about agents we should be at the agents' level of explanation. There are at least two different viewpoints that need to be disentangled: the agent's and the designer's [6]. Relative to the agents' world, the designer acts as Natural Selection or God does on our world. Even in the case that an agent's perception of the action of another agent is actually implemented as an information passed from a sender to a receiver, this should not be necessarily considered as a form of "communication", and correspondingly the information passed should not be necessarily labelled as a "message".

From the external viewpoint of the designer a message passing of this sort is designed in order to inform the agent who is observing. However from the viewpoint of the agent a simple perception is not necessarily communication.

2.2   Communication Is not Always Explicit

Communication is normally conceived as implemented through specialised actions such as those defined in the FIPA ACL protocol [18]. Such protocols are inspired by natural language or expressive signals where meaning is associated to a specific action by convention.

What about the case where the agent is aware of being observed (other agents believe that he is performing a given practical action) and he "intends that" [7] the others are interpreting his action? This sort of communication without a codified action but with a communicative intention is what we intend for Behavioural Implicit Communication [1]. What is relevant here is that the agent's execution plan is aimed to achieve a pragmatic goal as usual: i.e. an agent A is collecting trash to put it in a bin (as in [8]).

To implicitly communicate, the agent should be able to contextually "use" (or learn to use or evolve to use) the *observed* executed plan also as a sign, the plan is used as a message but it is not shaped, selected, or designed to be a message.

An agent B has the same goal but observing the other's action he decides to clean the other side of the road. Since the agent A knows that an agent B is observing him, the practical action he is executing can be used *also* as a message to B such as "I am cleaning here". Such a possibility can lead agents to avoid a specific negotiation process for task allocation and can finally evolve in an implicit agreement in what to do.

There seems to be at least three different conditions to support such a form of communication.

– The first is relative to environmental properties. The "observability" of the practical actions and of their traces is a property of the environment where agents live. One environment can "enable" the visibility of the others while another can "constrain" it, in the same way that sunny or foggy days affect our perception. An environment could also enable an agent to make himself observable or on the contrary to hide his presence on purpose.
– The second is related to the capacity of agents to understand and interpret (or to learn an appropriate reaction to) a practical action. A usual practical action can be a message when an agent knows the way others will

understand his behaviour. The most basic message will be that the agent is doing the action α. A more sophisticated form would imply the ability to derive pragmatic inference from it (what is the goal of doing? What can be implied?).

– The third condition is that the agent should be able to understand (and observe) the effect that his actions has on the others so that he can begin acting in the usual way *also* because the other understand it and react appropriately.

Behavioural Implicit Communication is in this sense a parasitical form of communication that exploits a given level of visibility and the capacity of the others to categorise or react to his behaviour.

A general definition for BIC is:

the agent (source) is performing a usual practical action α but he also knows and lets or makes the other agent (addressee) observe and understand such a behaviour, i.e. to capture some meaning μ from that "message", because this is part of his (motivating or non motivating) goals in performing α.

2.3   BIC Is not Always Stigmergy

The need for an environment for a multi-agent system is often associated with the goal of implementing stigmergy as a decentralised coordination mechanism. Besides, being *the production of a certain behaviour as a consequence of the effects produced in the local environment by previous behaviour or indirect communication through the environment* [4], stigmergy seems very similar to the form of communication we are arguing for.

However these general accepted definitions makes the phenomenon too broad. It is too broad because it is unable to distinguish between the communication and the signification processes. As we have seen in Subsection 2.1 we do not want to consider the hostile agent's actions or the escaping prey as communicative actions notwithstanding that the effects of their actions elicit and influence the actions of other agents. Besides, every form of communication is mediated by the environment exploiting some environmental channel (i.e. air for audio signals).

As in BIC, real stigmergic communication does not exploit any *specialised communicative* action but just usual practical actions (i.e. the nest building actions). In fact we consider stigmergy as a subcategory of BIC, being communication via long term *traces*, physical *practical* outcomes, *useful* environment modifications which preserve their practical end but acquire a communicative function. In this perspective, stigmergy to a special form of BIC where the addressee does not perceive the *behaviour* (during its performance) but perceives other *post-hoc traces* and outcomes of it.

Usually stigmergy is advocated as a coordination mechanisms that can achieve very sophisticated forms of organisation with no need for intelligent behaviour. However there also exist interesting form of stigmergic communication at the intentional level. Consider a sergeant who – while crossing a mined field – says "walk on my prints!" to his soldiers. From that very moment any print is a mere consequence of a step, plus a stigmergic (descriptive "here I put my foot" and prescriptive "put your foot here!") message to the followers.

2.4   Coordination Is not Always Cooperation

Coordination is that additional part or aspect of the activity of an agent specifically devoted to deal and cope with the dynamic environmental interferences, either positive or negative, i.e. with opportunities and dangers/obstacles [19]. Coordination can be non social as when an agent coordinate with a moving object. For instance, it can be *unilateral, bilateral* and *reciprocal* (see Fig. 1) without being cooperative as when a leopard curves left and right and accelerates or decelerates on the basis of the *observed* path and moves of its escaping prey; but at the same time the gazelle jumps left or right and accelerates or not in order to avoid the leopard and on the basis of the *observed* moves of it. This is an observation based but not a communication/message based (BIC) *reciprocal* coordination.

For the goals of this paper, we distinguish five different forms of coordination:

Unilateral — X intends to coordinate with Y by observing Y's actions.

Bilateral — In this case we have the unilateral form of coordination for both agents, so: X intends to coordinate with Y by observing Y's actions, and viceversa: Y intends to coordinate with X by observing X's actions.

Unilateral-AW — In this case we have a unilateral form of coordination, but with a first form of awareness: X intends to coordinate with Y by observing Y's actions, and Y is aware of it (i.e. knows to be observed).

Reciprocal — In this case the we have both a bilateral form of observation based coordination and awareness by both the agents: X intends to coordinate with Y by observing Y's actions, Y is aware of it, Y intends to coordinate with X by observing X's actions and X is aware of it.

Mutual — This case extends the reciprocal form by introducing the explicit awareness of each other intention to coordinate: X intends to coordinate with Y by observing Y's actions, Y is aware of it, Y intends to coordinate with X by observing X's actions, X is aware of it, X is aware of Y's intention to coordinate, and Y is aware of X's intention to coordinate.

Behavioural implicit communication is necessary for mutual coordination while it is possible and useful in the other kinds of observation-based coordination.

3   Toward a Shared Environment: Objective and Intentional Observability

The goal of this paper is to instrument an agent working environment with properties and services that can enable the observation-based forms of coordination discussed above, BIC in particular. In other words, we aim at defining an abstract model of an agent environment, which could be engineered on top of a

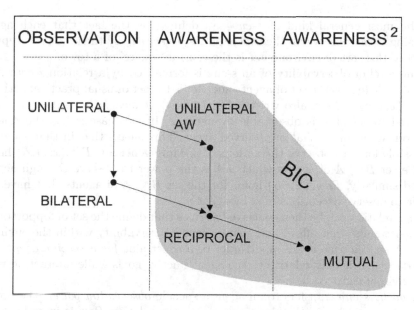

Fig. 1. Forms of coordination in relation to observation capability and awareness

MAS infrastructure, so as to be exploited by agents living in the MAS to exploit BIC for their cooperation. Given this objective, it will be fundamental to identify a formal model of this support, in order to ease its engineering on top of existing MAS infrastructures: accordingly in this section the abstract model of the shared environment enabling observability is introduced and in Section 4 its formal semantics is described.

Agents that live in a *common environment* (*c-env*) are agents whose actions and goals interfere (positively or negatively) and need coordination to manage this interference. In a pure *c-env*, actions and their traces are state transitions that can ease or hamper the individual agents' goals. An example is a ground that is common for different insects species but where no interspecies communication is possible. Agents can observe just the state of the environment and act on that basis without having access to the actions of their peers. Even a trace is seen as part of the environment and not as a product of other agents. A general property of a *c-env* is that it enables agents to modify its state and keep track of it.

We propose a notion of *shared environment* (*s-env*), that is a particular case of a *c-env* that enables (1) different forms of observability of each other action executions, as well as (2) awareness of this observability. These features will be shown to support (unilateral, bilateral, reciprocal, mutual) coordination.

3.1   Observability in Shared Environments

Each s-env is defined by the level of observability that it can afford. The level of observability is the possibility for each agent to observe, *i.e.* to be informed about, another agent's actions or their traces.

The most general kind of *s-env* can defined by the fact that each agent accessing it *can* observe all the others and is *observable* by them. A prototypical model of this sort of environment is the central 'square' of a town.

The level of observability of an s-env is formalised by a relation $Pow : A \times A \times Act$, where A is the set of agents and Act is the set of usual practical actions. When $\langle x, y, \alpha \rangle \in Pow$, also written $Pow(x, y, \alpha)$, it means that action $\alpha \in Act$ executed by agent y is observable by agent x. In this case x has the role of observer agent and y that of observed agent. This means that in that *s-env*, it is possible for x to observe the actions of y. More generally, $Pow(x, B, \alpha)$ holds for the set $B \subseteq A$ of agents which x has the power to observe through action α, and similarly, $Pow(B, y, \alpha)$ holds for the set $B \subseteq A$ of agents that have the power to observe executions of α by agent y.

Pow relation can be then conceived as rules that define the set of 'opportunity and constraints' that afford and shape agents' observability within the environment. A specific rule is an opportunity or a constraint *for a specific agent* and in particular it is only relative to the agent's active goals while interacting with that environment.

A *public s-env* transfers to an agent a specific *observation power*: the power to be informed about others' actions. So, as the relation *Pow* is introduced to statically describe the set of opportunities and constraints related to agents' observability, a relation *Obs* (a subset of *Pow*) has to be introduced to characterise the state of the s-env at a given time, so that $Obs(x, y, \alpha)$ means that agent x is actually observing executions of action α by agent y. That is, $Obs(x, y, \alpha)$ means that an execution of action α by agent y will be perceived by x.

To take into account the agent's viewpoint over observation, we introduce the concept of agent *epistemic state (ES)*, representing the beliefs the agent has because of his observation role. The ES of an agent x includes its *environmental knowledge* which is then given by information *(i)* on the agents he is observing, *(ii)* on the agents that are observing him, and *(iii)* on the action executions that he is observing. We generalise, and write $B_z obs(x, y, \alpha)$ for agent z believing that x is observing executions of action α by z, and $B_x done(y, \alpha)$ for x believing that y has executed action α.

3.2   Observation Is Interaction with the Environment via Epistemic Actions

The epistemic state of an agent evolves through *epistemic actions*, which are actions aimed at acquiring knowledge from the environment [20]. In our framework epistemic actions are formalised as a class of *interactions* with the environment. Typically, an epistemic action is fired by an agent intention, by which the s-env reacts updating the epistemic state of the agent. To model agent's intention, we introduce the concept of motivational state: besides the epistemic state, an agent is characterised by a *motivational state* (MS).

A first case of epistemic action is used by the agent which is willing to know whether he is observing another agent, whether another agent is observing him, or generally, whether an agent x is observing an agent y. So, suppose the MS of

z includes intention $I_z check(x, y, \alpha)$, which means that agent z intends to know whether x observes executions of α by y. At a given time, an epistemic action is executed by which the ES of agent z will include the belief about whether $Obs(x, y, \alpha)$ holds or not.

Similarly, an agent may have the intention $I_x obs(x, y, \alpha)$ in exploiting the observability power of the environment to observe y's actions α. The intention activates the observation service provided by the s-env, causing: *(i)* the $B_x obs(x, y, \alpha)$ knowledge to be added to agent's epistemic state (i.e. agent x knows that he is observing actions by agent y); (ii) the element $Obs(x, y, \alpha)$ to be added to the set defining Obs relation (meaning that the s-env enables the observation for agent x of actions α executed by agent y) In other words, we can think that the appearance of an intention in the motivation state of the agent causes the execution of an epistemic action toward the environment, enabling agent observations.

Similarly, an agent may want to stop observing actions. When the intention $I_x drop(x, y, \alpha)$ appears in the agent motivational state, the effects of $obs(x, y, \alpha)$ are reversed, i.e. no longer the agent continues to observe action α in the future.

Now we are ready to link the MS state of the agent, Obs rules and the ES state of the agent: according to the semantics of the actions, the execution of an action α by agent y (denoted as $done(y, \alpha)$) causes the creation of a new belief $B_x done(y, \alpha)$ in the epistemic state of all the agents x of the environment such that $Obs(x, y, \alpha)$ holds.

4 Formal Model

In the following, we provide a syntax and an operational semantics for modelling MAS according to the conceptual framework defined in previous sections. This formalisation has the primary goal of been a precise description of the concepts described in previous section, and of their impact on the dynamic evolution of a MAS. Then, given the operational character of the model, it can be used as an abstract reference implementation for an infrastructure supporting s-envs, as well as to pave the way towards the application of some analysis tool.

We let metavariables x, y, z range over agent identifiers, and α, β over usual practical actions.

The syntax of MAS configurations is as follows:

$S ::= 0 \mid A \mid E \mid S \,\|\, S$	MAS Configuration
$A ::= 0$	Agent Configuration
$\mid B_x \phi$	Belief of x
$\mid I_x \phi$	Intention of x
$\mid A \,\|\, A$	Composition
$E ::= 0$	Environment Configuration
$\mid Pow(x, y, \alpha)$	x has the power to observe y's α
$\mid Obs(x, y, \alpha)$	x is observing y's α
$\mid E \,\|\, E$	Composition

$$
\begin{array}{lll}
\phi ::= & & \text{Formulas} \\
& obs(x, y, \alpha) & x \text{ is observing } y\text{'s } \alpha \\
\mid & coord(x, y, \alpha) & x \text{ coordinates with } y \text{ through } \alpha \\
\mid & check(x, y, \alpha) & \text{check whether } x \text{ is observing } y\text{'s } \alpha \\
\mid & drop(x, y, \alpha) & \text{prevent } x \text{ from observing } y\text{'s } \alpha \\
\mid & done(x, \alpha) & x \text{ executes actions } \alpha \\
\mid & \neg\phi \mid I_x\phi \mid B_x\phi & \text{Structured formulas}
\end{array}
$$

The operator for parallel composition is assumed to be commutative, associative, and to absorb the empty configuration 0.

The metavariable S ranges over configurations of the MAS, which at our abstraction level are a parallel composition of agent configurations and environment configurations. Environment configurations are parallel composition of terms, each denoting either the power of agent x to observe action α executed by agent y ($Pow(x, y, \alpha)$), or the fact that the environment is currently supporting the fact that x is observing action α executed by agent y ($Obs(x, y, \alpha)$). Agent configurations are parallel compositions of mental properties, namely beliefs (B) and intentions (I) qualified by the agent x, and about a formula ϕ. Notice that we model a MAS configuration as a multiset of either agent and environment properties, without a separation, by simply following the abstraction process induced by the formalism adopted.

A formula ϕ can be believed and/or intended by an agent. Atomic formulas are: *(i)* $obs(x, y, \alpha)$, used to express that x is observing executions of α by y, *(ii)* $coord(x, y, \alpha)$, used to express that x coordinates its behaviour with y by observing executions of α, *(iii)* $check(x, y, \alpha)$, used to check if x is observing executions of α by y, *(iv)* $drop(x, y, \alpha)$, used to prevent x from observing executions of α by y, and *(v)* $done(x, \alpha)$, used to express an that x executes/has executed α. Moreover, formulas can be structured ones: $\neg\phi$ expresses negation of ϕ, $I_x\phi$ and $B_x\phi$ that agent x intends/believe ϕ, respectively. A number of assumptions on such formulas are clearly to be made as usual, e.g. that $\neg\neg\phi \equiv \phi$ or $B_x\phi \equiv B_x B_x\phi$, but we abstract away from this aspect for it plays no significant role in this paper.

The operational semantics is defined by the following rewrite rules for system configurations.

$$
\frac{-}{I_z check(x, y, \alpha) \parallel Obs(x, y, \alpha) \parallel S \to B_z obs(x, y, \alpha) \parallel Obs(x, y, \alpha) \parallel S} \text{ [CHK]}
$$

$$
\frac{Obs(x, y, \alpha) \notin S}{I_z check(x, y, \alpha) \parallel S \to B_z obs(x, y, \alpha) \parallel S} \text{ [NCHK]}
$$

$$
\frac{-}{I_z drop(x, y, \alpha) \parallel B_z obs(x, y, \alpha) \parallel Obs(x, y, \alpha) \parallel S \to B_z \neg Obs(x, y, \alpha) \parallel S} \text{ [YDRP]}
$$

$$
\frac{Obs(x, y, \alpha) \notin S}{I_z drop(x, y, \alpha) \parallel B_z obs(x, y, \alpha) \parallel S \to B_z \neg obs(x, y, \alpha) \parallel S} \text{ [NDRP]}
$$

$$\frac{\overline{\quad}}{I_z obs(x,y,\alpha) \,\|\, Pow(x,y,\alpha) \,\|\, S \to B_z obs(x,y,\alpha) \,\|\, Pow(x,y,\alpha) \,\|\, Obs(x,y,\alpha) \,\|\, S} \quad \text{[ASK]}$$

$$\frac{I_x done(x,\alpha) \,\|\, S \to I_x done(x,\alpha) \,\|\, S'}{I_x done(x,\alpha) \,\|\, Obs(y,x,\alpha) \,\|\, S \to I_x done(x,\alpha) \,\|\, Obs(y,x,\alpha) \,\|\, B_y done(x,\alpha) \,\|\, S'} \quad \text{[OBS1]}$$

$$\frac{Obs(y,x,\alpha) \notin S}{I_x done(x,\alpha) \,\|\, S \to B_x done(x,\alpha) \,\|\, S} \quad \text{[OBS2]}$$

$$\frac{\overline{\quad}}{A \,\|\, S \to A' \,\|\, S} \quad \text{[AG]}$$

Rule [CHK] says that if agent z intends to check/know if x is observing y's action α and this is the case, then such an intention will be turned into a belief. Dually, rule [NCHK] deals with the case where this is not the case ($Obs(x,y,\alpha)$ does not occur in the system configuration), so that z will believe that $obs(x,y,\alpha)$ does not hold.

Rule [YDRP] says that if agent z know that x is observing y's action α (which is the case) and wants to stop him, term $Obs(x,y,\alpha)$ is dropped from the environment and z's belief is updated correspondingly. By rule [NDRP] we deal where the similar case, but supposing the agent had a wrong belief (x was not actually observing y's actions α), which is dealt with trivially.

Rule [ASK] is about agent z willing that x observes y's actions α: if this is allowed ($Pow(x,y,\alpha)$), x's beliefs will be updated as well as the environment state.

Rule [OBS1] and [OBS2] recursively define how the environment broadcasts information about an action to all the observers. When agent x wants to execute α, each observer y (rule [OBS1]) will be recursively added the belief $B_y done(x,\alpha)$: when none needs to be managed, x intention can simply become a fact, that is, he will belief the action to be executed.

The final, trivial rule [AG] is used to represent the fact that at any given time some agent configuration can change autonomously, thus modelling any belief revision or intention scheduling.

Notice that formulas $B_z coord(x,y,\alpha)$ or $I_z coord(x,y,\alpha)$ never appear in this semantics. This is because the fact that an agent coordinates its behaviour with another is not an aspect influencing/influenced by the environment: it is rather a mental property characterising the forms of observation-based coordination an agent participates to thanks to the s-env support.

5 Applications of the Model

The formal model described above serves multiple purposes:

- clearly and rigorously identifying basic primitives / general-purpose mechanisms which can be composed to specify various type of observation-based coordination patterns;

- helping the engineering of the approach on top of MAS infrastructures. The operational semantics provides a rigorous description of the observation features we aim at supporting at the infrastructure level. So it is a fundamental guide for designer and developers of MAS infrastructures which want to support BIC;
- supporting agent reasoning. By formally defining the observability rules characterising environment configuration, we promote their inspection and formal reasoning by intelligent agents, so as to automate the analysis of the dynamic behaviour of the MAS: recognising failures, providing suggestions, and so on.

A formal semantics makes it possible to establish some rigorous properties about observed events and observation rules of the environment, which necessarily impact on the reasoning process of observing / observed agents. In other words, the environment (infrastructure) provides some guarantees which can be taken as assumptions by agents exploiting the services, so as to alleviate their reasoning process: for instance, the environment can guarantee agents to observe *all* the actions executed by a certain other agent in the right order.

In this section we deepen this issue showing how concepts and applications related to the s-env notion can be formally addressed by our model.

5.1   Specifying Observation-Based Coordination

The formal framework can be adopted to specify rigorously the forms of coordination devised in Section 2. Given two agents x and y, an action α, and the system configuration S we introduce the following predicates:

- Unilateral

$$Uni(x, y, \alpha, S) \triangleq I_x coord(x, y, \alpha) \in S \ \wedge \ Obs(x, y, \alpha) \in S$$

- Unilateral with Awareness

$$UniAW(x, y, \alpha, S) \triangleq Uni(x, y, \alpha, S) \ \wedge \ B_y obs(x, y, \alpha) \in S$$

- Bilateral

$$Bi(x, y, \alpha, S) \triangleq Uni(x, y, \alpha, S) \ \wedge \ Uni(y, x, \alpha, S)$$

- Reciprocal

$$Rec(x, y, \alpha, S) \triangleq UniAW(x, y, \alpha, S) \ \wedge \ UniAW(y, x, \alpha, S)$$

- Mutual

$$Mut(x, y, \alpha, S) \triangleq Rec(x, y, \alpha, S) \ \wedge \ B_x I_y coord(y, x, \alpha) \ \wedge \ B_y I_x coord(x, y, \alpha)$$

So forms of unilateral coordination are obtained by instrumenting the environment configuration with the simple rule $Pow(x, y, \alpha)$ and with agent x manifesting the intention $I_x(obs(x, y, \alpha))$, causing the instrumentation of the environment with the rule $Obs(x, y, \alpha)$.

Bilateral coordination can be obtained by extending previous approach to include also y observation of x's actions, instrumenting the environment with the rules $Pow(y, x, \alpha)$ and $Obs(y, x, \alpha)$, the latter instantiated by the intention of the agent y $I_y obs(y, x, \alpha)$.

The unilateral and bilateral forms of coordination can be extended then with forms of awareness, by agents intention $I_y check(x, y, \alpha)$ enabling y awareness of the observability of his actions to x – obtaining the unilateral-aw form – and $I_x check(y, x, \alpha)$, enabling also x awareness of the observability of his actions to y – obtaining the reciprocal form of coordination.

5.2   From Overhearing to Oversensing

As an example scenario possibly enjoying the features of s-envs we consider overhearing. This has been introduced in MAS as a technique / architecture to realise forms of collaboration and coordination non-preplanned, typically in unstructured and unpredictable environments, based on unobstrusive observation and unsolicited suggestion [21]. Roughly speaking, overhearing consists in one agent – the overhearer – sniffing messages exchanged by two or more agents. The overhearer collects the messages and makes them available to suggester agents through a sort of publish / subscribe service: suggesters subscribe their interest to be notified by the overhearer when a certain type of event occurs concerning the communication among observed agents.

Overhearing has been used for supporting group formation in open environments [22], monitoring the interactive behaviour of organization – in particular implicit organisation [23], to enable awareness among agents [24], plan and conversation dynamic recognition [25].

Overhearing can be suitably implemented on top of the abstract model of environment described in this paper. In our case the overhearer agent disappears, since its functionalities are directly provided by the s-env environment (infrastructure), which is responsible to enable interactions (communications) among agents. The publish / subscribe service among the overhearer agent and suggester agents is mapped onto the s-env services.

Each suggester agent manifests its intention to overhear certain communication events concerning the interaction of agents $a_1, \ldots a_n$ by formulating the intentions:

$$I_s obs(s, a_1, communication\text{-}event)$$
$$\ldots$$
$$I_s obs(s, a_n, communication\text{-}event)$$

Specific examples can be:

$$I_s obs(s, customer, ask(customer, service\_provider, price(X, Y)))$$
$$I_s obs(s, service\_provider, inform(service\_provider, \_, \_))$$

Here, all the requests made by the customer agent to a service provider about some good prices are observed, along with all the information provided by the service-provider. Actually, our model supports an extension of overhearing toward oversensing, i.e. applying the principle of overhearing to a general model of action / interaction, which includes – but is not limited to – communication.

6   Other Examples of BIC Coordination

Mutual coordination is at the basis of BIC, requiring not only observation based coordination and forms of awareness, but agents awareness of each other intention to coordinate.

Actually, tacit messages can be exchanged also in different other forms of coordination. In coordination the most important message conveyed by BIC is not the fact that I intend to do (and keep my personal or social commitments – which is crucial in cooperation), or my reasons and motives for acting, or the fact that I'm able and skilled. It is more relevant communicating (informing) about when, how, where I'm doing my act/part in the shared environment, so that you can coordinate with my behaviour while knowing time, location, shape, etc.

In what follows some examples of coordination with tacit messages are provided that are inspired mainly from the teamwork literature.

6.1   Information on the Other Members' Activity: "I Am Ready"

In [7] a trade off in the amount of information team members must maintain on each other intentions is discussed, particularly when a step involves only an individual or a sub-team. This intention tracking does not need a complete plan recognition but simply that the individual or the sub-team intend to execute that step. Consider as an example a sort of teamwork which is to drive an underground train. A coordination problem for the driver is to close the doors when all passengers are on board and this can be difficult when a station is overloaded. The driver is able to observe using a mirror the passengers rush in taking his train. Passengers usually don't know to be observed and they are not communicating their intentions. However usually before leaving a station the drivers make a first attempt to close the door which, although it is a practical action, is mainly used as a message like "The train is leaving". The driver does not intend to really close the door. However whether passengers understand the message or simply infer the driver's intention to leave, they often go off the train and let the train leave safely the station. This is a case of bilateral coordination where only the drivers' actions can be considered as messages.

6.2   Joint Persistent Goals Achievement: "I Have Done It"

Joint intention theory [7, 26, 27] has been proposed as a framework for multi-agent coordination in a team. The team members are required to jointly commit to a joint persistent goal G. It also requires that when any team member acquires the belief that G has been achieved or turns out to be unachievable or irrelevant, a mutual belief about this event should be attained. Because of the domain is usually of partial observability, the team member is commonly designed to signal this fact to the other agent through *explicit communication*. However, in real world domains, explicit communication has a cost and sometimes the expected cost of mis-coordination can outweigh it [28]. Behavioural implicit communication can be adopted in such cases even if it is possibly ambiguous because it can turn out to be good enough and better of not communicating at all. Drawing on [28] consider such scenario. Two helicopters with different abilities have a joint goal of reaching together a final destination but encounter a dangerous radar unit. Only one of them is capable of destroying the radar and should decide to communicate a message like "I destroyed the radar" to the other. However sending these message could be too expensive and risky (i.e. by being intercepted). If the destroyer believes that the other helicopter is following him and is observing him, by simply keeping on track to destination he can assume that the other will receive his silent message anyway and will keep the commitment to reach the final destination. This is a case of mutual coordination with tacit messages because also the follower's action of keeping the track can be considered as a message.

7   Conclusion

In this paper we have proposed a model of a shared environment for observation based coordination which can enable behavioural implicit communication between the agents. The BIC approach and the related shared environment supporting framework can be suitably implemented in infrastructures supporting the MAS. In particular *governing infrastructures* – i.e. infrastructures providing abstractions and services also for governing / constraining agent interaction [6] – can be suitably adopted for the purpose, representing the s-env as a first class issue.

The requirement for a MAS infrastructure in order to support the observation-based coordination are:

- It must provide explicit abstractions storing, managing and enacting *pow* and *obs* rules, as the set of rules defining respectively the observability level of the environment and the set of rules defining actually what observations are taking place;
- It must have access to the motivational state of the agents, in order to dynamically check for agent intentions, causing epistemic actions and then the updating of the *obs* rules of the environment;
- It must have access to the epistemic state of the agents, in order to dynamically update it according the action execution events and the *obs* rules dynamically characterising the shared environment.

The concept of observation artifact is strictly related to the *coordination artifact* abstraction [10], which represents first class runtime entities provided to agents to support their coordination. TuCSoN is a coordination infrastructure for MAS

supporting the coordination artifact abstraction [11]: accordingly suitable infrastructure can be devised to support effectively observation artifacts, as runtime
entities enhancing the observation capabilities of agents.

Acknowledgements

The authors are grateful to the anonymous reviewers, whose work, constructive
remarks and criticisms have greatly helped improving the quality of this paper.

This research is under the auspices of: MIUR (the Italian Ministry of Education, University and Research), COFIN 2003 project "Fiducia e diritto nella
società dell'informazione", paper no. 3; and EC (the European Community),
FP6 project "AgentLink III".

References

1. Castelfranchi,   C.:   When   doing   is   saying – the   theory
   of   behavioral   implicit   communication.   Draft.   Available   at
   http://www.istc.cnr.it/doc/62a_716p_WhenDoingIsSaying.rtf (2003)
2. Ciancarini, P., Omicini, A., Zambonelli, F.: Multiagent system engineering: the coordination viewpoint. In Jennings, N.R., Lespérance, Y., eds.: Intelligent Agents VI
   — Agent Theories, Architectures, and Languages. Volume 1767 of LNAI., Springer-
   Verlag (2000) 250–259
3. Theraulaz, G., Bonabeau, E.: A brief history of stigmergy. Artificial Life **5:2**
   (1999) 97–117
4. Beckers, R., Holland, O., Deneubourg, J.L.: From local actions to global tasks:
   Stigmergy in collective robotics. In Brooks, R.A., Maes, P., eds.: Artificial Life IV.
   MIT Press (1994)
5. Schumacher, M.: Objective Coordination in Multi-Agent System Engineering –
   Design and Implementation. Volume 2039 of LNAI. Springer-Verlag (2001)
6. Omicini, A., Ossowski, S.: Objective versus subjective coordination in the engineering of agent systems. In Klusch, M., Bergamaschi, S., Edwards, P., Petta, P.,
   eds.: Intelligent Information Agents: An AgentLink Perspective. Volume 2586 of
   LNAI: State-of-the-Art Survey. Springer-Verlag (2003) 179–202
7. Grosz, B., Kraus, S.: Collaborative plans for complex group action. Artificial
   Intelligence **86** (1996) 269–357
8. Rao, A.S.: A unified view of plans as recipes. In Hölmstrom-Hintikka, G., Tuomela,
   R., eds.: Contemporary Action Theory. Volume 2: Social Action. Kluwer Academic
   Publishers (1997)
9. Huber, M., Durfee, E.: Deciding when to commit to action during observation based
   coordination. In: 1st International Conference on Multi-Agent Systems (ICMAS-
   95), Menlo Park, CA, USA, AAAI Press (1995) 163–170 Proceedings.
10. Omicini, A., Ricci, A., Viroli, M., Castelfranchi, C., Tummolini, L.: Coordination
    artifacts: Environment based coordination for intelligent agents. In: Autonomous
    Agents and Multi-Agent Systems. (2004) 3rd International Joint Conference (AA-
    MAS 2004), New York, July 2004.
11. Omicini, A., Zambonelli, F.: Coordination for Internet application development.
    Autonomous Agents and Multi-Agent Systems **2:3** (1999) 251–269 Special Issue:
    Coordination Mechanisms for Web Agents.

12. Noriega, P., Sierra, C.: Electronic institutions: Future trends and challenges. In Klusch, M., Ossowski, S., Shehory, O., eds.: Cooperative Information Agents VI. LNAI. Springer-Verlag (2002) 14–17
13. Watzlavich, P., Beavin, J., Jackson, D.: Pragmatics of human communication: a study of interactional patterns, pathologies, and paradoxes. W.W. Norton &Co., Inc., New York (1967)
14. Omicini, A., Ricci, A., Viroli, M., Rimassa, G.: Integrating objective & subjective coordination in multiagent systems. In: 19th ACM Symposium on Applied Computing (SAC 2004), Nicosia, Cyprus, ACM (2004) 449–455 Special Track on Coordination Models, Languages and Applications.
15. Keil, D., Goldin, D.: Modeling indirect interaction in open computational systems. In: IEEE 12th International Workshops on Enabling Technologies: Infrastructure for Collaborative Enterprises (WET ICE 2003), 1st International Workshop "Theory and Practice of Open Computational Systems" (TAPOCS 2003), Linz, Austria, IEEE CS (2003) Proceedings.
16. Helbing, D., Keltsch, J., Molnar, P.: Modelling the evolution of human trail systems. Nature **388**() (1997) 47–50
17. Parunak, H.V.D., Breuckner, S., Sauter, J., Odell, J.: A preliminary taxonomy of multi-agent interaction. In Giorgini, P., Müller, J., Odell, J., eds.: Agent-Oriented Software Engineering IV. LNCS. Springer-Verlag (2004) 4th International Workshop (AOSE 2003), Post-Proceedings.
18. FIPA: FIPA   Communicative   Act   Library   Specification.   (2000) http://www.fipa.org.
19. Castelfranchi, C.: Modelling social action for AI agents. Artificial Intelligence **103** (1998) 157–182
20. Castelfranchi, C., Lorini, E.: Cognitive anatomy and functions of expectations. In: Cognitive Modeling of Agents and Multi-Agent Interactions. (2003) Workshop at IJCAI. Proceedings.
21. Aiello, M., Busetta, P., Dona', A., Serafini, L.: Ontological overhearing. In: Intelligent Agents VIII. Volume 2333 of LNAI. Springer-Verlag Berlin (2002) 175–189
22. Legras, F., Tessier, C.: Lotto: Group formation by overhearing in large teams. In Jennings, N.R., Sierra, C., Sonenberg, L., Tambe, M., eds.: 3rd international Joint Conference on Autonomous Agents and Multiagent Systems (AAMAS 2004), New York, USA, ACM (2004)
23. Rossi, S., Busetta, P.: Towards monitoring of group interactions and social roles via overhearing. In: CIA 2004. Volume 3191 of LNAI. Springer-Verlag Berlin (2004) 47–61
24. Novik, D., Ward, K.: Mutual beliefs of multiple conversants: a computational model of collaboration in air traffic control. In: AAAI-93, Washington, DC, USA (1993) 196–201
25. Gutnik, G., Kaminka, G.: Toward a formal approach to overhearing: algorithm for conversation identification. In Jennings, N.R., Sierra, C., Sonenberg, L., Tambe, M., eds.: 3rd international Joint Conference on Autonomous Agents and Multiagent Systems (AAMAS 2004), New York, USA, ACM (2004)
26. Cohen, P., Levesque, H.: Teamwork. Technical report, SRI-International, Menlo Park, CA, USA (1991)
27. Jenning, N.R.: Controlling cooperative problem solving in industrial multi-agent systems using joint intentions. Artificial Intelligence **75:2** (1995) 195–240
28. Pynadath, D., Tambe, M.: The communicative multiagent team decision problem: Analyzing teamwork theories and models. Journal of Artificial Intelligence Research (2002)

Swarming Distributed
Pattern Detection and Classification

Sven A. Brueckner and H. Van Dyke Parunak

Altarum, 3520 Green Court, Suite 300, Ann Arbor, MI 48105-1579
1.734.302-{4683, 4684}
{sven.brueckner, van.parunak}@altarum.org

Abstract. Swarming agents in networks of physically distributed processing nodes may be used for data acquisition, data fusion, and control applications. We present an architecture for active surveillance systems in which simple mobile agents collectively process real-time data from heterogeneous sources at or near the origin of the data. We motivate the system requirements with the needs of a surveillance system for the early detection of large-scale bioterrorist attacks on a civilian population, but the same architecture is applicable to a wide range of other domains. The pattern detection and classification processes executed by the proposed system emerge from the coordinated activities of agents of two populations in a shared computational environment. Detector agents draw each other's attention to significant spatio-temporal patterns in the observed data stream. Classifier agents rank the detected patterns according to their respective criterion. The resulting system-level behavior is adaptive, robust, and scalable.

1 Introduction

Fine-grained agents swarming in a large-scale physically distributed network of processing nodes may be designed to perform three major tasks. They may use local sensors to acquire data and guide its transmission, they may fuse, interpolate, and interpret data from heterogeneous sources, and they may take or influence command and control decisions.

In previous projects, we developed swarm intelligent agent systems for command and control [11] [4] and for data acquisition and transmission [6]. This paper presents a swarming agent architecture for distributed pattern-detection and classification.

Driven by the need for more efficiency and agility in business and public transactions, more and more data becomes digitally available in real time in increasingly finer-grained global computer networks. These heterogeneous data streams reflect many aspects of the behavior of individuals or small groups in a population (e.g., traffic flow, shopping and leisure activities, healthcare needs). A new generation of active surveillance systems that integrate a large number of spatially distributed heterogeneous data streams may be used in various applications, for instance, to protect a civilian population from bioterrorist attacks, to support real-time traffic coordination systems, to monitor the physiological state of outpatients, or to manage public access to sensitive natural resources efficiently.

D. Weyns et al. (Eds.): E4MAS 2004, LNAI 3374, pp. 232–245, 2005.

Active surveillance of population-level activities includes the detection and classification of spatio-temporal patterns across a large number of real-time data streams. Approaches that analyze data in a central computing facility tend to be overwhelmed with the amount of data that needs to be transferred and processed in a timely fashion, especially in networks with restricted bandwidth and processing capabilities. Also, centralized processing raises proprietary and privacy concerns that may make many data sources inaccessible. Our proposed pattern detection and classification architecture avoids these problems through consequent decentralization. Instead of transferring the data to a centralized processing facility, we transfer the processes (fine-grained agents) to the data sources. As a consequence, significantly less data needs to be transferred over long distances and access restrictions may be guaranteed through proven local processes.

We apply swarm intelligence techniques (for introductions see [9] or [2]) to globally coordinate our local data processing. The swarm intelligence design approach adapts robust, self-organizing coordination mechanisms observed in distributed natural systems (e.g., social insect colonies) to engineered systems. One of the most powerful global coordination mechanisms in distributed biological systems is stigmergy [7], from the Greek words *stigma* "sign" and *ergos* "work". The work performed by the agents in the environment in turn guides their later actions – a feedback loop that establishes dynamic information flows across the population and guides its operation.

The remainder of this paper is structured as follows. In Section 2 we introduce one specific active surveillance problem. The following major Section 3 specifies our proposed architecture and its operation in detail. Section 4 presents a software demonstration that illustrates the proposed mechanisms. We conclude in Section 5.

2 The Biosurveillance Problem

In the event of a large-scale bioterrorist attack on a civilian population, triggering the emergency response system even at the first positive diagnosis of a disease caused by a CDC-class A bioterrorist pathogen (e.g., airborne anthrax) is still too late to prevent thousands of deaths, a breakdown of the public health system, and civil disorder. Such a disaster can only be prevented when the emerging epidemic is caught while the symptoms of the infected people are still unspecific and very similar to common diseases (e.g., influenza).

New sensor and information technology may be used to detect an attack from the subtle changes in population behavior that usually precede the first medical diagnosis by a significant amount of time. Behavioral patterns in the community are likely to change as people fall ill. This change is reflected in many different population activity indicators (e.g., school absenteeism, traffic patterns) that are increasingly accessible in real-time. A system that surveys multiple data points in real-time may be more successful in triggering an alert than any single data source.

The detection and classification of subtle changes in population activity requires the integration of a wide variety of non-specific real-time data sources into the operation of the surveillance system. The providers of the data are often very sensitive to proprietary and privacy concerns. For instance, local sales figures of various over-the-counter remedies at individual pharmacies are an invaluable contribution to biosurveillance, but the owner of the data (the merchant) must be assured that this data does not reach its competitors. Also important is data from the public healthcare system, such as the number of patients inquiring about certain symptoms at their physician. But the surveillance system is only permitted to work with anonymized data.

The use of non-specific data sources for the early detection of an epidemic in a population requires the integration of many population activity indicators to achieve the required sensitivity and specificity. Furthermore, to guarantee the early detection of an outbreak, the system must operate on real-time data that is updated at least several times a day. As a result, there is an immense amount of data that needs to be processed in a timely fashion.

A biosurveillance system must be robust against cyber attacks and component failures, cheap and unobtrusive in its day-to-day operation, intuitive in its reporting, and designed for low-cost adaptivity and scalability along various dimensions, such as for instance:

- spread and complexity of population patterns,
- types and locations of data sources,
- detected symptoms and diseases, or
- detected attack patterns

3   Architecture and Operation

We consider a distributed swarming agent architecture the most appropriate answer to the challenge of detecting spatio-temporal patterns in a network of heterogeneous sources of potentially proprietary real-time data. Instead of attempting to stream a tremendous amount of data into a central processing facility, we propose to integrate the external sources into a network for mobile agent computing. Essentially, this network of agent processing nodes is a massively parallel computer for pattern detection and classification with a unique way of self-organizing the processing tasks.

Into our network of processing nodes we deploy large populations of extremely simple mobile agents (small footprint) that coordinate their activities in stigmergetic interactions. Using artificial pheromones – spatio-temporally localized numerical variables – the agents dynamically organize themselves around patterns observed in the data streams.

The emergence of globally coordinated behavior through stigmergetic interactions among many fine-grained software agents in a shared computational environment is facilitated by an application-independent component of the distributed runtime environment that emulates actual pheromone dynamics (aggregation, evaporation, dispersion) in the physical world. The operation of this component – we call it the pheromone infrastructure – is described in detail in the following section.

Our heterogeneous agent system continuously executes two parallel processes: pattern detection and pattern classification. More populations of agents could be deployed at any time, for instance to introduce additional criteria in the detection process, or to add more classification schemes.

The agents executing the detection process ("Detectors") continuously process the input data and search for spatio-temporal structures. Detectors use pheromones of one set of flavors to focus their search dynamically on suspicious areas of the network, while a second set is used to communicate the result of the detection process. In the software demonstration that we present in Section 4, Detectors search for unusually high differences in the data streams of neighboring locations in the network.

"Classifier" agents are responsible for the classification of the detected patterns according to a specified scheme. If multiple schemes are applied in parallel, then there are Classifiers of as many sub-populations as there are schemes and each sub-population uses a different pheromone flavor to communicate its results. The pattern classification scheme used in our demonstration correlates the detected patterns with a particular, dynamically changing geographic direction (wind). Patterns that show a strong alignment with the chosen direction are highlighted by the Classifiers.

In the following sections we first review the operation of the pheromone infrastructure. Then we present the agents of the detection and classification processes in detail.

3.1 Support for Stigmergy

Our agents coordinate their activity and communicate their results through markers in a shared dynamic environment. These stigmergetic interactions give rise to a robust self-organizing system-level behavior that rests on the feedback between the dynamics of the individual agents and the processes that manipulate information in the agents' environment (Figure 1).

Marker-based stigmergy in social insect colonies uses chemical markers (pheromones) that the insects deposit on the ground in specific situations (e.g., food found). Multiple deposits at the same location aggregate in strength. Members of the colony who sense pheromones of a particular flavor may change their behavior (e.g., follow pheromone trail to food source). Pheromone concentrations in the environment disperse in space and evaporate over time, because pheromones are highly volatile substances.

[4] specifies and analyzes an application-independent component for distributed agent runtime environments that emulates the dynamics of pheromone aggregation, dispersion, and evaporation for fine-grained software agents. The pheromone infrastructure represents concentrations of pheromones as scalar values assigned to a particular location in a discrete space. Different pheromone flavors are distinguished through values of additional tags attached to a pheromone. A tag is a particular attribute that may carry a value from a given domain. For instance, all pheromones in the application described here share a tag for a discretized time value.

The spatial structure of the pheromone infrastructure is captured in a network of places. A place is a location where agents may deposit or sense pheromones and where the infrastructure manipulates local concentrations. We use places to represent the structure of the problem space in which the agents coordinate their activities. This space may be the physical space (e.g., city blocks), temporal space

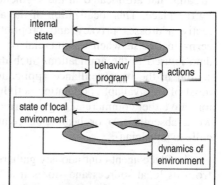

Fig. 1. Stigmergy links environmental dynamics with agent processes

(e.g., a machine schedule), or even some abstract graph (e.g., role graph in a template for a robotic team that executes a specific mission).

Each deposit of a pheromone at a particular place specifies a number of tags and a numerical concentration value. The strengths of all deposits at the place that specify the same tags are added together. The pheromone's propagation factor specifies the proportion of the deposit that is passed to neighboring places. A factor of zero prevents all propagation. The evaporation factor specifies the rate of reduction of the pheromone concentration at a place over time.

Previously, we applied the pheromone infrastructure to manufacturing control [4] and combat coordination [11]. In the proposed biosurveillance application, which we use in this paper as an example for our distributed pattern detection and classification approach, we represent the spatial and social structure of the protected population in our network of places. A place "covers" a unique segment of the region in which the system is deployed and neighborhood relations among places reflect physical neighborliness (adjacency of segments) as well as social connectedness (population movement and interaction patterns) of these segments (Figure 2).

The spatial structure of the pheromone dynamics immediately carries over into the structure of the agent processing network as well as into the spatial structure of agent activities itself. A Place agent provides the services of a place in the pheromone infrastructure and the agent is executed at a processing node that is preferably located inside the geographic segment covered by the place. The agent provides the swarming agents of the actual application with access to the local data sources in the segment, it implements the local pheromone dynamics, it provides topological information, and it manages the local agent directory for dynamic interactions among agents currently resident on the place.

Access to Data Sources.—In our architecture we process real-time data streams from heterogeneous and spatially distributed sources without transferring the data to a centralized computing resource. Rather, we use mobile agents to process the data near its respective source in a network of processing nodes. A Place agent occupies the processing node and provides the application agents with a unified interface (XML-based) to the data streams that are located in the segment covered by the place. This localization of the access directly addresses privacy and proprietary concerns that arise when commercial or protected data is used in the application. Such data is essential in the biosurveillance application, since most of the available population activity indicators are either commercial (e.g., pharmacy sales, work absenteeism) or healthcare related (e.g., calls to physician).

The Place agent continuously gathers the data from its local sources and stores it at the processing node to provide fast access by the agents. The data samples are tagged with the time the sample was taken and data above a certain age

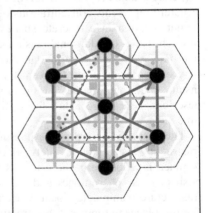

Fig. 2. Places may represent segments of the region and are connected in spatial and social relations

(the data availability horizon) is deleted by the Place agent. Thus, the application agents may operate on a set of value profiles (samples over time), one for each individual local source.

Pheromone Services.—Providing interaction protocols that allow the application agents to deposit pheromones and sense local concentrations, and executing the dynamics of pheromone aggregation, dispersion, and evaporation are the main tasks of a Place agent. The details of this important service and the emergent characteristics of the pheromone dynamics are specified and formally analyzed in [4].

Topological Information.—The agents of the application move dynamically through the network of processing nodes. To ensure the scalability of our architecture and to provide robustness to node failures and topology changes, no global map of the place network is provided. Instead, application agents request local topology information from their local Place agent at the time of their move. In return they receive a list of direct neighbors of the place (spatial and social neighborhood) and they are only permitted to move to these locations.

Directory Services.—The dynamical nature of our agent architecture does not permit fixed interaction structures. Rather, agents choose their interaction partners dynamically, depending on their current situation (e.g., agent location, local pheromone concentrations, internal agent state). The Place agents act as facilitators by providing the application agents with local directory information concerning other application agents on the same place. Consequentially, all agent interactions are localized, which focuses the system's attention and reduces the need for communication bandwidth, a feature that will be crucial in real-world applications (see for instance [1]).

3.2 Pattern Detection Process

Our Detector agents face the problem of finding global patterns across spatially-distributed heterogeneous real-time data sources while they are only able to process data locally. Thus, it is actually the population of Detectors that identifies a pattern, not the agents themselves. Also, the Detectors have to calibrate their joint sensitivity dynamically, since the same local values may be considered part of a clear pattern at one time and barely distinguishable at another depending on the overall data stream.

These two population tasks break down to two questions for the individual agent: a) where to focus the search; and b) what to declare part of a pattern. The first question addresses the dynamically changing spatial and temporal focus of an agent. Detector agents are able to move from place to place and they can shift their focus at different periods in the local data streams (Figure 3). Thus, an agent needs guidance for its spatial and temporal moves.

The second question addresses the problem of normalization across space and time. If the agents were able to access all the data streams at once, they could easily determine the maximum value and normalize all the data. Then, a threshold would separate background locations from components of a pattern. Without the global access to data, Detector agents have to find other means to determine that threshold.

Given the decentralized nature of the agent environment and the scale of the Detector population – in the hundreds or even thousands depending on the size of the system – both questions have to be answered collectively. We establish two coordination

processes among the De-
tector agents, one based
on pheromones in the
shared environment to
guide the agents' move-
ment, the other one based
on repeated direct inter-
actions (face-offs) among
the agents to establish the
current global maximum.

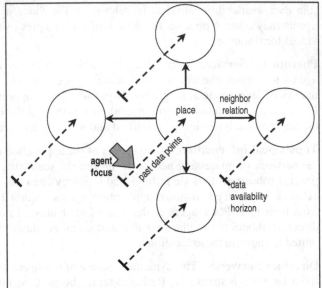

3.2.1 Guiding the Focus
A Detector tries to align
its focus with the location
of a pattern in the heterogeneous data stream. A
location designates not
only a region in space,
but also a point in time in
the recent past, since the
data in the stream chan-
ges over time. The spatial

Fig. 3. The Spatio-temporal focus of an agent moves through the "space" covered by the system

focus of the agent is simply its current place in the pheromone infrastructure, while its
temporal focus is set in an internal variable. Thus, the agent moves its focus either by
moving to a neighboring place, or by incrementing or decrementing its internal variable. Movements are restricted to the region covered by the pheromone infrastructure
and by the horizon, beyond which data is no longer stored at the places. As real time
advances, an agent's temporal focus may become invalid (outside the horizon), in
which case the agent's focus is automatically moved to remain at the horizon.

With every movement of its focus, a Detector agent assesses the evidence that the
data of the local real-time sources in its spatio-temporal focus is part of a pattern. The
definition of a pattern depends on the particular application of the detection mechanism. For instance, in the software demonstration that we present in Section 4, the Detectors search for locations where the data shows a strong spatial gradient. Other applications, for instance biosurveillance, may search for spatio-temporal locations
where the observed data significantly deviates from an established normal baseline.

The Detectors collectively coordinate their search, using pheromones to guide their
individual movements. This stigmergic coordination mechanism balances two conflicting trends: Detectors are *attracted* to locations which other Detectors identified as
part of a potential pattern, but Detectors are at the same time *repelled* by large concentrations of other Detectors. The attractive force recruits agents to potential patterns
to reinforce the finding of other agents. The repulsive force limits the recruitment to
prevent the system from being locked into only one solution. In recruitment mechanisms in nature such a limit is "built in" automatically by spatial limitations, since two
physical entities cannot occupy the same space at the same time.

Agents dynamically create the attractive and repulsive forces through individual
context-dependent pheromone deposits. The "Search" pheromone (P_S) has two major

flavors; $P_S(A)$ concentrations are considered attractive, while $P_S(R)$ concentrations repel
agents from a spatio-temporal location. The
place at which a P_S pheromone concentration is
sampled determines the spatial component of
the location to which the pheromone refers. The
temporal component is expressed with an additional tag attached to each P_S pheromone, specifying a point in time in the past. Deposits of
pheromones with different tags are not aggregated into one concentration by the infrastructure. Thus the collection of all P_S pheromones

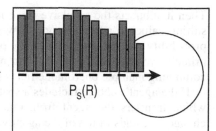

Fig. 4. The local pheromone concentrations translate into a force profile
over time

at the same place with the same major flavor may be interpreted as a force profile
over time (Figure 4).

Regularly repeated deposits of a pheromone at a fixed spatio-temporal location
quickly take the local pheromone concentration to an analytically predictable fixed
point, which depends on the deposit rate and the evaporation and propagation factor
of the particular pheromone flavor [4]. These deposits may be generated by the same
or by different agents and any agent that knows the configuration of the pheromone is
able to estimate the deposit rate from the sampled concentration, assuming that the
fixed point has been reached when the sample is taken.

A Detector regularly, at a globally fixed rate, deposits one unit of the $P_S(R)$ pheromone at its current place. The pheromone is tagged with the current value of the internal variable that determines the agent's temporal focus. Thus all deposits from
agents with the same focus aggregate into one local pheromone concentration. The
fixed point reached by this concentration directly reflects the number of agents that
share the same focus.

Deposits to the $P_S(A)$ pheromone are only generated regularly by a Detector if the
agent is convinced that it is currently focused on a part of a pattern. Once the evidence
computed by the agent has passed a certain threshold (see next Section), the agent
starts depositing one unit of the attractive pheromone at regular intervals. Thus, the
local $P_S(A)$ pheromone concentration relates directly to the "belief" of the Detector
population that this location is part of a distinguishable pattern.

Both flavors of the P_S pheromone propagate in space and time. A deposit of the
pheromone with a particular temporal focus tag at a specific place immediately triggers weaker deposits at neighboring places and nearby points in time. This propagation mechanism, implemented in the Place agents, is a straight-forward temporal extension of the spatial propagation mechanism. It creates a smooth distributed force
field over the represented space and time for each major flavor of the P_S pheromone.

A Detector agent regularly executes a movement decision cycle. Each cycle begins
with the agent's sampling the $P_S(A)$ and $P_S(R)$ concentrations at and nearby its current
focus. The agent may choose to move only in space (neighboring place), only in time
(increment/decrement temporal focus variable), or in both space and time; and for every
potential new location of its focus, the agent samples the pheromone concentrations.

In its movement decision the agent combines the two opposing forces. For each potential new location it computes the relative attractive force and the relative repulsive
force by normalizing the sampled $P_S(A)$ and $P_S(R)$ concentration for each option.

Then it subtracts the repulsive force from the attractive force and normalizes the resulting values to add up to one. Now each of these normalized values represents the probability that the agent selects the particular location and the agent spins an appropriately weighted roulette wheel to make its choice. We present the advantages of combining multiple pheromone fields in the decision process in [5].

If the agent's choice includes a spatial movement, it executes its mobility protocol, which transfers the agent from one processing node to the next and which also changes the registration of the agent with a place. The temporal component of a move only requires the agent to change its internal variable.

The probabilistic movement of the Detector agents' focus guided by the dynamically changing force fields does not cover the whole search space evenly, but rather concentrates the agents near detected patterns. To ensure that the system as a whole remains adaptive to newly emerging patterns and also to provide sufficient ergodicity for the threshold adaptation process, we restrict the lifespan of an agent to a fixed number of movements. At the same time, each Place agent introduces new agents at a fixed rate, dynamically balancing the global population size and ensuring a minimum number of visits at each place.

3.2.2 Adapting the Threshold

The significance that a Detector agent assigns to the evidence presented in the data it currently observes depends on the overall situation in the system and thus requires global information. The current threshold above which the agent starts depositing attractive pheromones represents an estimate of the global background level, and must be collectively established across the Detector population.

We use a variant of Particle Swarm Optimization (PSO) [8], inspired by flocking, herding, and schooling behavior in animal populations, to adjust the threshold. Bird flocks coordinate their movement as individual birds align their heading and velocity with that of their nearby neighbors and move in the direction of the center of the flock [12]. In PSO, the task of a swarm of agents is to search some space. Agents are distributed over the space, and periodically compare their estimates of the function being searched with other nearby agents, adjusting their own best information on the basis of that of their neighbors. Most PSO implementations house all the agents on a single processor, and "nearby" is typically defined in terms of the data structure housing the agents.

We adapt this model to coordinate the deposit threshold across the Detector population. A Detector agent starts depositing $P_S(A)$ pheromones when the locally observed evidence passes a globally fixed percentage threshold of the maximum evidence presented anywhere in the system at that moment. To estimate this global maximum value across the agent population, agents individually keep a short term memory of their local observations and at regular intervals compare their estimate of the maximum with other randomly encountered agents. Because our agents are distributed over a network, their PSO interactions are defined by collocation in the network of place agents.

A Detector agent keeps a memory of the observed evidence during a fixed number of last steps and carries an estimate of the current global maximum evidence in the system. If, at any time the agent observes an evidence value larger than its current maximum estimate, it updates its estimate. At regular intervals, an agent randomly selects one of the other Detector agents that currently share the same place ("random encounter") and initiates a face-off interaction. In this interaction, the agents exchange and then modify their estimates to reflect the observations of the respective other.

A simple set of rules guides the exchange. Let m_a be the maximum of the observed values of agent a and let M_a denote the agents current estimate of the global maximum (m_b and M_b denote the same values for agent b). After the exchange M_a and M_b are set to the same value computed as

$$(max[m_a,M_b]+max[m_b,M_a]+max[m_a,m_b])/3 . \tag{1}$$

Thus, both agents adopt the mean of their estimates tempered by the actual observations of the respective interaction partner.

The random face-offs among the agents and the fact that their movements cover the whole search space ensure that the individual estimates eventually approximate the global maximum. Changes in the actual maximum value are soon detected and communicated among the Detector agents.

3.2.3 Communicating the Result

Deposits of the $P_S(A)$ pheromone indicate the presence of a potential pattern in the observed data streams. The purpose of this pheromone is to attract other Detector agents to this location, so it must be propagated to neighboring locations that may not be part of the pattern.

In addition to the "Search" pheromone (P_S) we introduce a "Find" pheromone (P_F) that allows the Detector population to clearly mark a detected pattern. Deposits of P_F pheromones, unlike those of P_S pheromones, are not propagated by the infrastructure (zero propagation factor). Also, the P_F pheromone evaporates much more slowly than the P_S pheromone, and thus it takes longer for the local concentrations to approximate the fixed point under repeated deposits.

Whenever a Detector agent deposits a $P_S(A)$ pheromone, it also deposits a P_F pheromone with the same temporal focus tag. Thus, at locations where the agents perceive sufficient evidence for the presence of a pattern, there will be a buildup of P_F concentrations. The slower evaporation of the pheromone ensures that only if there is sustained evidence of a pattern will the P_F pheromone concentrations reach a significant strength.

The global pattern of P_F pheromone concentrations is the output of the pattern detection process. This pattern may be visualized for human operators and it also serves as input for the pattern classification process, described in the next section.

3.3 Pattern Classification

The pattern classification process seeks to highlight those of the detected patterns that express a particular spatial or temporal characteristic. For instance, in our demonstration we highlight only those patterns that extend in a particular spatial direction. Other classification schemes might, for instance, highlight patterns that join places with a particular characteristic or that extend across specific types of neighborhood relations among places.

Each applied classification scheme requires a population of Classifier agents that probabilistically move their individual focus across the spatio-temporal locations represented in the infrastructure according to the hypothesized pattern. Any Classifier, regardless of its association with a particular scheme, samples local P_F pheromone locations which identify the patterns to the classification process. The chosen classification scheme is encoded into the agent's movement and pheromone deposit decision logic.

In general, Classifiers tend to linger at locations that belong to a pattern with a high ranking in the classification scheme and they also tend to deposit more pheromones there. All Classifiers deposit "Class" pheromones (P_C) to communicate their findings. Each scheme is associated with a different flavor of the P_C pheromone.

The global pattern of P_C pheromone concentrations is the output of the pattern classification process. Again, this pattern may be presented to human operators and it may also serve as input to additional processes, which, for instance, may cross-correlate various classifications. At this point, we do not yet present any such potential extensions.

4 Demonstration

To demonstrate the potential of distributed pattern detection and classification in the domain of biosurveillance, we implemented a simple scenario. The demonstration also serves as a verification of the main proposed coordination algorithms.

In our demonstration we tile an abstract region with 75 by 75 rectangular places. Each place has eight neighbors – the places touching its edges and corners. We do not represent additional social relationships between places since we do not model an actual population.

We restrict ourselves to homogenous, static, and normalized data sources. We integrate three types of data sources into the system, of which at each place there exists one input stream. We assume that each data source at each place only delivers a fixed value between zero and one. In our visualization of the demonstration, we interpret each source as a component of a color value (RGB). For example, Red might represent over-the-counter tissue sales, Green antihistamine sales, and Blue workplace absenteeism. Thus, each place has a background color that represents its local input data.

Our Detector agents search for places whose local data is significantly different than the data in its neighborhood (e.g., higher sales of a certain class of over-the-counter remedies). Thus, at each step from one place to the next an agent measures the difference in the observed data and it assigns high evidence to a large differential.

Figure 5 shows the input pattern that our fixed data sources present to the agents. Besides random background data, there is a horizontal, a vertical, and a diagonal pattern of high differential values. Such a global picture is only available to human experimenter. The agents are restricted to the local input data at their respective current place and also users of most deployed systems are not likely to be able to see the whole pattern, since it may be impossible to transfer all the data in time.

The pattern detection process presented in Section 3.2 has two major components. The Detector agents coordinate their movements to focus on potential patterns and they exchange information in random encounters to estimate the global maximum in the presented evidence. In our demonstration we only use static and normalized data sources and thus we did not implement the estimation mechanism. We only focus on spatial patterns, not temporal ones.

Figure 6 shows a snapshot of the local concentrations of the $P_S(A)$ pheromone, which the Detectors use to attract each other to potential patterns. The lighter the color of a place, the higher is its local pheromone concentration. We populated our 75 by 75 places infrastructure with 1000 Detectors, each of which is permitted to take 400 steps before it is replaced by a new agent at a random location.

The non-propagating and only slowly evaporating P_F pheromone indicates where the Detector population believes the current patterns are. The pattern is now reduced to a few pheromone concentrations, which easily can be shipped to

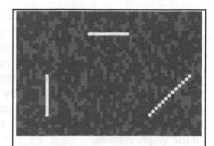

Fig. 5. Global input pattern presented to the detection and classification processes in our demonstration

the user for review. Also, each local concentration is effectively normalized since it is created under a global perspective provided by the movement of agents across the region. Figure 7 shows a snapshot of the P_F pattern as the local concentrations have stabilized. In our simulations, the agents quickly converged on the presented pattern and established a stable P_F concentration field.

We implemented one pattern classification scheme in our demonstration. Assuming that a detected pattern may relate to an epidemic outbreak of a disease caused by an airborne bioterrorist pathogen, our Classifier agents highlight those patterns that are aligned with the direction of the wind.

We deploy 1000 Classifiers, which have a strong tendency (weighted probabilities) to move in a given direction across the infrastructure. The agents deposit a non-propagating, slowly evaporating P_C pheromone. Thus, high stable concentrations of this pheromone indicate patterns that are aligned with the direction of the wind.

Fig. 6. Pattern of $P_S(A)$ pheromones that coordinates the Detectors' movements

An agent-internal confidence level determines the probability that a Classifier deposits a P_C pheromone. The agent's confidence grows if in successive steps it sees high P_F concentrations and it decreases as it passes through a sequence of low concentrations. So, as an agent moves along a detected pattern, it becomes increasingly likely that this pattern is aligned with direction given to the agent population.

The agent's confidence level also influences its movement decision. With a low confidence, the agent rapidly proceeds to its given direction. But, as the agent's confidence grows, so does its probability to take a step in the opposite dirtion. As a consequence, Classifiers tend to linger on

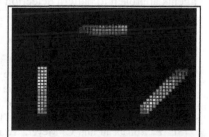

Fig. 7. Pattern of P_F pheromones that represents the Detectors' findings

patterns that induce high confidence levels, which, in turn, result in increased P_C pheromone deposit rates at the location of the pattern.

Figure 8 shows the result of the pattern classification process in our demonstration. The wind was assumed to run diagonally across the region and thus of the three detected patterns (Figure 7), only the diagonal one is highlighted in the P_C pheromones.

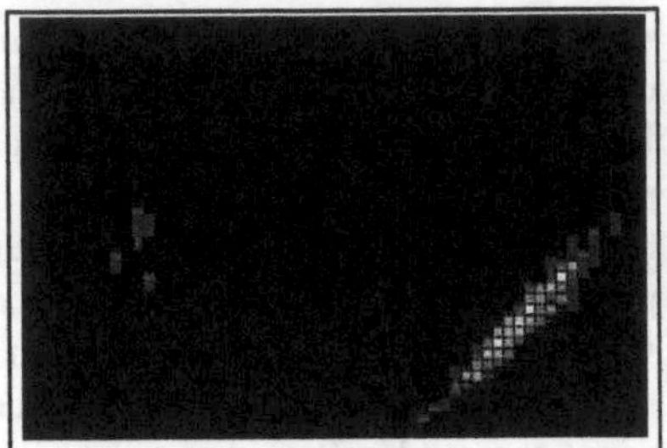

Fig. 8. Pattern of P_C pheromones that highlights the diagonal pattern

5 Conclusion

In this paper we presented a swarming agent architecture for the distributed detection and classification of spatio-temporal patterns in a heterogeneous real-time data stream. We motivate our decentralized approach with the requirements for an active surveillance system for epidemic outbreaks caused by a large-scale bioterrorist attack on a civilian population, but the same architecture may be applied to a wide variety of other surveillance applications, such as financial transactions, network diagnosis, or power grid monitoring.

In our approach we deploy large populations of simple mobile agents in a physically distributed network of processing nodes. At each such node we install a service agent that is part of the application independent runtime environment and that enables the agents to share information indirectly through their common computational environment. The indirect information sharing permits the application agents to coordinate their activities across entire populations.

This architecture may be adapted to the detection of various spatio-temporal patterns and new classification schemes may be introduced at any time through new agent populations. The system is scalable in space and complexity because of the consequent localization of processing and interactions. The system protects the potentially proprietary or private data through simple provable local processes that execute at or near the actual source of the data.

We successfully implemented a subset of the proposed mechanisms in a simplified software demonstration. The observed robustness, scalability and fast convergence to an acceptable solution provide strong evidence for the potential of our swarming agents approach to pattern detection and classification.

References

[1] D. Anhalt. The Changing Nature of Commercial Satcom and its Impact on US Military Advantage. Satellite 2001, Office of Net Assessment, Washington, DC, 2001.

[2] E. Bonabeau, M. Dorigo, and G. Theraulaz. Swarm Intelligence: From Natural to Artificial Systems. New York, Oxford University Press, 1999.

[3] E. Bonabeau and C. Meyer. Swarm Intelligence: A Whole New Way to Think About Business. Harvard Business Review, 79(May), 2001.

[4] S. Brueckner. Return from the Ant: Synthetic Ecosystems for Manufacturing Control. Ph.D. Thesis at Humboldt University Berlin, Department of Computer Science, 2000.

[5]   S. Brueckner and H.V.D. Parunak. "Multiple Pheromones for Improved Guidance." Proceedings of the 2nd DARPA-JFACC Symposium on Advances in Enterprise Control. Minneapolis, MN, USA. July, 2000.

[6]   S. Brueckner and H.V.D. Parunak. "Analysis and Design of Self-Organizing Systems of Fine-Grained Agents." ERIM white paper available from the authors. July, 2001.

[7]   P.-P. Grassé. La Reconstruction du nid et les Coordinations Inter-Individuelles chez Bellicositermes Natalensis et Cubitermes sp. La théorie de la Stigmergie: Essai d'interprétation du Comportement des Termites Constructeurs. Insectes Sociaux, 6:41-84, 1959.

[8]   J. Kennedy, R. C. Eberhart, and Y. Shi. Swarm Intelligence. San Francisco, Morgan Kaufmann, 2001.

[9]   H. V. D. Parunak. 'Go to the Ant': Engineering Principles from Natural Agent Systems. *Annals of Operations Research*, 75:69-101, 1997.

[10] H. V. D. Parunak, A. D. Baker, and S. J. Clark. The AARIA Agent Architecture: From Manufacturing Requirements to Agent-Based System Design. Integrated Computer-Aided Engineering, 8(1):45-58, 2001.

[11] H. V. D. Parunak, S. A. Brueckner, J. Sauter, and J. Posdamer. Mechanisms and Military Applications for Synthetic Pheromones. In Proceedings of Workshop on Autonomy Oriented Computation, 2001.

[12] C. W. Reynolds. Flocks, Herds, and Schools: A Distributed Behavioral Model. Computer Graphics, 21(4 (July)):25-34, 1987.

[13] G. Theraulaz, S. Goss, J. Gervet, and J. L. Deneubourg. Task Differentiation in Polistes Wasp Colonies: A Model for Self-Organizing Groups of Robots. In Proceedings of First International Conference on Simulation of Adaptive Behavior, pages 346-355, MIT Press, 1991.

Digital Pheromones for
Coordination of Unmanned Vehicles

H. Van Dyke Parunak, Sven A. Brueckner, and John Sauter

Altarum, 3520 Green Court, Suite 300, Ann Arbor,
MI 48105-1579
1.734.302-{4684, 4683, 4682}
{van.parunak, sven.brueckner, john.sauter}
@altarum.org

Abstract. One of the parade examples of agent coordination through a shared environment is the use of chemical markers, or pheromones, for path planning in insect colonies. We have developed a digital analog of this mechanism that is well suited to problems such as the control of unmanned robotic vehicles, and extended it in novel ways to provide a rich set of tools for robotic control. We introduce the approach, describe the mechanisms we have developed, and summarize the technology's performance in a series of scenarios reflecting military command and control.

1 Introduction

Many social insect species coordinate the activities of individuals in the colony without direct communication or complex reasoning. Instead, they deposit and sense chemical markers called "pheromones" in a shared physical environment that participates actively in the system's dynamics. The resulting coordination is robust and adaptive. Seeking such characteristics in engineered systems, we have developed a software runtime environment that uses digital pheromones (data structures inspired by the insect model) to coordinate computational agents using mechanisms similar to those of social insects.

We have applied digital pheromone mechanisms to the problem of controlling air combat missions, with special emphasis on unmanned air vehicles. [11]. In the course of our experimentation, we have developed several mechanisms that are promising for agent coordination in general. This report describes pheromone-based movement control as a variety of potential-field-based methods (Section 2), reviews the mechanisms we have developed (Section 3), and describes their performance in several air combat scenarios (Section 4).

2 Potential Fields via Pheromones

From an engineering perspective, pheromones are a particularly attractive way to construct a potential field that can guide coordinated physical movement.

D. Weyns et al. (Eds.): E4MAS 2004, LNAI 3374, pp. 246–263, 2005.

2.1 Potential Fields

Potential-based movement systems are inspired by electrostatics. The (vector) electric field $\vec{E}(\vec{r})$ at a point in space is defined as the force felt by a unit charge at that point. We define a (scalar) potential field

$$\varphi_{21} = -\int_{P_1}^{P_2} \vec{E} \bullet d\vec{r} \tag{1}$$

by integrating this vector field from an arbitrary reference point to each point in the space. Conversely, the field may be expressed as the gradient of the potential, $\vec{E} = -\nabla\varphi$, and a massless charged particle will move through space along this gradient. In electrostatics, the field is generated by the physical distribution of charges according to Coulomb's law. Einstein's extension of the formalism to gravity leads to a gravitational field generated by the physical distribution of mass. Thus the movement of a massive charged particle will follow a composition of two fields.

The notion of movement guided by a potential gradient has been applied to other situations in which the field is generated, not by natural physical phenomena, but by synthetic constructs. A parade example is robot navigation [14], which automatically maps from a given distribution of targets and obstacles to a movement plan. In such applications, the designer of the field is not limited to two components of the field (electrostatic and gravitational), but can include many different fields to represent different classes of targets and obstacles.

We use a potential field to guide unmanned robotic vehicles (URV's) through the battlespace (Figure 1). In this scenario, robotic vehicles seek to destroy the tank farm, which is defended by two missile batteries. The vehicles climb an attractive gradient centered on the tank farm while avoiding repulsive gradients centered on the threats. To be useful in warfighting, this field requires four characteristics (mnemonically, "4-D"):

Diverse.—It must fuse information of various types and from various sources, including targets to be approached, threats to be avoided, and the presence of other URV's with whom coordination is required.

Distributed.—Centralized processing of a potential field imposes bottlenecks in communications and processing, and generates localized vulnerabilities to attack. Ideally, the potential field should be stored close to where the information that it integrates is generated, and close to where it will be used.

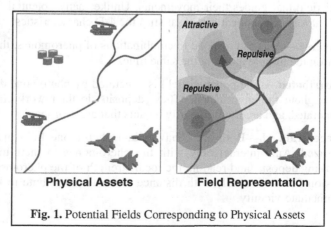

Physical Assets   **Field Representation**

Fig. 1. Potential Fields Corresponding to Physical Assets

Decentralized.—Efficiency and robustness also dictate that components of the system be able to make local decisions without requiring centralized control, ideally on the basis of nearest-neighbor interactions with one another.

Dynamic.—The battlespace is an uncertain and rapidly changing environment, and the methods and architecture used to construct and maintain the field must be able to incorporate such changes rapidly into the field.

An architecture inspired by insect pheromones satisfies these requirements, and can be applied to warfighting scenarios.

2.2 Digital Pheromones

Insects coordinate without direct communication, by sensing and depositing pheromones (chemical markers) in the environment [10]. For example, the networks of paths that they construct joining their nests with available food sources form minimum spanning trees [5], minimizing the energy ants expend in bringing food into the nest. This structure emerges as individual ants wander, depositing and sensing pheromones.

The real world provides three operations on chemical pheromones that support purposive insect actions.

It *aggregates* deposits from individual agents, fusing information across multiple agents and through time.

It *evaporates* pheromones over time. This dynamic is an innovative alternative to traditional truth maintenance. Traditional knowledge bases remember everything they are told unless they have a reason to forget something, and expend large amounts of computation in the NP-complete problem of detecting inconsistencies that result from changes in the domain. Ants immediately begin to forget everything they learn, unless it is continually reinforced. Thus inconsistencies automatically remove themselves within a known period.

It *diffuses* pheromones to nearby places, disseminating information for access by nearby agents.

The pheromone field constructed by the ants in the environment is in fact a potential field that guides their movements. Unlike many potential fields used in conventional robotics applications, it satisfies the 4-D characteristics:

Diverse.—Ants can respond to combinations of pheromones, thus modifying their reaction to multiple inputs at the same time.

Distributed.—The potential field is generated by pheromone deposits that are stored throughout the environment. These deposits do their work close to where they are generated, and are used primarily by ants that are near them.

Decentralized.—Both ant behavior and pheromone field maintenance are decentralized. Ants interact only with the pheromones in their immediate vicinity, by making deposits and reading the local strength of the pheromone field. Because diffusion falls off rapidly with distance, deposits contribute to the field only in their immediate vicinity.

Dynamic.—Under continuous reinforcement, the pheromone field strength stabilizes rapidly, as a concave function of time (proportional to

$$\int_0^t E^\tau d\tau \; ,$$

(2)

where $E \in (0,1)$ is the evaporation rate) [2]. Thus new information is quickly integrated into the field, while obsolete information is automatically forgotten, through pheromone evaporation.

An implementation of digital pheromones has two components: the *environment* (which maintains the pheromone field and performs aggregation, evaporation, and diffusion), and the *walkers* (which deposit and react to the field maintained by the environment). Our implementation has two corresponding species of agents. A set of *place agents* with a Neighbor relation defining adjacency makes up the environment, and each walker is represented by a *walker agent.*

Each place agent maintains a scalar variable corresponding to each pheromone flavor. It augments this variable when it receives additional pheromones of the same flavor (whether by deposit from a walker or by propagation from a neighboring place), evaporates the variable over time, and propagates pheromones of the same flavor to neighboring place agents based on the current strength of the pheromone. The underlying mathematics of the field developed by such a network of places, including critical stability theorems, are described elsewhere [2]. If the strength of the pheromone at a location drops below a threshold, the software no longer processes that pheromone, and it disappears.

In principle, there are no restrictions on the graph of place agents. In physical movement problems, each place agent is responsible for a region of physical space, and the graph of place agents represents adjacency among these regions. There are different ways in which place agents can be assigned to space. In the work reported here, we tile the physical space with hexagons, each representing a place agent with six neighbors.

A walker agent inhabits one place agent at any given time. It can read the current strength of pheromones at that place as a function of their flavors, and deposit pheromones into the place. It can also determine from the place agent the relative strength of a given flavor at the place and at each of its neighbors. A walker moves from one place to another by spinning a roulette wheel whose segments are weighted according to this set of strengths.

Such techniques can play chess [4] and do combinatorial optimization [1], and we have applied them to manufacturing [2] and military C^2 [11].

3 Basic Mechanisms

We have explored several basic mechanisms essential to the engineering deployment of pheromone mechanisms. These fall into three broad categories: combinations of multiple pheromones, using history in movement decisions, and ghost agents. Some of the results discussed in this section are expounded at more length in other publications, but are drawn together here so that they can be more readily considered as an integrated system.

3.1 Pheromone Vocabulary

There are two ways in which the pheromone vocabulary can be multiplied. First, different flavors may reflect different features of the environment (e.g., Red (hostile) air defenses, Blue (friendly) bases). These flavors have different *semantics*. Second, different flavors with the same semantics (e.g., all generated by the same feature) may differ in their evaporation or propagation rate or threshold, thus having different *dynamics*.

Pheromones with Different Semantics.—We explored the effect of increasing the semantics of a pheromone vocabulary in the context of the classic missionary-cannibal problem [12]. Three missionaries and three cannibals are together on one bank of a river, with a dugout canoe capable of carrying only one or two people. If at any time the cannibals outnumber the missionaries on either bank of the river, they will eat them. The problem is to plan a sequence of moves that gets all six people safely across the river.

At each decision epoch, only those agents on the bank with the boat make a movement decision. Each such agent decides whether to move by evaluating a personal choice function that returns a real number between 0 and 1, evaluating a random variable uniformly distributed on [0,1], and comparing these two values. If the random number is less than the value of the choice function, the agent volunteers to move. The actual riders in the boat are chosen randomly from the list of candidates.

The details of the agent's decision are embedded in its choice function, which is a function of the levels of the available pheromones. In principle, each individual agent could have its own choice function, but in our experiments all Missionaries share one choice function and all Cannibals share another.

We explore the performance of the system for various combinations of three pheromones: a bank pheromone that tells agents where they are, an undifferentiated population pheromone deposited by both Missionaries and Cannibals, and distinctive Missionary and Cannibal pheromones. Our performance metric is the number of steps necessary for the system to move the agents from one bank to the other. Because of the stochastic nature of the decisions, different runs often yield different num-

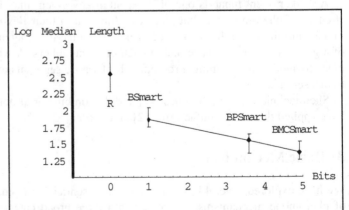

Fig. 2. Performance and Pheromone Vocabulary (Error bars show inter-quartile spread)

bers of steps, and we report the median run length over 100 runs.

Figure 2 shows the result for one series of experiments, comparing three different pheromone configurations. "R" indicates the performance for agents executing a random walk. "BSmart" shows the performance when the agents have access only to a pheromone indicating which bank they inhabit (thus one bit of information). The performance at "BPSmart" results from telling them in addition the total population on their bank. Since there are six possible populations on either of two banks, the information available is $Log_2(2*6) = 3.58$. "BMCSmart" reflects the

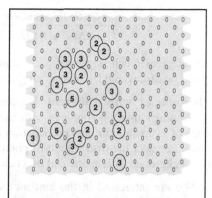

Fig. 3. Test Distribution of Pheromone Sources

performance when missionaries and cannibals deposit distinct pheromones. There are 4*4 possible equilibrium values on each bank, but no agent will ever sense the combination {0,0}, so the total information available is $Log_2(2*(4*4-1)) = 4.91$. Figure 2 shows that log performance is linear in information content, so performance is exponential in information content.

In these experiments, the agent's choice function explicitly takes into account the levels of the different pheromones. An alternative approach, used in our air combat applications, computes a weighted function of the various input pheromones to create a single "net pheromone" whose gradient walkers then follow. In this case, the basic pheromone flavors are:

- *RTarget*: emitted by a red (hostile) target.
- *GTarget*: emitted by a blue (friendly) agent who has encountered a red target and is returning to base.
- *GNest*: emitted by a blue agent who has left the base and is seeking a target.
- *RThreat*: emitted by a red threat (e.g., missile battery)

In addition, we provide the blue agent with *Dist*, an estimate of how far away the target is.

Initially, we experimented with an equation of the form

$$\frac{\theta \cdot RTarget + \gamma \cdot GTarget + \beta}{\alpha \cdot RThreat + \delta \cdot Dist + \beta}, \tag{3}$$

where α, β, γ, δ, and θ are tuning factors, easily manipulated in a genetic algorithm or particle swarm optimization [15, 16]. β avoids singularities when other terms are 0. This form attracts blue agents to targets or to the trails of other blue agents who have found targets, avoids threats, and seeks to minimize distance to the target. While yielding reasonable performance, this equation left some performance gaps. Manual manipulation of the equation yielded the alternative form

$$\frac{\theta \cdot RTarget + \gamma \cdot GTarget + \beta}{(\rho \cdot GNest + \beta)(Dist + \varphi)^{(\delta + \alpha(RThreat+1))} + \beta}, \tag{4}$$

which gives much improved performance. While more complex, this latter equation could be discovered by genetic programming.

Pheromones with Different Dynamics.—Another technique involving multiple pheromones uses pheromones with the same semantics but differing dynamics (e.g., rates of evaporation E and propagation F and threshold S) [3]. To motivate this mechanism, consider the distribution of pheromone sources shown in Figure 3. Each source (or background 0) is at one cell of a hexagonal grid.

We are interested in the guidance that the pheromone field offers a walker at a given place. Let fi be the pheromone strength at place i. The guidance gj available to a walker at place j is

$$g_j = \underset{i \in \{j\} \cup N(j)}{Max} \left(\frac{f_i}{\sum f_i} \right) - \frac{1}{1 + N(j)}. \tag{5}$$

Guidance thus ranges from 0 (if all accessible places have the same pheromone strength) to 1 (if only one place has pheromone and all the others have none).

Figure 4a,b shows the distribution of guidance (white = 1, black = 0) for two different propagation parameters F. When F is low (left plot), most places in the target-rich region at the left of the figure have high guidance, but the pheromones do not propagate across the targetless right side of the figure, yielding a broad "valley" with low guidance. When F is high (right plot), propagation merges signals from individual sources, yielding low guidance in the target-rich region but a much narrower valley on the right. Thus high propagation gives good long-range guidance but poor short-range guidance, while low propagation gives good short-range guidance but poor long-range guidance.

A reasonable resolution is to have each source deposit multiple pheromones with different dynamics. A walker picks its next step first by measuring the guidance available from each flavor, then computing its movement based on the pheromone with highest guidance. Figure 4c shows the guidance field from six flavors with different dynamics, yielding both high guidance in the target area, and propagation of pheromones across most of the eastern valley.

3.2 History

A walker's movement through the graph of places should balance several factors. A strong field gradient enables deterministic hill climbing that the walker should exploit. However, a weak gradient may result from noise in the system. In this case, it does not provide reliable guidance. We would prefer that the walker continue moving in the general direction of its previous steps if there is one, and otherwise that it explore more broadly.

To balance deterministic hill climbing and stochastic exploration, the walker moves from one place to another by spinning a roulette wheel whose segments are

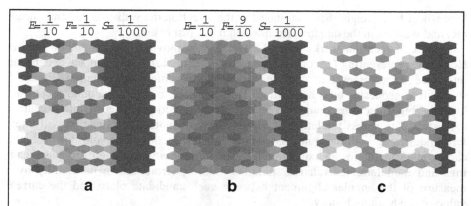

$$E=\frac{1}{10} \quad F=\frac{1}{10} \quad S=\frac{1}{1000} \qquad E=\frac{1}{10} \quad F=\frac{9}{10} \quad S=\frac{1}{1000}$$

a   b   c

Fig. 4. Guidance fields for low (*a*) and high (*b*) propagation parameters, and for a range of six different propagation parameters (*c*)

weighted according to the relative strengths of a pheromone flavor (or weighted combination of flavors) in the place and its neighbors. The mapping function from relative pheromone weight to segment width determines the degree of stochasticity in the walker's behavior. If s_i' is the perceived pheromone concentration at place i, the normalized weight p_i at that place is

$$p_i = \frac{s_i'}{\sum_{j=1} s_j'}, \tag{6}$$

where the summation ranges over place i and its neighbors, and the probability p_i' that the walker will move to that place is

$$p_i' = \frac{e^{\beta * p_i}}{\sum_{j=1} e^{\beta * p_j}}. \tag{7}$$

The parameter β determines the degree of stochasticity in the walker's movement. On a hex grid, when $\beta < 4$, selection probabilities are more similar than the pheromone strengths would indicate, favoring exploration, while $\beta > 5$ tends to emphasize stronger gradients, favoring exploitation.

To balance hill climbing against previous direction, we assign momentum to the walker. Models of actual ant behavior usually restrict the ant's ability to smell pheromones to some angle on either side of its current orientation. In our implementation, this technique takes the form of multiplying each segment in the walker's rou-

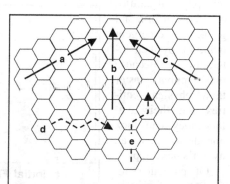

Fig. 5. Path anisotropy in a hex lattice

lette wheel by a weight that is strongest in the direction the walker is currently heading, and weakest in the direction from which it has just come.

Such a momentum works well if the walker is moving over continuous space. However, representing (continuous) space as a (discrete) graph of place agents can introduce anisotropies that confuse a simple momentum computation. Figure 5 shows five geodesics on a hex lattice. Trajectories a, b, and c maintain a constant heading, but trajectories d and e experience local direction changes while executing a shortest path across the lattice. A straightforward momentum function will interfere undesirably with these necessary changes of direction. To avoid this problem, each walker maintains an exponentially-weighted moving average of its past headings and modulates the relative strengths of the pheromones in its vicinity by a measure of the angular alignment between each candidate place and the current value of the heading history.

3.3 Ghost Agents

So far, we have distinguished stationary *place agents* (corresponding to regions of the problem space, and forming a graph structure representing the connectivity of that space) from *walker agents* (mobile agents that are associated with one place agent at a time and move among them according to the edges in the place network). For some purposes, it is useful to further refine the concept of walkers into two species.

The walker associated with a single physical robot is its avatar. In Hindu mythology, the term refers to an incarnation of a deity, hence, an embodiment or manifestation of an idea or greater reality. In our system, an avatar is the manifestation in our system of the greater reality (ground truth in the battlespace). A physical entity has only one avatar, which travels with the physical entity that it represents. It moves from one place agent to another only when its parent entity moves physically from one region to another. Thus its speed is limited by the physical speed of its associated entity.

One avatar may send out many unembodied walkers, or *ghosts*. Ghosts move as fast as the network among place agents can carry them. Because they are more numerous than physical entities and their associated avatars, they can do "what-if" explorations that physical entities could not afford, and generate emergent behavior by their interactions. Because they move faster than physical entities and their avatars, they can look ahead to plan an avatar's next steps.

Of particular interest to robotic applications is the emergence of dis-

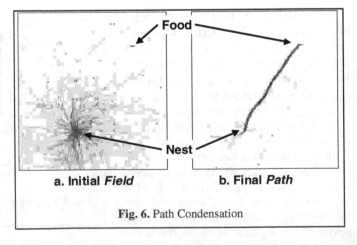

a. Initial *Field*   **b. Final *Path***

Fig. 6. Path Condensation

crete paths in the pheromone field as many ants concurrently read and reinforce it. For example, Figure 6a shows the pheromone field deposited by a swarm of ants wandering out from their nest (at the lower left of the figure) in search of food (at the upper right). Initially, the field is roughly circularly symmetrical, and

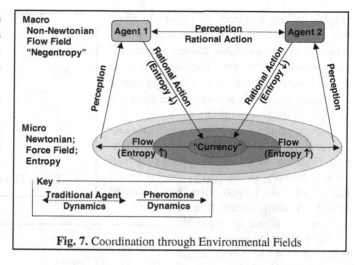

Fig. 7. Coordination through Environmental Fields

serves to guide food-bearing ants back home. Once some ants find the food and begin returning home, this field rapidly collapses into a path (Figure 6b).

At first glance, this dynamic [6] violates second-law tendencies to increasing disorder in systems consisting of many components. Left to themselves, large populations tend to disorder, not organization. Natural systems can organize at the macro level because their actions are coupled to a flow field at a micro level. Agents *perceive* and orient themselves to the flow field and reinforce that field by their *rational action*, as shown by the solid lines in Figure 7 [8]. Metaphorically, they drain unwanted entropy from the macro level (where organization is desired) to the micro level (where disorder is tolerated).

Traditional coordination mechanisms ignore the micro level completely, as agents perceive and act directly on one another (dashed line in Figure 7). We link agents through the environment so that perception and action serve both to coordinate multiple agents and to control overall disorder.

We validate this mechanism of emergent coordination explicitly through experiments that compute the entropy over time of the pheromone molecules at the micro level and the agents at the macro level [13]. The increase in entropy at the micro level (through Brownian motion of pheromone molecules) more than balances the decrease in entropy experienced by walkers following the pheromone gradient.

The path emergence illustrated in Figure 6 is the result of interactions among many walkers. Each walker's behavior is highly stochastic, performing a real-time Monte Carlo search of its local vicinity, and contributing to the emergence of a long-range path. In engineering applications, it may not be

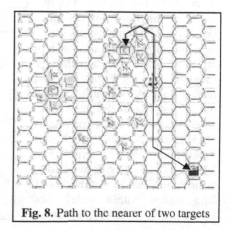

Fig. 8. Path to the nearer of two targets

feasible to ask hundreds of physical robots to explore the domain in this manner, nor is it necessary. As an avatar moves, it continuously sends out ghosts. The interaction of the ghosts forms the path, which is being constantly revised to accommodate dynamic changes in the environment.

Our experiments show this path formation dynamic to be extremely robust and adaptive. Figure 8 shows the formation of a path from a friendly airbase (lower right) to the nearer of two targets (the house-shaped icons), avoiding threats (the radar icons). If we increase the strength of the left-hand target to twice that of the closer target, the path will lead there instead. Figure 9 shows a path to a target protected by a gauntlet of threats, a configuration that resists classical potential field methods.

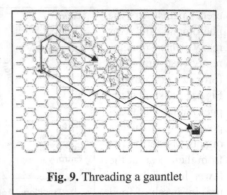

Fig. 9. Threading a gauntlet

When ghost agents choose between two targets, they cannot tell whether one target's pheromone is stronger because it is depositing at a higher rate, or because it is nearer than the other target. We explore the balance between these factors by setting up two targets T_1 and T_2 diametrically opposite one another from the ghosts' origin, with varying ratios of distance and strength. Then we compute the percentage p_1 of runs (out of a total of 45) that form a path to T_1 rather than to T_2. Figure 10 plots of this probability as a function of the strength and distance ratios. The dots represent experimental observations, between which other values are linear interpolations. Most of the plot is dominated by regions in which p_1 is either 1 or 0. The region within which both strength and distance play an ac-

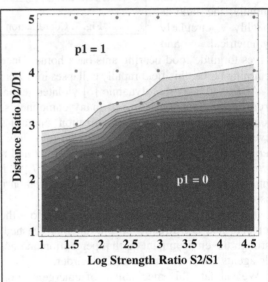

Fig. 10. Trade between target strength and distance

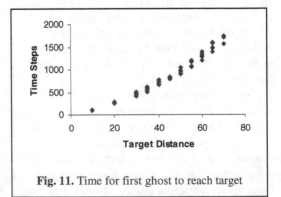

Fig. 11. Time for first ghost to reach target

tive role in target selection is relatively narrow. As both ratios grow, the difference in distance overwhelms the difference in strength.

Another important trade in understanding the behavior of ghost agents is between time and distance. When they are far from a target, ghost agents execute a random walk. Closer to the target, they can sense the target's pheromone field, and climb its gradient. One might expect that the number of steps required to reach a target would increase precipitously as the distance between a ghost's origin and its target grows. In fact, the transition is quite well behaved (Figure 11).

4 Operational Scenarios

We have demonstrated these mechanisms in military air operations in four increasingly sophisticated scenarios.

4.1 SEADy Storm

SEADy Storm [7] is a war game used to explore technologies for controlling air tasking orders. The battlespace is a hexagonal grid of sectors, each 50 km across). Friendly (Blue) forces defend a region in the lower left against invading Red forces that occupy most of the field. Red's playing pieces include ground troops (GT's) that are trying to invade the Blue territory, and air defense units (AD's, surface-to-air missile launchers) that protect the GT's from Blue attack. Blue has bombers (BMB's) that try to stop the GT's before they reach the blue territory, and fighters tasked with suppressing enemy air defenses (SEAD's).

Each class of unit has a set of commands from which it periodically chooses. Ground-based units (GT and AD) choose a new command every 12 hours, while air units (BMB and SEAD) choose every five minutes, reflecting the time it would take the resource to cross a sector. The commands fall into three categories (Table 1). GT cannot attack Blue forces, but can damage BMB's if they attack GT.

Blue can attack AD and GT when they are moving or attacking, and AD may attack any Blue forces that are not moving or waiting. Each unit has a strength that is reduced by combat. The strength of the battling units, together with nine outcome rules, determine the outcome of such

Table 1. Unit Commands in SEADy Storm

	Move	Attack	Wait
AD	Relocate	Fire (on any	Hide
		Blue aircraft)	Deceive
GT	Advance		Hide
SEAD	NewSectors	AttackAD	Rest
BMB	NewSectors	AttackAD	Rest
		AttackGT	

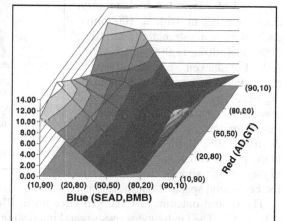

Fig. 12. Red Strength in Blue as a function of force composition

engagements. Informally, the first five rules are:

1. Fatigue: The farther Blue flies, the weaker it gets.
2. Deception: Blue strength decreases for each AD in the same sector that is hiding.
3. Maintenance: Blue strength decreases if units do not rest on a regular basis.
4. Surprise: The effectiveness of an AD attack doubles the first shift after the unit does something other than attack.
5. Cover: BMB losses are greater if the BMB is not accompanied by enough SEAD.

Rules 6-9 specify the percentage losses in strength for the units engaged in a battle, based on the command they are currently executing. For example, Rule 9 states: "If BMB does "AttackGT" and GT does "Advance": a GT unit loses 10% for each BMB unit per shift; a BMB unit loses 2% per GT unit per shift."

The primary parameter explored in the experiments reported here is the proportion of SEAD in the Blue military, and of AD in the Red military. Each side began with a 100 units, each with unit strength, and 10%, 20%, 50%, 80%, or 90% of SEAD or AD. The uneven spacing reflects a basic statistical intuition that interesting behaviors tend to be concentrated toward the extremes of percentage-based parameters. In current military doctrine, 50% is an upper limit on both AD and SEAD. We explore higher values simply to characterize the behavioral space of our mechanisms.)

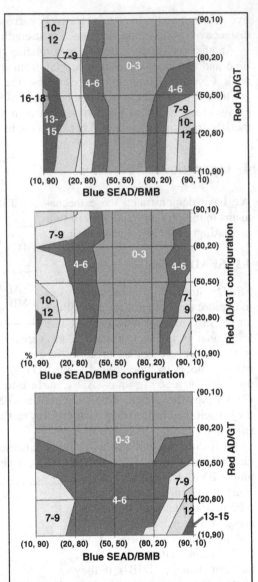

Fig. 13. Population of Red in Blue without pheromones (*top*), with pheromones attracted to both targets and threats (*center*), and attracted to targets but repelled by threats (*bottom*)

The central outcome is total Red strength in Blue territory at the end of the run (Figure 12). The landscape shows several interesting features, including

- a "valley" of Blue dominance for all Red ratios when Blue SEAD is between 50% and 80%, with slightly increasing Red success as the AD proportion increases;
- clear Red dominance for lower SEAD/BMB ratios, decreasing as SEAD increases;
- a surprising increase in Red success for the high SEAD and low AD levels.

Figure 13 compares the population of Red in Blue territory as a function of red and blue force composition for three different Blue control strategies. In the top plot, Blue does not use pheromones at all. The variations are due to the intrinsic dynamics of the combat, yielding a narrow valley up the center of the plot where Red's population is 3 or less (the criterion for Blue victory). When Blue uses pheromones to seek out Red targets and threats (middle plot, shown in profile in Figure 13), the wider valley reflects improved Blue performance. In the bottom figure, when Blue uses pheromones to avoid threats and approach targets, the valley with the lowest Red population is about the same area but of a very different shape than in the previous case, but the next level of Red occupation (4-6) is much larger, showing a reduction in higher levels of Red occupation.

A detailed discussion of the dynamics of this scenario and effects when we change the modeling formalism is available at [9].

4.2 CyberStorm

At the next level of sophistication, we expand the range of unit types. Red now has armored and infantry battalions, air defense units, distinct headquarters types for regiments, air defense, and the entire corps, and fueling stations. Blue has three types of fighters and two types of bombers. The environment includes bridges and road crossings (which speed the movement of ground units that encounter them) and oil fields (which Red seeks to attack and Blue seeks to protect). Combat outcome is based on the percentage survival of the oil fields.

Using this enriched environment, we have explored a variety of issues around blue decision-making. In these experiments (as in SEADy Storm), Blue resources move directly in response to Red pheromones, without using ghosts. Our experiments show that reasonable numbers of Blue resources cannot sample the pheromone field adequately to overcome the stochasticity inherent in the domain. As a result, outcomes vary widely with random seeds. These experiments demonstrated the need for ghost agents to sample the primary pheromone field at a statistically more significant level, and preprocess it for use by Blue avatars and the physical resources with which they are associated.

4.3 Super Cyber Storm

We exercised the ghost agents on a third model of the domain, which includes a significantly wider range of entity types, combat resolution on the basis of individual weapon type rather than unit type, more realistic dependencies among entities (for example, the effectiveness of Red air defense now depends on the status of other Red air defense units), and most importantly, a "pop-up" Red capability that lets us increase greatly the range of changes in Red's visibility as a scenario unfolds. This environment permits us to assess the effectiveness of ghost-based pheromones in dealing with pop-up threats.

First, we make all Red threats visible and stationary, and let the ghosts plan paths to the target for each of 181 offensive Blue missions against an entrenched Red force. We compute these paths using two different propagation parameters for Red threat pheromones, one that permits paths to fly relatively close to the threats, and another that keeps paths relatively far from the threats. Then we turn on Red movement and hiding behaviors, and compare the outcome of two sets of runs. In one set, Blue does not use ghosts or pheromones at all, but simply flies each mission on its precomputed path. This mode

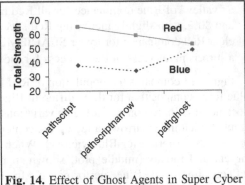

Fig. 14. Effect of Ghost Agents in Super Cyber Storm

of operation corresponds to traditional pre-planned flight itineraries, except that our pre-planned paths, based on complete knowledge of Red's locations at the time of planning, are superior to those that could be constructed in a real conflict. In the other set of runs, Blue ignores precomputed paths and relies on ghosts to form paths for its missions dynamically. We assess the outcome of each run by the total remaining strength of Blue and Red assets at the end of the set of missions.

Figure 14 shows the medians over five runs of Red and Blue total unit strengths for three configurations. In "pathscript," each mission flies the path precomputed for it using a high Red propagation parameter, leaving a conservative margin around Red threats. In "pathscriptnarrow," Blue again flies precomputed paths, this time using paths computed with a lower Red propagation parameter, and permitting Blue to come closer to Red locations. These less conservative paths lead to increased combat between Blue aircraft and Red threats, and both Red and Blue losses increase compared with "pathscript." In "pathghost," Blue missions ignore precomputed paths and send out ghosts to compute their paths dynamically as the mission unfolds. In this mode of operation, Blue's losses are least, since it can now avoid pop-up Red threats. As a result, it can deliver more weaponry to its assigned targets, increasing Red's losses in comparison with the other two scenarios.

4.4 Swarming UAV Experiment

Recently, these algorithms have been applied successfully to an experiment on the effectiveness of swarming UAV's (unmanned air vehicles) in suppressing antiaircraft threats in a wargame simulation conducted by the U.S. military. The pheromone approach shows significant performance improvements over the baseline. The public report has not been released, but will be by the time the final version of this paper is available, and details will be included in the publication version.

The U.S. Army Space and Missile Defense Battlelab, in support of the Joint Forces Command, used a subset of the ADAPTIV algorithms in a limited-objective experiment to determine the effects of employing affordable Swarming UAV's against an enemy's mobile strategic Surface to Air Missiles (SAM's; SA20's) utilizing an anti-access strategy [17]. The study considered four cases. The base case was drawn from a previous JFCOM study, Unified Vision 00, which utilized Global Hawks as UAV's. The comparison cases envisioned a swarm of smaller UAV's, with flight characteristics typical of a LOCASS-type platform. The study cases were 1) UAV's with sensors only, 2) UAV's with both sensors & munitions, and 3) UAV's with sensors/ munitions/jammers. The munitions on armed UAV's were deployed by flying the UAV into the target, thus sacrificing the UAV. The matrix also included excursions for each of the study cases that varied the quantities (10, 50,100) of UAV's in the swarm. The base case and study case excursions resulted in a total of 10 excursions with 10 runs each. The results were then analyzed for statistically supported comparisons across several measures of effectiveness (MOE's). The results for UAV's with sensors, weapons, and jammers were the same as those for UAV's with only sensors and weapons.

- Percent of Red assets detected: all swarming cases significantly outperformed the base case, and larger swarms significantly outperformed smaller ones. Sensor-only cases were slightly better than cases with multi-function UAV's, presumably because the population of armed UAV's decreases over the run as some UAV's function as weapons. The greatest difference was 30% detection (base case) vs. 95% detection (100 sensor-only UAV's).
- Percent reduction of successful TBM launches: no significant difference from base case.
- Percent of Red assets destroyed (by type): the smallest swarm of sensor-only UAV's did not significantly outperform the base case, but all other swarms did. Larger swarms significantly outperformed smaller ones, and swarms in which UAV's were armed outperformed those in which UAV's carried only sensors. The greatest difference for each category of Red asset is between the base case and a swarm of 100 armed UAV's. The differences are 25% destroyed vs. 63% for TBM TEL's, 5% vs 56% for tombstone radars, and 6% vs. 68% for SAM TEL's.
- Percent of Blue assets destroyed: no significant difference from base case. (UAV's are considered expendable, and not counted among blue assets for the purpose of this statistic.) When measured as a percentage of total missions flown, this metric drops slightly for larger swarms and for armed UAV's compared with unarmed ones, but the differences are still within the margin of error of the experiment.
- System Exchange Ratio (SER): the base case had a SER of 0.51, indicating that Blue lost twice as many assets as Red. All swarms except the 10-unit sensor-only swarm significantly outperformed the baseline. Larger swarms outperformed smaller ones, and armed UAV's outperformed unarmed ones. The best SER, for a swarm of 100 armed UAV's, was 4.56.

It has been observed that the improved performance in these scenarios is due to the increased number of sensors deployed in the battlespace, not to the use of a swarming algorithm per se. However, no competing algorithm can coordinate a hundred UAV's effectively. Current command and control mechanisms require multiple human operators per UAV, and coordination across such a team poses formidable problems. The swarming approach is valuable precisely because it does not require a large cadre of operators.

In September and October of 2004, these mechanisms were used to control physical UAV's in a demonstration at the Aberdeen Proving Grounds, Aberdeen, MD.

5 Summary

Digital pheromones are a powerful mechanism for controlling the movement of agents through space. They provide the elegance of potential field methods, with particular support for integrating diverse information sources, processing information in a completely distributed and decentralized environment, and coping with dynamic changes in the landscape. In exploring successively complex military scenarios, we have developed a toolkit of methods and mechanisms, including pheromone vocabularies that vary in both semantics and dynamics, mechanisms for incorporating agent momentum into movement decisions, ghost agents to preprocess the pheromone field and reduce stochasticity at the level of physical resources, and visualization mechanisms to enable human stakeholders to understand and monitor the emergent behavior of the system.

Acknowledgments

This work is supported in part by the DARPA JFACC program under contract F30602-99-C-0202 to ERIM CEC, under DARPA PM's COL D. McCorry and MAJ S. Heise, Chief Technologist Steve Morse, and Rome Labs COTR's C. Defranco and T. Busch. The experiment described in Section 4.4 was conducted under the auspices of the Joint Experimentation Directorate of the US Joint Forces Command. The views and conclusions in this document are those of the authors and should not be interpreted as representing the official policies, either expressed or implied, of the Defense Advanced Research Projects Agency or the US Government. Realization of these concepts owes much to our research team, including E. Feibush, E. Greene, O. Gilmore, R. Matthews, and M. Nandula. Portions of this technology are covered by US and international patents pending.

References

[1] E. Bonabeau, M. Dorigo, and G. Theraulaz. *Swarm Intelligence: From Natural to Artificial Systems*. New York, Oxford University Press, 1999.

[2] S. Brueckner. *Return from the Ant: Synthetic Ecosystems for Manufacturing Control*. Dr.rer.nat. Thesis at Humboldt University Berlin, Department of Computer Science, 2000. Available at http://dochost.rz.hu-berlin.de/dissertationen/brueckner-sven-2000-06-21/PDF/Brueckner.pdf.

[3] S. Brueckner and H. V. D. Parunak. Multiple Pheromones for Improved Guidance. In *Proceedings of Symposium on Advanced Enterprise Control*, 2000.

[4]   A. Drogoul. When Ants Play Chess (Or Can Strategies Emerge from Tactical Behaviors? In *Proceedings of Fifth European Workshop on Modelling Autonomous Agents in a Multi-Agent World (MAAMAW '93)*, pages 13-27, Springer, 1995.

[5]   S. Goss, S. Aron, J. L. Deneubourg, and J. M. Pasteels. Self-organized Shortcuts in the Argentine Ant. *Naturwissenschaften*, 76:579-581, 1989.

[6]   D. Helbing, F. Schweitzer, J. Keltsch, and P. Molnár. Active Walker Model for the Formation of Human and Animal Trail Systems. Institute of Theoretical Physics, Stuttgart, Germany, 1998. Available at http://xxx.lanl.gov/ps/cond-mat/9806097.

[7]   A. Kott. SEADy Storm. In A. Kott, editor, *JFACC*, Carnegie Group, Inc., 2000. Available at http://www.altarum.net/cec/projects/adaptiv/SeadyStorm-v1.2.doc.

[8]   P. N. Kugler and M. T. Turvey. *Information, Natural Law, and the Self-Assembly of Rhythmic Movement*. Lawrence Erlbaum, 1987.

[9]   H. V. Parunak, S. Brueckner, J. Sauter, and R. Matthews. Distinguishing Environmental and Agent Dynamics: A Case Study in Abstraction and Alternative Modeling Technologies. In A. Omicini, R. Tolksdorf, and F. Zambonelli, Editors, *Engineering Societies in the Agents' World (ESAW'00)*, vol. LNAI 1972, *Lecture Notes in Artificial Intelligence*, pages 19-33. Springer, Berlin, 2000. Available at http://www.altarum.net/~vparunak/esaw00.pdf.

[10]   H. V. D. Parunak. 'Go to the Ant': Engineering Principles from Natural Agent Systems. *Annals of Operations Research*, 75:69-101, 1997. Available at http://www.altarum.net/~vparunak/gotoant.pdf.

[11]   H. V. D. Parunak. Adaptive control of Distributed Agents through Pheromone Techniques and Interactive Visualization. In H. V. D. Parunak, J. Sauter, and R. S. Matthews, editors, ERIM CEC, 2000. Available at www.altarum.net/cec/projects/adaptiv/.

[12]   H. V. D. Parunak and S. Brueckner. Ant-Like Missionaries and Cannibals: Synthetic Pheromones for Distributed Motion Control. In *Proceedings of Fourth International Conference on Autonomous Agents (Agents 2000)*, pages 467-474, 2000. Available at http://www.altarum.net/~vparunak/MissCann.pdf.

[13]   H. V. D. Parunak and S. Brueckner. Entropy and Self-Organization in Multi-Agent Systems. In *Proceedings of The Fifth International Conference on Autonomous Agents (Agents 2001)*, pages 124-130, ACM, 2001. Available at www.altarum.net/~vparunak/agents01ent.pdf.

[14]   E. Rimon and D. E. Kodischek. Exact Robot Navigation Using Artificial Potential Functions. *IEEE Transactions on Robotics and Automation*, 8(5 (October)):501-518, 1992.

[15]   J. Sauter, H. V. D. Parunak, S. A. Brueckner, and R. Matthews. Tuning Synthetic Pheromones With Evolutionary Computing. In *Proceedings of Genetic and Evolutionary Computation Conference Workshop Program, 2001*, pages 321-324, 2001. Available at http://www.altarum.net/~vparunak/ECOMAS2001.pdf.

[16]   J. A. Sauter, R. Matthews, H. V. D. Parunak, and S. Brueckner. Evolving Adaptive Pheromone Path Planning Mechanisms. In *Proceedings of Autonomous Agents and Multi-Agent Systems (AAMAS02)*, pages 434-440, 2002. Available at www.altarum.net/~vparunak/AAMAS02Evolution.pdf.

[17]   SMDC-BL-AS. Swarming Unmanned Aerial Vehicle (UAV) Limited Objective Experiment (LOE). U.S. Army Space and Missile Defense Battlelab, Studies and Analysis Division, Huntsville, AL, 2001. Available at
https://home.je.jfcom.mil/QuickPlace/experimentation/PageLibrary85256AB1003BBEA
7.nsf/h_0036FB98FFD2ACCA85256AB2004161B0/D7680995272C266B85256B20004
E1BF0/?OpenDocument.

Motion Coordination in the Quake 3 Arena Environment: A Field-Based Approach

Marco Mamei and Franco Zambonelli

Dipartimento di Scienze e Metodi dell'Ingegneria,
University of Modena and Reggio Emilia
Via Allegri 13, 42100 Reggio Emilia, Italy
{mamei.marco, franco.zambonelli}@unimo.it

Abstract. This paper focuses on the problem of orchestrating the movements of bot agents in the videogame Quake 3 Arena. Since the specific patterns of movement that one may wish to enforce may be various, and serve different purposes (have bots meet somewhere, move in formation, or surrounding human players), a general and flexible approach is required. In this paper we discuss how the Co-Fields coordination model can be effectively exploited to this purpose. The key idea in Co-Fields is to model the agents' environment by means of application-specific computational force fields, leading agents' activities to a globally coordinated and adaptive motion behavior. The Co-Fields model is described both in general terms and in the specific Quake 3 Arena implementation, and several application examples are presented to clarify it. Also, the paper outlines the general applicability of the approach besides the Quake scenario and in areas such as mobile computing and mobile robots.

1   Introduction

Quake 3 Arena (Q3A) [1] belongs to the kind of first-person shooter (FPS) computer games. The player controls a character (bot) fighting against other artificial bots (i.e., software agents). The most important tasks are staying alive and killing opponents. The game provides a first-person perspective on the current situation, see figures 4, 5, 7.

Bots in FPS have continually become more complex and more intelligent. The original bots were completely oblivious to their environment and used fixed scripts to attack the human player. Current bots, such as those found in Q3A and Unreal Tournament [2], are actually autonomous goal-oriented agents. They collect health and other power-ups, and they have a variety of tactics such as circle-strafing and popping in and out of doorways [3].

Although current bots perform very well as single players, the mechanisms to let them cooperate and coordinate each other activities (for example to surround an enemy) are still under-developed [4, 2].

The aim of this paper is to present an approach to the problem of coordinating the movements of a set of Q3A bots. The goals of bots' coordinated

D. Weyns et al. (Eds.): E4MAS 2004, LNAI 3374, pp. 264–278, 2005.
© Springer-Verlag Berlin Heidelberg 2005

movements can be various: letting them to meet somewhere, distribute themselves accordingly to specific spatial patterns, surround an enemy, or simply move in the environment without interfering with each other.

In our perspective, any type of coordination - there included in videogames - is built upon two main building blocks: *(i)* interaction mechanism *(ii)* context awareness. With regard to the former point, it is obvious that coordination requires some form of interaction (e.g. communication): bot agents need to communicate someway in order to decide/plan/synchronize their actions. With regard to the latter point a bot agent can meaningfully coordinate with other agents only if it is somehow aware of "what is around", i.e., its context (i.e. operational environment).

Starting from these considerations, we focus on the problem of dynamically providing bots with effective interaction mechanisms and with simple, easy to be obtained, and expressive contextual information.

To achieve our goal, we take inspiration from the physical world, i.e., from the way particles in our universe move and globally self-organize accordingly to that contextual information which is represented by potential fields. In particular, in our approach, the environment and contextual information are represented in the form of distributed computational fields (Co-Fields). Each agent of the system can generate and have propagated by the environment specific fields, conveying application-specific information about the local environment and/or about itself. Agents can locally perceive these fields and move accordingly, e.g. following the fields' gradient. The result is a globally coordinated and adaptive movement, achieved with very little efforts by agents.

The paper is organized as follows: Section 2 motivates and describes field-based coordination as realized by the Co-Fields model. Section 3 explains how the model has been implemented in Q3A. Section 4 presents some motion coordination examples in Q3A. Section 5 discusses how the ideas presented can be applied in a wide range of other scenarios and presents related work. Finally, Section 6 concludes.

2   The Co-fields Approach

Let us consider the problem of letting a team of bots to meet somewhere in the Q3A dungeon. As anticipated in the introduction, to achieve this task, bots need some kind of interaction mechanism and some form of contextual information.

The mainstream solution for the above demands is to provide bots with a map of the dungeon and with some kind of communication channel that bots can use to agree on a specific location for the meeting. Although such solution may appear natural, it may require bots to execute complex algorithms to decide and negotiate where to meet and how to go there. This typically ends-up in brittle, static and not-adaptive solutions.

From a general perspective, the problem is that context-awareness is gathered by means of general purpose, not expressive and rather difficult to be processed description of the environment. The acquired information tends to be strongly separated from its usage by the agents, typically forcing them to execute complex algorithms to elaborate, interpret and decide what to do with that information.

On the contrary, if the context would have been represented expressively to facilitate agents in the achievement of a specific task, agents would trivially use that information to decide what to do. For example, in the above meeting application, if the agents would be able to perceive in their environment something like a "red carpet" leading to the meeting room, it would be trivial for them to exploit the information: just walk on the red carpet!

So the point is: how can we create the "red carpet"? How can we effectively represent context for the sake of specific coordination problems?

An intriguing possibility is to take inspiration from the physical world, and in particular from the way masses and particles in our universe move and globally self-organize their movements accordingly to that local contextual information that is represented by gravitational and electro-magnetic fields. These fields are sorts of "red carpets": particles achieve their tasks simply by following the fields.

This idea is at the basis of field-based coordination models [5]. Following this approach, agents achieve their goals not because of their capabilities as single individuals, but because they are part of an auto-organized system that leads them to the goals achievement. Such characteristics also imply that the agents' activities are automatically adapted to the environmental dynamic, which is reflected in a changing field-based representation, without forcing agents to re-adapt themselves. More in detail, the Co-Fields approach is centered on a few key concepts:

1. Contextual information is represented by "computational fields", spread by agents and/or by the environment, diffused across the environment, and locally sensed by agents;
2. A motion coordination policy is realized by letting the agents move following the local shape of these fields, the same as a physical mass moves in accord to the locally sensed gravitational field;
3. Both environment dynamics and agents' movements may induce changes in the fields' surface, thus inducing a feedback cycle (point 2) that can be exploited to globally achieve global and adaptive motion coordination.

2.1 Computational Fields

A computational field is a distributed data structure characterized by a unique identifier, a location-dependent numeric value, and a propagation rule identifying how the field should distribute in the network and how its value should change during the distribution. Fields can be static or dynamic, basically a field is static if once propagated its magnitude does not change over time; it is dynamic if its magnitude does. A field can be dynamic because for example its source moves and the field, with some propagation delay, changes accordingly its magnitude, or because for example its propagation rule its designed to remain active and to change field value after some time. Fields are locally accessible by agents depending on their location, providing them a local perspective of the global situation of the system. For instance, with reference to the case study, a Quake bot, call it the "prey" can spread in the map network infrastructure a computational field (let's call it PRESENCE field) whose value monotonically increases as it gets farther from the bot. Such field implicitly enables any other bots; call them the "predators", from wherever in the dungeon, of sensing the presence of the "prey" and its distance. Also, by sensing the local gradient of the PRESENCE field, the "predators" could also know in which direction the "prey" can be found (see figure 1).

2.2 Motion Coordination

In Co-Fields, the simple principle to enforce motion coordination is to have agents move following the local shape of specific fields. For instance, a "predator" bot looking for a "prey" bot can simply follow downhill the corresponding PRESENCE field. Dynamic changes in the environment and agents' movements induce changes in the fields' surface, producing a feedback cycle that consequently influences agents' movement. For instance, should the "prey" bot be moving around in the dungeon, the associated PRESENCE field would automatically update its shape to reflect the new situation. Consequently, any agent/bot looking for a "prey" would automatically re-adapt its movement accordingly. Should there be multiple "prey" bots, they could decide to sense each other's PRESENCE fields so as to stay as far as possible from each other to better escape from "predators".

In general, a Co-Fields based system can be considered as a simple dynamical system and can be effectively modeled as that (see [6] for details on Co-Fields modeling): agents are seen as balls rolling upon a surface, and complex adaptive movements are achieved not because of the agents wills and skills, but because of dynamic re-shaping of this surface. Of course, such a physical inspiration and the strictly local perspective in which agents act promote a strictly greedy approach in agents' movement: agents act on the basis of their local viewpoint, disregarding if a small sacrifice now (i.e., climbing a Co-Fields hill instead descending it) can possibly lead to greater advantages in the future. In a circular track for example, a "predator" looking for a "prey" that is moving clockwise, instead of greedily follow downhill the PRESENCE field (as the Co-Fields approach promotes), could better decide to move uphill to meet the "prey" counterclockwise. However, this is a general drawback of distributed problem solving, where efficiency reasons often rule out the possibility of globally informed decisions by distributed agents.

2.3 Application-Specific Coordination

The achievement of an application-specific coordination task is rarely relying on the evaluation, as it is, of an existing computational field (as in the case of a "predator" looking for a "prey" and simply following the specific PRESENCE field of that "prey". Rather, in most cases, an application-specific task relies on the evaluation of an application-specific coordination field, as a combination of some of the locally perceived fields. The coordination field is a new field in itself, and it is built with the goal of encoding in its shape the agent's coordination task. Once a proper coordination field is computed, agents can achieve their coordination task by simply following (deterministically or with some probabilistic rule) the shape of their coordination field uphill or downhill (depending on the specific problem) as if they were walking upon the coordination field associated surface (see figure 1). For instance, in the case study, for "prey" bots to stay as far as possible from each other, they can follow uphill a coordination field CF resulting from the combination (the sum) of all the computational fields of each "prey":

$$CF = \sum_{i=1}^{n} PRESENCE_i$$

At the moment, we still have not identified a general methodology to help us identify, given a specific motion pattern to be enforced, which fields have to be defined, how they should be propagated, and how they should be combined in a coordination field. We are confident some methodology to help in that direction can be found in the future, and would possibly make Co-Fields applicable to a wider class of distributed coordination problems even beyond motion coordination. Nevertheless, the immediate applicability of Co-Fields is guaranteed by two important considerations:

1. It is possible to get inspiration and of reverse engineer a wide variety of motion patterns found in Nature. For example, swarm intelligence phenomena [7, 8] such as bird flocking, ant foraging and bee dances provide a variety of useful motion patterns and can all be modeled with Co-Fields [9].
2. Complex motion patterns can be divided into simpler movements (e.g. moving along a square can be divided into following sequentially the four lines composing the square edges). Thus, although it might be impossible to perform complex motion patterns by following only one field, such complex motions patterns could be easily achieved by following sequentially a number of different fields.

3   Implementation

As anticipated in the introduction, to test the validity of our approach, we implemented the Co-Fields model within the videogame Quake 3 Arena (Q3A).

There are mainly two options to exploit Q3A as an environment simulation for multi-agent system:

1. write an *external* program (client-bot) that connects to the game as a human player. This bot receives (via a suitable interface) a world representation (roughly similar to the 3D scene view a human player can see) and can perform actions by sending commands to the game engine (roughly similar to joystick commands). With this approach the goal is to create a bot that actually plays the game as a human player [10, 3].
2. write an *internal* modification (*mod*) of the game. A mod is a package of changes made to the game altering the way in which the game was designed

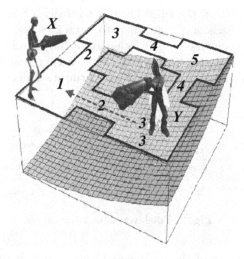

Fig. 1. Agent X propagates a PRESENCE field whose value has the minimum where Agent X is located. Agent Y senses that PRESENCE field to approach agent X by following downhill the PRESENCE field's gradient

to work. A mod can involve something as simple as changing the speed at which a rocket moves across a room or as complex as a complete overhaul of the look and feel and even the rules of the game [11].

In our work we ventured with the latter approach for a very specific reason. Since fields must be spread across the whole Q3A world, it appears difficult to realize such functionality with a client-bot that is functionally equivalent to a human player. Some kind of deeper modification appears to be required.

From a general perspective, this fact can be regarded as an example of the importance of explicitly modeling the environment in a multi-agent system. In fact, the power of the Co-Fields approach derives primarily from the fact that the field-based representation of the environment provides agents with handy information to achieve a specific task. This frees the agents from the burden of mutually interacting to acquire suitable context information.

3.1   Quake 3 Arena Internals

Q3A has been designed as two separate interlocking components: the 3D engine (proprietary) and the game logic (open-source). Mods are created modifying the open-source part of Q3A and recompiling it with the rest of the code. In this way, a mod programmer can disregard all the low-level details about the 3D display and concentrate on high-level topics like bots' behavior and game logic.

Before explaining how Q3A has been modified to implement Co-Fields, it is fundamental to give some remarks on the bots general architecture. A bot is build with a layered structure: the first layer manages the bot I/O operations, the second one manages the execution of complex actions (e.g. walking to a room, picking-up a weapon, etc.), the third layer is basically a finite state automaton governing high-level decisions (e.g. when to attack, when to withdraw, etc.). Eventually, the fourth one models the behavior of the commander when a squad of bots is involved (see figure 2). Q3A works as a time-based simulation. Each bot is given a 1/10 sec time-frame in which to run its code.

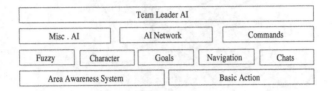

Fig. 2. Bot layered architecture

Although the purpose of the bot layered architecture is to mask to the programmer the intricacies of dealing with low-level details and to focus only on high-level artificial intelligence issues, for the purpose of implementing Co-Fields, there are two low-level parts worth to be considered: the Area Awareness System (AAS) and the bot's Goals.

The AAS is the component in charge of providing the bot with a representation of the Q3A world. Specifically, a bot perceives the world as a set of not-overlapping, adjacent, convex areas. These areas are mainly used for navigation purposes; routes in the Q3A world are basically a sequence of areas to be traversed.

A bot is a goal-oriented agent, whose execution is mainly intended to pursue some goals. There are either long-term goals (e.g. look for an enemy) and nearby goals (e.g. pick a power-up while looking for an enemy). The fundamental point to understand is that when, modifying the bots' behavior, we tend to remain on the high levels of its architecture. This means that bots are not controlled by means of an algorithm prescribing something low-level like (e.g. walk north 10m, then turn left, then fire). But with something high-level and goal-oriented as (e.g. look for heavy-weapons then hunt for enemies, until not injured).

3.2   Implementing Co-fields

To implement Co-Fields one has basically to: *(i)* have fields spread in the Q3A world, *(ii)* change the way in which bots perceive their environment. Bots must be provided with a field-based representation of the environment, *(iii)* the goal of moving following fields' gradients must be introduced.

In our implementation, each bot propagates only one field (such a fixed number is imposed by Q3A that does not allow dynamic memory allocation). Each field is stored in an array having a number of cells equals to the number of areas composing the Q3A world. Each cell stores the value of a field in a specific area. In our implementation such a value is always a function of the distance between the area considered and the area in which the bot (source) is located. At every time-frame of the game, all the arrays are updated to reflect the current system situation (see code in figure 3).

In standard (i.e. not modified) Q3A, bots perceive the world by means of a set of areas as provided by the AAS. The AAS provides various information on the kind and content of the areas (e.g. the area is full of water, contains a power-up, etc.). In our modifications, we enriched such a model, to provide bots with also the information on the kind of fields being spread in the areas and their magnitudes.

Each bot is also associated with an array representing its coordination field. Such an array is evaluated by composing the above described fields' arrays. Specifically, each bot selects the area where to move by looking, in its coordination field array, for neighbor areas where the gradient goes e.g. downhill. Then, the bot is committed to the long term goal LTG_PATROL to the selected area. This brings the bot to go (and patrol) the selected area. The looping of these actions at each time-frame, lets the bot follow downhill its coordination field.

```
int client;
// these are pointers to some areas in Q3A world
aas_areainfo_t infoarea; aas_entityinfo_t ent_field;
// with the following command ent_field points
// to the area occupied by bot client
BotEntityInfo(client, &ent_field);
for (i=1;i<=numareas;i++)
{
  // The following command, within the for-cycle
  // lets infoarea points to every area in the world
  trap_AAS_AreaInfo( i, &infoarea);
  // The field value is equal to the distance between the
  // bot and the area. It is thus a field increasing its
  // magnitude as it gets farther from the source.
  dist = Distance(ent_field.origin,infoarea.center);
  FIELD[client][i]=dist;
}
```

Fig. 3. Fragment of the Q3A modified file "ai_main.c".A PRESENCE field is spread in Q3A world

4   Examples of the Use of Co-fields

To clarify the usage of Co-Fields in Q3A, we detail here some specific motion coordination problems that bots may be in need to face.

4.1   Exploiting the PRESENCE Fields: Meetings and Predations

We have previously shown how the PRESENCE field can be exploited to detect where a bot is located in the Q3A map and how it can be reached. Moreover,

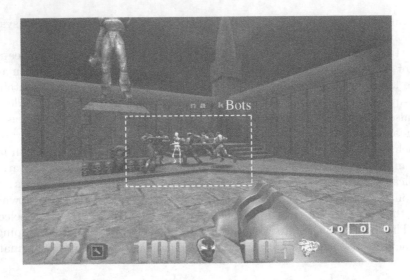

Fig. 4. A snapshot of the meeting process in Quake 3 Arena. All the bots have met

the PRESENCE field can be exploited to enforce a variety of other interesting motion patterns.

As a first example, let's consider a "meeting" application to help a team of bots to dynamically meet with each other. Although different policies can be enacted to let a team of bots to meet somewhere (e.g., a specific point or by a specific bot), here we concentrate on having the bots collaboratively walk towards each other and eventually meet in some dynamically determined intermediate point. If each member i of the group generate a PRESENCEi field, then each bot i of them can evaluate its coordination field by taking the maximum PRESENCE field of all the other bots:

$$CF_i = max(PRESENCE_{j \neq i})j = 1, 2, ..., n$$

and then follow such coordination field downhill. While the coordination fields continuously change due to the concurrent movements of all the members of the team each following its own coordination fields, the result is that the bots gradually approach towards each other, until collapsing in a single point. In other words, because agents actually attract each other, the system naturally converge to the situation in which all the agents are in the same point.

Figure 4 shows a snapshot of Q3A with bots involved in the meeting process. The key point to emphasize is that the meeting process, and Co-Fields in general, is adaptive: it works well even independently of the characteristics of the environment (e.g., of the map), without having to change a bit in the code of agents or in the structure and propagation of computational fields.

As another example exploiting the PRESENCE fields, consider a team of bots ("predators") moving in an environment with the goal of surrounding and kill the human player ("prey"). By getting inspiration from the behavior of wolves, which succeed in collaboratively surround a prey using the simple strategy of approaching the prey while trying to stay as far as possible from each other, we can define the coordination field of a generic predator i in this way:

$$CF_i^{pred} = PRESENCE^{prey} - \sum_{j=1, j\neq i}^{n} PRESENCE_j^{pred}$$

expressing that the predators follow downhill the PRESENCE field of the prey (to reach it) and, at the same time, tries to stay far from all other predators. The result (see figure 5) is that predators, rather than simply approaching the prey, are able to surround it.

Fig. 5. Snapshot of the surrounding process in Quake 3 Arena. The bots surround the player by closing all the escape doorways (remember that the game offers a first person view)

4.2   Flocking

As another example, let us consider the problem of having bots move in the Q3A map by maintaining an equal distance to each other, so as to form a regular formation. In an ideal, continuous case, a field that could be used to realize that purpose could be the one in Figure 6(a). Let us call this field FLOCK, to correctly attribute the fact that algorithms for moving in a formation has been inspired by the movements of birds' flocks [8]. Each agent has to generate a FLOCK field with a minimum at a distance a from itself, where a is the distance that must be preserved between agents to maintain the formation, and continuously increasing for higher distances. Then, to guarantee that each agents stay at a distance a from any other agents, the FLOCK fields generated by all the agents in the environment (say, a total of n) must be composed in the following coordination field:

$$CF(x, y, t) = min(FLOCK_i(x, y, t) : i = 1, 2, ..., n)$$

where is the FLOCK field of the agent i, and CF is the coordination field. to be followed downhill by agents. In other words, each agent i in the system can evaluate its coordination field CF as a minimum combination of all the other agents' fields and simply follow downhill the coordination field obtained. Globally, the system self-organizes in an almost regular grid, because all the agents try to remain in one of the minimum points of the next agents' fields and thus they tend to maintain a regular distance of a (see figure 6(b) and figure 7).

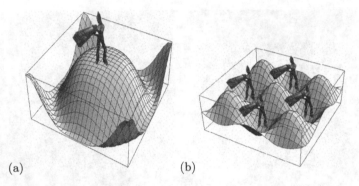

(a)   (b)

Fig. 6. (a) Single flock field (b) Global composition of the flock fields: bots maintain an almost regular grid formation

5   Other Application Scenarios and Related Work

Other than videogames, field-based coordination and the Co-Fields model well suit a wide array of application scenarios: from other videogames and movies to pervasive computing, robotics and material self-assembly.

5.1   Co-fields in Other Scenarios

The problem of coordinating the movements of a group agents has lots of interesting applications in several scenarios. Let us consider the exemplary pervasive computing problem of tourists visiting a museum assisted by personal digital assistants. Specifically, we can focus on how tourists can be supported in coordinating their movements with other, possible unknown, tourists. Such coordination activities may include scheduling attendance at specific exhibitions, having a group of students split in the museum according to teacher-specific laws, helping a tourist to avoid crowd or queues, letting a group of tourist to meet together at a suitable location, and even helping to escape accordingly to specific emergency evacuation plans.

Fig. 7. Snapshot of the flocking process in Quake 3 Arena. Bots moving maintaining regular distances from each other

To apply the Co-Fields model to this scenario, we need a computer infrastructure suitable in supporting fields propagation across the museum. Specifically, we can suppose that the museum is provided with an adequate embedded computer network. In particular, embedded in the museum walls (either associated to each artistic items or to each museum room), there will be a network of computer hosts, each capable of communicating with each other and with the mobile devices located in its proximity via the use of a short-range wireless link. The number of the embedded hosts and the topology of the network may depend on the museum, but the basic requirement is that the network topology mimics the topology of the museum plan (i.e. no network links between physical barriers, like walls). On each host there will be a middleware providing basic support for data storing (to store field values) and communication mechanisms (to propagate fields) [6]. Moreover, we can suppose that tourists are provided with a software agent running on some wireless handheld device, like a palm computer or a cellular phone, in charge of giving her/him suggestions on where to move.

Devices connect to nearby embedded hosts (to this end some kind of localization mechanism has to be enforced [12]). They can inject fields across the network and read field values in the neighborhood to enforce field-based coordination (e.g. move to the room where the gradient of a field goes downhill). With this regard, it is worth noting that the critical assumption made about the museum network topology is about not having people stumbling at walls while following gradients. More details on this Co-Fields application can be found in [13].

The above scenario and the associated motion coordination problems are of a very general nature, being isomorphic to a lot of scenarios ranging from other pervasive computing applications (such as, e.g., traffic management and forklifts activity in a warehouse, where navigators' equipped vehicles hint their pilots on where to go), to Internet-scale scenarios (e.g. in software agents exploring the Web, where mobile software agents coordinate distributed researches by moving on various Web-sites). Therefore, our Co-Fields model can be applied also in much diverse areas than the one considered [14, 13, 6].

5.2   Related Work

Several proposals, in the last few years, address the problem of supporting agents' activities with coordination approaches similar to Co-Fields.

In the videogame domain, one of the most remarkable examples is represented by the popular videogame "The Sims" [15]. "The Sims" exploits sorts of computational fields, called "happiness landscapes" and spread in the virtual city in which characters live, to drive the movements of non-player characters [16]. For instance, if a character is hungry, it perceives and follows a happiness landscape whose peaks correspond to places where food can be found, i.e., a fridge. After having eaten, a new landscape will be followed by the character depending on its needs. Although sharing the same inspiration, "Sims' happiness fields" are static and generated only by the environment. In Co-Fields, instead, fields are dynamic and can change over time, and agents themselves are able to generate fields to promote a stronger self-organization perspective.

Remaining in the entertainment domain, it is worth reporting that autonomous agents, coordinating their movements and their actions, have been employed in the recent movie "The Lord of the Rings, The Two Towers". In the Helm's deep battle, to enhance the scene realism, the 50000 fighting characters have been modeled by means of goal-oriented autonomous agents, developed within the Massive framework [17]. In this approach agents interact with each other on a strict local basis, without any long-range interactions. In our opinion, also this kind of approach could take advantage of integrating long-range, mediated interactions like those enabled by fields. These, in fact, would allow simulating large-scale tactics, like a global flanking or a global surrounding.

Also outside the entertainment domain, similar approaches can be conveniently used. Several projects in the last few years have worked to facilitate distributed-motion coordination. In robotics, the idea of potential fields driving robotic movement is not new [5]. For instance, one of the most recent manifestations of this idea, the Electric Field Approach [18] was used to control a team of Sony Aibo legged robots in the RoboCup domain. Following the EFA approach, each Aibo robot builds a field-based representation of the environment from the images captured by its head-mounted camera and decides its movements by examining the fields' gradients of this representation. Although close in spirit, EFA and Co-Fields differ from the implementation point of view. In Co-Fields, fields are distributed data structures actually spread in the environment; in EFA, fields are just an agent's internal representation of the environment and do not actually exist. Co-Fields require a supporting infrastructure to host field data structures, but they completely avoid the complex algorithms involved in field representation and construction.

Field-based approaches are taking over also in futuristic and fascinating scenarios such as self-assembly of agent-based micro-particles. One of the most successful approaches in this scenario has been proposed within the amorphous computing research [19]. The particles constituting an amorphous computer have the basic capabilities of propagating sorts of abstract computational fields in the network, and to sense and react to such fields. In particular, particles can transfer an activity state towards directions described by fields' gradients, so as to make coordinated patterns of activities emerge in the system independently of the specific structure of the network. Such mechanism can be used, among other possibilities, to drive particles' movements and let the amorphous computer self-assemble in a specific shape. Although conceived for a very specific scenario, this approach shares with Co-Fields the idea of having a single, physically inspired, mechanism to both diffuse contextual information and to organize adaptive motion coordination patterns. Finally, we want to emphasize again that, in our opinion [9], a lot of related work form the swarm intelligence research [7], there included flocks of birds, schools of fishes and packs of wolves [8], can all be modeled in terms of Co-Fields.

6   Conclusions and Future Work

While both a preliminary prototype implementation and the outcomes of our simulation shows the feasibility of the approach, a number of research directions are still open to improve its generality and its practical applicability. In addition to the already identified need for general methodologies to help designing specific coordination patterns in terms of Co-Fields, it will be important to explore the potential of Co-Fields in encoding more general distributed coordination patterns, possibly not related to motion.

Acknowledgements

Work supported by the Italian MIUR and CNR in the "Progetto Strategico IS-MANET, Infrastructures for Mobile ad-hoc Networks".

References

1. Quake 3 Arena: (http.//www.ldsoftware.com/games/quake/quake3-arena)
2. Unreal Tournament: (http://www.unrealtournament.com)
3. Liard, J.: It knows what you're going to do: Adding anticipation to a quakebot. In: Intenational Conference on Autonomous Agents, Montreal, Canada (2001)
4. Quake 3 Team Arena: (http://www.idsoftware.com/games/quake/quake3-teamarena)
5. Khatib, O.: Real-time obstacle avoidance for manipulators and mobile robots. The International Journal of Robotics Research 5 (1986) 90 – 98
6. Mamei, M., Zambonelli, F.: Programming pervasive and mobile computing applications with the tota middleware. In: IEEE International Conference On Pervasive Computing (Percom). IEEE CS Press, Orlando (FL), USA (2004)

7. Bonabeau, E., Dorigo, M., Theraulaz, G.: Swarm Intelligence. From Natural to Artificial Systems. Oxford University Press, Oxford (UK) (1999)
8. Parunak, H.V.: Go to the ant: Engineering principles from natural multi-agent systems. Annals of Operations Research **75** (1997) 69 – 101
9. Mamei, M., Leonardi, L., Zambonelli, F.: Co-fields: A unifying approach to swarm intelligence. In: Engineering Societies in the Agents World III: Third International Workshop, ESAW 2002. LNAI. Springer-Verlag, (Berlin, DE) 68 – 81
10. J. Liard, J.D.: Creating human-like synthetic characters with multiple skill levels: A case study using the soar quakebot. In: AAAI 2000 Fall Symposium Series: Simulating Human Agents. (2000)
11. Holmes, S.: Focus on MOD programming in Quake 3 Arena. Premier Press (2002)
12. Hightower, J., Borriello, G.: Location systems for ubiquitous computing. IEEE Computer **34** (2001) 57 – 66
13. Mamei, M., Zambonelli, F., Leonardi, L.: Co-fields: A physically inspired approach to distributed motion coordination. IEEE Pervasive Computing **3** (2004) 52 – 61
14. Mamei, M., Zambonelli, F., Leonardi, L.: Distributed motion coordination with co-fields: A case study in urban traffic management. In: 6th IEEE Symposium on Autonomous Decentralized Systems. IEEE CS Press, Pisa, Italy (2003) 63 – 70
15. The Sims: (http://thesims.ea.com)
16. Johnson, S.: Wild things. Wired **10** (2002)
17. Koeppel, D.: Massive attack. Popular Science (2002) 38 – 44
18. Johansson, S., Saffiotti, A.: Using the electric field approach in the RoboCup domain. In: RoboCup 2001: Robot Soccer World Cup V. LNAI. Springer-Verlag, (Berlin, DE) 399–404
19. Nagpal, R.: Programmable self-assembly using biologically-inspired multiagent control. In: Proceedings of the 1st Joint Conference on Autonomous Agents and Multi-Agent Systems. ACM Press, Bologna, Italy (2002) 418 – 425

Author Index

Lecture Notes in Artificial Intelligence (LNAI)